Second Edition

deutsch aktuell 1

Teacher's Edition

Wolfgang S. Kraft

EMC Publishing, Saint Paul, Minnesota

ABOUT THE AUTHOR

Wolfgang S. Kraft, a native of Germany, is Director of Foreign Languages of EMC Publishing. He graduated from the University of Minnesota with a B.A., B.S., and M.A. degrees, and has taught German at University High School, Minneapolis, Minnesota; White Bear Senior High School, White Bear Lake, Minnesota; Bethel College, St. Paul, Minnesota, as well as in several adult education programs.

Mr. Kraft also has been a Native Informant at NDEA Foreign Language Institutes, has participated on various foreign language panels, and conducted many foreign language workshops.

Besides writing and taking most of the pictures for *Deutsch: Aktuell*, Mr. Kraft has authored several other German programs among them *So sind die Deutschen* and *Passport to Germany*.

Mr. Kraft has traveled extensively throughout German-speaking countries to accumulate vital and up-to-date information indispensable in the development of *Deutsch: Aktuell*.

ISBN 0-8219-0074-9

Published by EMC Publishing
300 York Avenue
St. Paul, Minnesota 55101

Printed in the United States of America
0 9 8 7 6 5 4 3

CONTENTS

SCOPE AND SEQUENCE CHART

LEKTION	DIALOG	ERGÄN-ZUNG	AUSSPRA-CHEÜBUNG	ÜBUNGEN	LESESTÜCK 1
1	*Wo wohnst du?* (Buchenau/München)	greetings; numbers 0–10; addition; alphabet; names	short & long /a/	familiar & formal forms (*du, ihr, Sie*); personal pronouns; present tense; the letter ß; nouns	– – –
2	*Zu Hause* (Mülheim/Köln)	days of week; time units; numbers 11–20; time of day; addition/subtraction	short & long /i/	formation of questions; present tense of *haben; der, die, das; zu Hause/nach Hause*; cognates	*Susanne geht nach Hause* (Buchenau/München)
3	*Auf dem Bahnhof* (Frankfurt)	numbers 10–100; time of day; directions; neighboring countries	short & long /o/	definite article; *wer, wen, was*; present tense of *sein; kennen — wissen*; telling time; words used for emphasis	*Kerstins Schulweg* (Mülheim/Köln)
4	*In der Schule* (Bergisch-Gladbach)	months; seasons; school subjects; grades	/x/ & /ch/	indefinite article (nominative & accusative); plural (nominative & accusative); negation; command forms; *wo, wohin, woher; gern*	*Auf dem Weg zur Uni* (Würzburg)
5	*Gehen wir ins Kino!* (Deggendorf)	rooms; dates (calendar); family relations	short & long /u/ & /e/	modal auxiliaries; future tense; pronouns; verbs with separable prefixes	*Bei Familie Höhne* (Ost-Berlin)
A	– – –	– – –	– – –	*wo, wohin, wie, was, woher*; questions; singular — plural; geographical information; definite/indefinite article; sentence completion; short readings; pronouns	*Ein Tag bei Grubers*

ERWEITERUNG	RÜCKBLICK	LESESTÜCK 2	SPRACHSPIEGEL	KULTURECKE
addition questions *Wie heißt das...?* responses	– – –	– – –	– – –	1. *Greetings, Farewells and Introductions* 2. *,,Du" oder ,,Sie"?*
missing words telling time present tense numbers *Wie heißt das...?* questions	– – –	– – –	self-expression *Wie sagt man's?* *Zungenbrecher*	*What Time Is It?*
sentence completion *Wie heißt das...?* responses questions	*haben/sein;* telling time; numbers; *wer, wen, was, wie, wo*	*Deutschland — Land und Fläche*	dialog construction questions *Wie sagt man's?* *Zungenbrecher*	*Traveling by Train*
matching words *Wie heißt das...?* compound nouns questions	verb forms; question formation; *was, wer, wen, wo, woher, wohin;* sentence completion; *viel/viele*	*Die BRD — Länder und Hauptstädte*	*Wie heißt das...?* description *Wie sagt man's?* *Zungenbrecher*	1. *School Life in the BRD* 2. *School Life in the DDR*
Wie heißt das...? dates counterparts questions	definite article & plural forms; command forms; negation; compound nouns; months; seasons	*Österreich*	dialog construction description of day *Wie sagt man's?* *Zungenbrecher*	*Entertainment and Leisure-Time Activities*
– – –	– – –	– – –	– – –	Cultural Notes: greetings, telephone; money; train stations, streetcars & subways

LEKTION	DIALOG	ERGÄN-ZUNG	AUSSPRA-CHEÜBUNG	ÜBUNGEN	LESESTÜCK 1
6	*In der Bank* (Neustadt/ Weinstraße)	articles of clothing; colors	/sch/	dative (indirect object, verbs, *wem*, prepositions); *wieviel — wie viele*; compound nouns	*Heike und Birgit gehen einkaufen* (Mülheim/Köln)
7	*Im Hotel* (Deggendorf)	weather; means of transporta-tion	short & long /ü/	dative pronouns; verbs with stem vowel change	*In der Jugendherberge* (Bonn)
8	*Michaels Party* (Köln)	school items; musical instruments	short & long /ö/ & /ä/	possessive adjectives (nominative & accusative); comparison of adjectives & adverbs; *der*-words	*Monika geht gern tanzen* (Buchheim/München)
9	*Beim Sportwett-bewerb* (Leipzig)	sports; beverages	initial, middle & final /r/	present perfect tense (regular & irregular verbs); possessive adjectives (dative)	*Marathonlauf in Leipzig*
10	*Beim Reisebüro* (Wiesbaden)	metric units	/ai/, /oi/, & /au/	verbs with separable prefixes; verbs with inseparable prefixes; accusative prepositions	*Auf zur Zugspitze!*
B	*Auf dem Weg in die Stadt*	– – –	– – –	dialog construction; sentence completion; word definition; possessive adjectives; matching words; present perfect tense; verbs with stem vowel change	*In der Stadt*

ERWEITERUNG	RÜCKBLICK	LESESTÜCK 2	SPRACHSPIEGEL	KULTURECKE
word description & definition; questions; *Wie heißt das . . . ?*	*wer, wen, wem, was;* future tense; modal auxiliaries; verbs with separable prefixes; *kennen/wissen*	*Die Schweiz*	description questions *Wie sagt man's?* *Zungenbrecher*	*Shopping*
weather *Wie heißt das . . . ?* sentence formation sentence completion questions	modal auxiliaries; dative prepositions; sentence completion; verbs with stem vowel change; pronouns	A. *Bonn — die Hauptstadt der BRD* B. *Berlin (Ost) — die Hauptstadt der DDR*	dialog construction questions *Jugendherberge* *Wie sagt man's?* *Zungenbrecher*	1. *Foreign Influence in Germany* 2. *German Influence in the U.S.*
gern conversation word definition questions	pronouns; verbs with stem vowel change; dative prepositions; opposites, separable prefixes; conversation	*Die BRD — Landschaft*	dialog construction questions *Wie sagt man's?* *Zungenbrecher*	*Occupations*
Wie heißt das . . . ? questions	comparison of adjectives & adverbs; possessive adjectives; verb selection; *der-words*	*Die DDR — Land und Städte*	description of sport word definition essay *Wie sagt man's?* *Zungenbrecher*	*Sports*
questions word definition response *Wie heißt das . . . ?* metric units	present, future & present perfect tense; dative & accusative	*Die Romantische Straße*	dialog construction metric units *Wie sagt man's?* *Zungenbrecher*	*Vacationing*
– – –	– – –	*Wolfgang und Günter fahren zur Jugendherberge*	– – –	Cultural Notes: English in the German language; origin of town names; German hotel

INTRODUCTION

This new edition of *Deutsch: Aktuell* is the result of extensive research involving hundreds of teachers who have used the previous edition, numerous discussions at professional workshops and application of the state-of-the-art in the field of foreign language instruction.

The strength of *Deutsch: Aktuell* becomes apparent in the variety of exercises presented, as well as in the cultural coverage of all German-speaking countries (West Germany, East Germany, Switzerland, Austria and even Liechtenstein).

Recent trends in both foreign language methods and technology have made it possible to add microcomputer software to this basal textbook program. *Deutsch: Aktuell* is perhaps the most comprehensive German textbook series today. Each level of *Deutsch: Aktuell* now includes these components: *textbook*, *teacher's edition*, *workbook*, *test booklet*, *sound-filmstrips*, *tape program* and *microcomputer software*.

Deutsch: Aktuell is not just a reworked textbook, but a completely rewritten and redesigned textbook. The major improvements are the use of full-color photos and illustrations throughout, addition of creative and communication activities, more up-to-date situations showing everyday German life, the listing of both German-English and English-German vocabulary sections, easy chapter identification and, finally, a more systematic introduction of the grammar.

Extensive research and a survey revealed that more than 75% of the students who had used the first edition textbooks were able to finish each book in one year. For that reason, the level of difficulty has been maintained. Furthermore, the number of lessons in the textbook is still twelve (ten regular and two review). Based on an average school year, it is estimated that each lesson will take about three weeks to complete.

In summary, *Deutsch: Aktuell* teaches the language and culture of today. The material has been reviewed by many young adults in Germany and the various situations and themes were judged by them to be realistic and true to life.

A WORD ABOUT THIS TEACHER'S EDITION

The purpose of the front section of this teacher's edition is to provide a complete overview of *Deutsch: Aktuell 1* (Scope and Sequence Chart), outline the components of the program, suggest a step-by-step approach to teaching a lesson, introduce practical classroom expressions, and give a detailed description of each lesson — including objectives, recommended games and activities, as well as background notes on the cultural material presented.

This teacher's edition contains an annotated version of the student textbook. Marginal notes, printed in another color, include numerous comments and suggestions to expand the material and provide additional information that may be useful to the teacher. Furthermore, the teacher will find the answers to the oral exercises included in this teacher's edition.

A special note! A frequently discussed question is "Should the *du* or *Sie* form be used in teaching the language?" The answer is "both." However, in giving instructions in the various exercises and in questions, the *du* form was generally used because it is more difficult (because of verb endings) and needs more practice. Furthermore, students will communicate among each other using *du* and, therefore, will learn to use the *du* form in a natural way.

COMPONENTS

Deutsch: Aktuell is a two-level German language program designed to meet the needs of today's language students. Each level includes the following components:

- textbook
- teacher's edition
- workbook
- test booklet (end-of-unit *written* and *listening comprehension* tests)
- sound-filmstrips
- tape program (exercises and tests)
- microcomputer software

TEXTBOOK

The textbook contains a total of twelve lessons (ten regular and two review lessons), a grammar summary, a vocabulary summary (German/English *and* English/German) and an index. All the lessons (except the review lessons) have been structured in a similar manner so that the students will become accustomed to the various sections found in each of the regular lessons.

Lesson Format

Dialog — Each dialog dramatizes a situation typical of everyday life in German-speaking countries. The speakers in the dialogs represent a cross-section of age groups, although the emphasis is on scenes centered around young adults.

Most dialogs have been divided into several sections so that each section can be treated as a mini-dialog to facilitate the learning process. The dialogs are presented visually on the accompanying filmstrips. These on-location, full-color photos reenact the printed and audio material, thus providing a more meaningful situation. Each dialog exemplifies grammatical structures to be learned as well as those previously introduced. Its vocabulary is limited to words already presented, with the exception of new words to be learned within the context of the conversation.

Following the dialog are questions carefully structured to review the content of the dialog. Finally, there is the English version of the dialog that will assist the student in clarifying the meaning. This version is not a literal translation. Consequently, the student should be cautioned not to compare individual words.

Nützliche Ausdrücke — This section extracts useful and idiomatic expressions from the *Dialog* and *Lesestück 1*.

Ergänzung — This section expands the topic of the lesson theme and provides additional language and cultural information.

Ausspracheübung (Level 1 only) — This exercise is intended to improve the student's pronunciation of individual sounds. Sounds that may be especially difficult to master have been isolated and are contrasted with each other. Only words previously introduced are used.

Übungen — A grammar explanation leads off each exercise section. After the grammatical structure has been explained, several oral and written exercises illustrating the grammar point are introduced. For easy identification, the oral exercises have been marked with the symbol ▣ and the written exercises with the symbol �. Of course, many of the oral exercises can be changed to written ones and vice versa. The *du* form has been used in most exercises. The teacher may wish to change the instructions and/or question-answer exercises using *Sie*, depending on the circumstances.

Lesestück 1 — This reading selection (beginning with *Lektion 2*) introduces additional cultural situations that occur in everyday German life. This is another section where the student can see the visual sequence in the filmstrip. The new vocabulary is presented in the margin for easy reference. New words and phrases are indicated by the symbol °.

Questions follow the reading selection to help the teacher measure the student's comprehension of this material.

Erweiterung — Additional exercise material is presented in this section. A wide variety of communication exercises are provided to challenge the student's understanding of the grammatical and cultural content of the lesson.

Rückblick — The review section reenters the various grammatical structures learned in previous lessons. Continuous review of this type, along with that in the two review units, insures retention and reinforcement of previously learned material.

Lesestück 2 — This reading selection (beginning with *Lektion 3*) familiarizes the student with geographical and cultural features of West and East Germany, Austria and Switzerland. This section is also supported by the accompanying filmstrip section.

Sprachspiegel — This section (beginning with *Lektion 2*) provides numerous opportunities for the student to become involved creatively in language expression. Various mini-situations in the *Wie sagt man's?* section present topical themes that are particularly useful in colloquial speech. The student will be challenged to master some rather tricky *Zungenbrecher*. They add to the student's pronunciation and enjoyment.

Kulturecke — This section presents, in a mini-social studies format, a cross-cultural approach. The text is presented in English so that students, from the very beginning, can be exposed to important cultural information. In the filmstrips, on-location photography reinforces each cultural topic.

Vokabeln — The vocabulary section gives the student an easy reference source to the new words introduced in each lesson. The plural forms have been listed from the first lesson on, even though the plural as a grammatical structure is not formally introduced until later. The vocabulary meaning is confined strictly to those words introduced in the particular lesson. In cases where the meaning of the same German word changes, the word is listed again in subsequent lessons.

Grammar Summary — The grammar introduced in *Deutsch: Aktuell 1* has been summarized in this section for convenient reference.

Vocabulary — The total vocabulary has been listed here for easy reference. Each word or phrase is followed by a number indicating the lesson in which it appears for the first time. For convenient and flexible use, both German-English and English-German vocabularies have been provided.

Index — A complete index of all the grammar and cultural material is provided at the end of the book for easy reference and location.

TEACHER'S EDITION

This teacher's edition contains the following sections:

- scope and sequence chart
- components
- teaching approaches (model unit)
- classroom phrases
- useful names and addresses of organizations
- an introduction to each of the *Lektionen*
  1. instructional objectives
  2. *Allerlei* — suggestions on teaching the cultural material (activities, games, class or individual projects)
  3. background information for the *Dialog, Lesestück 1, Lesestück 2* and *Kulturecke*
- annotated version of the student textbook

WORKBOOK

The workbook expands the material introduced in the textbook. It includes numerous written exercises that reinforce the language skills and the culture covered in the textbook. An answer key for all exercises contained in the workbook is also available.

TEST BOOKLET

The test booklet includes two sections: (1) the student answer sheets for the *listening comprehension tests* for each lesson and (2) the *written tests* for each lesson.

Listening Comprehension Tests have been recorded and are part of the tape program. The tests provide various ways of checking how well students have learned the material of each lesson. A typical test includes a listening comprehension section, logical/illogical statements, sound discrimination and sections on culture. The recorded material (with an answer key) of all the listening comprehension tests is printed in the teacher's edition of the test booklet.

Written Tests have been prepared for each lesson. These tests are intended to be given to the students after each lesson has been completed. An answer key to the written tests has also been included in the teacher's edition of the test booklet.

SOUND-FILMSTRIPS

A total of ten full-color filmstrips (one for each regular lesson), a transcript and a map (Level 1 only) are part of each level. Each filmstrip contains an average of about 100 on-location photos, carefully coordinated with the printed and recorded sections of the *Dialog, Lesestück 1, Lesestück 2* and *Kulturecke*.

It should be stressed here that the photography scenes in the filmstrips were taken in many different parts of West Germany, East Germany, Austria and Switzerland. An attempt has been made to familiarize students with various aspects of German culture in different regions. Furthermore, the emphasis in the scenes has been placed on situations depicting everyday life, most of which involve young adults.

Different voices from many different parts of Germany have been recorded on the cassettes so that students will hear a variety of native speakers. Whenever appropriate, sound effects have been added, particularly in the *Dialoge*, in order to provide a more authentic and meaningful situation. The *Kulturecke* has been recorded both in English (for beginning students) and in German (for more advanced students). Teachers wishing to present the German version of the *Kulturecke* should begin the visual presentation with the title frame for this section and advance the cassette sound track to the beginning of the German material that follows the English equivalent.

The manual accompanying the sound-filmstrips includes the complete text of each lesson with indication of frame numbers for easy identification.

The map of German-speaking countries is an important part of this program. It represents the various geographical features discussed in *Deutsch: Aktuell*, usually in the *Lesestück 2*. This map is especially useful for a geographical review.

TAPE PROGRAM

The tape program is an integral part of *Deutsch: Aktuell*. The following material has been recorded on cassettes or reel-to-reel tapes:

Lektionen 1–10 (Cassettes/Tapes 1–10)

Dialog — introduced first as a listening experience and then broken into manageable phrases for student repetition.
Nützliche Ausdrücke — for student repetition.
Ergänzung — for student repetition.
Ausspracheübung — for student repetition.
Übungen — a variety of exercises such as substitution, transformation and communication. The specific exercises recorded have been marked in the textbook by the symbol ▣ .
Erweiterung — additional exercises to reinforce and expand the lesson content.
Lektionen A-B (Cassette/Tape 11) — A review lesson follows each fifth lesson and includes short reading selections, dialogs, useful expressions, exercises summarizing and reinforcing previously learned material, and cultural information.
Tests (Cassettes/Tapes 12–14) — A test that measures comprehension of the material covered is included for each of the ten regular lessons. Special emphasis has been placed on the listening skill, sound discrimination and understanding of the cultural material introduced in each lesson.

MICROCOMPUTER SOFTWARE

A set of ten diskettes (one per lesson) is available. The purpose is to review, reinforce and expand the grammatical and cultural material of each lesson. It is also an excellent device to give students who need help, a source for independent study.

TEACHING APPROACHES

Model Unit (Lektion 4)

Instructional approaches vary considerably among teachers. Furthermore, the length of each class period often differs from one school to the next. Consequently, it is impossible to provide a detailed plan for each individual lesson that would apply to all students using this material.

We have, however, selected one lesson from *Deutsch: Aktuell 1* to provide some guidelines for using the content successfully. Needless to say, teachers will find some useful information here but may not want to follow each individual suggestion as presented. We have chosen *Lektion 4* as our model unit — a lesson still in the early stages of this beginning program, yet including all the different sections of a typical lesson.

Since class periods vary in length, we have arbitrarily chosen a 50-minute period and planned the learning activities accordingly. On the basis of a 50-minute period and a schedule of 170 to 180 school days, it is estimated that *Deutsch: Aktuell 1* can be covered in its entirety (ten regular lessons and two review lessons) in one year at the high school level.

DAY 1

1. Warm-up
— Review some of the material from *Lektion 3*. For example, ask students questions using the time of the day. (*Wieviel Uhr ist es jetzt?*, *Um wieviel Uhr gehst du zur Schule?*, etc.) Go over numbers 1–100.
— You may also want to pick one or two exercises from the *Rückblick* section of *Lektion 4*. Be sure to personalize the material as much as possible.
2. Introduce *Lektion 4* by going over the main objectives of the lesson. You may refer to the section on "Instructional Objectives" listed in this teacher's edition (beginning *Lektion 4*).
3. Introduce the dialog *In der Schule* (p. 57).
— Play the recorded material to expose your students to the young adult voices. If possible, show the accompanying filmstrip sequence of the dialog portion while the students listen to the recorded section. After showing the on-location photo sequence, your students will understand the content much better.
— Have students point out similarities/differences that they have observed in viewing the filmstrip.
— Show the first third of the dialog section on the filmstrip once more while playing the recorded sound track. If filmstrips are not available, just play the recorded material.

— Practice pronunciation of the first section. Have students repeat individual sentences that you may want to break down into manageable phrases or words. Have students follow along in the textbook so that they can relate the sound to the printed words.

— Ask simple questions about the dialog as soon as students have a fairly good understanding of the material. You may want to ask more questions besides those provided in the textbook. (*Wo sind die drei Jungen und das Mädchen?, Wer ist der Schlaukopf?* — This is a good place to introduce the word *Dummkopf* — *Was machen Stefan, Dirk und Elke jetzt?*, etc.)

4. Introduce the months of the year listed in the *Ergänzung* (p. 59). Have students repeat each of the twelve months to assure good pronunciation. You may want to ask such questions as: *Welcher Monat ist jetzt?, Wann ist Sommer? (Herbst? Winter? Frühling?), Wann beginnt die Schule?*, and *Wie viele Tage hat der Januar, Februar (dieses Jahr), März...?* Point out the similarity (*April, August, September, November*) and the difference (*Januar, Februar, März, Mai, Juni, Juli, Oktober, Dezember*) in spelling the months.

5. Introduce the indefinite article (p. 61).

— Go over *Übungen 1–3*. You may have to review definite articles of some of the nouns listed if students make too many mistakes.

6. Do workbook exercise 18. Find out how quickly your students can do it. If there is no time, you can do this fun activity on another day.

Assignment

1. Study the first third of the dialog (p. 57).
2. Know the months of the year and the seasons (p. 59).

DAY 2

1. Review

— Play the first third of the dialog (p. 57). Ask questions.

— Have students role-play the parts of the dialog. Have them ask each other questions about it.

— Ask questions about the months of the year. (*Welcher Monat ist jetzt?, Und welcher Monat kommt danach?*, etc.) You may want to ask students to write out the months and check the spelling.

— Review the indefinite article. Pick a few nouns at random (from *Übungen 1–3*, p. 61) and check to be sure that students know the articles.

2. Introduce the second third of the dialog (p. 57). You may wish to play this section on the tape. Ask questions from the book or additional ones (*Wo ist dein Buch?, Wo steht Übung 1? Und wo ist der Dialog?, Verstehst du den Dialog?*) Have students read the individual parts and ask each other questions.

3. Introduce the school subjects that German students take (p. 59). Study the weekly school calendar and ask students which subjects they are taking: *Was für Fächer hast du? (Hast du diese Fächer jeden Tag?), Was für Fächer haben die Schüler in Deutschland?, Was für ein Fach ist schwer/leicht?*

This section is quite suitable for reviewing time. (*Wann hat dieser Schüler Physik (Englisch, Mathe...)?, Um wieviel Uhr beginnt die Chemiestunde?, Wie lange dauert diese Stunde?*)

4. Go over *Übungen 4–5* (pp. 61–62) You may wish to use the recorded section on tape and, at the same time, review *Übungen 1–3* (p. 61).

5. Do *Übung 6* (p. 62). This exercise could be done as a written exercise.

Assignment

1. Study the first two sections of the dialog (p. 57).
2. Complete *Übung 7* (p. 62).

DAY 3

1. Review

— Have students act out the first two sections of the dialog. Ask questions.

— Have students ask each other about the subjects they are taking. (*Welche Fächer hast du?, Wie viele Fächer hast du?, Wie oft hast du dieses Fach?*) At this point, you may want to have students fill out the *Stundenplan* — workbook exercise 16. (See also page TE21 of this front section).

— Go over *Übung 7* (p. 62).

2. Introduce *Lesestück 1* (p. 71). You may want to read the first paragraph to the class or play the sound track version (without the visual section on the filmstrip).

— Have students read individual sentences.

— Have students ask each other questions.

3. Introduce plural nouns (p. 62).

— Explain that plural nouns can be learned in groups. Point out the sections of nouns following the grammar explanation.

— Indicate that each lesson vocabulary (*Vokabeln*) and the vocabulary at the end of the book always have the plural forms listed.

— Go through *Übungen 8–10* (p. 65).

4. Go over the last part of the dialog (p. 57). You may want to play this section on tape. Ask questions and have students read the individual parts.

5. Introduce the game *Das nächste Wort*. (See description on page TE21 of this front section.)

Assignment

1. Do workbook exercises 1–2.
2. Study plural noun forms (pp. 63–64) and go over *Übungen 8–10* (p. 65).

DAY 4

1. Review

— Supply the singular form of nouns and have

students provide plural forms. Review *Übungen 8–10* (p. 65).
— Go over workbook exercises 1–2.
— Review the complete dialog. Ask many questions and have students take individual parts.
2. Cover *Übungen 11–12* (pp. 65–66). This can be done orally or in writing.
3. Introduce the German grading system in the *Ergänzung* (p. 60).
4. Have students ask each other: *Wie alt bist du?* Since the students most likely will be the same age, you may wish to have students count off in numbers (starting with 15 — as an example). Each student now has a different number and the question provides more interest.
5. Ask questions about section(s) covered in *Lesestück 1* the day before.
— Finish reading the selection. Ask questions and/or have students ask each other questions.
— Have students read out loud to practice pronunciation.
— You may want to play the recorded material accompanying the filmstrip material.
Assignment
1. Thoroughly study the complete *Dialog* and *Lesestück 1.*

DAY 5

1. Review
— Go over the complete dialog. Ask questions. Have students take parts.
— If available, show the sound-filmstrip section of the dialog and play the recorded version once more.
— Show the visual section of the filmstrip and have students supply the descriptive material. Encourage students first to reproduce the text material as accurately as possible. Then challenge your students to come up with adaptations, encouraging them to deviate as much as possible. This will bring out a great deal of creativity.
2. Show the complete audio-visual section of *Lesestück 1* (if available).
— Ask questions about individual sections covered before.
— Have students supply the narrative portion.
— Have students ask questions about the content.
3. Have students repeat the words listed in the *Ausspracheübung* (p. 60). Again, you may want to use the recorded section in the tape program. Check individual responses to be sure that your students can closely imitate words containing the /x/ and /ch/ sounds. If your students have difficulties, explain the formation of these sounds by using the annotated description provided in the *Ausspracheübung* of this teacher's edition.
4. Do workbook exercise 3. Go over it in class.

Assignment
1. Do workbook exercise 4.

DAY 6

1. Review
— Have students pronounce the individual words listed in the *Ausspracheübung* (p. 60).
— Review plural nouns. Spot check (using the list of nouns provided on pp. 63–64) to be sure that students know the plural forms.
— Go over workbook exercise 4.
2. Introduce negation (p. 66). Go over *Übungen 13–16* (pp. 66–67). Just for variety, you may want to have students answer the questions in the positive in *Übungen 13–15.*
3. Ask the questions provided in *Übung 32* (p. 74). Find out how many different answers your students come up with.
4. Go over exercise I of *Rückblick* (p. 74).
Assignment
1. Complete workbook exercises 5–6.

DAY 7

1. Review
— Ask some simple questions and have students come up with the negative form. You may want to have students ask each other questions that can be answered positively or negatively.
— Go over workbook exercises 5–6.
2. Complete *Übung 17* (p. 67). This exercise can be done orally, in writing, or both.
3. Have students read several of the short dialogs in the *Wie sagt man's?* section (pp. 78–79). The purpose of the mini-dialogs is to expose students to colloquial language that is of practical value in everyday speech. These sections are ideal for role-playing and asking of questions.
4. Introduce the game *Ratet mal!* (see description on page TE21 of this front section).
Assignment
1. Do *Übung 18* (p. 67).
2. Have students read *Kulturecke 1* (pp. 80–81).

DAY 8

1. Review
— Ask some questions and have students answer them negatively, or provide simple positive or negative statements and have students change them to the opposite.
— Go over *Übung 18* (p. 67).
2. Discuss *Kulturecke 1: School Life in the* BRD. How does the school system differ from our own?
3. If available, show the sound-filmstrip section of *Kulturecke 1.* Unquestionably, these pictures will strengthen the students' cultural understanding. Although the material has been discussed in English — to provide a clearer understanding — you still

may wish to ask some questions in simple German: *Wie alt sind die Schüler in der Grundschule? (Realschule? Gymnasium?)*, *Welche Fächer haben die Schüler auf dem Gymnasium?*, *Gehen alle Schüler auf ein Gymnasium?*, *Um wieviel Uhr kommen die Schüler aus der Schule?*

4. Do exercise II of *Rückblick* (p. 75).

5. Introduce the command form (pp. 67–68). Go over *Übungen 19–21* (pp. 68–69).

Assignment

1. Do *Übung 24* (p. 69).

2. Have students review *Übungen 19–21* (pp. 68–69).

DAY 9

1. Review

— Go over random sentences from *Übungen 19–21* (pp. 68–69). Mix up sentences using *du, ihr* and *Sie*.

— Have students read their answers of *Übung 24* (p. 69).

2. Do *Übungen 22–23* (p. 69).

3. Start reading *Lesestück 2* (p. 76). You may want to point out the various geographical features on the map accompanying *Deutsch: Aktuell*. Have students read sentences. You can also use the recorded material from the cassettes accompanying the filmstrips. Stop at the end of each paragraph and ask questions. (*Wo liegt...?, Welche Stadt ist die größte? Wie heißt das kleinste Land?*, etc.) You may want to have students start with the individual project "Map" as outlined on page TE21 of this front section. This could be a regular or extra credit assignment.

4. Go over section I of the *Sprachspiegel* (p. 78). Your students should be encouraged to come up with other teacher instructions in German (besides those presented) that they have probably heard from you. Encourage as much creativity as possible. Some of the instructions should be acted out by your students to make the situation more meaningful. (*Sag ein Wort!, Beantworte diese Frage!*, etc.)

Assignment

1. Do workbook exercises 7–8.

2. Review section(s) in *Lesestück 2* (pp. 76–77) read in class.

DAY 10

1. Review

— Go over workbook exercises 7–8.

— Ask questions about *Lesestück 2*. You may want to have individual students point to the various cities or *Länder* on a map.

2. Finish reading *Lesestück 2*. If available, show the filmstrip section of this reading selection. While showing the map pictures, you may ask some other questions (besides those listed in the book), such as *Wo liegt Schleswig-Holstein?, An welche Länder grenzt Bayern?, Wie heißt die Hauptstadt von Hessen?*, etc.

3. Do workbook exercise 9 orally or in writing. Encourage varied responses.

4. Have students read the remaining mini-dialogs in the *Wie sagt man's? (Sprachspiegel)* section (pp. 78–79), which has not been covered yet. Your students should try to act these out as much as possible. Be sure they understand each one.

5. Go over workbook exercise 10.

Assignment

1. Assign exercise II of *Sprachspiegel* (p. 78).

2. Do workbook exercise 17.

DAY 11

1. Review

— Select several students and have them read their version of *Auf dem Weg zur Schule (Sprachspiegel*, exercise II, p. 78). Have other students ask some questions. Encourage open-ended conversation as much as possible. Go over workbook exercise 17.

— Ask a few questions about *Lesestück 2* (pp. 76–77).

2. Do workbook exercise 11.

3. Introduce *wo, wohin* and *woher* (p. 69).

4. Go over *Übungen 25–26* (p. 70).

5. Do *Übung 29 (Erweiterung*, p. 73). After your students have matched the words, you may want to ask questions about some of these nouns or have them define some of the nouns in simple German. (*Was ist eine Schule?, Wie heißt ein Monat (oder alle zwölf)?, Warum brauchst du ein Buch?*, etc.)

Assignment

1. Do exercise III in *Rückblick* (p. 75).

2. Review idiomatic expressions learned in the *Dialog*, and *Lesestück 1*, listed in the *Nützliche Ausdrücke* (p. 58).

DAY 12

1. Review

— Ask questions using *wo, wohin* and *woher*. (*Wo wohnst du?, Woher kommst du?, Wohin gehst du heute nachmittag?*, etc.)

— Go over exercise III in *Rückblick* (p. 75).

— Have students cover up the left side (German) of *Nützliche Ausdrücke* and have them provide the German expressions.

2. Continue with exercise IV in *Rückblick* (p. 75). Encourage as much variation as possible. This exercise can be done orally or in writing.

3. Introduce the word *gern* (p. 70). Go over *Übungen 27–28* (pp. 70–71). Be sure to ask other questions, particularly with personal emphasis. (*Was machst du gern?, Was lernst du gern?, Was hast du gern?*, etc.)

4. Have students complete workbook exercise 15. If many errors are made, review location of cities using a map.

Assignment
1. Review *Kulturecke 1* and read *Kulturecke 2*.
2. Do workbook exercises 12–13.

DAY 13

1. Review
— Ask some questions using *gern*. Have students ask each other questions.
— Discuss important aspects of *Kulturecke 2* (pp. 82–84). You may want to ask some simple questions in German such as: *Wie alt sind die Kinder in einer Kinderkrippe (im Kindergarten)?*, *Wie viele Jahre gehen die Schüler auf die Oberschule?*, *Welche Fächer haben die Schüler?*, *Was ist die Große Pause?*, *Wie alt sind die Jungen Pioniere?*, *Was ist die FDJ?*, etc.
2. If available, show the accompanying filmstrip section (while playing the cassette) of *Kulturecke 2: School Life in the* DDR. You may want to show the picture sequence of *Kulturecke 1* first to refresh your students' memories. Discuss specific details and questions that might come up. The background information on page TE22 of this teacher's edition gives further insight into the cultural topic of German school life (*BRD* and *DDR*).
3. Do *Übungen 30–31* (pp. 73–74). *Übung 30* can be done orally or writing. Check for accuracy.
4. Complete exercise V in *Rückblick* (p. 75).
5. Have students attempt to say the tongue twister (*Zungenbrecher*, p. 79). This could be a fun activity. Find out who can say it the most times without stumbling.
Assignment
1. Review *Lektion 4*. You may want to point out specific portions that you feel your students need to practice and review.
2. Offer extra credit to students who report about the German school system (*DDR* and *BRD*). See workbook exercise 14.

DAY 14

1. Review *Lektion 4*. Be sure that your students understand the material. Clarify questions.
2. Describe the individual pictures in this lesson.
3. Have students start on the *Kreuzworträtsel*, workbook exercise 19. If not enough time, have them hand it in either the next day, or the day after the test.

DAY 15

NOTE: It may be advisable to hand out only the test section of *Lektion 4* (answer sheet for listening comprehension test and the written test pages) rather than the complete test booklet.
1. Play the recorded test material as your students mark their answer sheets. You may decide to play the German material twice to give your students an opportunity to understand each item thoroughly before completing it.
2. After your students have completed the listening comprehension test, they are now ready to begin the written test.
IMPORTANT! You may decide to give two tests (listening comprehension and written) on separate days depending on the time available during one class period.

CLASSROOM PHRASES

As early as the first day of instruction, the teacher may want to introduce students to frequently used classroom expressions so that the students get used to the spoken language right away. Here is a list of some of the more useful expressions.

Hört zu! Listen.
Wiederholt! Repeat.
Alle zusammen! Everybody.
Noch einmal. Once more.
Lauter, bitte. Louder, please.
Paßt auf! Pay attention.
Antwortet! Answer.
Fragt! Ask.
Macht eure Bücher auf, Seite...! Open your books to page...
Macht eure Hefte auf, Seite...! Open your notebooks/workbooks to page.
Nehmt ein Stück Papier 'raus! Take out a sheet of paper.
Nehmt einen Bleistift! Take a pencil.
Schreibt! Write.
Lest! Read.
Fangt jetzt an. Start now.
Weiter. Continue.
Macht eure Bücher zu! Close your books.
Macht eure Hefte zu! Close your notebooks/ workbooks.
Geht an die Tafel! Go to the blackboard.
Seht an die Tafel! Look at the blackboard.
Schreibt...an die Tafel! Write ... on the black-board.
Seht mich an! Look at me.
Das ist richtig. That's right.
Das ist falsch. That's wrong.
Das ist sehr gut. That's very good.
Gut! Good.
Prima! Great.
Ausgezeichnet. Excellent.
Wo ist der Fehler? Where's the mistake?
Buchstabiert es! Spell it.
Übersetzt ins Deutsche! Translate into German.
Danke. Thank you.
Hausaufgaben/Schularbeit. Homework.
Für morgen ... For tomorrow ...
Gebt mir eure Hausaufgaben (Schularbeit)! Give me your homework.

Wir haben eine Prüfung (einen Test). We're having a test.

Wer weiß es? Who knows it?

Auf deutsch, bitte! In German, please.

Seid ihr fertig? Are you finished?

Ruhe, bitte. Quiet, please.

To express themselves in class, students may want to learn the following basic expressions.

Ich weiß nicht. I don't know.

Ich verstehe das nicht. I don't understand that.

Was bedeutet...? What does...mean?

Wie sagt man...? How do you say...?

Ich habe eine Frage. I have a question.

USEFUL NAMES AND ADDRESSES

A number of organizations provide assistance to students and teachers in matters relating to German-speaking countries. This assistance ranges from answering questions about entry of the country (embassies) to supplying travel information, brochures and posters (tourist offices). The list below represents some of the most important sources of contact. There also may be local or regional organizations in your area. Contact the national organization(s) for specific information.

FEDERAL REPUBLIC OF GERMANY

Embassy of the Federal Republic of Germany
4645 Reservoir Road N.W.
Washington, D.C. 20007
(202) 298-4000

(assisting with travel plans)
German National Tourist Office
747 Third Avenue
New York, New York 10017
(212) 308-3300

(providing information, materials)
German Information Center
410 Park Avenue
New York, New York 10022
(212) 888-9840

(providing materials and information on train travel)
German Rail
747 Third Avenue
New York, New York 10017
(212) 308-3100

GERMAN DEMOCRATIC REPUBLIC

Embassy of the German Democratic Republic
1717 Massachusetts Avenue N.W.
Washington, D.C. 20036
(202) 232-3134

(providing information and materials)
U.S. Committe for Friendship with the GDR
130 East 16th Street
New York, New York 10003
(212) 473-1441

AUSTRIA

Embassy of Austria
2343 Massachusetts Avenue N.W.
Washington, D.C. 20008
(202) 483-4474

(providing travel information, materials)
Austrian National Tourist Office
545 Fifth Avenue
New York, New York 10017
(212) 697-0651

SWITZERLAND

Embassy of Switzerland
2900 Cathedral Avenue N.W.
Washington, D.C. 20008
(202) 745-7900

(providing travel information, materials)
Swiss National Tourist Office
608 Fifth Avenue
New York, New York 10020
(212) 757-5944

LIECHTENSTEIN

Liechtenstein is represented in the U.S. by the Embassy of Switzerland — address above.

Other organizations located in the Federal Republic of Germany and in the German Democratic Republic

FEDERAL REPUBLIC OF GERMANY

(providing information and materials)
Inter Nationes
Kennedyallee 91-103
D-5300 Bonn 2

(providing information on German government)
Press- und Informationsamt der Bundesregierung
Postfach 2160
Welckerstrasse 11
5300 Bonn 1

(providing information on the postal system)
Deutsche Bundespost
Posttechnisches Zentralamt
Postfach 1180
6100 Darmstadt

(providing information on camping)
Deutscher Camping-Club e.V.
Postfach 400428
Mandlstrasse 28
D-8000 München 40

(providing information on youth hostels)
Deutscher Jugendherbergs-Verband
Buelowstrasse 26
D-4330 Detmold 1

GERMAN DEMOCRATIC REPUBLIC

(providing information on various topics)
PANORAMA DDR
Auslandspresseagentur GmbH

Wilhelm-Pieck-Strasse 49
1054 Berlin
(*providing publications*)
Liga für Völkerfreundschaft der DDR
Thälmannplatz 8/9
1080 Berlin

TEACHING SUGGESTIONS

LEKTION 1

A. Instructional Objectives

After completing all the material in *Lektion 1*, the students should be able to:
1. greet each other in German
2. identify greetings, farewells and introductions
3. properly use *du* and *Sie*
4. identify all and use some of the boys' and girls' names listed
5. ask simple questions to determine where a person lives
6. use numbers 0–10
7. use personal pronouns
8. use the present tense of regular verb forms
9. say the German alphabet and spell familiar words using it
10. pronounce short and long /a/

B. Allerlei

1. Game — *Die Schreibmaschine*

You might play this game, using the vocabulary of *Lektion 1*, once you have presented the German alphabet and your class has practiced it. Use p. 4 of the textbook for practice. *Die Schreibmaschine* strengthens spelling accuracy in German. To set up the game, divide the class into two teams. Then assign a letter of the alphabet — including the letters *ä, ö, ü* and *ß* — to individual members of each team. In doing this, be sure each team has members that represent the whole alphabet. If the class is small, then assign several letters to single players.

Start the game by giving one team a word from the lesson to spell orally. They must do this so fast that they sound like a typewriter; hence, the name of the game. You may set a time limit for calling out letters, say one or two seconds. Let's take one example. The word is *gehen*. The student with the letter *g* calls out that letter in German and teammates with the appropriate letters complete, in turn, the spelling of *gehen*. By doing this, the team earns one point. Then the other team gets their shot at a word. Whenever a team fails, its rival gets a chance to spell the word and win another point. The game can last as long as you like, depending on the goal of the game.

2. Game — *Buchstabiert es!*

Divide the class into teams. Each team challenges the other(s) by asking them to spell a word. You may want to limit each word to five or six letters initially.

3. Class activity — Greetings

After practicing the greetings in the *Dialog*, *Ergänzung* and reading about them in the *Kulturecke 1*, act them out. Divide the class into groups of three. Have one group member introduce a second member to the third one. It might go something like this: "*Heike, das ist Stefan.*" Heike responds, "*Tag, Stefan!*" (or "*Grüß dich, Stefan!*"). As part of their greetings, students should shake hands in the German manner.

4. Class project — Pen pals

A number of organizations will make arrangements to get pen pals from German-speaking countries for American students based on the students' sex, age and interests. You may want to contact some of the organizations listed on page TE16 for assistance. Exchanging letters with German-speaking people will give your students a chance to communicate with their peers overseas. At first your students will correspond mostly in English, but this project should spur them on to write more in German.

C. Background Information

page 1 — This dialog sequence was photographed in Buchenau, a western suburb of Munich.

page 11 — Handshaking used to be a normal part of everyday greetings. However, in recent years, more and more Germans shake hands only when meeting strangers, when seeing friends or relatives after a prolonged absence, or when congratulating. The practice now varies so much in all regions and population groups that it is impossible to give a strict rule for all occasions. When in doubt, it is better for Americans to wait until the German makes the first move.

page 12 — A recent survey revealed that about one fourth of all adult Germans quickly change to "*du*" after having made friends, but more than 40% wait for quite some time. Men use "*du*" twice as often with friends as women do.

Many young people up to their mid-twenties normally use the "*du*" among each other. Students will say "*Sie*" to their teachers and professors and vice versa, unless the professors are exceptionally progressive-minded and insist on "*du*."

The foreigner in Germany is always well advised to use "*Sie*" (and the family name) first and then play it by ear. Usually it is the older person who suggests the switch to "*du*." If two Germans decide to associate on a "*du*" basis, they may even today celebrate the occasion, which is called "*Brüderschaft trinken*" (drink to brotherhood). Both hold their glass of wine or beer in their hands and hook their arms (holding the beverage) while sipping from their own glass. Then they shake hands and, (if women) kiss lightly, and announce their first name such as "*Ich heiße Monika.*" Although this "*Brüderschaft*" ceremony is regarded by many as ridiculous, it is often practiced for fun.

Americans, in becoming acquainted, automatically try to create a relaxed, informal atmosphere; Germans react with a kind of polite formality. Germans accept distance between strangers as a normal fact of life, and the "*Sie*" means just that. There is no offense implied.

LEKTION 2

A. Instructional Objectives

After completing all the material in *Lektion 2*, the students should be able to:

1. use the days of the week and time units
2. ask and tell time (full hour)
3. use numbers 11–20 and solve simple addition and subtraction problems
4. understand the time system used in Germany
5. form questions and statements
6. use the forms of *haben*
7. understand the usage of the definite article
8. understand the difference between *zu Hause* and *nach Hause*
9. pronounce short and long /i/

B. Allerlei

1. Game — *Ich telefoniere.*
Divide the class into several teams. Whisper a sentence to the first person on each team who in turn will whisper it to the next person, until the sentence gets to the last person on the team. The last person will announce what s/he heard. The team that has the closest version of the original sentence scores a point.

2. Game — *Wie heißt das Wort?*
Divide the class into teams. Each student is given a word in either German or English and asked to supply the equivalent in the other language to score a point for his/her team.

3. Class activity — German popular music
Your students will enjoy listening to currently popular German songs. Choose a recording with words that are fairly clear and easy to understand, perhaps a slow song such as a ballad. Before playing it in class, give a little background information on the singer and song. Next you might hand each student a sheet of the lyrics. Leave blank spaces on the sheets for words that students already know. Ask the students to write in the missing words while you play the selection several times. To cap off this activity, you might translate the whole song for your class.

4. Class activity — *Wer ruft an?*
Have your students bring two telephones to school (students could also improvise using the phone). Ask one of your students to answer the phone. Give the caller a name (see list in *Lektion 1*). Improvise

the phone ringing. The activity could go like this: (Student A = caller; Student B = person receiving call and disguising his voice).

Student B: *Hier Uwe Meier. Wer ist da?*
Student A: *Ich sage das nicht.*
Student B: *Bist du ein Junge oder ein Mädchen?*
Student A: *Ein Junge.*
Student B: *Wie viele Buchstaben hat dein Name?*
Student A: *Fünf.*
Student B: *Beginnt dein Name mit A...? B...C...*
(Student A says, "Nein" each time until the letter "P" comes up, at which time Student A can guess. If s/he doesn't get it, another student takes over with the 2nd letter, another with the 3rd letter, until the fifth — if needed)
Student B (or C-E): *Heißt du Peter?*
Student A: *Richtig.*

C. Background Information

page 15 — When answering the phone, whether at home or in the office, it is customary in Germany to give one's family name. About half of the German households have a telephone. Those who do not have a phone can make their calls from a *Bundespost*-owned telephone booth. Local calls cost 20 pfennigs. For more specific information on the German telephone system, refer to the section on this subject in *Lektion A* (p. 119).

page 24 — These three girls (Monika, Susanne and Katrin) attend the *Gymnasium* in Buchenau, a newer community outside Munich. Most of the apartment buildings and houses (including the high school) were built during the past ten to fifteen years. The *S-Bahn* (a city train) connects the many communities around such cities as Munich, Hamburg, Berlin and Cologne. Clearly-posted charts show the complete *S-Bahn* system including the many different connections with the *U-Bahn* (subway).

page 29 — To familiarize students with different times and the cultural differences involved in telling time, various clocks from all parts of the *BRD* and the *DDR* have been shown on the filmstrips. Here is a summary in sequence of the visuals shown:
Eisenach/Wartburg (DDR): a sundial located right inside the fortress where Martin Luther translated the Bible.
Ost-Berlin (DDR): the famous world clock on the *Alexanderplatz* showing the times from all parts of the world.
Würzburg (BRD): many clocks on top of a store in the center of the downtown shopping area.
Buchenau/München: near the *Gymnasium*.
Rothenburg ob der Tauber (BRD): the *Ratstrinkstube* where the famous *Meistertrunk* (which saved the town during the Thirty Year's War, 1618–1648) is recreated three times a day by moving figures in the right and left window. For more information see

Lektion 10, Lesestück 2 (including background information).

Leipzig (DDR): clock in front of the *Hauptbahnhof*, the largest terminal railroad station in Europe (26 tracks).

Sellin (DDR): clock located at the entrance to the beach of the Baltic Sea (*Ostsee*).

Würzburg (BRD): clock at the *Hauptbahnhof*.

Rothenburg ob der Tauber (BRD): clock at one of the many towers that are part of the city wall (*Stadtmauer*).

Essen (BRD): downtown shopping mall.

Mainz (BRD): church tower clock along the Rhine River.

Leipzig (DDR): clock in the old town of Leipzig.

Titisee (BRD): clock in this Black Forest town.

München (BRD): clock at the *Hauptbahnhof*.

München (BRD): clock next to entrance of the *S-Bahn*.

Eibsee (BRD): train schedule at the small station, located between Garmisch-Partenkirchen and the Zugspitze.

Bremen (BRD): church schedules announcing the times of various services.

Neustadt/Weinstraße (BRD): office hours of a local bank.

Konstanz (BRD): clock indicating departure times of the boats crossing Lake Constance (*Bodensee*).

LEKTION 3

A. Instructional Objectives

After completing all the material in *Lektion 3*, the students should be able to:

1. ask simple questions pertaining to purchasing a train ticket
2. understand all aspects of train travel in Germany
3. use numbers 10–100
4. ask and tell time (all)
5. identify (on a map) and say the neighboring countries of Germany
6. understand the general size of the *BRD* and *DDR*
7. use the accusative of *der*, *die* and *das* and the related question words *wer*, *wen* and *was*
8. use the forms of *sein*
9. know the difference between *kennen* and *wissen*
10. be familiar with words used for emphasis
11. pronounce the short and long /o/

B. Allerlei

1. Game — *Lotto*
After presenting and practicing the numbers from 0–100, you might hand out cards bearing these numbers (you may decide to use fewer numbers) and play the German version of "Bingo."

2. Game — *Summ!*
After presenting and practicing numbers 0–100, you might play this game. Similar to the English game called "Buzz," *Summ!* drills knowledge of numbers in German. The game starts with the students standing up and ends when only one of them remain on his/her feet. Students count off in German. The first student says *null*, the second *eins*, the third *zwei*, etc. They must watch out when an arbitrarily chosen number or its multiple comes up. Traditionally, the number 7 is used, though the game plays well with numbers like 5, 6 or 8. Students must also be alert when it's their turn to give either a number containing 7 (e.g., 17) or a multiple of 7 (e.g., 14, 21, 28). The student says *Summ!* in lieu of *sieben* or any number related to it. The teacher spots those responding incorrectly and asks each in turn to sit down. Of course, a student can slip up and be seated even when the number to be given has nothing to do with 7. The count picks up after the next student in line corrects the error by saying *Summ!* or the right number, depending on the type of mistake made. Though students compete against each other, the whole class will take pride in keeping this game going for longer and longer stretches.

3. Game — *Wer weiß die Antwort?*
A student from a team sees or hears a math problem (addition-subtraction) that s/he must state orally and give the correct answer in order to score a point for his/her team.

4. Individual project — Map
After learning the names of the neighboring countries in the *Ergänzung* and additional information (capitals of the *BRD* and the *DDR*) in *Lesestück 2*, each student could make a map of Germany (*BRD* and *DDR*). You might suggest that students use different colors to depict the various geographical features. Different colors should also be used for identifying the *BRD* and the *DDR*, as both of these countries are considered separate countries. Have students save the map for future use of other geographical features discussed in subsequent lessons.

5. Class activity — Train schedules
After the class reads and studies the *Kulturecke*, you might hand out copies of a German train schedule. (These can be obtained from German Rail, 747 3rd Avenue, New York, N.Y. 10017). Then ask students to use the schedule to plan a trip between two cities that you name, one as the point of departure and the other as the point of arrival. Students must decide which is the best train to take and give reasons for their choice (e.g., speed, good accommodations, cost).

C. Background Information

page 33 — In major train stations, the traveler will find luggage carts (*Koffer-Kulis*) for transporting luggage directly to the train. The traveler, departing from a station and looking for departure information, will find the following specific details listed on the *Abfahrt* schedule: *Zeit* (time of departure), *Zur Nr.* (train number), *Nach* (destination), *Gleis* (track) or *Bahnsteig* (platform). Major German stations, like the one in Frankfurt, have arrival and departure times listed on TV screens. Classes of cars are prominently marked "1" or "2" so the traveler can get into the compartment for which s/he bought tickets. If the train is expected to be crowded, it may be worthwhile to pay an additional nominal amount and get a *Platzkarte* (reserved seat).

page 45 — Conductors are no longer seen in streetcars. Tickets must be purchased prior to getting on. Every stop has ticket automats, usually marked "*Fahrausweise*" where tickets can be purchased. The fine for not having a ticket is 40 marks. Many students, especially those going to a *Realschule* or *Gymnasium* (like Kerstin and Gabi), have to take public transportation.

page 49 — The *BRD* (*Bundersrepublik Deutschland*) lies in the center of Europe, between the Scandinavian countries to the north, the Alpine countries to the south, the countries in Atlantic Western Europe and in Continental East Europe. Of the 61 million people living in the *BRD*, there are between 4 to 5 million foreigners. There were only 20 million people in the same area 100 years ago. The greatest population increase occurred immediately after World War II, when more than 14 million refugees and displaced people from Germany's eastern territories and from the *DDR* came in. Since 1974 the population has been declining. There are 247 people per square kilometer. Only the Netherlands and Belgium are more densely populated in Europe.

The *DDR* (*Deutsche Demokratische Republik*) is located to the east of the *BRD*. East of the *DDR* is Poland and southeast Czechoslovakia. The Baltic Sea (*Ostsee*) forms its northern frontier. The average population density is 154 inhabitants per square kilometer. This density could be compared with that of the states of New York and Maryland.

pages 52–54 — Ticket counters at a German train station are conspicuously located, usually in the main hall. You can buy a ticket at any window, often marked "*Fahrkarten — Inland.*" If you want to go outside of Germany, look for a window marked "*Ausland.*" The following types of tickets are most common: *eine Fahrkarte, einfach* (one-way ticket), *eine Fahrkarte, hin und zurück* (round-trip ticket), *eine Tagesrückfahrkarte* (a reduced ticket for one-day round trip within 50 kilometers from your departure point), *eine Sonderrückfahrkarte* (special, reduced round-trip ticket — particularly for weekend trips).

Furthermore, there are all kinds of reductions for groups (two adults and one child form a "minigroup"). Large reductions (usually 50%) are possible for holders of a *Senioren-Paß* (for young people

between 12 and 22), and a *Eurail* pass, which can be purchased in the U.S. prior to departure. The *Eurail* pass can save a tremendous amount of money for those who intend to use European trains extensively during their trip.

There are several types of trains (listed on the *Ankunft* and *Abfahrt* schedules).
1. Those listed in black type are *Nahverkehrszüge*, which are more or less "milk trains" that stop at every small town.
2. The first of the trains marked in red is the *Eilzug*. These trains are marked with an "E" before the train number. It is advisable to take this train for trips of 50 kilometers or less.
3. Next is the *D-Zug* and *D-City-Zug*, marked with a "D" or "DC" before the train number. These trains are faster and make fewer stops then the "E"-trains, but for distances under 50 kilometers you pay a bit extra — 3 marks, a so-called *Zuschlag* (supplement). D-City trains connect 73 German towns with the four main routes of the "Intercity" system.
4. The fourth kind of train has an "IC" (for *Intercity-Zug*) or "TEE" (for *Trans-Europa-Express*) before the train number. These comfortable long-distance trains are very fast and do not stop in smaller towns. But again, you pay extra for the fast service and comfort. The *Zuschlag* is 10 marks for first class and 3 marks for second class (including seat reservation — *Platzkarte*). The *TEE*-trains have only first class.

Your ticket will probably be punched once while you're on the train. The conductor may ask for "*Fahrkarten,*" or he may use the expression "*Ist noch jemand zugestiegen?*" This means "Has anyone here boarded since tickets were last checked?" Normally, you show your ticket only once.

German trains, like other European trains, have no drinking water. The water from the faucet in the lavatory is not drinkable. If you're thirsty, try to catch a vendor selling bottled drinks.

As for restroom facilities, you'll find them at the end of the car. There are no separate facilities for men and women. The sign on the door will say "*Toilette.*" The sign near the handle of the door will tell you whether the room is occupied (*besetzt*) or free (*frei*).

Except for *TEE* and *IC* trains, stops are not announced in the train, but over loudspeakers in the station. It's a good idea to check the schedule and know about when you'll arrive at your destination.

LEKTION 4

A. Instructional Objectives

After completing all the material in *Lektion 4*, the students should be able to:
1. name the months of the year and the seasons

2. ask and answer questions about their school subjects
3. ask the age of other students
4. describe how they get to school
5. describe a typical school day
6. list the ten *Länder* (including capitals) and know their location
7. discuss the similarities and differences of the school system in the *BRD* and *DDR*
8. use the indefinite article (*nominative* and *accusative*)
9. use plural nouns (*nominative* and *accusative*)
10. understand the difference between *kein* and *nicht* and be able to use both in sentences
11. form commands
12. form questions using the question words *wo*, *wohin*, *woher*
13. use *gern*
14. pronounce /x/ and /ch/

B. Allerlei

1. Game — *Das nächste Wort?*
The class is divided into two teams. A player from each team calls out any day, month, number, etc., that is part of a definite sequence. The corresponding person from the other team has to say the next item in the sequence. For example, Player 1 of Team A says "*Montag.*" Player 1 of Team B will have to say "*Dienstag.*" The same rules apply to the other categories. A point is scored for each correct answer.

2. Game — *Ratet mal!*
This game is similar to "Hangman." The object of this game is to guess a word. Confine words to categories like nouns, verbs, adjectives, etc. A student from one team goes to the board and thinks of a word. S/he writes blanks for each letter on the board. The other team (or the whole class) now guesses each letter in German (good review of the alphabet!). If the correct letter has been guessed, the student will write that letter on the first blank. If it's incorrect, s/he will draw the first part of the hanged man. This game will go on until either the complete word has been guessed or the hangman has been completed.

3. Class project — *Stundenplan*
Have your students make up a school schedule, including school days, class time(s), subjects and activities. The schedule does not have to represent their real school schedule but could be fictitious. Once every student has his/her own schedule, have students ask each other such questions as: *Wie viele Fächer hast du?*, *Was hast du am Montag?*, *Hast du Physik?*, *Wann?*, *Was für ein Fach hast du am Montag um zehn Uhr?*

4. Individual project — Map
Include the *Länder* (and their respective capitals) in the map started in *Lektion 3*. If your students did not draw a map, this might be a good place to start. Besides the *Länder*, your students should also include the other features discussed in *Lektion 3* (*Nachbarländer*).

C. Background Information
page 57 — These pictures were taken at the *Nicolaus Cusanus Gymnasium* in Bergisch-Gladbach. There are several separate buildings with the school yard in the center. The four students (Stefan, Dirk, Elke and Oliver) are in the schoolyard during their recess (*Große Pause*).

pages 71–73 — There are 38 major universities in the *BRD*, not counting technical universities, comprehensive universities, colleges of medicine and veterinary science or church-affiliated colleges. About 950,000 students are enrolled at these universities — more than five times as many as 20 years ago. About 52,000 are foreigners. Traditionally students are quite free to determine their own courses of study. Although many subjects are recommended and interim examinations are obligatory, the students can make up their own schedules from a wide selection of courses.

No tuition fees are charged at universities. If neither the students themselves nor their parents are able to pay for their living expenses, the *Land* (federal district) helps out. Every other student receives some financial assistance, depending on the parents' means.

The tremendous growth of university students has led to enrollment restrictions that became necessary for a number of courses. Not all applicants are able to study at the university of their choice. The criteria for acceptance is based on the average grades of the *Abitur*, waiting time and hardship.

pages 76–77 — The largest *Land* in physical size is *Bayern*; the largest in population is *Nordrhein-Westfalen*. As a matter of fact, it is Europe's most densely populated region, with 504 persons to the square kilometer (1,318 to the square mile). Some of the *Länder* including *Bayern*, *Hamburg* and *Bremen* have a long constitutional history. Other *Länder* such as *Rheinland-Pfalz* and *Niedersachsen* came into being only after 1945, with the sometimes rather arbitrarily-drawn borders of the former Zones of Occupation playing a part. After the dissolution of the *Land Preußen* in 1946, Prussia's western provinces became *Länder* of their own, such as *Schleswig-Holstein* or parts of newly-formed *Länder*. For instance, the *Land Nordhein-Westfalen* was created out of the *Rhine* province (minus the southern part) and the province of *Westfalen*. Hannover was merged with *Niedersachsen*, *Hessen-Nassau* and *Hessen*. Together with the onetime Bavarian *Rheinland-Pfalz*, the southern part of the Rhine province formed the *Land Rheinland-Pfalz*. The *Land Baden-Württemberg* came into being in

1952 on the strength of a plebiscite. The Saar Territory (detached from the Western Zones of Occupation before 1949) returned to the Federal Republic of Germany as *Saarland* on January 1, 1957, and became fully integrated economically on May 6, 1959.

pages 80–81 — *Kindergarten* (ages 3–6) is voluntary. Compulsory education begins with the age of 6 and lasts 9 years. At the age of 15, those who do not continue with their education must attend a vocational school once or twice a week as part of their training until the age of 18.

Children between 6 and 10 attend the primary school (*Grundschule*). Most children and their parents face the difficult decision of the choice of secondary school at the age of 10. They can go to either a secondary modern school (*Hauptschule*), an intermediate school (*Realschule*), the academically-oriented high school (*Gymnasium*) or, in some of the cases, the comprehensive school (*Gesamtschule*). In order to facilitate their choice and their transition to secondary education, an "orientation phase" (grades 5 and 6) was introduced in all the *Länder*. More than 15% of children leaving fourth grade are now going into these orientation courses.

More than 50% of all students attend the *Hauptschule*, 20% the *Realschule* and about 20 to 25% go to the *Gymnasium* (the remaining students attend special schools). Of the 15% out of the total school population graduating with the *Abitur* (final high school diploma), only about half of them are able to attend the universities since universities have been overbooked and presently take students only with a *Gymnasium* final grade average of 1.7 (1 = A, 2 = B).

pages 82–84 — This high school (*Johannes R. Becher Oberschule*) was named after the poet Johannes R. Becher, who became the first Minister of Culture of the *DDR*.

Pre-school education establishments (*Kinderkrippen* and *Kindergarten*) are built and maintained by the government as well as by enterprises in the socialist industry and agriculture. They are all government supervised, and are fitted out with a wide variety of toys and teaching aids appropriate for children of that age. Regular attendance by a doctor is also insured by the authorities.

The comprehensive school (*Oberschule*) is attended by children for a period of ten years. Great emphasis is placed on relating school matter to real life. The students must grasp what goes on in the production processes in a socialist society and prepare themselves not only for making a contribution to this later on, but for playing an active part in society generally, including cultural and intellectual life. The political and moral aspect of teaching is directed toward bringing up people who are committed not only to the communist future, but who are already developing communist pattern of thought and behavior.

The working class has a direct influence on the education the younger generation receives. Children in grades 7 to 10 spend a certain amount of time in selected factories or on farms as part of their curriculum. As part of this process, work-teams in factories or on farms often "adopt" a particular school or class.

Those children who complete the ten full years at the *Oberschule* may apply to stay another two years to take their *Abitur*, the diploma that entitles them to advanced level of study. Of all students leaving the *Oberschule*, 99% become apprentices.

LEKTION 5

A. Instructional Objectives

After completing all the material in *Lektion 5*, the students should be able to:

1. talk about going to a movie
2. identify and name rooms in a house or apartment
3. name the date
4. use the terms for family relationships
5. describe a typical day in their life
6. describe Austria (size, neighboring countries, cities, mountains, rivers and lakes)
7. discuss leisure-time activities in Germany and how they resemble or differ from our own
8. use modal auxiliaries (present tense)
9. use the future tense
10. use pronouns (nominative and accusative)
11. understand the use of verbs with separable prefixes in sentences
12. pronounce short and long /u/ and /e/

B. Allerlei

1. Game — *Was machst du während des Tages?*
Prepare a number of questions beforehand. These questions could be like the following: *Um wieviel Uhr stehst du auf?* (you may have to explain the meaning of *aufstehen*), *Was machst du dann?*, *Wann gehst du zur Schule?*, *Welches Fach hast du in der 1. Stunde?* (you can continue with "2. Stunde." "3. Stunde," etc.), *Was macht dein Vater?* (*deine Mutter?*), *Um wieviel Uhr kommst du aus der Schule?*

Hand out a blank sheet of paper to each student. As you ask each question at a time, have students write an answer starting at the top of the paper. After they are finished, tell students to fold the small section of the written portion so that it is not visible; then, have students pass their sheet to the next person and read the second question. Continue this procedure until you have all the questions. Be sure that students continue folding the paper each time an answer has been written so that none of the answers can be seen by the next student.

At the end ask students to unfold their paper and give a description by reading the answers to the question, "*Was machst du während des Tages?*" The story can be quite funny and add a great deal of amusement.

2. Game — *Konzentration*

To review the conjugation of the verbs, modal auxiliaries and the use of *werden*, you might play this game. It resembles the English game of the same name (Concentration). For each student, you write out a different verb (including modal auxiliaries) on an 8½ × 11 sheet of paper. Tape one of the sheets to the desk top of each student. It must hang over the desk edge. Students should move their desks into a circle, allowing them full view of the sheets.

Now the game begins. All students hit the tops of their desks with the palms of their hands twice and clap their hands twice. One assigned student (or the teacher) then calls out one of the verbs plus a subject in this basic "1–2" rhythm (*wissen — du*). Keeping the "1–2" beat, all students hit their desk twice, clap twice and the student who has the verb *wissen* calls out *du weißt*. Then all students again hit their desk twice, clap twice and the student with the verb *wissen* calls out another verb subject (e.g. *müssen — ihr*). This sets off another round of desk-tapping, hand-clapping and verb-calling. If a student misses his/her turn, mispronounces the verb or responds out of rhythm, the student flips his/her verb sheet up to signify s/he is out of the game. Continue playing, at as lively a pace as possible, until one student remains. This game may strike senior high students as infantile, but it's a challenge to play it right especially when it moves at a fast pace.

3. Class project — Calendars

Now that your students have learned the days of the week (*Lektion 2*), the months of the year (*Lektion 4*) and the date in German (this lesson), you might have them make German calendars. Some students could make a calendar of the entire year, while others could make a monthly calendar listing the holidays, special school events, tests, etc. for that particular month. A monthly calendar could be placed in a prominent place in the classroom. The rest of your students could make the calendars for upcoming months. All students should work on these projects as part of a team you form.

4. Individual project — *What else do Germans do in their spare time?*

After students have read and studied the *Kulturecke* (Entertainment and Leisure-Time Activities), you might assign this individual project to your better or interested students. Have them collect German magazines or newspapers (you may have some in your classroom) or ask them to contact the German Information Center, 410 Park Avenue, New York, NY 10022 for assistance. Needless to say, Germans are involved in other interesting leisure-time activities that your students might want to report about.

C. Background Information

page 87 — The film industry in the Federal Republic of Germany has been facing a crisis for years. In the 1950s the movie theaters attracted more than 800 million people, whereas only 115 million attended in the late 1970s. However, in recent years the German movie industry has seen a 17% increase, which is partially due to the fact that the quality of German films has improved markedly.

More than 25% of all movies shown in Germany have been imported from the U.S. Only one third of the films shown are of German origin. Contrary to theaters in this country, there are different price ranges in German theaters. The most reasonable seats are in the front row. The more expensive seats can be found toward the back and in the balcony.

pages 101–102 — Marzahn, a suburb of Ost-Berlin, is a totally new community that has been built the past 10 to 15 years. Tens of thousands of people live here, mostly in apartment buildings. Marzahn, as well as most newly created towns or cities, is self-sufficient. Schools, shops and youth centers are all part of this community. There are two main TV stations programmed by the *DDR*. However, people of Ost-Berlin can also watch the three TV stations that come from the *BRD*.

pages 105–106 — Austria is situated in southern central Europe, covering a part of the eastern Alps and the Danube region. Although it is land-locked, it has close contacts with the Mediterranean area. The country has a wide variety of landscape, vegetation and climate and, situated as it is at the heart of the continent, it has always been a junction for communication between the trade and cultural centers of Europe.

Austria has common boundaries with no fewer then seven countries that belong to a variety of social and economic systems. With the exception of the Magyars of Hungary, who belong to the Ural-Altaic group of peoples, Austria's neighbors belong to the major European nations, the Germanic, Romanic and Slavic groups.

Austria is a federal state consisting of nine provinces — Vorarlberg, Tirol, Salzburg, Carinthia, Styria, Upper Austria, Lower Austria, Vienna and the Burgenland. The colors of the Austrian flag are red, white and red, and the coat-of-arms is a single-headed eagle with a mural crown at its head, holding a hammer and sickle. These symbols represent the three most important sections of the population — the hammer for the workers, the sickle for the farmers and the crown for the middle classes. Between the eagle's talons is a broken chain, symbolizing the restoration of Austrian independence in 1945.

Vienna (population 1,615,000), the Austrian capital, is a federal province in its own right. It is situated in the eastern part of the country, surrounded on all sides by the province of Lower Austria, only about forty miles from the borders of Hungary and Czechoslovakia. One of the foundations of Vienna's development into a leading European city is its position at the junction between east-west trade route along the Danube and the long established communications link between the Baltic countries and the Mediterranean.

Graz (population 250,000) Austria's second largest city, was best known in the days of the monarchy as the place to which state officials liked to retire. It is now a thriving, modern city known to visitors from many countries, especially for its characteristic landmark, the clock-tower on the Schloßberg.

Linz (population 208,000), with its modern Danube port installations, is a major center for the production of iron, steel and chemicals.

Salzburg (population 137,000) is the capital of the province of *Salzburg*. The salt that gave both the city and the province their name has been mined in this region for centuries. Once the home of Mozart, it has developed since 1945 into a focal point for international tourist trade. All of the old city has been preserved and represents a work of art in its own right.

Innsbruck (population 120,000) is situated at the junction of numerous trancontinental communications links. The Inn Valley motorway extends west. The Brenner motorway is one of the most sophisticated super highways in Europe. Innsbruck (two Winter Olympic Games were held here) is a popular ski area for skiers coming from all over the world.

pages 108–110 — The *Litfaßsäulen* are named after Ernst Litfaß, a Berlin printer, who created such pillars in 1855. West-Berlin alone has over 2,000 of these columns. Tickets for any cultural or sports event can be purchased in ticket offices (*Vorverkauf*) usually found in the center of major cities. Germany has always offered extensive cultural enrichment. There are 300 theaters, 80 symphony orchestras, and 1,800 museums in the *BRD*.

Although it is called the *Oktoberfest*, most of this gigantic affair takes place during the latter part of September. It ends in early October. It is the Bavarian National Festival and, as such, the emphasis is on drinking beer. Incredible quantities of *Wiesenbier*, which is especially strong, are downed every year at the *Oktoberfest*, together with many tons of pork, sausages, roasted chicken, and oxen from the spit. Several million attend the festival each year.

The highlight of the *Karneval* in Cologne is the parade on *Rosenmontag*. This parade is usually four to five miles long. In slow procession, it winds through the city, with huge floats, horses, bands, funny groups of jesters wearing grotesque or comical masks, and "regiments" of Fools Guilds in their traditional, picturesque uniforms.

Soccer (*Fußball*) is the king of sports in Germany and attracts an average of 20 million spectators to both stadiums and TV sets every Saturday afternoon during the *Bundesliga* season.

Walking, hiking, swimming and gardening are most popular. About one third of the population take car rides once in a while, but two thirds of all families go for a walk (*Spazierengehen*) regularly on Sundays.

Young people between 13 and 15 years of age have little more free time than their parents. One third of the youngsters in this age group spend their leisure hours with a clique of ten or more, enjoying sports, swimming, exchanging records or cassettes. Of the 16- to 18-year-olds, 15% visit a disco occasionally on weekends.

LEKTION A

A. Instruction Objectives

After completing all the material in *Lektion A*, students should be able to:
1. understand the reading selection and talk about its content
2. complete all the exercises without any difficulty (grammar has been covered before)
3. use the various ways of greeting people in Germany
4. be familiar with the use of a private and public telephone in Germany
5. understand the basic coin and bank note units used in the *BRD* and *DDR*
6. be familiar with and discuss German railroad stations and streetcar systems

B. Allerlei

1. Game — *Wie viele Wörter kannst du bilden?*
Give your students (individual students or teams) a fairly long word. The object is to find as many new words in it as possible.

2. Game — *Ein Buchstabe, aber wie viele Wörter?*
Give your students (or teams) a letter and have them come up with as many words as possible. Example: The letter is "g" (*gehen, Gepäck, groß, Geld, Glück*). You may want to limit a more frequently appearing letter to nouns, verbs or adjectives.

3. Class activity — *Zungenbrecher*

You may want to select any of the five tongue twisters (*Zungenbrecher*) introduced in the first five lessons and see who can say each one the fastest.

LEKTION 6

A. Instructional Objectives

After completing all the material in *Lektion 6*, the students should be able to:

1. be familiar with the German terms for clothing items
2. identify and name different colors
3. describe shopping in a department store
4. describe Switzerland (size, neighboring countries, cities)
5. discuss similarities and differences in going shopping in Germany vs. in the U.S.
6. use the dative (indirect object, with verbs and after prepositions)
7. understand the difference between *wie viele* and *wieviel*
8. form compound nouns
9. pronounce /sch/

B. Allerlei

1. Game — *Ich gehe einkaufen.*

The object of the game is to remember what was said before and add another item. The first person, for example, says, "*Ich gehe einkaufen. Ich kaufe ein Hemd.*" The second person might say, "*Ich gehe einkaufen. Ich kaufe ein Hemd und eine Hose.*" The third person will repeat everything the second person said and add another clothing item. A student who cannot repeat what was previously said (or makes a mistake) is out of the game.

2. Class activity — Clothing and colors

After your students have learned the terms for clothing items and colors, you might have them do this activity. Pass out current issues of German magazines such as *Bunte Illustrierte*, *Stern*, *Quick* or others and tell students to find and clip out photos of the latest styles. The pictures they collect should display a wide variety of clothes in various colors. Next, they could write captions in German that name the items and colors depicted. For example, *Der Herr hat einen Anzug an. Er ist braun.* Finally, you might have your students present their work to the class, both showing their pictures and reading their captions.

3. Class activity — Going to the bank and department store

Have students make some paper money and coins (see denominations in *Lektion A*) and have them bring different clothing items to school. Improvise a shopping scene by setting up a bank and a department store (or clothing store). Assign parts (customers, clerk and/or cashier at bank and store).

Students should be free to act out a shopping situation according to their ideas. Depending on the caliber of your class, you may or may not decide to have students prepare beforehand.

4. Individual project — Switzerland

After your students have read and studied *Lesestück 2* (*Die Schweiz*), tell them to pretend they are going to Switzerland. Have them plan what they want to see. Ask them to write their travel plans (in English) after they decide what kind of itinerary they prefer — a wide-ranging tour, an extended stay at one favorite site, or visits to one type of attraction (e.g. ski resorts). Your students can find some valuable information through your school or local library, travel agents (with free brochures) or the Swiss National Tourist Office (608 Fifth Avenue, New York, N.Y. 10020) — providing travel brochures.

C. Background Information

page 123 — The German banking scene is dominated by three large commercial banks (Deutsche Bank, Dresdner Bank, and Commerzbank) with branch offices all across the *BRD*; in addition there are very sizeable regional banks and hundreds of savings banks (*Sparkassen*). The Post Office, too, offers banking services. Unless you plan to play the ever-fluctuating currency market, it may be advisable to convert your money to German traveler's checks prior to leaving the U.S. Checks made out in German currency are paid in full, whereas American traveler checks (payable in dollars) are converted and then a nominal fee for this transaction is added.

page 134 — It is important, particularly for Americans to try on clothing because not only the sizes, but also the cuts, vary. There are additional variations between clothing items from other countries — France, Italy, Greece, Spain, East European or Far East countries.

pages 138–39 — Though quite small in area, Switzerland, located in the center of the Western European continent, has a wealth of scenic beauty. The Alps, grouped around the Gotthard Massif are most impressive here; they reach their greatest altitude in Switzerland with the Dufour Peak of Monte Rosa which is 15,215 feet high. These impressive looking mountain ranges are visible far beyond the Swiss borders; they are the landmark of the country. Here too is the source of the rivers and streams that start as mountain waters, and eventually flow to all parts of Europe. The Rhine, after 235 miles in Switzerland, eventually flows to the North Sea. The Rhine reaches the French frontier 165 miles away from its source in the glaciers and turns south to the Mediterranean. The Inn feeds the Danube from the Grisons and so forms a link between Switzerland and the Black Sea; and finally the Ticino flows from the Gotthard to become a tributary of the Po, which in turn empties into the Adriatic. Over 40 rivers and more than 50 lakes have molded the face of Switzerland. North of the Alps, the landscape becomes broader and more peaceful, with hills, valleys and fertile fields, only to soar upwards, between the Rhine and the Rhone, to the ridges of the Jura, a totally different kind of mountains, covered with soft meadows and plunging steeply down into the valleys.

Of the total population of almost 6,400,000, there are over 900,000 foreigners living in Switzerland. Three fourths of the population lives in the Central Lowlands between the Alps and the Jura and over two fifths in cities and towns of more than 10,000.

pages 142–44 — The unit of currency in the *BRD*, the *Deutsche Mark* (DM), was created in 1948. Since then the DM has changed its value several times. For two weeks during the winter and summer (starting officially on the last Monday in January and the last Monday in July respectively), German shops have their big sales, called *"Winter- oder Sommerschlußverkauf."* In recent years, many shops have started with *Ausverkauf* much earlier than on the fixed dates, offering certain items at reduced prices as *Sonderangebot* (special offer). Large department stores are found in larger as well as average-size German cities. Some of the major department stores are *Hertie, Kaufhof, Horten* and *Karstadt.*

LEKTION 7

A. Instructional Objectives

After completing all the material in *Lektion 7*, the students should be able to:
1. develop a conversation centered around checking into a hotel
2. talk about the weather
3. identify and name important means of transportation
4. describe in simple language a German youth hostel
5. talk about the two German capital cities — Bonn and Berlin (Ost)
6. discuss foreign influence in Germany
7. discuss German influence in the U.S. and relate it to their own community, if possible
8. use dative pronouns
9. use verbs with stem vowel change *a-ä, e-i* and *e-ie*
10. pronounce short and long /ü/

B. Allerlei

1. Game — *Zwanzig Fragen*
Have one of your students think of an object, a person or a place. The other students should ask him/her questions that s/he will answer with "ja" or "nein." The goal of the game is to guess the object, person or place in twenty questions.

2. Game — *Die Wortpyramide*
Give your students a short word. For each letter of the word, your students will have to write out a word. Example: HOTEL = *h*aben, *o*der, *T*ag, *ein*, *Lehrer*. If you want to make this game more challenging, you could limit the word to a particular category (school, home, etc.) and/or specify how many letters the new words should have.

3. Class project — *Wo übernachten wir?*
Divide your students into several groups. Have each group prepare a situation (preferably in dialog form) describing their search for a place to stay overnight (youth hostel, hotel, friend's house). Encourage your students to be as creative as possible. Have each group present their version whenever time permits. They should act out their scenes and make up appropriate items (passport, ID card, registration form).

4. Individual project — *Jugendherbergen*
Ask students interested (for extra credit) to write a letter (requesting information) to Deutscher Jugendherbergs-Verband, Buelowstraße 26, D-4330 Detmold 1. Their letter should include anything they wish to know about German youth hostels not covered in this unit.

C. Background Information

page 147 — A traveler not familiar with travel in Germany would be wise to make use of either the *VARTA-Führer durch Deutschland* or the *MICHELIN Deutschland*. Both of these well-known guides list not only restaurants but also hotels. For the hotels, these guides give five or six different standards and additional information useful for the traveler.

Another way of finding a hotel is to look for the *Zimmernachweis*, usually in or near the main railroad station or the town. Here, you will receive the information about available hotel rooms in your price range. You will have to pay a nominal fee for having a hotel room booked through this office.

Many Americans traveling in Germany for the first time are sometimes disturbed by the need to fill out official forms when registering in a hotel (e.g., home address, date of birth, nationality). These forms must be filled out by all guests, Germans included. They are required by law.

pages 156–57 — As soon as groups or individuals arrive, they meet in the lobby where the Youth Hostel Director (*Herbergsvater*) assigns each the appropriate sleeping facilities and, when time permits, shows everyone around. In most youth hostels at least four people are accommodated in one room, usually in bunk beds. Young people can be seen playing games inside and outside the youth hostels. Of course, everyone participates in hiking. Consequently, youth hostels are normally found outside of towns where there are plenty of forests and other hiking areas.

Meals at a hostel are quite reasonable and nourishing. It is the responsibility of every group to pick up their meals from the kitchen counter where they are properly distributed and counted. Modern kitchen equipment has made the preparation and clean-up chores much more convenient today.

pages 160–61 — Why Bonn? Visitors may well ask themselves this question when traveling through Germany's spacious, modern cities. Why wasn't one of the many larger cities chosen as the capital, instead of the small university town? Wouldn't a city like Frankfurt have been more suitable? So thought almost half of the delegates to the Council of Parliament in May, 1949, whose last task after ratifying the constitution was finding a government seat for the new state. But the heavy destruction of Frankfurt — considered at that time as a possible capital — as well as other major German cities, was the deciding factor. In a close race, the birthplace of Beethoven (Bonn) won over that of Goethe (Frankfurt). In 1949, however, Bonn was considered, quite intentionally, to be only a provisional capital; the future of Berlin could not be anticipated. History took another course and Bonn today is more than ever the center of German political events.

pages 162–63 — Although Berlin is called by the people of the *DDR* "*die Hauptstadt der DDR*," technically and politically speaking it is "*Berlin (Ost)*" that should be considered the capital because after World War II Berlin was divided into four Zones of Occupation (American, British, French and Soviet). The three Zones occupied by the American, British and French soon became know as "*West-Berlin*" whereas the Soviet-occupied Zone became known as "*Ost-Berlin*." It is the latter which is the capital of the *DDR*.

Berlin (Ost) has a population of 1,090,000. The city is the center of the political and social life in the *DDR*. The main government organs (*Volkskammer, Staatsrat, Ministerrat*) as well as the various embassies can be found here. Furthermore, the city is one of the most important industrial areas of the country. The city is surrounded by numerous lakes and forests. The most popular is the *Großer Müggelsee*. Numerous museums, theaters and cultural places offer Berliners and tourists a variety of different events. Of particular significance are the *Deutsche Staatsoper* (*Unter den Linden*), the *Deutsche Theater*, the *Berliner Ensemble*, the *Museum für Deutsche Geschichte* and the *Palast der Republik*.

pages 165–66 — School-age children of foreigners receive a course of preparatory education lasting two years. They are then integrated into classes with German students. In addition to these lessons, they receive three to five hours of instruction in their native language every week. These lessons are given by teachers from their native country and cover the language, history, geography and religion of that country.

In the past few years, foreign children have been doing better in school than before, but they are still unsatisfactory on the whole. One child in every five does not even go to school, and about one half of foreign adolescents do not attend a vocational school. Only 50% of foreign students finish the *Hauptschule*, and only a few go to the *Realschule* or *Gymnasium*.

LEKTION 8

A. Instructional Objectives

After completing all the material in *Lektion 8*, the students should be able to:
1. know various school items
2. name important musical instruments
3. describe a typical leisure-time activity
4. describe the geographical features (landscape, mountains, rivers, lakes and islands) of the *BRD*.
5. discuss various occupations in Germany
6. use possessive adjectives (nominative and accusative)
7. use comparison of adjectives and adverbs
8. use *dieser, welcher, jeder*
9. pronounce short and long /ä/ and /ö/

B. Allerlei

1. Game — *Land, Stadt*...
Have students take out a sheet of paper and mark the following categories on top of the sheet: *Land, Stadt, Fluß, Berg, Name, Schule, Kleidung*. You may start with fewer categories. Ask one of the students to say the alphabet silently. When you say "Halt!," the student should reveal the letter, for example "R." The student then will try to find appropriate words under each category. For example: *Rumänien, Regensburg, Rhein, Renate, Radiergummi, Rock*. You may want to set a time limit of two minutes and stop the game if students can't finish. (In the list above, for instance, students may not know "*Rumänien*.") Give one point per word. If you like, you may want to have students work in small teams, and, of course, you can add other categories besides those indicated above.

2. Class activity — *Eine Party*
Have students describe a party orally or in writing. The description can be in dialog or narrative form. To make this situation more meaningful, you may help students with some additional vocabulary. Have them make up a short list (in English) so that you can give them these words in German. Students could act out a party or you may even turn this activity into an after-school affair (a good German club activity!).

3. Class Activity — *Was brauche ich für die Schule?*
Collect all the items listed in the *Ergänzung, No. 1*

(bag, briefcase, wastepaper basket) in a container and add other items students should know. Then, ask a question like "*Was habe ich in dieser Tüte (in dieser Schultasche, in diesem Papierkorb)?*" Rather than having students just guess these items, you may want to have them make a statement or ask a question, like "*Ich muß etwas schreiben. Haben Sie Papier?*"

4. Individual project — *Die BRD*

After your students have read *Lesestück 2* (*Die BRD — Landschaft*), tell them to pretend they are going to West Germany. Have them plan what they want to see. Ask them to write a short description (in German) including where they want to go and why. If you expect a more detailed description, you may want to have your students write it in English. For additional information, they should go to their library, local travel agency and/or write to the German Information Center, 410 Park Avenue, New York, N.Y. 10022.

C. Background Information

page 171 — Driver's training in Germany is much more expensive than in the U.S. It may cost as much as DM 1,000 (including all the lessons). Although you may take your driver's test before you're 18 (as Michael did in the *Dialog*), the driver won't receive the driver's license (*Führerschein*) until s/he turns 18.

pages 183–84 — Many teenagers take dancing lessons in Germany. It is customary for boys and girls to look for a dancing partner at the dance studio. Some of the young adults, like Monika in *Lesestück 1*, have gone through several dance courses with the same partner as the individual dancing steps are then practiced to perfection. Those who continue dancing for several years, eventually compete in dance competitions (*Tanzturnier*).

pages 187–88 — The most northerly stretch of the *BRD* is the base of the Jutland peninsula, an extensive low-lying plain with deeply indented fjords, flat farmland, wooded hills, moors and heather. As far down as the flat Lüneburg Heath south of Hamburg, this part of the country was formed by Ice Age glaciers.

The southern edge of this plain gives way to a succession of mountain chains of ancient geological formation, known as the Central Mountains, which include the Harz, the Teutoburger, Wald, the Rhön, the Taunus, the Rhineland Slate Mountains, the Black Forest and the Bavarian Forest. Because these central mountains are broken up into sharply defined groups with broad valleys, they form no obstacle to north-south communications either by land or by water. On Germany's southern border the Alps tower up, a chain of high, jagged mountains extending from Austria to France.

As a result of the very different nature of the soil and the location of natural resources, agriculture and industry are unevenly distributed across the country. The coastal area in the north is farming country with harbors and some industry. The Ruhr and the Rhine-Main areas are the industrial heart of Germany and the most thickly populated parts. On the Rhine and its tributaries, the main wine-growing areas are found. Hessen and the Saarland are agricultural and industrial regions with wooded, hilly countryside and numerous health spas. The Black Forest is a picturesque, mountainous and thickly wooded area, principally given over to land cultivation and forestry; many specialized industries have established themselves here as well. Bavaria, in the north, is heavily industrialized; but the south, on the other hand, is the Alpine country with mountain lakes and romantic castles, and incomparable vacation and winter sports area.

pages 190–92 — Foreigners who want to work in Germany must have a work permit that is issued by the employment office (*Arbeitsamt*) in the community where the applicant lives. Furthermore, an applicant needs a residence permit (*Aufenthaltserlaubnis*) that does not automatically exclude application for a work permit, passport and forms filled out by future employers. In general, work permits are available to non-Germans only if a German or other EEC-citizen cannot fill the job. However, a special work permit is issued to foreigners married to Germans.

LEKTION 9

A. Instructional Objectives

After completing all the material in *Lektion 9*, the students should be able to:
1. talk about their interest in a certain sports activity
2. name various kinds of beverages
3. describe a sports event at their school
4. discuss the geographical features (landscape, cities, rivers, mountains) of the *DDR*
5. discuss the various sports in Germany and compare differences and similarities with the U.S.
6. use the present perfect tense with regular and irregular verbs
7. use possessive adjectives (dative)
8. pronounce /r/

B. Allerlei

1. Game — *Erzähl eine Geschichte!*
Begin telling a story. Have each student add a sentence until the story has been completed. It might be fun to record the story and play it back.

2. Game — *Ich sehe etwas, was du nicht siehst*...
You may want to start this game by saying, "*Ich sehe etwas, was du nicht siehst. Es beginnt mit 'B'.*" The

class guesses what it is. The student who has guessed the right answer selects the next mystery word.

3. Individual project — *Welche Sportart treibst du gern?*
Have your students write a short essay based on their experiences in participating in sports. If some students are not active in sports, have them substitute such topics as *"Was für ein Musikinstrument spielst du?"* (*"Wie lange hast du schon gespielt? Wie gefällt es dir?..."*) or *"Hast du ein Hobby? Beschreibe es!"*

4. Individual project — Map
If you had your students make a map of Germany before (*Lektion 4*), you may either skip this activity or add other geographical features to their earlier map. Your students' map should include the various geographical features discussed in *Lesestück 2*. You may want to have the major cities, rivers, and mountains of the *BRD* (*Lektion 8, Lesestück 2*) included as well.

C. Background Information

page 195 — These boys were the finalists, selected from hundreds of other athletes, who participated in the district championships in Leipzig (*Bezirksmeisterschaft*).

pages 205–206 — The marathon run in Leipzig is an annual event in which the athletes come from all over the *DDR* to compete. The athletes represent the various sports clubs of their community. Runners are placed into age groups indentified by different colored numbers on their shirts (red = 18 to 32, green = 33 to 36, blue = 37 to 42, black = 43 to 50, brown = 51 and older).

pages 208–209 — Off the Baltic coast there are a number of islands. *Rügen* is the largest with an area of 358 square miles. The coastline gives way to a low-lying plain, intersected only by a few low ranges of hills and stretching as far south as the Halle-Leipzig area. The northern part of the plain contains lake districts, one not far from Berlin. The largest lakes are Lake Müritz and Lake Schwerin.

The south of the *DDR* is mainly highland with hilly areas forming an arc. From west to east these are the *Thüringer Wald*, with the *Großer Beerberg* that rises to 983 m (3,160 ft.) and the *Großer Inselberg* 916 m (3,000 ft.), the *Thüringer Schiefergebirge*, the *Vogtland*, the *Erzgebirge*, with the country's highest point, the *Fichtelberg*, 1,214 m (3,983 ft.), the *Elbsandsteingebirge*, the *Zittauer Gebirge* and the *Lausitzer Bergland*. In the west there are also the *Harz* Mountains with the *Brocken* (1,142 m or 3,737 ft.).

Forests cover 27% of the country's territory. There are extensive woodland areas in the highlands and in the northern lake districts.

pages 212–14 — Every fourth inhabitant of the *BRD* is a member of one of the 54,000 sports clubs.

Soccer (*Fußball*) is the king of sports in Germany. The big championship games and the European Cups and other international matches draw up to 70% of the German population to the TV sets. The *Fußball-Bundesliga* (Federal Soccer League) is the "first division" of German soccer, consisting of the 18 best teams. Every season two teams (in last place) are demoted, and two teams (the best from the second division) move up.

Next to soccer, gymnastics clubs (*Turnvereine*) have the most members — almost three million. Rifle, track and field, tennis, swimming, handball, and table tennis clubs follow, in that order.

LEKTION 10

A. Instructional Objectives
After completing all the material in *Lektion 10*, the students should be able to:
1. talk about a real or imaginary trip
2. understand and use the most important metric units
3. describe a trip to the *Zugspitze* and along the *Romantische Straße*
4. discuss the more well-known vacation areas of Germany
5. use verbs with separable and inseparable prefixes
6. use accusative prepositions
7. pronounce /ai/, /oi/ and /au/

B. Allerlei
1. Game — *Wir fahren nach Deutschland.*
Remembering what was said before is the object of this game (similar to *Lektion 6*, Game 1). The first student says, *"Wir fahren nach Deutschland. Wir nehmen einen Mantel mit."* The second student will repeat the first sentence and might say *"Wir nehmen einen Mantel und ein Kleid mit."* The third student repeats what the second one said and adds another word. A student who cannot repeat what was previously said or makes a mistake is out of the game. If you don't want to play this game, you may want to substitute places in Germany instead. For example, *"Wir fahren nach Bonn."* The next might say, *"Wir fahren nach Bonn und dann nach Hamburg."* The third student adds another place and the game continues in the same manner.

2. Game — *Wie lange kannst du sprechen?*
The teacher will give the students a specific topic and will ask them to talk about this subject as long as they can. Rather than having each student be on his/her own, you may want to form teams so that one can take over when the partner runs out of things to say. The teacher should allow students to stop for only about five seconds. Either the teacher or another student could keep track of the time. The person or team that speaks the longest is the winner.

3. Individual project — *Ich möchte nach...fahren.*
Have students write a short essay (in German) about where they would like to go. Have them select any place in the German-speaking countries. The essay should include the purpose of the trip, why a certain place was selected, how they will get there and what they will see. Here is an opportunity for creative writing and expression.

4. Class project — *Invite a native speaker.*
Have students find out if there are native speakers in town or people who have recently been in German-speaking countries. If such a person can be located, ask him/her about coming to your class. Before the speaker arrives, either you or your students should find out about this person. Depending upon his/her background, ask students to prepare questions in German (if the speaker is from a German-speaking country) beforehand. You should prepare your students as much as possible to make the visit worthwhile.

C. Background Information

page 217 — The number of German tourists who spend their vacation outside of Germany is considerably larger than the number of foreigners visiting Germany. For years the main tourist spots for Germans have been Austria, Italy, Spain, Yugoslavia, Holland, France and North Africa. During the past ten years, Germans have expanded their travel itinerary to countries beyond Europe.

pages 227–29 — Because of its height — nearly 10,000 ft. above sea level — and its favorable geographical position, the Zugspitze became a base of several scientific institutions. The weather station lodged in the meteorological tower of the *Münchner Haus* is concerned with weather research and weather forecasting. The *Bundespost* (Federal Post Office) runs an international wireless station for TV and telephone purposes with Austria and Italy. The Fraunhofer Society maintains a station in the tower of the cable car to the Zugspitze summit for physical research on the atmosphere. The Max-Planck Institute for Physics and Astrophysics measures cosmic radiation in the *Alu-Hütte*.

Germany's highest hotel (8,700 ft.) is located on the south slope of the Zugspitze. The Zugspitze palteau offers skiing for beginners as well as for experts.

pages 232–34 — Würzburg dates back to the 7th century when it was a Franconian duchy. The Marienberg Fortress was built in 1201 and later became the residence of many bishops. The Main-Franconian Museum has been housed here since 1946. It contains an excellent collection of works of art, most notably plastics by Tilman Riemenschneider.

Weikersheim is proud of this spacious Renaissance palace that was converted by the princess of Hohenlohe into a regional museum. There quarters were once reserved for the use of guests from Europe's royal families and today still show evidence of that period with its luxurious furniture, tapestries, portraits and porcelain.

In the *Herrgottskirche* of Creglingen, the visitor will find the greatest work of the wood-carver, Tilman Riemenschneider.

Rothenburg ob der Tauber is probably one of the most frequently visited towns in Germany. In 1631 women and children of Rothenburg begged General Tilly not to destroy the town. Today the Market Square is the center of life and the starting point of daily sightseeing tours. The *Meistertrunk*-scene with Tilly and Mayor Nusch is recreated at the gable (near the clock) of the *Ratsherrntrinkstube* at the Market Square. According to legend, Mayor Nusch's *Meistertrunk* saved the town.

It is said that Dinkelsbühl was enclosed by walls and moats already in 928. In the 15th century Dinkelsbühl reached its peak of development. Famous artisans, architects, scholars and merchants lived inside the walls. The Thirty Years' War, however, almost completely destroyed the town. This Free Imperial City of the Middle Ages has maintained its charm and culture, unharmed by any wars since that time.

A gigantic crater formed in Dinkelsbühl by the impact of a meteorite is said to have served as model terrain for the Apollo astronauts. A watchman still surveys the town from the top of the Gothic church of St. George. The old medieval wall still today encircles the town.

On the way to the Danube, and dominating the Wörnitz countryside, is Harburg Castle together with the township of the same name. The castle, which was never captured nor destroyed, is today a museum housing art treasures of the princess of Öttingen-Wallerstein, including Gothic tapestries, valuable manuscripts and works by Riemenschneider.

Both the Romantische Straße and the River Wörnitz have to cross the foothills of the Jura Mountains in order to reach the Danube. In Donauwörth, a former Free Imperial City, the way leads along one of the most spectacular routes in South Germany — the old Imperial road — down to the river.

Augsburg is the oldest city on the Romantische Straße with a history dating back 2,000 years (450 years as the capital of a Roman province, 500 years of power as a Free Imperial City and 1,400 years as a religious center).

pages 236–38 — The most frequently visited spots for German as well as foreign travelers are the Rhine, followed by the Black Forest, Bavaria with its Alps and royal castles, the great cities of Munich, Berlin and Hamburg, the "Romantic Road," the seacoast and the North Sea islands, the university city of Heidelberg, the Moselle and the Ahr, Cologne, Lake Constance the Swabia-Allgäu country, and the cities of Frankfurt and Düsseldorf.

There are about 240 health resorts such as Wiesbaden, Baden-Baden and Reichenhall. There are scenic lakes such as Lake Constance (Bodensee) Tegernsee, Chiemsee and Königsee. The Drachenfels — Europe's most climbed hill (it is only 1,056 feet high), the Feldberg in the Black Forest and the Zugspitze in the Alps are also tourist areas well-known outside of Germany. There are more Americans coming to Germany than people from any other country. Next to tourists from the U.S. come citizens of Holland, followed by those from the United Kingdom.

LEKTION B

A. Instructional Objectives
After completing all the material in *Lektion B*, the students should be able to:
1. understand the two reading selections and talk about their content
2. role-play the scene presented in the *Dialog*
3. complete all the exercises without any difficulty (grammar has been covered before)
4. find some other English words or phrases (besides those listed) while looking through some German newspapers and/or magazines
5. discuss various details presented centering around a German hotel

B. Class activity — Zungenbrecher
To review specific sounds (causing some difficulties), the teacher may want to select some of the tongue twisters presented throughout the book.

Second Edition

deutsch aktuell 1

Wolfgang S. Kraft

Consultants

Chief Consultant
Hans J. König
The Blake Schools
Hopkins, Minnesota

Monika Devrient
Städtisches Gymnasium
Mülheim, Germany

Karl-Heinz Gabbey
Buffalo Grove High School
Buffalo Grove, Illinois

Richard C. Helt
University of Arizona, Tucson

Anthony Jung
University of Nebraska at Omaha

Peter Klose
Grand Blanc High School
Grand Blanc, Michigan

Hildegard S. Morrell
Bellevue Senior High School
Bellevue, Washington

Roland Specht
Ruhr-Universität Bochum
Bochum, Germany

EMC Publishing, Saint Paul, Minnesota

ISBN 0-8219-0070-6

Published by EMC Publishing
300 York Avenue
St. Paul, Minnesota 55101

Printed in the United States of America
0 9 8 7 6 5 4 3

A Word to the Student

Many often ask, "Why study German? — What do I need it for?" Did you know that Germans make up the largest single ethnic group in this country and that most major U.S. companies have subsidiaries or branch offices in Germany? When you apply for a job, knowledge of a foreign language will be a great advantage for you with many companies. Knowledge of German will give you a better chance to get that job.

Studying German in our increasingly complex world has become an important asset for anyone who desires to learn more about today's world. But it is not just learning the language that will open the door to German-speaking countries — it is the knowledge and insight into the German culture. Understanding the German language and culture will help you to know your own language and culture better.

The strength of *Deutsch: Aktuell* is its realistic and up-to-date treatment of the German language and culture. As the word *aktuell* implies, it is a topical, contemporary program in which you will explore *all* German-speaking countries (West and East Germany, Austria and Switzerland). You will be exposed to topics that have been carefully selected on the basis of how typical they are or how frequently they occur in the daily lives of the people in the German-speaking countries.

Deutsch: Aktuell will teach you to communicate in German in everyday situations. Don't be afraid to express yourself. It's natural to make mistakes, but your language skills will become much stronger as you use the language. You will acquire the desire and confidence to communicate in German.

And now, I wish you the best of success and lots of fun, or as we say in German...
Viel Erfolg und viel Spaß!

Wolfgang Kraft

Lektion 1

Lektion 2

Lektion 3

Lektion 4

Lektion 5

Lektion 8

Lektion 9

Lektion 10

Lektion B

Deutsches Sprachgebiet

Nordsee

Ostsee

Rügen

Flensburg
Schleswig
Helgoland
Kiel
Holstein
Fehmarn
Lübeck
Rostock
Schwerin
Inseln
Bremerhaven
Emden
Wilhelmshaven
Hamburg
Oldenburg
Bremen

DEUTSCHE DEMOKRATISCHE REPUBLIK

Niedersachsen
Elbe
Oder
Berlin (Ost)

Osnabrück
Hannover
Braunschweig
Potsdam
Goslar
Magdeburg
Bielefeld
Dessau
Münster
Nordrhein-Westfalen
Cottbus
Dortmund
Harz
Saale
Essen
Halle
Duisburg
Düsseldorf
Kassel
Leipzig
Köln
Rhein
Erfurt
Dresden

BUNDES-REPUBLIK DEUTSCHLAND

Gera
Aachen
Bonn
Jena
Karl-Marx-Stadt
Fulda
Thüringer Wald
Erzgebirge
Zwickau
Koblenz
Hessen
Rheinland-Pfalz
Wiesbaden
Frankfurt/Main
LUXEMBURG
Mainz
Würzburg
Bayreuth
Trier
Darmstadt
Bayern
Saarland
Mannheim
Nürnberg
Saarbrücken
Heidelberg
Neustadt
Rothenburg
Karlsruhe
Regensburg
Baden-Baden
Stuttgart
Passau
Baden-Württemberg
Linz
Augsburg
München
Wien
Freiburg
Schwarzwald
Neusiedlersee
Titisee
Konstanz
Chiemsee
Salzburg
Oberammergau
Zugspitze
Bodensee
Garmisch-Partenkirchen
Basel
Zürich
Watzmann
ÖSTERREICH
Aare
Alpen
Vaduz
Innsbruck
Graz
Luzern
LIECHTENSTEIN
Grossglockner
Bern
Rhone
SCHWEIZ
Genf
Monte Rosa

Dialog

Wo wohnst du?

Grüß dich! is a common way of greeting each other in the southern part of Germany, particularly among young adults, friends and relatives. *Tag!* (short for *Guten Tag!*) is more common in the northern part of Germany. See detailed information in *Kulturecke 1* of this lesson.

ANDREAS:	Grüß dich, Monika!
MONIKA:	Grüß dich, Andreas! Wie geht's?
ANDREAS:	Nicht schlecht.
ANDREAS:	Kennst du Ingo?
MONIKA:	Nein.
ANDREAS:	Ingo ist mein Freund.
INGO:	Grüß dich, Monika! Wohnst du auch hier in Buchenau?
MONIKA:	Ja. Ich wohne da drüben. Und du?
INGO:	Ich wohne gleich hier um die Ecke.
MONIKA:	Was machst du jetzt, Andreas?
ANDREAS:	Ingo und ich gehen in die Stadt.
MONIKA:	Ich gehe auch in die Stadt.
INGO:	Komm doch mit!
MONIKA:	Gut, das ist mir recht.

Additional information about the *Dialog* (the same is true for subsequent *Dialoge*) is found in the "Background Information" section in the front portion of this teacher's edition.

Fragen über den Dialog (Questions about the Dialog)

1. Kennt Monika Ingo?
2. Wo wohnt Monika?
3. Wo wohnt Ingo?
4. Was machen Andreas und Ingo?
5. Was macht Monika?

Ask other questions such as: *Wo wohnst du?*, *Wie geht's?*, *Was machst du jetzt?*, *Gehst du in die Stadt?*, etc.

Where Do You Live?

ANDREAS:	Hi, Monika!
MONIKA:	Hi, Andreas! How are you?
ANDREAS:	Not bad.
ANDREAS:	Do you know Ingo?
MONIKA:	No.
ANDREAS:	Ingo is my friend.
INGO:	Hello, Monika! Do you live here in Buchenau, too?
MONIKA:	Yes. I live over there. And you?
INGO:	I live right around the corner.
MONIKA:	What are you doing now, Andreas?
ANDREAS:	Ingo and I are going downtown.
MONIKA:	I'm going downtown, too.
INGO:	Why don't you come along?
MONIKA:	O.K., that's all right with me.

Nützliche Ausdrücke (Useful Expressions)

Review these expressions after students have thoroughly covered the *Dialog*. Have students cover the German material (left side) as you review the expressions.

Grüß dich, Monika!*	Hi, Monika!
Wie geht's?	How are you?
Gleich um die Ecke.	Right around the corner.
Was machst du?	What are you doing?
Ich gehe in die Stadt.	I'm going downtown.
Komm doch mit!	Why don't you come along?
Das ist mir recht.	That's all right with me.

*Grüß dich! is commonly used in Southern Germany.

Wie geht's?

Ergänzung (Supplement)

Have students practice introducing each other and shaking hands.

1. Tag, Andreas!
   Guten Tag, Monika!
   Grüß dich, Ingo!

Have students ask each other questions. (*Heißt du Ralf? Ja, … — Nein, … Wie geht es dir?, Wo wohnst du*, etc.)

2. Wie heißt du?　　　　　　　　　Ich heiße Helga.
   Wie heißen Sie?　　　　　　　　Ich heiße Herr Lehmann.
   　　　　　　　　　　　　　　　Ich heiße Frau Schmidt.
   　　　　　　　　　　　　　　　Ich heiße Fräulein Meier.

   Wie heißt er?　　　　　　　　　Er heißt Hans.
   Wie heißt sie?　　　　　　　　　Sie heißt Tina.

3. Wie geht es dir, Kurt?　　　　　Nicht schlecht.
   Wie geht es Ihnen, Herr Müller?　Danke, gut.

4. Heißt er Ralf?　　　　　　　　Ja, er heißt Ralf.
   　　　　　　　　　　　　　　　Nein, er heißt nicht Ralf.
   　　　　　　　　　　　　　　　Er heißt Walter.

5. Wo wohnst du?　　　　　　　　Ich wohne da drüben.
   　　　　　　　　　　　　　　　Ich wohne gleich um die Ecke.
   　　　　　　　　　　　　　　　Ich wohne in Hamburg.

   Wohin geht Sabine?　　　　　　Sie geht in die Stadt.

Teach the numbers by having students repeat each one after you. As soon as they know the numbers, either write them on the board at random or make flashcards and have students identify each number as you show it.

6.

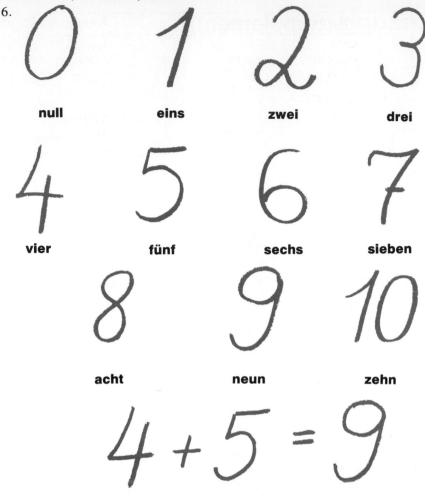

null   **eins**   **zwei**   **drei**

vier   **fünf**   **sechs**   **sieben**

acht   **neun**   **zehn**

Vier plus fünf ist neun.

It is important that students know the German alphabet as soon as possible. You many want to break it into sections. Have students say the alphabet backwards and forwards. Then use some of the words or names they know and ask students to spell them. Listen to their pronunciation.

Das Alphabet					
a	ah	**k**	kah	**u**	uh
b	beh	**l**	ell	**v**	fau
c	tseh	**m**	emm	**w**	weh
d	deh	**n**	enn	**x**	iks
e	eh	**o**	oh	**y**	üpsilon
f	eff	**p**	peh	**z**	tset
g	geh	**q**	kuh	**ä**	äh
h	hah	**r**	err	**ö**	öh
i	ih	**s**	ess	**ü**	üh
j	jot	**t**	teh	**ß**	ess-tset

4

This is a good place to ask questions such as: *Wie heißt du?, Buchstabiere deinen Namen!* (Give an example in German to explain the last expression.) The names listed are the most common German names today.

Namen für Jungen		Namen für Mädchen	
Achim	Jörg	Alexandra	Katja
Alexander	Jürgen	Andrea	Katrin
Andreas	Kai	Angelika	Kerstin
Axel	Karsten	Anja	Manuela
Benjamin	Klaus	Annette	Maren
Bernd	Lars	Barbara	Marianne
Björn	Manfred	Beate	Marlis
Boris	Manuel	Bettina	Martina
Carsten	Marc	Bianca	Melanie
Christian	Marco	Birgit	Michaela
Daniel	Marcus	Britta	Miriam
Dennis	Martin	Carmen	Monika
Dieter	Matthias	Christa	Nadine
Dirk	Michael	Christiane	Nadja
Erich	Nils	Christine	Natalie
Felix	Norbert	Claudia	Natascha
Florian	Oliver	Cornelia	Nicole
Frank	Patrick	Daniela	Nina
Franz	Peter	Diana	Petra
Fritz	Rainer	Doris	Renate
Georg	Ralf	Elke	Rita
Gerd	Rudolf	Erika	Ruth
Gerhard	Rüdiger	Eva	Sabine
Günter	Sebastian	Gabi	Sandra
Hans	Simon	Gerda	Sibylle
Harald	Stefan	Gisela	Sigrid
Hartmut	Steffen	Heidi	Silke
Heiko	Sven	Heike	Silvia
Helmut	Thomas	Helga	Simone
Herbert	Thorsten	Ilse	Sonja
Hermann	Timo	Inge	Stefanie
Holger	Tobias	Ingrid	Stephanie
Ingo	Torsten	Irene	Susanne
Jan	Udo	Jennifer	Tanja
Jens	Uwe	Jessica	Tina
Joachim	Volker	Julia	Ursula
Jochen	Walter	Jutta	Waltraud
Johannes	Wolfgang	Katherina	Yvonne

Ausspracheübung (Pronunciation Exercise)

To assure a more exact pronunciation of the sounds listed, you may wish to refer to the linguistic description provided.

short /a/		long /a/	
machst	Hans	Tag	Helga
Stadt	acht	da	Tina
das	Hamburg	ja	
was	Walter	Fragen	
Andreas	danke	Monika	
Ralf			

[a] short *a* — sound (*was*): The tip of the tongue touches the lower incisors while the mouth is slightly opened. Except for a low rise of the tongue in the mediodorsal region, the tongue lies low and flat. No contact is made with the palate. The velum is raised.

[ɑ:] long *a* — sound (*da*): The tip of the tongue touches the lower incisors while the mouth is wide open. The tongue lies low and flat. The low position of the tongue, with the relatively large jaw angle, prevents contact of the tongue with the palate.

Übungen (Exercises)

The Familiar Form: *du* (singular) and *ihr* (plural)

The familiar form is used when you speak to relatives, close friends, children and animals.

Examples: (Ingo's mother is speaking to her son.) *Kennst du Monika?* Do you know Monika?

For additional information on the familiar and formal forms, refer to *Kulturecke 2* of this lesson.

(Andreas is talking to his friends.) *Was macht ihr?* What are you doing?

The Formal Form: *Sie* (singular and plural)

The formal form is used when you speak to adults and to those you are not addressing by their first name.

Examples: (Thomas is talking to his teacher.) *Gehen Sie in die Stadt, Herr Schulz?* Are you going downtown, Mr. Schulz? (Mrs. Müller talks to some customers.) *Wo wohnen Sie jetzt, Herr und Frau Meier?* Where are you living now, Mr. and Mrs. Meier?

NOTE: The formal form *Sie,* in both the singular and plural, is capitalized.

Personal Pronouns

	Singular	Plural
1st person	ich I	wir we
2nd person	du you	ihr you
3rd person	er he sie she es it	sie they
formal form	Sie you	Sie you

Present Tense Verb Forms

In the present tense in English, there are basically two different verb forms for all persons. For instance, *come* can be used for all persons, except third person singular where it is *come(s).* In German, however, the verb has more forms, as can readily be seen in the chart.

To use the proper verb form, you need to know the infinitive of the particular verb. The infinitive of the English verb *went, gone* or *goes* is *to go.* The infinitive of a German verb ends with *-en* (in a few cases *-n*) as in geh*en*, mach*en*, or wohn*en*. The infinitive is a combination of the stem of the verb and the ending (INFINITIVE = STEM + ENDING).

Example: INFINITIVE = STEM + ENDING
gehen   =   *geh*   +   *en*

When the stem of a verb is known, you need to know the appropriate ending for the particular singular or plural form.

The present tense of regular verbs is characterized by the endings indicated below.

Singular	ich geh-e du geh-st er sie } geh-t es	I go you go he goes she goes it goes
Plural	wir geh-en ihr geh-t sie geh-en Sie geh-en (sg. & pl.)	we go you go they go you go

NOTE: Should the stem of the verb in the 2nd person singular end in *s, ß, x or z,* then the *s* of the ending is dropped.

Examples: *du heiß-t* (your name is)
du putz-t (you are cleaning)
du mix-t (you are mixing)
du lös-t (you are loosening)

The Letter *ß (ess-tset)*

The letter *ß* is equivalent to *ss.* The *ß* is used in these positions:
a. at the end of a word (Grü*ß* dich!)
b. before a consonant (hei*ß*t)
c. after a long vowel or vowel combination (Stra*ß*e, wei*ß)*
The *ß* is never used when all the letters in a word are capitalized.

Example: *Straße* but *STRASSE*

Nouns

All nouns in German are capitalized.
Examples: *die Stadt, der Tag*

Folgt den Beispielen! (Follow the examples.)

1. Ich wohne hier.   Ich wohne hier.
   Andreas   Andreas wohnt hier.
   Andreas und Monika   Andreas und Monika wohnen hier.
   wir   Wir wohnen hier.
   du   Du wohnst hier.
   Frau Meier   Frau Meier wohnt hier.

2. Wie heißt sie? (Monika)   Sie heißt Monika.
   Wie heißt er? (Andreas)   Er heißt Andreas.
   Wie heißt sie? (Frau Schmidt)   Sie heißt Frau Schmidt.

Wie heißt er? (Herr Lehmann)	Er heißt Herr Lehmann.
Wie heißt sie? (Fräulein Meier)	Sie heißt Fräulein Meier.
Wie heißt er? (Ingo)	Er heißt Ingo.

3. Was machst du jetzt?

Variation: Have students answer the question. Use different pronouns.

	Was machst du jetzt?
wir	**Was machen wir jetzt?**
Monika	Was macht Monika jetzt?
Ingo und Andreas	Was machen Ingo und Andreas jetzt?
Herr Schmidt	Was macht Herr Schmidt jetzt?
ihr	Was macht ihr jetzt?
er	Was macht er jetzt?

4. Andreas kennt Ingo.

	Andreas kennt Ingo.
Monika	Monika kennt Ingo.
Herr und Frau Meier	Herr und Frau Meier kennen Ingo.
ich	Ich kenne Ingo.
wir	Wir kennen Ingo.
Herr Lehmann	Herr Lehmann kennt Ingo.

5. Change each of the following sentences from the familiar to the formal form.

Variation: Change sentences to familiar form, plural *(ihr)*.

1. Wie heißt du?
2. Wohnst du da drüben?
3. Wie geht's?
4. Du kennst Frau Meier.
5. Du gehst in die Stadt.
6. Was machst du jetzt?
7. Wo wohnst du?

6. Beantwortet diese Fragen! (Answer these questions.)

1. Wie geht's?
2. Wo wohnst du?
3. Wie heißt du?
4. Was machst du jetzt?
5. Kennst du Monika? Ja,…
6. Wohnst du gleich um die Ecke? Ja,…
7. Gehst du in die Stadt? Ja,…

7. Select one of the words from the list to complete each sentence.

1. Wie _____?
2. Ingo _____ mein Freund.
3. Ich _____ in die Stadt.
4. Frau Lehmann _____ gleich um die Ecke.
5. Er _____ Andreas.

6. Was _____ ihr jetzt?

7. _____ Sie da drüben, Herr Schmidt?

8. Das ist mir _____.

heißt	recht
macht	ist
gehe	wohnt
wohnen	geht's

8. Provide an appropriate response in German.

1. Grüß dich! Wie geht's?   Encourage as many different responses as possible.
2. Wohnst du hier?
3. Was machst du?
4. Wohnt Monika in Buchenau?
5. Heißt er Herr Meier?

Erweiterung (Expansion)

Folgt den Beispielen!

9. Eins plus drei ist…?   Eins plus drei ist vier.

Fünf plus zwei ist…?   Fünf plus zwei ist sieben.

Acht plus eins ist…?   Acht plus eins ist neun.

Drei plus drei ist…?   Drei plus drei ist sechs.

Zwei plus acht ist…?   Zwei plus acht ist zehn.

Vier plus fünf ist…?   Vier plus fünf ist neun.

10. Kennt er Monika?   Ja, er kennt Monika.

Variation: Have students answer with *nein.* Provide an example.

Wohnt sie hier?   Ja, sie wohnt hier.

Geht Andreas in die Stadt?   Ja, Andreas geht in die Stadt.

Wohnt Ingo gleich um die Ecke?   Ja, Ingo wohnt gleich um die Ecke.

Heißt er Herr Meier?   Ja, er heißt Herr Meier.

Heißt sie Fräulein Lehmann?   Ja, sie heißt Fräulein Lehmann.

11. Write out each problem and answer in German.

1. $2 + 5 =$ _____
2. $3 + 3 =$ _____
3. $8 + 1 =$ _____
4. $4 + 1 =$ _____
5. $2 + 2 =$ _____

12. Wie heißt das auf deutsch?

1. What's your name?
2. Where do you live?
3. Andreas is my friend.
4. That's O.K. with me.
5. Do you know Mrs. Meier?
6. I live over there, too.
7. Hello, Monika!
8. Why don't you come along.
9. Three plus six is nine.
10. Five plus one is six.

13. Decide whether or not the response to each question or statement is appropriate. If it is inappropriate, write a response that makes sense.

1. Wie geht's?
   Nein.
2. Wo wohnst du?
   Da drüben.
3. Was machst du?
   Das ist mir recht.
4. Wie heißt er?
   Er heißt Elke.
5. Guten Tag, Frau Meier!
   Gut.
6. Kennen Sie Fräulein Lehmann?
   Ja.
7. Vier und fünf ist...?
   Nein.
8. Was macht ihr jetzt?
   Wir gehen in die Stadt.
9. Wie geht es Ihnen, Herr Schmidt?
   Nicht schlecht.
10. Wohnen Sie hier?
    Ja, gut.

14. Beantwortet diese Fragen! Have students come up with different answers.

Was machst du jetzt?

Wie heißt du?

Wo wohnst du?

Wie geht es dir?

Gehst du in die Stadt?

Wie heißt er?

Wie heißt sie?

Kulturecke 1 (Culture Corner)

Greetings, Farewells and Introductions

"Hello" and "Hi" have become almost international greetings these days, and many younger Germans use them when dealing with each other. Their own language, however, did not originally include such short, informal greetings. The normal German greeting is *"Guten Tag."* Often the first word is dropped, and you'll simply hear *"Tag"* or people just mumble *"n' Tag."* In Southern Germany you will rarely hear *"Guten Tag"* but rather *"Grüß Gott."* Young people in Southern Germany will also greet each other with *"Grüß dich."* In Austria people often greet each other with *"Servus."*

In the morning, most Germans greet each other with *"Guten Morgen,"* or simply *"Morgen"* whereas in the evening they say *"Guten Abend"* or again just mumble *"n' Abend."* It is quite customary for strangers in smaller towns to greet each other. Men will even tip their hats. When entering a town or city, the visitors are often greeted with a sign that says *"Willkommen."*

"Auf Wiedersehen" or simply *"Wiedersehen"* means *"good-bye." "Tschüs"** is a very casual form of *"Wiedersehen,"* primarily used in Northern Germany. It comes closest to the American "See you!" or "So long!" Ending a telephone conversation, most Germans say *"Auf Wiederhören"* or simply *"Wiederhören."* It means "Hope to hear you again," just as *"Auf Wiedersehen"* means "Hope to see you again." If a German says *"Bis bald!"* (until soon) or *"Bis dann!"* (until then), he or she usually has a specific time in mind. A German does not need to say "Good-bye, hope to see you again," because *"Auf Wiedersehen"* means exactly that.

On leaving a party at night, when Americans would say "Good night," most Germans will not say *"Gute Nacht"* but *"Auf Wiedersehen."* People living in the same house would say *"Gute Nacht."* And, of course, family members say it when they go to bed.

*The standard way of spelling "Tschüs" is with "s." However, Germans will also spell it with "ss" (Tschüss) or with "ß" (Tschüß).

Bis bald!

Auf Wiederhören!

Servus!

Germans do a lot more handshaking than Americans. Germans not only shake hands when being introduced but many still consider a handshake as part of the everyday greeting. To a German, it means little more than saying "Hello." A nod of the head usually accompanies the handshake. When meeting acquaintances in the street, in shops or elsewhere in public, Germans usually shake hands only if they intend to have a little chat.

What do you say when introducing people to each other in Germany? You say *"Darf ich bekannt machen?"* or *"Darf ich vorstellen? — Herr Meier — Herr Schmidt."* The two shake hands, smile and say *"Guten Tag, Herr Meier"* and *"Guten Tag, Herr Schmidt"* to each other. A friendly nod of the head when shaking hands would be in order, too.

Americans who are used to saying "How are you?" when being introduced, may be tempted to say *"Wie geht es Ihnen?"* when being introduced to a German. This is not customary, however, unless you are at the doctor's office and he inquires about your health. *"Wie geht es Ihnen?"* or short *"Wie geht's?"* is a greeting for someone you already know.

Kulturecke 2

„Du" oder „Sie"?

Both words *"du"* and *"Sie"* mean "you." However, *"du"* is considered the informal mode and *"Sie"* the formal mode of address. For Germans, there is nothing stiff about *"Sie."* For instance, people may work in an office for years and still call each other *"Sie,"* yet the atmosphere can be very friendly and pleasant. So, who calls each other *"du"*? Primarily blue-collar workers, students and military personnel or the police force say *"du"* to each other.

In social life, people you know well — called *"Bekannte"* (acquaintances) — are addressed with *"Sie,"* while close, personal friends — called *"Freunde"* — are addressed with *"du."* Young people, too, quickly tend to use the *"du"* form among each other.

All members of a family say *"du"* to each other. Children are always addressed with *"du"* until mid-adolescence. Among each other, children use the *"du"* form as well. The *"du"* form is also used in prayers and church services. Finally, you always address animals with *"du,"* regardless of whether they are small or large.

Family members address each other with "du."

The vocabulary section is intended for reference only. Words have been arranged in alphabetical sequence for easy reference. Although the definite article is not introduced until *Lektion 2*, the nouns and the articles along with their respective plural forms are listed.

Vokabeln

acht eight
auch also, too
da there
    da drüben over there
danke thanks
das the, that
deutsch German
drei three
du you (familiar singular)
die **Ecke,-n** corner
eins one
er he
es it
die **Frau,-en** Mrs., woman
das **Fräulein,-** Miss
der **Freund,-e** boyfriend, friend
fünf five
gehen to go
    Wie geht's? How are you? (familiar)
gleich immediately, right away
    gleich um die Ecke right around the corner
gut good, well, O.K.
heißen to be called, named
    Wie heißt du? What's your name?
der **Herr,-en** Mr., gentleman
hier here
ich I
ihr you (familiar plural)
in in
ist is
ja yes
jetzt now
der **Junge,-n** boy
kennen to know (someone)
kommen to come
    Komm doch mit. Why don't you come along?
machen to do, make
das **Mädchen,-** girl
mein my
der **Name,-n** name
nein no
neun nine
nicht not
null zero
plus plus
recht right
    Das ist mir recht. That's all right with me.
schlecht bad
sechs six
Sie you (formal)
sie she, they
sieben seven

die **Stadt,-̈e** city
der **Tag,-e** day
    Tag! Hello! (conversational), Hi!
    Guten Tag! Hello!
um around
    um die Ecke around the corner
und and
vier four
was what
wie how
Wie geht's? How are you? (familiar)
wir we
wo where
wohnen to live
zehn ten
zwei two

Wo wohnen Sie?

Dialog

Zu Hause

Point out that Germans give their family name when answering the phone.

am Telefon

HEIKE:	Heike Gruber.
SVEN:	Tag, Heike. Hier ist Sven. Ich komme bald rüber.
HEIKE:	Um wieviel Uhr?
SVEN:	Um vier.
HEIKE:	Ich habe dann keine Zeit.
SVEN:	Schade. Na, dann bis morgen.
HEIKE:	Tschüs bis morgen.

Consider the verb with a separable prefix as an expression at this point.

im Zimmer

BIRGIT:	Warum bleibst du zu Hause?
HEIKE:	Ich habe heute viel zu tun.
BIRGIT:	Wie langweilig! Du, ich brauche etwas Geld.
HEIKE:	Schon wieder? Wieviel denn?
BIRGIT:	Zehn Mark. Petra und ich gehen zur Eisdiele.
HEIKE:	Du hast Glück. Ich habe noch etwas Geld.
BIRGIT:	Keine Angst! Du bekommst das Geld morgen zurück.
HEIKE:	Bis später.

Treat the dative preposition and article (*zur* Eisdiele) as an expression at this stage.

Fragen über den Dialog

1. Wo ist Heike?
2. Hat Heike heute Zeit?
3. Warum bleibt Heike zu Hause?
4. Was braucht Birgit?
5. Wieviel Geld bekommt Birgit?
6. Was machen Birgit und Petra heute?

At Home

on the telephone

HEIKE: Heike Gruber.

SVEN: Hello Heike. This is Sven. I'm coming over soon.

HEIKE: What time?

SVEN: At four.

HEIKE: I won't have time then.

SVEN: Too bad. Well, then 'til tomorrow.

HEIKE: See you tomorrow.

in the room

BIRGIT: Why are you staying at home?

HEIKE: I have a lot to do today.

BIRGIT: How boring! Say, I need some money.

HEIKE: Again? How much?

BIRGIT: Ten marks. Petra and I are going to the ice cream parlor.

HEIKE: You're lucky. I still have some money.

BIRGIT: Don't worry. You'll get the money back tomorrow.

HEIKE: See you later.

Review the expressions that have appeared in the *Dialog* and *Lesestück*. You may want to use these expressions and develop a conversation with your students. (*Kommst du rüber?*, *Um wieviel Uhr kommst du?*, *Bleibst du heute zu Hause?*, *Hat er/sie viel zu tun?*, etc.)

Nützliche Ausdrücke

Er kommt rüber.	He's coming over.
Um wieviel Uhr?	At what time?
Schade.	Too bad.
Ich bleibe zu Hause.	I'm staying home.
Hast du viel zu tun?	Do you have a lot to do?
Wie langweilig!	How boring!
Du hast Glück.	You're lucky.
Keine Angst!	Don't worry! Don't be afraid!
Sie geht auf ein Gymnasium.	She goes to a secondary school.
Ich bin pünktlich.	I'm punctual. I'm on time.
Was ist los?	What's the matter?
Schreibt ihr heute eine Arbeit?	Are you taking a test today?
Sie sprechen über…	They talk about…
Hast du Lust?	Would you like to?
Ist es möglich?	Is it possible?
Steigen Sie ein?	Are you getting in(to)?

Ergänzung

Expand the material. Ask questions such as: *Heute ist Dienstag.*, *Welcher Tag ist morgen?*

1.   Welcher Tag ist heute? Heute ist Montag.

2.   die Sekunde, die Minute, die Stunde, der Tag, die Woche, der Monat, das Jahr

3.   Review numbers *0-10* and introduce *11-20*. Use flashcards or the board and show numbers at random for students' response.

Have students respond to different times using a paper clock you have made or the illustrations on the board.

4.   Wieviel Uhr ist es? (Wie spät ist es?)

Expand this material by posing other problems using numbers *0-20.*

Es ist zwölf.
Es ist zwölf Uhr.

Es ist zehn.
Es ist zehn Uhr.

Es ist eins.
Es ist ein Uhr.

Es ist vier.
Es ist vier Uhr.

Es ist sieben.
Es ist sieben Uhr.

5.   Wieviel ist acht plus fünf? Acht plus fünf ist dreizehn.
     Wieviel ist elf minus sieben? Elf minus sieben ist vier.

Ausspracheübung

Have students repeat words. If students have problems discriminating between short and long /i/, use the description on sound formation provided.

short / i /	long / i /
ich	viel
mit	wie
in	wieviel
ist	Eisdiele
bis	sie
immer	die
nicht	wir
Monika	vier

[ɪ] **short *i* — sound (*in*):** The tongue arches up and toward the front. The lips are slightly open. There is little contact between the tongue and the hard palate.

[i:] **long *i* — sound (*die*):** The tip of the tongue either rests on the inner edge of the lower incisors or slightly behind them. The lips tend to be spread.

Übungen

Formation of Questions

Point out to students that the intonation drops at the end of a question. Practice a few questions to be sure your students develop the right intonation pattern in forming questions.

To form a question you must use the so-called inverted word order. The subject and the verb of the sentence are interchanged.

Examples: *Kommen Sie später?* Are you coming later?
Gehen wir in die Stadt? Are we going downtown?
Heißt sie Christine? Is her name Christine?
Geht Thomas nach Hause? Is Thomas going home?

You can readily see that the formation of questions in German is simpler than in English where most questions use the form of "to do" (do you?, does he?, etc.).

The inverted word order is also used with such question words as those listed below:

Wie? (how)   *Wie* heißen Sie?
Wo? (where)   *Wo* wohnst du?
Wohin? (where to)   *Wohin* gehen Sie?
Was? (what)   *Was* machst du jetzt?
Woher? (where from) *Woher* kommt er?

Folgt den Beispielen!

Personalize these exercises by having some students ask the questions (answers of exercises) and others answer them. Students should be encouraged to vary the questions.

1. Du hast keine Zeit.   Hast du keine Zeit?
   Monika wohnt da drüben.   Wohnt Monika da drüben?
   Andreas geht in die Stadt.   Geht Andreas in die Stadt?
   Ihr bekommt das Geld.   Bekommt ihr das Geld?
   Heike bleibt zu Hause.   Bleibt Heike zu Hause?
   Herr Schmidt kennt Sven.   Kennt Herr Schmidt Sven?

2. München ist eine Stadt.   Ist München eine Stadt?

   Wir haben viel zu tun.   Haben wir viel zu tun?

   Ich brauche etwas Geld.   Brauche ich etwas Geld?

   Sie gehen zur Eisdiele.   Gehen Sie zur Eisdiele?

   Sven kommt bald rüber.   Kommt Sven bald rüber?

   Er wohnt in Buchenau.   Wohnt er in Buchenau?

3. Kennst du Katrin?   Ja, ich kenne Katrin.

   Gehst du in die Stadt?   Ja, ich gehe in die Stadt.

   Wohnst du hier?   Ja, ich wohne hier.

   Bleibst du zu Hause?   Ja, ich bleibe zu Hause.

   Brauchst du Geld?   Ja, ich brauche Geld.

   Hast du viel zu tun?   Ja, ich habe viel zu tun.

4. Habt ihr fünf Mark?   Ja, wir haben fünf Mark.

   Fragt ihr Heike?   Ja, wir fragen Heike.

   Habt ihr etwas Zeit?   Ja, wir haben etwas Zeit.

   Bleibt ihr hier?   Ja, wir bleiben hier.

   Bekommt ihr Geld?   Ja, wir bekommen Geld.

   Wohnt ihr da drüben?   Ja, wir wohnen da drüben.

   Kommt ihr um sieben?   Ja, wir kommen um sieben.

Variation: Have students deviate from the specific answers in Übungen 3-4 and have them form other answers.

5. **Change each statement to a question.**

   1. Susanne ist heute nicht pünktlich.
   2. Sie haben viel zu tun, Herr Gruber.
   3. Wir gehen nicht in die Stadt.
   4. Sven kommt um zwei Uhr aus der Schule.
   5. Ihr wohnt in München.
   6. Du brauchst etwas Geld.
   7. Er hat keine Angst.
   8. Monika kennt Susanne.
   9. Herr und Frau Lehmann gehen zur Eisdiele.
   10. Wir warten eine Weile.

6. **Beantwortet diese Fragen!**

Encourage varied responses.

   1. Wo wartest du?
   2. Um wieviel Uhr kommst du aus der Schule?
   3. Warum gehst du in die Stadt?
   4. Brauchst du etwas Geld?
   5. Hast du viel zu tun?
   6. Wieviel Uhr ist es jetzt?
   7. Warum hast du keine Zeit?
   8. Warum bleibst du zu Hause?

Present Tense of *haben* (to have)

Although most verbs show the regular pattern of conjugation (stem + ending), there are several verbs which do not follow this pattern, as in the case with *haben*.

Singular	ich habe du hast er sie } hat es	I have you have he has she has it has
Plural	wir haben ihr habt sie haben Sie haben (sg. & pl.)	we have you have they have you have

Folgt den Beispielen! Limit the forms of *haben* to the few examples given in *Übungen 7-9*. Avoid direct object usage which will be discussed in *Lektion 3*.

7. Heike hat zehn Mark. Und Monika?   Monika hat auch zehn Mark.
    Wir haben zwölf Mark. Und du?   Ich habe auch zwölf Mark.
    Andreas hat fünf Mark. Und Sabine?   Sabine hat auch fünf Mark.
    Herr und Frau Lehmann haben zwanzig   Wir haben auch zwanzig Mark.
        Mark. Und ihr?
    Ich habe zwei Mark. Und Peter?   Peter hat auch zwei Mark.
    Wir haben fünfzehn Mark. Und ihr?   Wir haben auch fünfzehn Mark.

8. Hast du viel zu tun?   Hast du viel zu tun?
        Frau Meier   Hat Frau Meier viel zu tun?
        ihr   Habt ihr viel zu tun?
        Sven   Hat Sven viel zu tun?
        wir   Haben wir viel zu tun?
        Heike und Birgit   Haben Heike und Birgit viel zu tun?

9. Haben Sie Glück?   Hast du Glück?
    Haben Sie etwas Geld?   Hast du etwas Geld?
    Haben Sie eine Cola?   Hast du eine Cola?
    Haben Sie zwanzig Mark?   Hast du zwanzig Mark?
    Haben Sie keine Angst?   Hast du keine Angst?
    Haben Sie eine Idee?   Hast du eine Idee?

10. Supply the correct form of *haben*.

1. Wir _____ keine Zeit.
2. Ich _____ viel zu tun.
3. _____ du etwas Geld?
4. Monika _____ eine gute Idee.
5. _____ ihr keine Angst?
6. Herr und Frau Schmidt _____ keine Lust.
7. _____ Sie fünfzehn Mark?

The Definite Article (Nominative Singular): *der, die, das* (the)

Explain to students that an article must be learned with each new noun.

In German there are three variations of the definite article in the nominative singular, i.e. *der, die* and *das*. The nominative is used to identify the subject.

Examples: *Der Junge heißt Peter. Die Idee ist gut. Das Gymnasium ist in der Nähe.*

It is extremely important to learn these articles that accompany the individual nouns. You should refer to these as masculine *(der)*, feminine *(die)*, and neuter *(das)*. Be aware, however, that the *nouns* associated with either of the three articles are not necessarily "masculine" or "feminine" or "neuter" by context—i.e., the article for a man's tie *(die Krawatte)* is feminine.

	Singular		
	masculine	*feminine*	*neuter*
nominative	der	die	das

Folgt dem Beispiel!

11. *der, die* oder *das?*

Tag	der Tag
Name	der Name
Zeit	die Zeit
Uhr	die Uhr
Geld	das Geld
Eisdiele	die Eisdiele
Mark	die Mark
Ecke	die Ecke
Freund	der Freund
Gymnasium	das Gymnasium

12. Supply the proper definite article.

1. Wie heißt _____ Junge?
2. Wo ist _____ Schule?
3. _____ Idee ist gut.
4. _____ Telefon ist da.
5. _____ Frau wohnt gleich um die Ecke.
6. Wie heißt _____ Mädchen?
7. _____ Stadt ist langweilig.
8. _____ Herr kommt pünktlich.

zu Hause and *nach Hause*

There is a distinct difference in using these two phrases. *Zu Hause* means *at home;* whereas *nach Hause* has the meaning *(going) home.*

Examples: *Wo ist Heidi? Sie ist zu Hause.*
Wohin geht Uwe? Er geht nach Hause.

13. *zu Hause* oder *nach Hause?*

1. Wann gehen Sie _____?
2. Katrin kommt um fünf Uhr _____.
3. Warum bleibst du heute _____?
4. Heike ist nicht _____.
5. Auf dem Weg _____ sprechen sie über die Schule.
6. Ich warte _____.
7. Hast du etwas Geld _____?

Cognates Have students go through a German newspaper or magazine to see how many cognates they can find.

Words that look alike in German and English and have the same meaning are called *cognates.* Although you can look them up in the vocabulary section, you won't have any problem identifying the meaning of a cognate. Here are some examples of cognates:

Telefon	*Diskothek*	*Butter*	*Hotel*	*Bank*
Chance	*Bus*	*Englisch*	*Eis*	*Amerika*

die Diskothek   das Eis   das Hotel

Lesestück (Reading Selection)

Susanne geht nach Hause

Monika geht auf ein Gymnasium° in Buchenau. Buchenau ist eine Stadt in der Nähe° von München. Jeden° Tag kommt Monika um ein Uhr aus der Schule°.

     Monika wartet° oft, bis Susanne und Katrin aus der Schule kommen. Alle drei gehen dann zusammen° nach Hause. Katrin ist immer pünktlich. Beide warten eine Weile. Endlich° kommt Susanne. Sie kommt oft zu spät°. Susanne ist heute nicht froh°. Sie ist verärgert°.

     Katrin fragt° Susanne: ,,Was ist los?" Susanne sagt°: ,,Ich habe heute viel zu tun. Wir schreiben morgen° eine Arbeit." Auf dem Weg° nach Hause sprechen sie oft über die Schule. Monika fragt: ,,Warum gehen wir nicht in die Stadt?" Katrin sagt: ,,Das ist eine gute Idee." Susanne hat auch Lust, aber heute ist es nicht möglich°.

     Alle drei gehen jetzt schnell zur Haltestelle°. Die S-Bahn° kommt in fünf Minuten. Monika sagt zu Susanne und Katrin: ,,Ich kaufe° noch schnell° eine Cola." Ein Kiosk ist gleich in der Nähe. Da kommt auch schon° die S-Bahn. Susanne sagt zu Monika und Katrin: ,,Tschüs bis morgen." Sie steigt ein°, und Monika und Katrin gehen in die Stadt.

secondary school
nearby/every
from school
waits
together
finally
late/happy
angry
asks/says
tomorrow
on the way

possible
to the stop/train

buy/quickly
already
gets in

Tschüs bis morgen!

Fragen über das Lesestück

1. Wo ist Buchenau?
2. Um wieviel Uhr kommt Monika aus der Schule?
3. Warum wartet Monika?
4. Wer kommt zu spät?
5. Warum ist Susanne verärgert?
6. Was ist eine gute Idee?
7. Was kommt in fünf Minuten?
8. Was kauft Monika?
9. Was macht Susanne jetzt?
10. Was machen Monika und Katrin?

Erweiterung

14. What words are missing? Ask students to write out the missing words to assure correct spelling.

elf, _____, dreizehn, vierzehn, _____, sechzehn, _____, achtzehn, neunzehn, _____
Montag, _____, Mittwoch, _____, Freitag, Sonnabend, _____
Sekunde, _____, Stunde, _____, Woche, _____, Jahr

15. *Wieviel Uhr ist es?* **Use a complete sentence to answer.**

1. 1:00
2. 8:00
3. 12:00
4. 3:00
5. 6:00
6. 9:00

16. Select one of the words from the list below and supply the correct form.

1. Ich _____ um zwei Uhr aus der Schule.
2. _____ du Katrin?
3. Wir _____ eine Arbeit.
4. Herr Lehmann _____ in München.
5. _____ ihr jetzt nach Hause?
6. Birgit _____ zehn Mark.
7. Er _____ keine Angst.
8. Sie _____: ,,Was ist los?"
9. Sven _____ heute zu Hause.
10. Heike _____: ,,Tschüs bis morgen."

kommen	haben	gehen
fragen	schreiben	heißen
sagen	bleiben	brauchen
wohnen		

Folgt den Beispielen!

17. *Wieviel Uhr ist es?*

Wieviel Uhr ist es? (zwei)	**Es ist zwei Uhr.**
Wieviel Uhr ist es? (zehn)	Es ist zehn Uhr.
Wieviel Uhr ist es? (fünf)	Es ist fünf Uhr.
Wieviel Uhr ist es? (zwölf)	Es ist zwölf Uhr.
Wieviel Uhr ist es? (sieben)	Es ist sieben Uhr.
Wieviel Uhr ist es? (neun)	Es ist neun Uhr.

18. *Wieviel ist…?*

Wieviel ist zwei plus drei?	**Zwei plus drei ist fünf.**
Wieviel ist sechs plus fünf?	Sechs plus fünf ist elf.
Wieviel ist vierzehn plus fünf?	Vierzehn plus fünf ist neunzehn.
Wieviel ist acht plus sieben?	Acht plus sieben ist fünfzehn.
Wieviel ist vier plus neun?	Vier plus neun ist dreizehn.
Wieviel ist eins plus elf?	Eins plus elf ist zwölf.

19.

Wieviel ist zehn minus vier?	**Zehn minus vier ist sechs.**
Wieviel ist zwölf minus neun?	Zwölf minus neun ist drei.
Wieviel ist siebzehn minus sieben?	Siebzehn minus sieben ist zehn.
Wieviel ist zwanzig minus zehn?	Zwanzig minus zehn ist zehn.
Wieviel ist acht minus fünf?	Acht minus fünf ist drei.
Wieviel ist dreizehn minus elf?	Dreizehn minus elf ist zwei.

20. **Wie heißt das auf deutsch?**

1. Don't be afraid!
2. Stay at home!
3. That's a good idea.
4. He is angry.
5. How boring!
6. We have a lot to do.
7. How much money do we have?
8. She is always on time.
9. It's not possible.
10. What's the matter?

21. **Complete the conversation by providing appropriate responses.** Encourage varied responses.

1. Um wieviel Uhr kommst du aus der Schule?
2. Was machen wir dann?
3. Das ist eine gute Idee.
4. Ja, morgen schreiben wir eine Arbeit.

22. Welcher Tag ist es?

1. Heute ist Sonntag. Morgen ist _____.
2. Morgen ist Donnerstag. Heute ist _____.
3. Heute ist Freitag. Morgen ist _____.
4. Morgen ist Mittwoch. Heute ist _____.
5. Heute ist Donnerstag. Morgen ist _____.
6. Morgen ist Montag. Heute ist _____.

23. *Beantwortet die Fragen!* **Use the cues provided. Be sure to write out the numbers.**

1. Wieviel Geld brauchst du? (ich / 10 Mark)
2. Wieviel Geld braucht Sven? (er / 17 Mark)
3. Wieviel Geld braucht ihr? (wir / 8 Mark)
4. Wieviel Geld brauchen Sie? (ich / 20 Mark)
5. Wieviel Geld braucht Susanne? (sie / 12 Mark)

Beantwortet diese Fragen!

24. Wo wohnst du? (gleich um die Ecke)　　Ich wohne gleich um die Ecke.

Was brauchst du?
(etwas Geld)　　Ich brauche etwas Geld.

Was macht ihr um drei Uhr?
(zur Eisdiele gehen)　　Wir gehen zur Eisdiele.

Um wieviel Uhr kommst du aus der
Schule? (zwei Uhr)　　Ich komme um zwei Uhr aus der Schule.

Was schreibt ihr?
(eine Arbeit)　　Wir schreiben eine Arbeit.

Was macht Katrin?
(nach Hause gehen)　　Katrin geht nach Hause.

25. Wieviel Uhr ist es jetzt?

Warum bleibst du zu Hause?

Hast du viel zu tun?

Wo wartest du?

Um wieviel Uhr gehst du nach Hause?

Was fragst du?

Warum gehst du in die Stadt?

Was brauchst du?

To help students answer each question you may want to provide a list of clues. (*Wieviel Uhr ist es jetzt? — zwei, fünf*, etc.; *Wo wartest du? — da drüben, an der Haltestelle, zu Hause*, etc.)

26. *Um wieviel Uhr kommst du?* **Indicate when you are coming by using these periods of time:** *heute morgen, heute vormittag, heute mittag, heute nachmittag,* **or** *heute abend.*

1. Ich komme um 11 Uhr.
2. Ich komme um 20 Uhr.

3. Ich komme um 16 Uhr.
4. Ich komme um 12 Uhr.
5. Ich komme um 9 Uhr.
6. Ich komme um 14 Uhr.
7. Ich komme um 6 Uhr.

Sprachspiegel
Encourage various responses.

Answer these questions with as much detail as possible, using the vocabulary and expressions you have learned so far.

1. Warum gehst du am Montag in die Stadt?
2. Was machst du am Sonntag?
3. Wer kommt rüber? Und warum?
4. Wer ist am Telefon?
5. Brauchst du etwas Geld? Warum?
6. Was ist schade?
7. Warum haben wir Glück?
8. Was ist nicht möglich?

Wie sagt man's? (How is it said?)

Have students read these mini-dialogs aloud. Ask them to act them out as realistically as possible.

Ich heiße Silvia. Und du?
Anja.

Tag, Volker. Wie geht's?
Danke, gut.

Mein Name ist Christine Weber. Wie heißen Sie?
Herr Schneider.

Heißt du Birgit?
Nein, Inge. Birgit ist da drüben.

Hast du etwas Zeit?
Nicht jetzt.
Und später?
Dann schon.

Gehst du in die Stadt?
Ja, heute nachmittag.

Was kaufst du?
Eine Cola.
Ich auch.

Tag, Volker. Wie geht's?

Zungenbrecher (Tongue Twister)

Fritz fischt frische Fische.
(Fritz catches fresh fish.)

If your students have no problems with this tongue twister, offer this original version:
Fischers Fritz fischt frische Fische, frische Fische fischt Fischers Fritz.

Kulturecke

What Time Is It?

In ancient times, people were just as interested in determining the time of the day as we are today. Different methods such as a sundial were used. Today, of course, we have a more sophisticated way of telling time, not only in our country but all over the world.

One of the most important phrases to know in any language is "What time is it?" In Germany you will find many clocks that will answer your question immediately. However, sometimes you will need to ask someone for the time. The most common ways to ask the time are *"Wieviel Uhr ist es?"* or *"Wie spät ist es?"* Here are some examples of expressing time in German:

6:00 = *Es ist sechs Uhr.*
9:00 = *Es ist neun.*
3:30 = *Es ist halb vier.*
8:30 = *Es ist acht Uhr dreißig.*
9:15 = *Es ist Viertel nach neun.* or *Es ist ein Viertel zehn.* or *Es ist neun Uhr fünfzehn.*
12:45 = *Es ist Viertel vor eins.* or *Es ist drei Viertel eins.*
8:05 = *Es ist fünf Minuten nach acht Uhr.* or simply *Es ist fünf nach acht.*
1:20 = *Es ist zwanzig Minuten nach eins.* or *Es ist ein Uhr zwanzig.*
11:50 = *Es ist zehn Minuten vor zwölf Uhr.* or *Es ist elf Uhr fünfzig.*
9:55 = *Es ist fünf vor zehn.* or *Es ist neun Uhr fünfundfünfzig.*
11:33 = *Es ist elf Uhr dreiunddreißig.* or *Es ist drei Minuten nach halb elf.*

A city hall clock. (Ulm)

die Weltzeituhr (Ost-Berlin)

Germans use a 24-hour system. (Bremen)

Germans do not use the *A.M./P.M.* system. The traveler will have to become familiar with the 24-hour system in a hurry, particularly when dealing with the official language used on radio and TV or at train stations. The 24-hour system is used primarily to avoid misunderstandings. There is no problem with the numbers 1 to 12, as they designate the *A.M.* period of time. Figures 13 to 24 indicate the hours that we call *P.M.* A Rhine steamer leaving at 1:20 P.M., for instance, would be announced as *13.20 (dreizehn Uhr zwanzig).*

An old-fashioned clock seller. (Schwarzwald)

Wieviel Uhr ist es? (Mainz)

Vokabeln

der **Abend,-e** evening
aber but
achtzehn eighteen
alle all
am (or: **an dem**) at the, on the
die **Angst,-̈e** fear
   Keine Angst! Don't worry! Don't be afraid!
die **Arbeit,-en** work
   eine Arbeit schreiben to take a test
auf to, on
aus from, out of
bald soon
beide both
bekommen to get, receive
bis until
bleiben to stay, remain
brauchen to need
die **Cola,-s** cola

dann then
denn used for emphasis
   Wieviel Geld brauchst du denn? Well, how much money do you need?
der **Dienstag** Tuesday
der **Donnerstag** Thursday
dreizehn thirteen
ein(e) a, an
einsteigen to get in(to), board
die **Eisdiele,-n** ice cream parlor
elf eleven
endlich finally
etwas some, a little
fragen to ask
der **Freitag** Friday
froh happy, glad
fünfzehn fifteen
das **Geld** money

das **Glück** luck
    Glück haben to be lucky
das **Gymnasium,-sien** secondary school
    Sie geht auf ein Gymnasium.
    She goes to a secondary school.
    haben to have
die **Haltestelle,-n** stop (for
    bus, streetcar or train)
das **Haus,-̈er** house
    nach Hause gehen to go home
    zu Hause at home
    heute today
    heute abend this evening
die **Idee,-n** idea
    immer always
das **Jahr,-e** year
    jeden (form of **jeder**) each, every
    kein no
    keine Zeit no time
der **Kiosk,-e** kiosk
    langweilig boring
    los: was ist los? What's the matter?
die **Lust** pleasure, joy
    Sie hat Lust... She would like to...
die **Mark** German monetary unit
    minus minus, less
die **Minute,-n** minute
der **Mittag,-e** noon
der **Mittwoch** Wednesday
    möglich possible
der **Monat,-e** month
der **Montag** Monday
der **Morgen** morning
    heute morgen this morning
    morgen tomorrow
    na well
der **Nachmittag,-e** afternoon
die **Nähe** nearness, proximity
    in der Nähe nearby
    neunzehn nineteen
    noch still, yet
    oft often
    pünktlich punctual, on time
    rüberkommen (colloquial)
    to come over
die **S-Bahn,-en** city train, suburban express
    train
    sagen to say
der **Samstag** Saturday
    schade too bad
    schnell fast, quick(ly)
    schon already
    schreiben to write
die **Schule,-n** school
    sechzehn sixteen
die **Sekunde,-n** second
    siebzehn seventeen
der **Sonnabend** Saturday

der **Sonntag** Sunday
    spät late
    Wie spät ist es? What time is it?
    How late is it?
    später later
    sprechen to speak, talk
    sprechen über to talk about
    steigen: Sie steigt ein. She gets in(to).
die **Stunde,-n** hour
das **Telefon,-e** telephone
    Tschüs! See you! (sometimes spelled
    Tschüss! or **Tschüß!**)
    tun to do
die **Uhr,-en** clock, watch
    Wieviel Uhr ist es? What time is it?
    Es ist vier Uhr. It's four o'clock.
    um at
    Um wieviel Uhr? At what time?
    verärgert angry
    viel much
    vierzehn fourteen
    von from, of
der **Vormittag,-e** forenoon
    wann when
    warten to wait
    warum why
der **Weg,-e** way
    auf dem Weg on the way
die **Weile** while
    eine Weile a while
    welcher which
    wer who
    wieder again
    wieviel how much?
    Um wieviel Uhr? At what time?
die **Zeit,-en** time
das **Zimmer,-** room
    zu at, too, to
    zur (or: **zu der**) to the
    zurückbekommen to get back
    zusammen together
    zwanzig twenty
    zwölf twelve

Dialog

Point out that train travel is much more popular in Germany (and Europe) than in the U.S.

Auf dem Bahnhof

Each train station has a schedule marked *"Ankunft"* and *"Abfahrt."*

Reflexive verbs will be discussed in Level 2. Treat this as an expression.

HERR MEISTER: Wir haben zu viel Gepäck.

FRAU MEISTER: Ja, du hast recht.

HERR MEISTER: Warte!...Hier ist ein Koffer-Kuli.

FRAU MEISTER: Prima. Um wieviel Uhr fahren wir denn nach Dortmund?

HERR MEISTER: Hier ist der Fahrplan. Abfahrt nach Dortmund: 8 Uhr 28, Gleis 7.

FRAU MEISTER: Es ist schon Viertel nach acht. Beeilen wir uns!

HERR MEISTER: Immer mit der Ruhe, Schatz! Wir bekommen die Fahrkarten am Schalter 2.

Point out that there are two seating classes on German trains.

HERR MEISTER: Zwei Fahrkarten nach Dortmund, bitte.

BEAMTER: Zweiter Klasse?

HERR MEISTER: Nein, erster Klasse.

BEAMTER: Hin und zurück?

HERR MEISTER: Nein, nur einfach.

BEAMTER: Einen Moment. Mal sehen, was der Computer zeigt. Ja, alles ist klar. Das macht 80 Mark.

HERR MEISTER: Hier ist Gleis 7.

FRAU MEISTER: Der Zug ist noch nicht da.

HERR MEISTER: Ah, dort kommt er schon. Ich trage die Tasche und den Koffer.

FRAU MEISTER: Warte! Nicht so schnell!

HERR MEISTER: Dieser Platz ist sehr bequem.

FRAU MEISTER: Wir haben wieder einmal Glück.
Der Zug ist auch nicht zu voll.

HERR MEISTER: Ja, wie sagt man doch: ,,Ende gut, alles gut!"

Fragen über den Dialog

1. Haben Meisters viel Gepäck?
2. Wohin fahren sie?
3. Um wieviel Uhr fahren sie?
4. Wo bekommen Meisters die Fahrkarten?
5. Fahren Herr und Frau Meister zweiter Klasse?
6. Ist der Zug schon da?
7. Wie ist der Platz?
8. Ist der Zug zu voll?

At the Railroad Station

MR. MEISTER: We have too much luggage.

MRS. MEISTER: Yes, you're right.

MR. MEISTER: Wait!…Here is a luggage cart.

MRS. MEISTER: Great. What time are we going to Dortmund?

MR. MEISTER: Here is the schedule. Departure to Dortmund: 8:28 A.M., track 7.

MRS. MEISTER: It's already a quarter after eight. Let's hurry!

MR. MEISTER: Take it easy, dear! We'll get the tickets at counter 2.

MR. MEISTER: Two tickets to Dortmund, please.

OFFICIAL: Second class?

MR. MEISTER: No, first class.

OFFICIAL: Round trip?

MR. MEISTER: No, just one-way.

OFFICIAL: One moment. Let's see what the computer is showing. Yes, everything is O.K. That's 80 marks.

MR. MEISTER: This is track 7.

MRS. MEISTER: The train isn't here yet.

MR. MEISTER: Ah, there it is already. I'll carry the bag and the suitcase.

MRS. MEISTER: Wait! Not so fast!

MR. MEISTER: This seat is very comfortable.

MRS. MEISTER: We're lucky again. The train is not too crowded.

MR. MEISTER: Yes, as they say, "All is well, that ends well."

Nützliche Ausdrücke

Review these expressions, which have been introduced in the *Dialog* and *Lesestück 1.*

Du hast recht.	You're right.
Prima.	Great.
Beeilen wir uns!	Let's hurry!
Immer mit der Ruhe!	Take it easy!
Alles ist klar.	Everything is O.K.
Das macht 10 Mark.	That's 10 marks.
Ich habe Glück.	I'm lucky.
Die Matheaufgaben sind ganz leicht.	The math problems are quite easy.
Das glaube ich nicht.	I don't believe that.
Sie ist sehr klug.	She is very smart.
Er weiß es.	He knows it.
Es dauert ein paar Minuten.	It takes a few minutes.
Gehst du zu Fuß?	Are you walking?

Sie gehen zu Fuß.

Die Aufgaben sind ganz leicht.

Weiß sie es?

Ergänzung

1.

10	20	30	40	50
zehn	**zwanzig**	**dreißig**	**vierzig**	**fünfzig**

60	70	80	90	100
sechzig	**siebzig**	**achtzig**	**neunzig**	**hundert, einhundert**

21	22	23	24
einundzwanzig	**zweiundzwanzig**	**dreiundzwanzig**	**vierundzwanzig**

2. Wieviel Uhr ist es?

Es ist halb drei.

Es ist Viertel vor zehn.

Es ist fünf Minuten vor vier.

Es ist Viertel nach sechs.

Es ist zehn Minuten nach zwölf.

3. Wie heißen die Nachbarländer von Deutschland?
   Dänemark, Holland (die Niederlande), Belgien, Luxemburg, Frankreich,
   die Schweiz, Österreich, die Tschechoslowakei, Polen

4. Nord, Ost, Süd, West *oder*: der Norden, der Osten, der Süden, der Westen

Have students look at a map and ask such questions as: *Wo liegt Kiel?… Stuttgart?… Frankfurt?…*

Point to a map and ask students : *Wie heißt dieses Land?… Wo liegt es?…* You may want to ask students to write out the names of countries.

Ausspracheübung

Practice words at a fast pace. Make sure students know the difference between short and long /o/. Describe the formation of the sound, if necessary.

short / o /	long / o /
komm	wohne
doch	so
von	Monat
Woche	Montag
noch	Bahnhof
Bonn	Dialog
bekommst	schon
oft	Cola
dort	froh
Ost	ohne
Nord	groß

[ɔ] **short** *o* — **sound** (*dort*): The lips are rounded and somewhat protruded. The tip of the tongue lies at the lower teeth or slightly drawn back from them.

[o:] **long** *o* — **sound** (*wo*): The lips form a small, almost round opening. The front of the tongue lies flat and usually the tip of the tongue touches the inner surface of the lower incisors.

Übungen

The Definite Article (Accusative Singular)

In the sentence *Ich frage das Mädchen* (I ask the girl.) *Ich* is called the subject (nominative), *frage* the verb, and *das Mädchen* the direct object (accusative) of the sentence.

	Singular		
	masculine	*feminine*	*neuter*
nominative	der	die	das
accusative	den	die	das

NOTE: From the chart above, you can readily see that the *die* and *das* articles do not change in the accusative and that *der* changes to *den*.

An *n* is added to certain masculine nouns when they are direct objects (accusative). In this category, the following nouns have been introduced so far: *der Herr, der Junge, der Beamte*.

Examples: *Seht ihr Herrn Meister? Wir brauchen den Jungen. Karin fragt den Beamten.*

Folgt den Beispielen!

If students have difficulties (*Übungen 1-2*), review the articles of nouns learned so far.

1. Was liegt da drüben? (Tasche)   Die Tasche liegt da drüben.

   Fahrplan   Der Fahrplan liegt da drüben.

   Geld   Das Geld liegt da drüben.

Uhr	Die Uhr liegt da drüben.
Vorort	Der Vorort liegt da drüben
Stadt	Die Stadt liegt da drüben.

2. Wo ist der Schalter? **Wo ist der Schalter?**

   Gepäck **Wo ist das Gepäck?**

   Eisdiele Wo ist die Eisdiele?

   Herr Wo ist der Herr?

   S-Bahn Wo ist die S-Bahn?

   Platz Wo ist der Platz?

   Mädchen Wo ist das Mädchen?

3. Wo ist der Zug? **Der Zug ist in Dortmund.**

   (in Dortmund)

   Wo ist der Koffer-Kuli? **Der Koffer-Kuli ist da drüben.**

   (da drüben)

   Wo ist die Eisdiele? Die Eisdiele ist um die Ecke.

   (um die Ecke)

   Wo ist das Geld? Das Geld ist hier.

   (hier)

   Wo ist der Koffer? Der Koffer ist dort.

   (dort)

   Wo ist die Frau? Die Frau ist zu Hause.

   (zu Hause)

4. Sehen Sie den Bahnhof? **Ja, ich sehe den Bahnhof.**

   Fahrplan **Ja, ich sehe den Fahrplan.**

Although verbs with stem vowel change are not introduced until *Lektion 7*, you may want to personalize this by asking a question such as: *Was siehst du?* If necessary, provide words (*Fahrplan, Bahnhof,* etc.)

   Computer Ja, ich sehe den Computer.

   Zug Ja, ich sehe den Zug.

   Platz Ja, ich sehe den Platz.

   Schalter Ja, ich sehe den Schalter.

5. Was hast du? (Tasche) **Ich habe die Tasche.**

   Uhr Ich habe die Uhr.

   Mark Ich habe die Mark.

   Cola Ich habe die Cola.

   Fahrkarte Ich habe die Fahrkarte.

   Arbeit Ich habe die Arbeit.

6. Wir sehen das Geld. **Wir sehen das Geld.**

   Junge **Wir sehen den Jungen.**

   Telefon Wir sehen das Telefon.

   Gymnasium Wir sehen das Gymnasium.

   Mädchen Wir sehen das Mädchen.

   Gleis Wir sehen das Gleis.

7. Kaufst du die Fahrkarte? **Kaufst du die Fahrkarte?**

Variation: Use the following to answer the question: *Ja, ich kaufe die Fahrkarte.*

   Tasche **Kaufst du die Tasche?**

   Koffer Kaufst du den Koffer?

Computer	Kaufst du den Computer?
Cola	Kaufst du die Cola?
Fahrplan	Kaufst du den Fahrplan?

8. Was kennst du? (Platz) — **Ich kenne den Platz.**
   Stadt — **Ich kenne die Stadt.**
   Haltestelle — Ich kenne die Haltestelle.
   Vorort — Ich kenne den Vorort.
   Mädchen — Ich kenne das Mädchen.
   Schule — Ich kenne die Schule.

9. Was brauchst du? (Fahrplan) — **Ich brauche den Fahrplan.**
   Was kaufst du? (Tasche) — **Ich kaufe die Tasche.**
   Was hast du? (Geld) — Ich habe das Geld.
   Was bekommst du? (Fahrkarte) — Ich bekomme die Fahrkarte.
   Was brauchst du? (Koffer) — Ich brauche den Koffer.

10. Supply the correct form of the words given in parentheses.

1. Wir tragen (the luggage) _____.
2. Fragen Sie doch (the official) _____!
3. Um wieviel Uhr kommt (the train) _____?
4. Seht ihr (the ticket counter) _____?
5. Ich brauche (the luggage cart) _____.
6. Die Jungen bekommen (the money) _____.
7. (The streetcar) _____ kommt gleich.
8. Wann beginnt (the school) _____?
9. (The telephone) _____ ist da drüben.
10. Er fragt (the girl) _____?

11. Beantwortet diese Fragen! Encourage varied responses.

1. Wer kommt um acht Uhr?
2. Was brauchst du denn?
3. Warum bist du verärgert?
4. Wen fragst du?
5. Warum hast du Glück?
6. Was dauert ein paar Minuten?
7. Wo ist die Haltestelle?
8. Wann kommt der Zug?

   9. Was ist eine gute Idee?

 10. Wohin gehst du?

12. **Provide the appropriate form of the definite article (*der, die, das*).**

   1. Wo ist _____ Fahrplan?

   2. Fragen Sie doch _____ Beamten!

   3. Ich trage _____ Koffer.

   4. Wie ist _____ Platz?

   5. Hast du _____ Gepäck?

   6. Wir brauchen _____ Geld.

   7. Wann kommt _____ Straßenbahn?

   8. Er fragt _____ Mädchen.

Question Words: *Wer? Wen? Was?*

Both question words *wer* (who) and *wen* (whom) ask about a person. To inquire about objects, you must use the question word *was* (what).

Wer inquires about the subject of the sentence, whereas *wen* asks about the direct object of the sentence. You can use either word whether masculine, feminine or neuter.

Examples: *Karin wohnt da drüben. **Wer** wohnt da drüben?*
                *Ich frage **den Beamten**. **Wen** frage ich?*
                *Wir brauchen **etwas Geld**. **Was** brauchen wir?*

Folgt den Beispielen!

13. Wer wohnt da drüben?   Herr Meister wohnt da drüben.
    (Herr Meister)

    Wer hat Glück? (ich)   Ich habe Glück.

    Wer geht auf das Gymnasium?   Katrin und Susanne gehen auf das Gymnasium.
    (Katrin und Susanne)

    Wer kennt Heike? (Birgit)   Birgit kennt Heike.

    Wer hat viel zu tun? (wir)   Wir haben viel zu tun.

    Wer bleibt zu Hause? (ihr)   Ihr bleibt zu Hause.

14. Wen fragt sie? (Junge)   Sie fragt den Jungen.

    Wen sehe ich? (Gabi)   Ich sehe Gabi.

    Wen brauchen wir?   Wir brauchen den Beamten.
    (Beamter)

    Wen kennt ihr?   Ihr kennt Herrn Gruber.
    (Herr Gruber)

    Wen fragst du?   Du fragst die Frau.
    (Frau)

    Wen seht ihr?   Ihr seht das Mädchen.
    (Mädchen)

15. Du bekommst *acht Mark*.   Was bekommst du?

15.

Du bekommst *acht Mark*.	Was bekommst du?
Ich frage *den Beamten*.	Wen frage ich?
Herr Meister kauft *die Fahrkarte*.	Was kauft Herr Meister?
Wir haben *viel Zeit*.	Was haben wir?
Andreas kennt *das Mädchen*.	Wen kennt Andreas?
Die Jungen tragen *den Koffer*.	Was tragen die Jungen?
Ich sehe *Birgit*.	Wen sehe ich?
Er hat *viel Glück*.	Was hat er?
Wir schreiben *die Arbeit*.	Was schreiben wir?

Side note left margin:

You may want to ask two questions for each sentence. (Du bekommst acht Mark... Wer bekommt acht Mark?/ Was bekommst du?)

16.

Herr und Frau Meister gehen in die Stadt.	Wer geht in die Stadt?
Ich frage *Susanne*.	Wen frage ich?
Mein Freund wohnt in Deutschland.	Wer wohnt in Deutschland?
Wir haben die Tasche.	Wer hat die Tasche?
Petra fragt *Frau Meier*.	Wen fragt Petra?
Sven kommt heute nicht.	Wer kommt heute nicht?
Ich sehe *Herrn Gruber*.	Wen sehe ich?
Du bleibst zu Hause.	Wer bleibt zu Hause?

17. Change the following sentences to questions. Use the correct question word — *wer*, *wen* or *was* — in your questions. Variation: Have students change sentences to simple questions. *(Frau Schmidt kauft die Tasche...Kauft Frau Schmidt die Tasche?)*

1. Frau Schmidt kauft *die Tasche*.
2. Ich kenne *Herrn Meister*.
3. *Andreas* kommt um vier Uhr nach Hause.
4. *Mein Freund* geht heute in die Stadt.
5. Wir brauchen *etwas Geld*.
6. Ihr seht *die S-Bahn*.
7. *Die Stadt* ist nicht weit von hier.
8. *Der Beamte* hat den Fahrplan.
9. Ich sehe *Kerstin*.
10. Sven fragt *die Frau*.

Present Tense of *sein* (to be)

The conjugation of *sein* is irregular.

Singular	ich bin du bist er sie } ist es	I am you are he is she is it is
Plural	wir sind ihr seid sie sind Sie sind (sg. & pl.)	we are you are they are you are

Folgt den Beispielen!

Practice the forms of *sein* further (*Übungen 18-19*) by asking personalized questions. (*Bist du heute abend zu Hause? Bist du pünktlich zu Hause?*, etc.)

18. Katrin ist immer pünktlich.
    Monika und Susanne

    ich

    ihr

    Herr und Frau Meister

    wir

Katrin ist immer pünktlich.
Monika und Susanne sind immer pünktlich.
Ich bin immer pünktlich.
Ihr seid immer pünktlich.
Herr und Frau Meister sind immer pünktlich.
Wir sind immer pünktlich.

19. Sind Sie heute abend zu Hause?

    ihr

    du

    Herr Schmidt

    wir

    die Mädchen

    ich

Sind Sie heute abend zu Hause?
Seid ihr heute abend zu Hause?
Bist du heute abend zu Hause?
Ist Herr Schmidt heute abend zu Hause?
Sind wir heute abend zu Hause?
Sind die Mädchen heute abend zu Hause?
Bin ich heute abend zu Hause?

20. **Supply the correct form of *sein*.**

    1. Warum _____ Heike verärgert?
    2. _____ du um acht Uhr zu Hause?
    3. Herr und Frau Lehmann _____ nicht da.
    4. Der Bahnhof _____ sehr weit von hier.
    5. _____ Sie Frau Meier?
    6. Ihr _____ immer so pünktlich!
    7. Ich _____ sehr froh.
    8. Das _____ eine gute Idee.
    9. Wo _____ ihr denn, Andreas und Susanne?
    10. Wieviel _____ drei und sechs?

kennen and *wissen*

Both words, *kennen* and *wissen*, mean "to know." However, *kennen* means "to know a person or a place," whereas *wissen* means "to know something" (as a fact).

Examples: *Kennst du Sabine?* but: *Weißt du, wer Sabine ist?*
Wir kennen Hamburg. but: *Wir wissen, wo Hamburg liegt.*

The verb *wissen* has irregular forms when it is used with *ich, du* and *er (sie, es).*

ich weiß	wir wissen
du weißt	ihr wißt
er ⎫	sie wissen
sie ⎬ weiß	Sie wissen
es ⎭	

Folgt dem Beispiel!

21. Weißt du das nicht?	**Weißt du das nicht?**
der Junge	**Weiß der Junge das nicht?**
ihr	Wißt ihr das nicht?
der Beamte	Weiß der Beamte das nicht?
Kerstin und Gabi	Wissen Kerstin und Gabi das nicht?
ich	Weiß ich das nicht?
wir	Wissen wir das nicht?

22. *kennen* oder *wissen*? Provide the correct form of the appropriate verb.

Expand the verb of wissen by asking questions such as: Weißt du/Wißt ihr, um wieviel Uhr der Zug kommt?,...die Klasse beginnt?,...wie der Junge heißt, etc. Encourage students to ask each other.

1. _____ Sie, um wieviel Uhr der Zug kommt?
2. Ich _____ Peter. Er ist sehr klug.
3. _____ du den Beamten?
4. Ich _____ nicht, was er macht.
5. _____ Kerstin die Matheaufgaben?
6. Wir _____, wo Peter wohnt.
7. _____ ihr das Mädchen?
8. Ja, wir _____ Herrn Schulz.

Telling Time (A.M. or P.M.)

Review telling time. Have a student act as the teacher. S/he should indicate different times on the board or use a clock.

Germans use the numbers 1 to 12 for A.M. and 13 to 24 for P.M. The 24-hour system is used particularly with official time announcements (radio, television, schedules, for example). However, when you ask someone on the street what time it is and the time of the day is obvious, then only the numbers 1 to 12 are used.

Examples: It's 4 P.M. *Es ist 16 Uhr.* (radio announcer)
Es ist 4 Uhr. (your friend answering)

When dealing with official time announcements, you will not hear the words *halb, (ein) Viertel, vor* or *nach,* but instead the announcer first will indicate the last full hour and then the minutes.

Examples: It's 8 P.M. *Es ist 20 Uhr.*
It's 9:18 P.M. *Es ist 21 Uhr 18.*

Words Used for Emphasis

A number of German words are used strictly for emphasis. Such words are *aber, auch, denn, doch* and *ja.* These words cannot be translated but are particularly important in conversational usage.

Examples: *Komm um sieben Uhr!* Come at seven o'clock.
*Komm **doch** um sieben Uhr!* Why don't you come at seven o'clock.
Wohin gehst du? Where are you going?
*Wohin gehst du **denn**?* Where *are* you going? or Tell me, where are you going?

44

Lesestück 1

Kerstins Schulweg

Kerstin wohnt in Mülheim, einem Vorort° von Köln. Jeden Tag, von Montag bis Freitag, geht Kerstin um halb acht zur Schule. Bis zur Haltestelle sind es nur° fünf Minuten zu Fuß. An einem Automaten kauft sie Fahrkarten° für die Straßenbahn°.

Gabi, Kerstins Freundin, kommt auch immer pünktlich. Kerstin begrüßt° Gabi. Sie kennt Gabi schon ein paar Jahre. Beide sind gute Freundinnen. Sie warten nicht sehr lange. Dann kommt auch schon die Straßenbahn und beide Mädchen steigen ein.

Gabi und Kerstin sprechen oft über die Schule. „Sind die Matheaufgaben nicht wieder einmal sehr schwer°?" fragt Gabi. „Das glaube ich nicht. Sie sind eigentlich ganz leicht," antwortet° Kerstin. „Du bist ja auch sehr klug. Du weißt immer so viel," sagt Gabi.

Beide Mädchen fahren drei Haltestellen mit° der Straßenbahn. Das dauert nur acht Minuten. Von der Haltestelle gehen sie noch zwei Ecken zu Fuß. Sie gehen jetzt etwas schneller. Sie haben nicht viel Zeit. Die Schule beginnt um acht Uhr.

suburb

only

tickets/streetcar

greets

hard

answers

with

Kerstin kauft Fahrkarten an einem Automaten.

Die Straßenbahn kommt.

Sie gehen zur Schule.

Lektion 3

Fragen über das Lesestück

1. Was ist Mülheim?
2. Um wieviel Uhr geht Kerstin zur Schule?
3. Wie weit ist es bis zur Haltestelle zu Fuß?
4. Was kauft Kerstin dort?
5. Kommt Gabi zu spät?
6. Was kommt bald?
7. Sind die Matheaufgaben für Kerstin schwer?
8. Fahren Kerstin und Gabi lange?
9. Wie weit gehen sie dann zu Fuß?
10. Um wieviel Uhr beginnt die Schule?

Erweiterung

23. Use the appropriate word from the list below to complete each sentence.

1. Gehst du in die Stadt? Heute ist es nicht _____!
2. Ich weiß das nicht. Die Matheaufgaben sind zu _____ .
3. Fahren Sie hin und zurück? Nein, nur _____ .
4. Angelika kommt um drei Uhr. Sie ist immer _____ .
5. Ich habe jetzt keine Zeit. Das ist aber _____ .
6. Komm mit! Wir fahren nach Bonn. Das ist mir _____ .
7. Warum bist du so _____ ? Wir schreiben heute eine Arbeit.
8. Wir haben viel zu tun. Wie _____ !

recht	verärgert
schade	möglich
langweilig	einfach
pünktlich	schwer

24. Wie heißt das auf deutsch?

1. Four tickets to Germany, please.
2. The seat is not comfortable.
3. Why is she so smart?
4. I'm walking.
5. Mr. Meier believes that.
6. It takes only five minutes.
7. Are you buying the suitcase?
8. What does the computer show?

25. Respond to each question or statement with a complete sentence that is meaningful.

1. Die Schule beginnt um acht Uhr.
2. Warum bist du so froh?

Encourage students to come up with a variety of different responses.

3. Die Matheaufgaben sind ganz leicht.

4. Ich habe viel zu tun.

5. Wie weit ist die Haltestelle zu Fuß?

6. Was fragt er?

7. Da kommt schon die Straßenbahn.

8. Der Platz hier ist sehr bequem.

9. Hast du immer so viel Glück?

10. Ich fahre hin und zurück.

26. Supply the missing words.

1. Fahren Sie hin und zurück? Nein, nur (one-way) _____ .

2. Wo ist (track five) _____ ?

3. (Let's hurry!) _____ ! (The train) _____ ist schon da.

4. Ich kaufe (the ticket) _____ .

5. Gabi ist Kerstins (girlfriend) _____ .

6. Wir haben (much time) _____ .

7. Brauchen Sie (the telephone) _____ ?

8. Hast du (the luggage cart) _____ ?

27. Beantwortet die Fragen! Have students use their imagination to answer these questions. Encourage varied responses.

Wo bekommst du die Fahrkarten?

Was zeigt der Computer?

Warum haben wir Glück?

Wohin fahren wir?

Wie weit gehst du zu Fuß?

Warum wartest du?

Kommst du oft zu spät nach Hause?

Was kaufst du?

Rückblick (Review) If students have difficulties dealing with *haben*, you may want to pick out some additional exercises from *Lektion 2*.

I. Provide the proper form of *haben* or *sein*.

1. Warum _____ Sie so verärgert?

2. _____ du etwas Zeit?

3. Endlich _____ ihr da!

4. Wir _____ oft Glück.

5. Die Idee _____ sehr gut.

6. Helmut und Stefan _____ immer pünktlich.

7. Monika _____ eine Cola.

8. _____ ihr das Geld?

9. Welcher Tag _____ morgen?

10. Du _____ ganz klug.

II. Write the complete answer (including numbers) to the question: *Wieviel Uhr ist es?* Use the 24-hour system.

1. 6:00 P.M.
2. 10:00 A.M.
3. 11:30 A.M.
4. 3:15 A.M.
5. 11:15 P.M.
6. 2:26 P.M.
7. 7:12 A.M.
8. 9:55 A.M.
9. 4:13 P.M.

III. Write out the answer to the question: *Wieviel ist…?*

1. $5 + 8 = ?$
2. $26 - 17 = ?$
3. $15 + 18 = ?$
4. $60 - 20 = ?$
5. $100 - 91 = ?$
6. $31 + 25 = ?$

IV. *Wer? — Wen? — Was? — Wie? — Wo?* Use the appropriate question word to form a question about each sentence. Be sure to ask the complete question.

1. Sie kennt *Julia und Christa* sehr gut.
2. Er heißt *Jörg*.
3. Achim und Renate wohnen *in der DDR*.
4. Wir schreiben *eine Arbeit*.
5. *Mein Freund und ich* gehen in die Stadt.
6. Hamburg liegt *im Norden*.
7. Ihr fragt *Fräulein Müller*.
8. Heike braucht *das Geld*.

Er kennt das Mädchen gut.

Lesestück 2

For additional details about *Lesestück 2,* refer to "Background Information" (in this and subsequent lessons) in the front section of this teacher's edition. The new words in this and the subsequent material from the *Lesestück 2* are listed in the margin as well as in the end vocabulary of the book, but not in the *Vokabeln* section at the end of each lesson.

Use a map to make the content more meaningful.

Deutschland — Land und Fläche

Deutschland hat ungefähr° 78 Millionen Einwohner°. Über 61 *approximately/inhabitants*
Millionen wohnen in der BRD (Bundesrepublik Deutschland), fast° *almost*
17 Millionen in der DDR (Deutsche Demokratische Republik).

Deutschland paßt° 22 mal in die Vereinigten Staaten, ohne° *fits/without*
Alaska und Hawaii. Die BRD ist ungefähr so groß wie° der Staat *as big as*
Oregon. Die DDR ist ungefähr so groß wie der Staat Tennessee. In
der Bundesrepublik ist die weiteste Entfernung° von Norden nach *farthest distance*
Süden 830 km (Kilometer), von Osten nach Westen 450 km. Die
weiteste Entfernung von Norden nach Süden in der Deutschen Demokratischen Republik ist 500 km und von Osten nach Westen
350 km.

Bonn ist die Hauptstadt° der Bundesrepublik. Diese Stadt *capital*
liegt im Westen der BRD. Ost-Berlin ist die Hauptstadt der Deutschen Demokratischen Republik und liegt im Osten der DDR.

Bonn ist die Hauptstadt der BRD.

Ost-Berlin ist
die Hauptstadt der DDR.

Fragen über das Lesestück

1. Wie viele Einwohner hat Deutschland?
2. Wie groß ist die Bundesrepublik und wie groß ist die DDR?
3. Was ist die weiteste Entfernung von Norden nach Süden in der DDR und in der BRD?
4. Wo liegt Ost-Berlin? Und Bonn?

Sprachspiegel

I. Create your own dialog by using the information given. Be as creative as possible.

After the dialog has been written out, you may want to have students act out their scenes.

You and your friend have arrived at the railroad station one hour before your train is leaving. You have plenty of time. You've got a lot of luggage, and you suggest to your friend that you get a cart. S/he suggests that you carry the luggage instead. You give your friend money so that s/he can buy the tickets. S/he tells the clerk at the window that you want to buy a second class ticket for yourself and your friend. S/he asks where both of you are going. You tell him/her that you are going to Köln. S/he tells your friend the total amount, and s/he pays. Since you've got some time, your friend suggests that you go to the kiosk around the corner to buy a cola.

II. Pretend to be an official at a railroad station answering questions of tourists who are not familiar with the station or the German train system.

Have one student read the questions in the book and another student answer them.

1. Wo steht der Zug nach Hamburg, bitte?
2. Wo bekomme ich Fahrkarten?
3. Wie viele Haltestellen sind es bis München?
4. Um wieviel Uhr kommt der Zug aus Österreich?
5. Wo ist Gleis 10?
6. Ist der Platz so bequem wie erste Klasse?
7. Was ist die Entfernung von hier nach Bonn?
8. Wie viele Einwohner hat diese Stadt?

Wie sagt man's?

Have students read or act out these mini-dialogs. You may want to ask some questions for each one. In the second dialog, for example, you could ask questions such as: *Was kommt in 20 Minuten?, Wo kommt der Zug?, Wann kommt der Zug?,* or *Hat er/sie noch Zeit?*

Ja, bitte?
Nach München bitte, hin und zurück.
Erster oder zweiter Klasse?
Zweiter Klasse, bitte.

Wann kommt der Zug?
In zwanzig Minuten. Gleis fünf.
Dann habe ich ja noch Zeit.

Wieviel kostet die Fahrkarte?
50 Mark.
Und nach Hamburg?

Zwei Fahrkarten, bitte.
Wohin denn?
Nach Köln.
Das macht 92 Mark.

Wo ist die Haltestelle?
Dort drüben.
Wann kommt die Straßenbahn?
In fünf Minuten.

Gehst du zu Fuß?
Zur Schule?
Nein, in die Stadt.
Das ist zu weit.

Sie weiß so viel.
Sie ist ja auch sehr klug.
Glaubst du das?
Nein, das weiß ich.

Zungenbrecher

Es klapperten die Klapperschlangen bis die Klappern schlapper klangen.
(The rattlesnakes rattled until the rattles sounded weaker.)

Break down the tongue twister into small sections and have students repeat them. Find out who can say it
several times without stumbling.

Kulturecke

Traveling by Train

Traveling by train in Germany can be rewarding or frustrating for the foreign traveler. If you're well prepared, you won't have any problems coping with this new and exciting adventure. When traveling between major cities, look for the main railroad station (*Hauptbahnhof*), usually located in the heart of the city. Should you depart from a small station, simply ask for the *Bahnhof*.

Upon entering a main station, become acquainted with the facilities. If you need information about a certain train, look for the schedules usually posted in a prominent location behind a glass window. There are normally two such schedules. One is marked "*Abfahrt*" (departure), the other "*Ankunft*" (arrival). The first schedule gives destinations, times of departure and other valuable information. In case you want to study these details in more privacy and at leisure, you should look for the information office, marked either "*Reiseauskunft*" or "*Information*." There you can buy a printed train schedule for a nominal fee. For information on local train travel, many major stations have automats marked "*Reisezugauskunft*" that will provide you with requested information after you have pushed the proper buttons. The major stations have begun to install large overhead departure schedules that indicate the departure time, type of train, destination and other information such as possible changes. If you are in a hurry or need speedy personal attention, look for an official wearing a dark blue cap with a golden band marked "*Information*." This official usually has a detailed train schedule and will have an answer to your question at his finger tips.

The facilities at train stations are generally well marked. Know the German names and you'll have no difficulty finding your way around. Buy your ticket at any window marked "*Fahrkarten*." Let's assume you want to travel to Frankfurt. To ask for a ticket, simply say to the clerk, "*Nach Frankfurt, bitte.*" If your ticket is to be one-way, add the word "*einfach*," which means literally "simple." If you want a round-trip ticket, say "*hin und zurück*," which means "there and back."

After you have purchased your ticket, you may decide to check your luggage instead of taking it directly to the train. Look for a sign which is marked "*Reisegepäck-Annahme*." Many travelers, however, prefer to take their luggage with them on the train. To check your luggage temporarily until departure, you should look for coin-operated lockers marked "*Schließfächer*."

Every station, large or small, usually has some eating facilities. In major stations you may find the words "*Cafeteria*," "*Imbiß*," which is a snack bar, and "*Restaurant*." If you don't want to sit down at a table, try to locate a snack bar that offers hot dogs, cold sandwiches and beverages. Those who would like to take some of the delicious German chocolates or candies on their trip can buy these goodies at specialty stands. Would you like to read some newspapers, magazines or books? Look for a stand marked "*Zeitschriften-Bücher*." Germans rarely go to visit friends or relatives in other towns without taking a small gift along, such as candy or more typically flowers. It is quite common to find flower shops at the station.

If you have little luggage to carry, you won't have any problems taking it directly to the train. However, if you have more luggage than you can carry easily, look for a luggage cart marked "*Koffer-Kuli*." You can place the luggage on the cart and wheel it right to the train. There is no charge for the use of these carts. Be sure to give yourself plenty of time to get to the train. The trains of the German Railroads (*Deutsche Bundesbahn*) are punctual and won't wait for you.

Most Germans travel second class (*Zweite Klasse*). Second class usually has vinyl seats; it's not luxurious but fairly comfortable. First class seats (*Erste Klasse*) are more plush and rather expensive. These accommodations are recommended only if you want to assure your-

Traveling by train is quite popular in Germany.

The *Intercity (IC)* trains connect major cities.

The *Abfahrt* schedule lists departing trains.

der Hauptbahnhof (München)

A specialty stand. (München)

self a seat during the rush period. If you're not sure, you can purchase a second class ticket and pay the difference after you have boarded the train. Check also to determine whether your car is a *Raucher* (smoker) or a *Nichtraucher* (non-smoker). Most cars have sections for both. Shortly before departure there will be the final call over the loudspeaker and a warning to step back and close the doors. Except at the major railroad stations, an official still blows the whistle to give the signal that the train is about to pull out.

Once the train has left the station, you can relax and examine your surroundings. You will find the compartment and the other facilities quite comfortable. Remember, most Germans travel by train and not by plane as in the U.S. Therefore, special care is taken to assure a pleasant environment on trains. If you don't want to bring your own sandwiches, you can have a warm or cold meal in the *Speisewagen* (dining car). Don't be surprised if someone else sits down at your table after asking you "*Ist hier noch frei?*" This is quite common in most German restaurants. If you want to take a nap, you can recline your seat. On a longer trip, you can reserve sleeping quarters in the *Schlafwagen* (sleeper) or in a *Liegewagen* (couchette) for an additional fee.

There are several types of trains, differing in the distance and speed of their runs. Most foreigners want to cover distances quickly. Therefore, you may prefer to travel in a *D-Zug*. A D-Zug makes fewer stops and connects more than 70 German cities. The fastest trains are the *Intercity* and the *TEE* (*Trans-Europa-Express*). These never stop in smaller towns. The Intercity trains link 40 major German cities and usually run at two-hour intervals. And, finally, should you fly in or out of Frankfurt — coming from or going to the area of Köln — Lufthansa, the German Airlines, will transport you in their Airport Express. This true adventure takes you past fairy tale-like castles along the Rhine.

Lufthansa Airport Express. (Köln)

Compartments are very comfortable.

Train travel can be relaxing.

Vokabeln

alles everything
an at
antworten to answer
der **Automat,-en** automat
der **Bahnhof,-̈e** (train) station
sich **beeilen** to hurry
    Beeilen wir uns! Let's hurry.
beginnen to begin
begrüßen to greet
Belgien Belgium
bequem comfortable
bitte please
bitte schön here you are
die **Bundesrepublik Deutschland** Federal Republic of Germany
der **Computer,-** computer
Dänemark Denmark
dauern to last
die **Deutsche Demokratische Republik** German Democratic Republic
Deutschland Germany
diese (form of **dieser**) this
dieser this
doch used for emphasis
dort there
eigentlich actual(ly), real(ly)
einfach simple, one-way
einmal once
    wieder einmal once again
das **Ende** end
fahren to drive, go
die **Fahrkarte,-n** ticket
der **Fahrplan,-̈e** schedule
die **Fläche,-n** area, surface
Frankreich France
die **Freundin,-nen** girlfriend
für for
der **Fuß,-̈e** foot
    zu Fuß on foot, walk
    zu Fuß gehen to walk
das **Gepäck** luggage, baggage
glauben to believe, think
das **Gleis,-e** track
groß big, large
halb half
hin und zurück round trip
kaufen to buy
der **Kilometer,-** kilometer
klar clear, O.K.
die **Klasse,-n** class
    zweiter Klasse second class
klug smart
der **Koffer,-** suitcase
der **Koffer-Kuli,-s** luggage cart

das **Land,-̈er** country, land
lange long
leicht easy
liegen to lie, be located
Luxemburg Luxembourg
mal times
man one, they, you people
die **Matheaufgaben** (pl.) math problems
die **Million,-en** million
mit with
der **Moment,-e** moment
nach to, after
das **Nachbarland,-̈er** neighboring country
die **Niederlande** Netherlands
der **Norden** north
nur only, just
der **Osten** east
Österreich Austria
paar: ein paar a few, some
der **Platz,-̈e** seat, place
prima great, splendid
die **Ruhe** peace, silence
    Immer mit der Ruhe! Take it easy.
der **Schalter,-** (ticket) counter
der **Schulweg,-e** way to school
die **Schweiz** Switzerland
schwer difficult, hard
sehen to see, look
    Mal sehen… Let's see…
sehr very
sein to be
so so
der **Staat,-en** state
die **Straßenbahn,-en** streetcar
der **Süden** south
die **Tasche,-n** bag
tragen to carry
die **Tschechoslowakei** Czechoslovakia
über over, above
die **Vereinigten Staaten** United States
das **Viertel,-** quarter
    Es ist Viertel nach acht. It's a quarter after eight.
voll full, crowded
der **Vorort,-e** suburb
der **Westen** west
wie viele how many
wissen to know
zeigen to show
der **Zug,-̈e** train

Dialog

In der Schule

hear
repeat 2x, phrase by phrase
then full sent.

also
in FS.

STEFAN:	Wo bleibt denn der Schlaukopf wieder?
DIRK:	Keine Angst! Er kommt schon.
ELKE:	Ihr seid so ungeduldig. Immer mit der Ruhe! Wir lösen die Physikaufgaben auch ohne Oliver. Seht mal, wer da kommt!
OLIVER:	Na, ihr drei? Seid ihr sauer?
STEFAN:	Verlier keine Worte! Wir brauchen deine Hilfe.

though the dropping of the "" (in Ich hab'*…vs.* Ich *?e…) is usually avoided in* *itten language, it is quite* *nmon in colloquial usage.*

DIRK:	Ich hab' mein Buch hier. Die Aufgabe steht auf Seite 97.
STEFAN:	Ich verstehe die Formeln gar nicht.
ELKE:	Lerne sie doch auswendig!
STEFAN:	Dein Vorschlag ist wirklich praktisch.

OLIVER:	Die Aufgabe ist doch ganz einfach! Lest die Beschreibung gründlich! Dann gebraucht diese Formel hier.
DIRK:	Warum bist du denn so klug?
OLIVER:	Ja, ich lerne eben fleißig. Man sagt ja: ,,Übung macht den Meister!"

Fragen über den Dialog

1. Warum ist Stefan ungeduldig?
2. Wer kommt?
3. Was brauchen Stefan, Dirk und Elke?
4. Wo steht die Aufgabe?
5. Was versteht Stefan nicht?
6. Was sagt Oliver? Ist die Aufgabe einfach oder schwer?
7. Warum weiß Oliver so viel?

At School

STEFAN:	Where is the genius?
DIRK:	Don't worry. He'll come.
ELKE:	You're so impatient. Take it easy. We'll solve the physics problems without Oliver. Look who's coming!
OLIVER:	Well, you three? Are you angry?
STEFAN:	Don't waste any words! We need your help.
DIRK:	I've got my book here. The problem is on page 97.
STEFAN:	I don't understand the formulas at all.
ELKE:	Why don't you memorize them?
STEFAN:	Your suggestion is really practical.
OLIVER:	The problem is quite simple. Read the description carefully. Then use these formulas here.
DIRK:	Why are you so smart?
OLIVER:	Well, I just study hard. They say, "Practice makes perfect."

Nützliche Ausdrücke

Practice these expressions that students have learned in the *Dialog* and *Lesestück 1*.

Du Schlaukopf!	You genius!
Sei nicht so ungeduldig!	Don't be so impatient!
Verlier keine Worte!	Don't waste any words!
Es steht auf Seite…	It's on page…
Ich verstehe das nicht.	I don't understand that.
Lerne es auswendig!	Memorize it!
Lest es gründlich!	Read it carefully!
Ich lerne fleißig.	I'm studying hard.
Übung macht den Meister!	Practice makes perfect!
Er wohnt in einer Wohnung.	He is living in an apartment.
Er klingelt an der Tür.	He is ringing the doorbell.
Sie gehen lieber zu Fuß.	They prefer to walk.
Der Blick ist besonders schön.	The view is especially beautiful.
Ich spreche gern Deutsch.	I like to speak German.
Sie sitzt auf einer Bank.	She is sitting on a bench.
Sie besprechen ein Buch.	They discuss a book.
Sie üben Englisch.	They practice English.

Der Blick ist
sehr schön.
(Kaiserstuhl)

Ergänzung

repeat 1 x

You may want to use a calendar to practice further the words for the twelve months. You could ask questions such as: *Wie heißen die Monate im Sommer?*, *Wann (In welchem Monat) beginnt die Schule?*, etc.

1. Wie heißen die zwölf Monate?

Herbst*
September, Oktober, November

Sommer*
Juni, Juli, August

Winter*
Dezember, Januar, Februar

Frühling*
März, April, Mai

*All names of the months and seasons are "**der**" words.*

2. Was für Fächer haben die Schüler?
   Deutsch, Englisch, Mathematik (Mathe), Geschichte, Erdkunde, Chemie, Biologie, Physik, Musik, Kunst, Sport.
   Personalize your questions. (*Was für Fächer hast du?*, *Wie oft hast du Deutsch — Englisch, Geschichte... — ?*, etc.)

Stundenplan

Klasse: **8 b**   Zimmer: _____   Klassenleiter: *Schröder*

Zeit	Montag	Dienstag	Mittwoch	Donnerstag	Freitag	Sonnabend
8⁰⁰–8⁴⁵	Mathe	Chemie	Deutsch	Erdkunde	Geschichte	Deutsch
8⁵⁰–9³⁵	Deutsch	Biologie	Deutsch	Musik	Geschichte	Mathe
9³⁵–9⁵⁰	Große	Pause				Schwimmen
9⁵⁰–10³⁵	Englisch	Sport	Englisch	Kunst	Latein	Schwimmen
10⁴⁰–11²⁵	Latein	frei	Biologie	Englisch	Latein	
11²⁵–11⁴⁰	Große	Pause				
11⁴⁰–12²⁵	Latein	Mathe	Französisch	Französisch	Deutsch	
12³⁰–13¹⁵		Französisch	Physik	Chemie	Französisch	

Explain the difference in the grading system (A, B, C, D, F vs. 1, 2, 3, 4, 5, 6). Both grades 5 and 6 are failing grades.

3. Was für Noten bekommen die Schüler?

4. Wie alt bist du? Ich bin sechzehn (Jahre alt).

Practice the /x/ and /ch/ sounds until students can imitate them very closely. Use the sound description to further illustrate the formation of these sounds.

Ausspracheübung

[x] *ch* — **sound (*doch*):** The lips are open. The jaw angle due to the preceding vowel is relatively large.

[ç] *ch* — **sound (*ich*):** The lips are slightly open and the jaw angle is small. With the apex against the lower

/ x /	/ ch /
doch	ich
noch	nicht
Buch	recht
auch	gleich
acht	Mädchen
machen	sprechen
Woche	pünktlich
nach	gründlich
brauche	dreißig
einfach	sechzig

The apex is usually against the lower teeth. The dorsum arches steeply upward and backward toward the velum and forms a constriction at the velum. The friction of the air stream passing through this constriction produces the characteristic friction noise.

teeth, the rest of the tongue arches forward and up toward the palate.

60

Übungen

The Indefinite Article (Nominative and Accusative Singular)

	Singular		
	masculine	*feminine*	*neuter*
nominative	ein	eine	ein
accusative	einen	eine	ein

The articles in the *ein*-group are called indefinite because they do not specifically identify the noun with which they are associated. All articles you have learned so far, i.e., *der, die, das,* are "*der*-words" (definite articles). In English the indefinite article is either *a* or *an*.

Examples: *ein Buch* (a book)

NOTE: You will see from the above that only the accusative of the masculine article differs from the nominative (*ein, einen*). This is also true of the definite article.

Folgt den Beispielen!

1. Der Student wohnt hier.   Ein Student wohnt hier.
    das Mädchen   Ein Mädchen wohnt hier.
    der Herr   Ein Herr wohnt hier.
    die Freundin   Eine Freundin wohnt hier.
    der Schüler   Ein Schüler wohnt hier.
    die Frau   Eine Frau wohnt hier.

students have some
ifficulties with
'bungen 2-3, you may want
review the articles for the
ouns listed. You could also
nange the questions into
1swers. *Wo ist der Bahnhof?*
a drüben., *Wo ist das*
lefon? Ich weiß das nicht.,
c.

2. Wo ist der Bahnhof?   Wo ist ein Bahnhof?
    Telefon   Wo ist ein Telefon?
    Straßenbahn   Wo ist eine Straßenbahn?
    Schule   Wo ist eine Schule?
    Fahrplan   Wo ist ein Fahrplan?
    Buch   Wo ist ein Buch?

3. Brauchen Sie einen Fahrplan? **Brauchen Sie einen Fahrplan?**
    Telefon   **Brauchen Sie ein Telefon?**
    Fahrkarte   Brauchen Sie eine Fahrkarte?
    Computer   Brauchen Sie einen Computer?
    Uhr   Brauchen Sie eine Uhr?
    Koffer   Brauchen Sie einen Koffer?
    Tasche   Brauchen Sie eine Tasche?

4. Lernst du die Formel?   Lernst du eine Formel?
    Findet Katrin die Eisdiele? Findet Katrin eine Eisdiele?
    Die Mädchen lesen das Buch. Die Mädchen lesen ein Buch.

Ich verstehe die Aufgabe.

Wir gebrauchen das Wort.

Fragen Sie den Beamten?

Kauft Jürgen die Fahrkarte?

Ich verstehe eine Aufgabe.

Wir gebrauchen ein Wort.

Fragen Sie einen Beamten?

Kauft Jürgen eine Fahrkarte?

5. Ich lerne das Wort auswendig.

Formel

Aufgabe

Übung

Buch

Beschreibung

Ich lerne ein Wort auswendig.

Ich lerne eine Formel auswendig.

Ich lerne eine Aufgabe auswendig.

Ich lerne eine Übung auswendig.

Ich lerne ein Buch auswendig.

Ich lerne eine Beschreibung auswendig.

Variation: Ask questions. (*Was lernst du auswendig?* — *Wort. Ich lerne das/ein Wort auswendig.*)

6. Complete the following sentences.

1. Er sucht (a schedule) _____.
2. Fragen Sie doch (an official) _____!
3. Kaufst du (a cassette) _____?
4. Löst ihr (a problem) _____?
5. Dirk und Stefan gebrauchen (a formula) _____.
6. Wir sehen (a train) _____.
7. Die Mädchen lesen (a book) _____.
8. Wann schreibst du (a test) _____?
9. Ich verstehe (an exercise) _____.
10. Brauchen Sie (a suitcase) _____?

7. Form complete sentences using the indefinite article.

Beispiel: *ich / haben / Buch*
Ich habe ein Buch.

1. wir / tragen / Tasche
2. wer / kaufen / Computer
3. Haltestelle / sein / um die Ecke
4. wo / stehen / Straßenbahn
5. verstehen / Sie / Wort
6. Katrin / Heike / kaufen / Cola
7. haben / du / Platz
8. Jörg / bekommen / Uhr
9. Frau Werner / brauchen / Telefon
10. suchen / ihr / Schule

Plural Forms of Nouns and Definite Article (Nominative and Accusative)

For singular nouns you must know the gender, that is to say, you must know whether the noun is a *der, die,* or *das*-word. In the plural, however, all nouns, regardless of their gender, are *die* in the nominative and the accusative.

As you can see from the list below, most nouns undergo certain changes from the singular to the plural. There is no definite rule for the formation of plural nouns. You must learn each plural form when you learn a new noun. For simplification, all important nouns that you have learned up to this lesson, have been placed into groups whenever the change from the singular to the plural follows certain patterns.

	Singular			Plural
	masculine	*feminine*	*neuter*	
nominative	der	die	das	die
accusative	den	die	das	die

Students should learn the plural forms of all the nouns that they have learned so far.

Plural of Nouns

no change

der Computer	die Computer
der Einwohner	die Einwohner
das Fräulein	die Fräulein
der Kilometer	die Kilometer
der Koffer	die Koffer
das Mädchen	die Mädchen
der Schalter	die Schalter
der Schüler	die Schüler

add *-n*, *-en* or *-nen*

die Aufgabe	die Aufgaben
die Eisdiele	die Eisdielen
die Fahrkarte	die Fahrkarten
die Fläche	die Flächen
die Formel	die Formeln
die Fremdsprache	die Fremdsprachen
die Haltestelle	die Haltestellen
die Idee	die Ideen
der Junge	die Jungen
die Kassette	die Kassetten
die Klasse	die Klassen
die Minute	die Minuten
der Name	die Namen
die Note	die Noten
die Reise	die Reisen
die Schule	die Schulen
die Seite	die Seiten
die Sekunde	die Sekunden
die Straße	die Straßen
die Tasche	die Taschen
die Vokabel	die Vokabeln
die Arbeit	die Arbeiten
der Automat	die Automaten

die Bedeutung	die Bedeutungen
die Beschreibung	die Beschreibungen
die Entfernung	die Entfernungen
der Herr	die Herren
die S-Bahn	die S-Bahnen
der Staat	die Staaten
die Straßenbahn	die Straßenbahnen
der Student	die Studenten
die Tür	die Türen
die Übung	die Übungen
die Uhr	die Uhren
die Universität	die Universitäten
die Wohnung	die Wohnungen
die Freundin	die Freundinnen

add -e or ̈e	
der Bus	die Busse
der Freund	die Freunde
das Gleis	die Gleise
das Jahr	die Jahre
der Kiosk	die Kioske
das Regal	die Regale
der Tag	die Tage
das Telefon	die Telefone
der Vorort	die Vororte
der Weg	die Wege
der Ausdruck	die Ausdrücke
die Bank	die Bänke
der Fahrplan	die Fahrpläne
der Fuß	die Füße
der Platz	die Plätze
der Schlaukopf	die Schlauköpfe
die Stadt	die Städte
der Vorschlag	die Vorschläge

add ̈er	
das Buch	die Bücher
das Fach	die Fächer
das Haus	die Häuser
das Land	die Länder
das Wort	die Wörter*

add -s	
das Büro	die Büros
die Cola	die Colas
der Kuli	die Kulis
das Sprachlabor	die Sprachlabors

*The word "das Wort" has two different plural forms depending on the meaning. Das Wort (die Wörter) means "the word" (several words in a sentence) but das Wort (die Worte) means "the word" (saying or quotation). The first form (das Wort/die Wörter) is used more frequently and will be stressed throughout this book.

Folgt den Beispielen!

8. Die Aufgabe steht da.   **Die Aufgaben stehen da.**

Variation: Ask a question. (Was steht da? — Aufgaben. Die Aufgaben. Die Aufgaben stehen da.)

der Zug	Die Züge stehen da.
die Beschreibung	Die Beschreibungen stehen da.
der Automat	Die Automaten stehen da.
das Mädchen	Die Mädchen stehen da.
die S-Bahn	Die S-Bahnen stehen da.

9. Versteht ihr das Buch?   **Versteht ihr die Bücher?**

Variation: Ask the question. (Versteht ihr das Buch? Ja, wir verstehen das Buch. or Nein, wir verstehen das Buch nicht.)

die Vokabel	Versteht ihr die Vokabeln?
der Schüler	Versteht ihr die Schüler?
der Beamte	Versteht ihr die Beamten?
die Frau	Versteht ihr die Frauen?
die Formel	Versteht ihr die Formeln?
der Vorschlag	Versteht ihr die Vorschläge?

10. Sie suchen die Kassette.   **Sie suchen die Kassetten.**

Variation: Change sentences to questions/answers.

der Ausdruck	Sie suchen die Ausdrücke.
das Wörterbuch	Sie suchen die Wörterbücher.
das Büro	Sie suchen die Büros.
die Schule	Sie suchen die Schulen.
der Bahnhof	Sie suchen die Bahnhöfe.
die Aufgabe	Sie suchen die Aufgaben.
das Regal	Sie suchen die Regale.

11. **Change the following sentences from the singular to the plural.**

     Beispiel: *Ich trage die Tasche.*
                    Wir tragen die Taschen.

1. Der Junge versteht die Aufgabe.
2. Der Vorschlag ist nicht praktisch.
3. Wo liegt die Stadt?
4. Fragst du den Beamten?
5. Findet das Mädchen das Haus?
6. Ich schreibe die Übung.
7. Der Schüler lernt das Wort.
8. Wie heißt der Monat?

12. **Provide the plural form as indicated.**

1. ein Tag: zwei _____
2. ein Telefon: drei _____

3. eine Freundin: beide _____

4. eine Uhr: viele _____

5. ein Koffer: ein paar _____

6. ein Platz: zehn _____

7. ein Nachbarland: fünf _____

8. eine Straßenbahn: nicht viele _____

9. ein Herr: ein paar _____

10. ein Fahrplan: so viele _____

Negation

The word *kein* means "no" and negates nouns.

Examples: *Ich habe kein Geld.* (I have no money.)
Sie hat keine Fahrkarte. (She has no ticket.)

The endings of *kein* are identical to those of the *ein*-words.

Examples: *Er kauft ein Buch. Er kauft kein Buch.*
Ich suche einen Platz. Ich suche keinen Platz.

The word *nicht* means "not" and negates verbs, adjectives and adverbs.

Examples: *Ich komme nicht.* (I am not coming.)
Er schwimmt nicht gut. (He isn't swimming well.)

With a few exceptions, *nicht* appears after the subject, verb and object, whichever comes last in the sentence.

Examples: *Wir fragen nicht.* (We aren't asking.)
Wir fragen den Jungen nicht. (We aren't asking the boy.)

Folgt den Beispielen!

13. Gibt es da ein Sprachlabor?

    Gibt es da ein Büro?

    Gibt es da eine Uni?

    Gibt es da eine Eisdiele?

    Gibt es da einen Bahnhof?

    Gibt es da ein Haus?

Variation: Answer questions with "Ja,..." (Übungen 13-15)

Nein, da gibt es kein Sprachlabor.

Nein, da gibt es kein Büro

Nein, da gibt es keine Uni.

Nein, da gibt es keine Eisdiele.

Nein, da gibt es keinen Bahnhof

Nein, da gibt es kein Haus.

14. Sagst du ein Wort?

    Hast du eine Kassette?

    Brauchst du einen Vorschlag?

    Suchst du einen Beamten?

    Findest du eine Straße?

    Lernst du eine Aufgabe?

    Kaufst du einen Computer?

Nein, ich sage kein Wort.

Nein, ich habe keine Kassette.

Nein, ich brauche keinen Vorschlag.

Nein, ich suche keinen Beamten.

Nein, ich finde keine Straße.

Nein, ich lerne keine Aufgabe.

Nein, ich kaufe keinen Computer.

15. Verstehst du das?

    Ist die Schule weit von hier?

    Bist du sauer?

Nein, ich verstehe das nicht.

Nein, die Schule ist nicht weit von hier

Nein, ich bin nicht sauer.

Geht Andreas nach Hause?	Nein, Andreas geht nicht nach Hause.
Suchst du es?	Nein, ich suche es nicht.
Wohnt Kerstin in Hamburg?	Nein, Kerstin wohnt nicht in Hamburg.
Kommt er pünktlich?	Nein, er kommt nicht pünktlich.
Steht der Zug da drüben?	Nein, der Zug steht nicht da drüben.

16.

Variation: Ask questions.
(*Kommt Sabine aus
Deutschland? Ja,…/Nein,…*)

Sabine kommt aus Deutschland.	Sabine kommt nicht aus Deutschland.
Frau Müller geht in die Stadt.	Frau Müller geht nicht in die Stadt.
Wir sprechen schnell.	Wir sprechen nicht schnell.
Findet Jürgen die Kassette?	Findet Jürgen die Kassette nicht?
Übt Ursula viel?	Übt Ursula nicht viel?
Der Beamte weiß es.	Der Beamte weiß es nicht.
Bist du zu Hause?	Bist du nicht zu Hause?

17. Restate these sentences in the negative.

> **Beispiele:** *Der Schüler fragt. Der Schüler fragt nicht.*
> *Brauchst du einen Koffer? Brauchst du keinen Koffer?*

Variation: Change questions
to statements and statements
to questions.

1. Haben Sie einen Computer?
2. Wir kaufen eine Cola.
3. Sie sprechen schnell.
4. Kommt ihr aus der Schule?
5. Heute abend gehen sie in die Stadt.
6. Warum schreibt er eine Arbeit?
7. Hast du Geld?
8. Der Student geht nach Hause.
9. Bekommen Sie eine Karte?
10. Oliver weiß das.

18. Answer the following questions in the negative.

Have students answer
questions in the positive.

1. Gehst du pünktlich in die Schule?
2. Bist du sauer?
3. Lernst du die Beschreibung auswendig?
4. Weißt du die Bedeutung?
5. Glaubst du das?
6. Hast du viel Zeit?
7. Kommt die S-Bahn in fünf Minuten?

The Command Form

Familiar Command

To form commands in English, the speaker simply takes the infinitive without "to," e.g., "go," "run" or "write." In German, the familiar command form in the singular is constructed by eliminating the "*en*" from the infinitive, i.e., by maintaining the stem.

Examples: *Geh! geh(en)* Go!   Point out to your students that commands in German require an
exclamation mark.
Schreib! schreib(en) Write!
Frag! frag(en) Ask!

NOTE: Frequently an "e" is added to the stem so that it would also be correct to say "*Schreibe!*, *Gehe!*, *Frage!*" However, an "e" *must* be added if the stem ends in *-d*, *-t* and *-ig*.

Examples: *Warte!* Wait!

When you address more than one person, the familiar (plural) form is as follows:

   Geht! Schreibt! Fragt!

It is helpful to remember that the familiar plural command is the same as the second person plural without *"ihr."*

NOTE: The ending "et" instead of just "t" is added to a verb stem that ends with *-d* or *-t*. *Wartet hier! Findet das!*

Formal Command

The singular and the plural formal command are formed by inverting subject and verb.

   Gehen Sie! Schreiben Sie! Fragen Sie!

You will notice right away that this formation is identical to the construction of a question. There is, however, a distinct difference in the intonation of a question and a formal command.

Command Forms of *haben* and *sein*

The following are the command forms for *haben* and *sein*:

Hab keine Angst!	*Sei pünktlich!*
Habt keine Angst!	*Seid pünktlich!*
Haben Sie keine Angst!	*Seien Sie pünktlich!*

The *wir*-Command Form *(Let's…)*

The *wir*-command form is used when asking for some action in the sense of *Let's* (do something)…!

Examples: *Gehen wir!* Let's go!
                 Fragen wir den Beamten! Let's ask the official!

Folgt den Beispielen!

19. Du bleibst nicht lange.   Bleib nicht lange!
      Du kaufst die Fahrkarte.   Kauf die Fahrkarte!
      Du sagst das Wort.   Sag das Wort!
      Du lernst fleißig.   Lern fleißig!
      Du kommst bald.   Komm bald!
      Du gehst in die Stadt.   Geh in die Stadt!
      Du wartest dort.   Warte dort!

20. Sie sprechen Deutsch.   Sprechen Sie Deutsch!
      Sie fragen den Herrn.   Fragen Sie den Herrn!
      Sie suchen die Straße.   Suchen Sie die Straße!
      Sie lösen die Aufgabe.   Lösen Sie die Aufgabe!
      Sie lesen das Buch.   Lesen Sie das Buch!
      Sie gebrauchen die Formel.   Gebrauchen Sie die Formel!
      Sie fahren zur Uni.   Fahren Sie zur Uni!

21.	Ihr habt keine Angst.	**Habt keine Angst!**
	Ihr schreibt die Arbeit.	Schreibt die Arbeit!
	Ihr hört die Beschreibung.	Hört die Beschreibung!
	Ihr glaubt das nicht.	Glaubt das nicht!
	Ihr lernt es auswendig.	Lernt es auswendig!
	Ihr besprecht die Übung.	Besprecht die Übung!
	Ihr seht den Computer.	Seht den Computer!

22.	Schreibst du das Wort?	**Schreib das Wort!**
	Warten Sie dort?	Warten Sie dort!
	Lernt ihr die Aufgabe?	Lernt die Aufgabe!
	Suchen Sie die Kassette?	Suchen Sie die Kassette!
	Gehst du zu Fuß?	Geh zu Fuß!
	Kommt ihr bald nach Hause?	Kommt bald nach Hause!
	Hast du keine Angst?	Hab keine Angst!

23.	Ihr seid pünktlich.	**Seid pünktlich!**
	Du bist froh.	Sei froh!
	Sie sind fleißig.	Seien Sie fleißig!
	Ihr seid schnell da.	Seid schnell da!
	Du bist nicht ungeduldig!	Sei nicht ungeduldig!
	Sie sind um drei Uhr hier.	Seien Sie um drei Uhr hier!

Practice additional command forms by asking students to give instructions. These can be phrases you have used in the class. (*Geh an die Tafel!*, *Schreib das Wort…an die Tafel!*, *Mach dein Buch auf!*, etc.)

24. Convert these sentences into commands.

> **Beispiel:** *Du sitzt hier.*
> *Sitz hier!*

1. Du lernst den Ausdruck auswendig.
2. Sie schreiben nicht.
3. Ihr fragt den Studenten.
4. Sie gehen zu Fuß.
5. Ihr kommt pünktlich.
6. Du bist nicht so langweilig.
7. Sie haben keine Angst.
8. Du kaufst die Bücher.

Wo, wohin and *woher*

Wo (where) is a question word asking about a location, whereas *wohin* (where to) and *woher* (where from) are question words asking about direction.

Examples: *Wo wohnst du?* Where are you living?
Wohin gehst du? Where are you going (to)?
Woher kommst du? Where are you coming from?

Folgt dem Beispiel!

25. Klaus geht *in die Stadt.*

Heike wohnt *in München.*

Die Jungen kommen *aus der Schule.*

Die Haltestelle ist *da drüben.*

Die Studenten fahren *nach Deutschland.*

Das Mädchen kommt *aus Hamburg.*

Wohin geht Klaus?

Wo wohnt Heike?

Woher kommen die Jungen?

Wo ist die Haltestelle?

Wohin fahren die Studenten?

Woher kommt das Mädchen?

Ask additional questions.
(*Klaus geht in die Stadt. —*
Wer geht in die Stadt?, Was
macht Klaus?)

26. *Wo? Wohin?* **Use one of the two question words to form questions.**

1. Herr und Frau Meister fahren *nach Dortmund.*
2. Jürgen wohnt *in Würzburg.*
3. Monika bleibt heute *zu Hause.*
4. Die Studenten gehen *zur Uni.*
5. Die Straßenbahn steht *an der Haltestelle.*
6. Mein Freund geht *nach Hause.*

gern

The word *gern* used with a verb indicates liking something or someone.

Examples: *Ich lese gern.* I like to read.
Gehst du gern zu Fuß? Do you like to walk?
Hat er das Mädchen gern? Does he like the girl?

Folgt dem Beispiel!

27. Was machst du gern?

Bücher lesen

in die Stadt fahren

die Aufgaben lösen

die Kassette hören

den Beamten fragen

den Vorschlag machen

Deutsch sprechen

Ich lese gern Bücher.

Ich fahre gern in die Stadt.

Ich löse gern die Aufgaben.

Ich höre gern die Kassette.

Ich frage gern den Beamten.

Ich mache gern den Vorschlag.

Ich spreche gern Deutsch.

28. **Answer these questions by using *gern* in your answers.**

1. Was machst du gern?
2. Wohin gehst du gern?

3. Was schreibst du gern?
4. Wen fragst du gern?
5. Wer lernt die Aufgaben gern?
6. Wo sitzt sie gern?

Have students ask each other additional questions using *gern*.

Omission of Article

The article is omitted whenever there is a reference to an occupation or a nationality.

Examples: *Jürgen ist Student.*
Herr Schulz ist Beamter.
Herr und Frau Lehmann sind Amerikaner.

Lesestück 1

Auf dem Weg zur Uni

on F.S.

Jürgen ist Student an der Universität Würzburg. Er wohnt in einer Wohnung° in der Nähe von der Universität. Auf dem Weg zur Uni wohnt auch Ursula, seine Freundin. Jürgen geht oft zu Ursula, klingelt an der Tür und wartet, bis sie aus dem Haus kommt. Das dauert auch nicht lange. Ursula begrüßt Jürgen. Dann gehen beide zu Fuß weiter.

apartment

Jürgen und Ursula sind Studenten.

Sie sprechen gern Englisch.

Jürgen und Ursula gehen nicht gern auf der Straße°. Dort ist immer zu viel Verkehr°. Sie gehen lieber auf einem Feldweg° zur Uni. Dort ist es sehr ruhig°, und auch der Blick auf die Stadt Würzburg ist besonders schön. Natürlich° sprechen Jürgen and Ursula oft über ihr Studium. Beide studieren Fremdsprachen°. Sie sprechen besonders gern Englisch. Jürgen hat Lust im nächsten Jahr nach England zu fahren. Ursula hat auch Lust, aber eine Reise° nach England kostet sehr viel, und sie hat dafür° zu wenig Geld.

An der Haltestelle sehen sie auf den Fahrplan. Da steht, um wieviel Uhr der Bus kommt. Nach der Uni fahren sie vielleicht° in die Stadt. Heute haben sie viel Zeit. Manchmal° sitzen sie auf einer Bank und besprechen ein Buch auf Englisch. Ursula kennt viele Vokabeln. Sie lernt die neuen Wörter° immer auswendig. Englisch ist für Jürgen manchmal etwas schwer. Es gibt immer so viele neue Wörter. Ursula hat ein Wörterbuch°. Jürgen findet dort schnell die Bedeutung° für die Wörter und Ausdrücke.

street
traffic/field path
quiet
of course
foreign languages

trip
for that

perhaps
sometimes

new words

dictionary
meaning

Um wieviel Uhr kommt der Bus?

Jürgen sucht eine Kassette.

Was machen sie im Sprachlabor?

Um halb zwei gehen Jürgen und Ursula zum Sprachlabor°. *language lab*
Ursula bekommt eine Kassette in einem Büro°. Jürgen sucht° eine *office/looks for*
andere Kassette auf einem Regal°. Er findet sie auch gleich. Dann *shelf*
gehen sie ins Sprachlabor und üben Englisch — hören°, sprechen *listening*
und verstehen°. *understanding*

Fragen über das Lesestück

1. Wo ist Jürgen Student?
2. Wohnt er weit von der Uni?
3. Fahren Jürgen und Ursula zur Uni?
4. Warum gehen Jürgen und Ursula nicht gern auf der Straße?
5. Was studieren beide?
6. Was kostet viel?
7. Warum sehen beide auf den Fahrplan?
8. Warum fahren Jürgen und Ursula vielleicht später in die Stadt?
9. Was tun sie manchmal?
10. Was ist für Jürgen etwas schwer?
11. Was bekommt Ursula in einem Büro?
12. Wohin gehen sie dann? Was machen sie dort?

Erweiterung

29. Match each word from the list with the most appropriate word on the left.

1. Koffer - _____
2. Buch - _____
3. Gymnasium - _____
4. Englisch - _____
5. Bremen - _____
6. Gleis - _____
7. Mark - _____
8. Monat - _____
9. DDR - _____
10. Tag - _____
11. Herbst - _____
12. Zeit - _____

Land   Bahnhof
Stadt   Geld
Schule   Seite
Jahreszeit   Uhr
Oktober   Gepäck
Fach   Mittwoch

30. Wie heißt das auf deutsch?

1. Memorize the description!
2. The exercise is on page 36.
3. I don't understand the suggestion.

4. They like to speak English.
5. Are you discussing the book, Elke and Sabine?
6. They prefer to read.
7. Are you always so impatient, Peter?
8. I'm 18 years old.

31. **Complete each word by adding another noun of one or more syllables.**

   Beispiel: *Physik* _____
   Physikaufgabe

   1. Halte_____
   2. Eis_____
   3. Nachbar_____
   4. Feld_____
   5. Straßen_____
   6. Bundes_____

   7. Schlau_____
   8. Fahr_____
   9. Haupt_____
   10. Jahres_____
   11. Fremd_____
   12. Sprach_____

32. **Beantwortet die Fragen!** Encourage different responses.

   Wie alt bist du?

   Was verstehst du nicht?

   Was brauchst du?

   Wohin gehst du?

   Was machst du besonders gern?

   Was kostet viel?

   Was für Fächer hast du?

   Was machst du heute nachmittag?

   Verstehst du die Lektion?

Rückblick

If students have difficulties with any of these exercises, you may want to go back to the particular lesson in which the grammar point was discussed and pick out some pertinent exercises.

I. Provide the proper verb form.

   1. (kaufen) _____ ihr die Kassetten?
   2. (lesen) Die Studenten _____ die Bücher.
   3. (wissen) Das _____ ich nicht.
   4. (fragen) _____ doch die Frau, Andreas!
   5. (sein) _____ Sie verärgert, Herr Lehmann?
   6. (üben) Wir _____ die Wörter.
   7. (haben) _____ keine Angst, Susanne und Monika!
   8. (lernen) Die Schüler _____ es auswendig.
   9. (brauchen) Ich _____ kein Geld.
   10. (suchen) Was _____ du denn, Sabine?
   11. (finden) Jürgen _____ Englisch etwas schwer.
   12. (verstehen) _____ ihr die Beschreibung?

II. Form questions from these statements.

1. Ursula geht nicht zur Uni.
2. Die Eisdiele ist gleich um die Ecke.
3. Die Schule beginnt um acht Uhr.
4. Peter hat eine Freundin.
5. Die Studenten fahren nach Deutschland.
6. Ihr versteht die Vokabeln.
7. Er weiß die Bedeutung.
8. Hamburg liegt im Norden.
9. Hessen grenzt an die DDR.
10. Wir bekommen etwas Geld.

III. Form questions by asking for the italicized words. Use these question words: *was, wer, wen, wo, woher, wohin.*

1. Die Eisdiele ist *in der Nähe*.
2. *Herr Meister* wartet auf dem Bahnhof.
3. Beide fahren *nach Hause*.
4. Um ein Uhr kommen sie *aus der Schule*.
5. Wir fragen *einen Beamten*.
6. Die Schüler lernen *die Bedeutung*.
7. Ich kenne *Katrin* nicht.
8. Die Mädchen haben *fünfzig Mark*.
9. Die S-Bahn steht *dort drüben*.
10. Die Studenten gehen *zur Uni*.

IV. Complete the following sentences.

1. Wir gehen gern _____.
2. Sie hat zu wenig _____.
3. Die Schüler besprechen _____.
4. Eine Reise nach Deutschland _____.
5. Ich habe Lust, aber _____.
6. Heute nachmittag fahren sie _____.
7. Er wohnt _____.
8. Ich kaufe _____.

V. Complete these sentences by using either *viel* or *viele*.

1. München hat _____ Einwohner.
2. Ich habe nicht _____ Geld.
3. Wie _____ Kassetten braucht ihr?
4. Lernt ihr _____ Wörter auswendig?
5. Haben Sie _____ Zeit?
6. Wir haben _____ zu tun.
7. In Nordrhein-Westfalen gibt es _____ Städte.
8. _____ Studenten gehen zur Universität in Würzburg.

Lesestück 2

To illustrate the various geographical features discussed, you may want to point them out on a map. After students are thoroughly familiar with *Lesestück 2*, have them ask each other questions.

Die BRD — Länder und Hauptstädte

Die Nationalfahne° der BRD ist schwarz-rot-gold°. Bonn, die Hauptstadt, liegt am Rhein im Westen der BRD. Die Bundesrepublik besteht aus° zehn Ländern.*

national flag/ black-red-gold

consists of

Im Norden liegt *Schleswig-Holstein*. Dieses Land grenzt an° Dänemark und die DDR. Kiel ist die Hauptstadt von Schleswig-Holstein. Das Land und die Stadt *Hamburg* liegen auch im Norden. Hamburg ist die größte° Stadt in der Bundesrepublik. Das kleinste° Land ist *Bremen*. Es liegt nur ungefähr 90 Kilometer von Hamburg entfernt°. *Niedersachsen*, ein anderes° Land im Norden der BRD, grenzt im Westen an die Niederlande und im Osten an die DDR. Die Hauptstadt von Niedersachsen heißt Hannover.

borders on

largest/smallest

away/another

* *Berlin (West) is also considered a **Land** but does not have the same voting power in the congressional houses in Bonn as the ten **Länder** located in the Federal Republic.*

München ist die Hauptstadt von Bayern.

Mainz ist die Hauptstadt von Rheinland-Pfalz.

Düsseldorf liegt in
Nordrhein-Westfalen.

Hannover liegt
im Norden der BRD.

Die meisten Einwohner hat das Land *Nordrhein-Westfalen*.
Dieses Land grenzt an die Niederlande und Belgien. Düsseldorf ist
die Hauptstadt von Nordrhein-Westfalen. In der Mitte° der Bun-   *middle*
desrepublik liegt *Hessen*. Hessen grenzt an die DDR. Die Hauptstadt heißt Wiesbaden. Ein anderes Land ist *Rheinland-Pfalz*. Es
grenzt an Belgien, Luxemburg und Frankreich. Die Hauptstadt von
Rheinland-Pfalz ist Mainz. Genauso wie° Bonn liegt auch diese   *just like*
Stadt am Rhein. Das *Saarland* grenzt an Luxemburg und
Frankreich. Saarbrücken ist die Hauptstadt vom Saarland.**

Das Land *Baden-Württemberg* liegt im Südwesten der Bundesrepublik und grenzt an Frankreich und die Schweiz. Die Hauptstadt von Baden-Württemberg ist Stuttgart. Das größte Land in der
Bundesrepublik ist *Bayern*. Bayern liegt im Süden und grenzt an die
Schweiz, Österreich, die Tschechoslowakei und die DDR. München ist die Hauptstadt von Bayern.

Es gibt eigentlich noch ein anderes Land — *West-Berlin*. West-
Berlin liegt in der DDR und hat einen besonderen° Status.   *special*

The definite article is used before the name **Saarland (das Saarland), **Schweiz** (die Schweiz) and **Tschechoslowakei** (die
Tschechoslowakei).

Fragen über das Lesestück

1. Wie viele Länder gibt es in der Bundesrepublik?
2. Wie heißt die Hauptstadt von Schleswig-Holstein?
3. Wie heißt die größte Stadt in der BRD?
4. Wo liegt Bremen?
5. Welches Land hat die meisten Einwohner?
6. Welches Land liegt in der Mitte der BRD?
7. An welche Länder grenzt Rheinland-Pfalz?
8. Wo liegt Baden-Württemberg?
9. Wie heißt das größte Land?
10. Wo liegt West-Berlin?

Sprachspiegel

I. Pretend you are a teacher talking to your students. Use the command form where appropriate. *Wie heißt das auf deutsch?*

1. Write the descriptions.
2. Memorize the formulas.
3. Where are the books? The problem is on page 56.
4. Read page 56.
5. Don't be so impatient.
6. I don't understand what you are saying.
7. The expression is quite simple.
8. Read it carefully.
9. Practice the words.
10. Go to the language lab.

This is a good review of command forms. You may want to add some other important expressions that your students heard you say.

II. *Auf dem Weg zur Schule.* **Describe (in narrative style) the following sequence, using the cues merely as a guideline.**

This exercise could be changed to a dialog as well.

You're walking to school…picking up your friend on the way…waiting several minutes before s/he comes out of the house…taking the streetcar at the stop nearby…talking about several items concerning school…getting off…checking the schedule at the stop…indicating a desire to go to the ice cream parlor after school…showing your dictionary to your friend…finding a word/vocabulary item…hurrying to school because the first class begins soon.

Wie sagt man's?

Have students read these mini-dialogs with meaning. They can act them out and change some to be more creative.

Woher kommst du?
Aus Bremen.
Wohnst du schon lange hier?
Seit März.

Wie alt bist du?
Siebzehn. Und du?
Schon neunzehn.

Verstehen Sie Deutsch?
Ein wenig.
Prima. Sprechen wir etwas!

Wie lange bleibst du noch?
Bis fünf Uhr.
Gut, ich brauche deine Hilfe.

Was lernst du denn so fleißig?
Die Deutschaufgaben.
Sind sie schwer?
Nein, ganz einfach.

Warum bist du denn so ungeduldig?
Die Kassette ist so lang.
Übe den Dialog doch später!
Ja, du hast recht.

Bist du sauer?
Ich brauche eine Tasche.
Hier ist meine.
Habe ich aber Glück!

Was suchst du denn?
Das Sprachlabor.
Es ist gleich um die Ecke.
Danke.

Zungenbrecher

Brauchbare Bierbrauerburschen brauen brausendes Braunbier.
(Useful beer brewery fellows are brewing foaming brown beer.)

Have students say the tongue twister as fast as possible without stumbling.

Kulturecke 1

School Life in the *BRD*

School life in the Federal Republic of Germany is considerably different from our own. There is practically no social life at a German school. Although schools offer physical education classes — and many have modern facilities — students wishing to participate in various sports activities usually join local sports clubs.

In the first four grades, ages 6 to 10, all children must attend the elementary school (*Grundschule*). These younger children usually carry briefcases or satchels strapped to their backs. During their years in the *Grundschule*, children are accustomed already to a sizeable stack of homework.

At the age of 10, or after fourth grade, most children and their parents face the difficult decision of which of three different schools to attend. Most students go to the *Hauptschule* where they receive a basic education for the next five years. The second choice is the *Realschule*. Here the students will remain for the next six years and receive training for higher level but non-academic occupations of all kinds. Finally, study at the *Gymnasium*, grades 5 to 13, leads to the *Abitur*, the final certificate that is a prerequisite for attending a university. Students going to the *Gymnasium* have a very concentrated curriculum. It is not uncommon for these students to take as many as ten or more different subjects a week. A typical schedule readily shows the emphasis on academic subjects.

In recent years, the *Gesamtschule* has become the answer for many children whose parents and teachers cannot make the proper choice of which school to attend after fourth grade. The *Gesamtschule* is an orientation for the two years following the *Grundschule*. It gives students an opportunity to switch, based on their ability, to any of the other three schools after the sixth grade.

Many students carry briefcases.

Was für ein Fach haben diese Schüler?

Students use bulletin boards to make announcements.

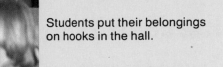
Students put their belongings
on hooks in the hall.

Sports activities are
not part of school life.

A special problem has been created by the numerous children of foreign workers (*Gast-arbeiter*) living in Germany. These children have to become immersed in the German language and culture at a rapid pace. Many schools offer special classes for these children before they can be integrated into the German educational system.

How do students get to school? In recent years, school buses have become a more and more popular way to get to school, although many students walk to school. Others take public transportation or ride their bikes. Some of the older students ride their mopeds, which are usually parked in a specially designated area in the parking lot. There are also a few cars in the parking lot that students over 18 years of age have been allowed to drive.

Most school buildings were built during the past twenty years. There are differences from American schools. Upon entering a *Gymnasium* in the area of Köln, for example, it becomes immediately apparent that students do not have any lockers. This is true in most German schools. Students put their belongings, such as coats and motorcycle helmets, on hooks in the hall. In the main hallway are bulletin boards that are used by the students and administrators to make various announcements. This school, as in most other German schools, offers no warm meals. Students can bring their own bag lunches or purchase various snacks and cold beverages at a counter and from several automats. However, the lunch counter is open only during recess (*Große Pause*).

At the *Gymnasium,* students must prove themselves. Only 15% of all students receive their *Abitur.* Teachers do not have a classroom of their own. For most subjects, students stay with the same classmates in the same room. The earlier grades at the *Gymnasium* offer rather general subjects, while upper grades introduce such subjects as English literature and philosophy.

German students generally spend fewer hours at school than American students, staying only until noon or 1:00 to 2:00 P.M. However, many of them have school on Saturday as well. And, of course, after school, students must spend considerable time doing their homework.

Kulturecke 2

School Life in the *DDR*

Education in the German Democratic Republic starts with pre-school care, which is provided for children whose parents work. Parents can take their children from the age of five months to three years to day nurseries, called *Kinderkrippen*. The *Kindergarten* is responsible for the education of children between the ages of three and six. The attendance of children at both *Kinderkrippen* and *Kindergarten* is free of charge, except for a very nominal amount that is paid for meals.

The backbone of the educational system is the ten-year general polytechnical school, called *Oberschule*. It has been a tradition to welcome first-graders with *Schultüten*, huge cones filled with candies and cookies. These cones are displayed in many stores before the start of the school year.

Let's visit the *Johannes R. Becher Oberschule* in Leipzig, a typical school located in a newer community. Immediately at the entrance of the school is a picture of Johannes R. Becher with an inscription intended to inspire the students of this school. The main objective of the school is shown on a bulletin board nearby. The statistics of the best athletes in the school are displayed here. Along the hallway are many colorful displays that further demonstrate the importance of working together with people in the DDR and those of other countries.

Looking down the hallway, one immediately notices that there are no lockers for students. This is true for most schools in the German Democratic Republic. Students have specified areas outside the classrooms for hanging up their jackets or coats and leaving their briefcases or other items.

From the first grade on, youngsters receive a general education that will prepare them for their later life in the socialist society of the German Democratic Republic. In the third grade, students continue with their basic studies in reading, writing and mathematics, but they are also given some insight into the world of work and the community around them. Over two-thirds of all first through fourth graders stay after school at the *Schulhort*, which has been established so students can take part in sports, games or hobbies while their parents are at work.

At the sixth grade, the spectrum of subjects taught widens considerably. Students begin their second year of study of Russian, their first foreign language. Furthermore, sixth graders are required to expand their knowledge in natural and social sciences as well as mathematics. Before entering a seventh grade classroom, one immediately recognizes the emphasis placed on technology and the natural sciences by examining the colorfully decorated classroom door. In this classroom, seventh grade students are studying physics. After the teacher has introduced a specific topic, students work out problems in their textbooks. Next door is an eighth grade chemistry class attentively listening to the lesson presented. Students are encouraged to assist the teacher in the chemistry experiments.

A glance at a tenth grade schedule reveals the general character of instruction at that level. Besides Russian, another foreign language, English, has been added to the schedule. Advanced mathematics and science, as well as courses on civic and polytechnic instruction, have also been included. The latter course is an introduction to socialist production where students are asked to donate their time to working in factories or on farms.

It is quite common for tenth graders to be asked to clean the school building thoroughly during the last two or three weeks of their school year. While some clean the building, others take care of the shrubs and trees around the school or even paint benches in the school yard. At the end of tenth grade, students complete their required schooling with a final examination and receive the so-called *Abschlußzeugnis* (final grade report). Students may continue for another

First graders are welcomed
with *Schultüten*.

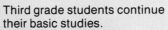
Third grade students continue
their basic studies.

Some tenth grade students
clean the building.

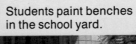
Students paint benches
in the school yard.

Most students can eat
a warm meal at school.

School meals cost 55 pfennigs.

two years (*Erweiterte Oberschule*) after which they will receive their *Abitur* and become eligible to attend the university.

Between 10:00 A.M. and 11:00 A.M. students usually have a recess (*Große Pause*) of about 15 to 20 minutes. During this time all students go to the school yard to play, talk to their friends or eat a snack. Over 70 percent of all students eat a warm meal at school. The school cafeteria serves warm meals between 11:30 A.M. to 1:00 P.M. for a cost of 55 pfennigs. Each class is assigned a specific block of time to eat. It is customary for the teacher to eat with the students.

Many youngsters belong to the Ernst Thälmann Pioneer organization (*Junge Pioniere*), recognized by their white blouses or shirts, and the Free German Youth (*Freie Deutsche Jugend* or *FDJ*), who wear blue blouses or shirts. The *Junge Pioniere* are 6 to 14 years of age; they can join the *FDJ* youth group at 14. These youth groups have a direct influence in school affairs through their elected committees. In particular, the older group, the *FDJ,* has strong communication ties with the parent-teacher association of the school.

Vokabeln

alt old
der **April** April
die **Aufgabe, -n** problem, exercise
der **August** August
der **Ausdruck,-̈e** expression
ausreichend sufficient
auswendig lernen to memorize,
   learn by heart
die **Bank,-̈e** bench
die **Bedeutung,-en** meaning, significance

befriedigend satisfactory
die **Beschreibung, -en** description
besonders especially
besprechen to discuss
die **Biologie** biology
der **Blick** view
das **Buch,-̈er** book
das **Büro,-s** office
der **Bus,-se** bus
die **Chemie** chemistry
dein your

das **Deutsch** German (language, subject in school)
der **Dezember** December
eben just
England England
das **Englisch** English (language, subject in school)
englisch English
die **Erdkunde** geography
das **Fach,-̈er** (school) subject
der **Februar** February
der **Feldweg,-e** field path
finden to find
fleißig hard-working, industrious
die **Formel,-n** formula
die **Fremdsprache,-n** foreign language
der **Frühling,-e** spring
gar nicht not at all
geben to give
    es gibt there is (are)
gebrauchen to use, apply
gern gladly, with pleasure
    gern gehen like (enjoy) to walk
die **Geschichte** history
gründlich thorough, careful
der **Herbst,-e** fall, autumn
die **Hilfe** help, assistance
hören to listen, hear
ihr their
im (or: **in dem**) in the
ins (or: **in das**) in(to) the
die **Jahreszeit,-en** season
der **Januar** January
der **Juli** July
der **Juni** June
die **Kassette,-n** cassette
klingeln to ring
    an der Tür klingeln to ring the doorbell
kosten to cost
die **Kunst** art
das **Land,-̈er** "state" in the **BRD**
lernen to learn
    auswendig lernen to memorize, learn by heart
lesen to read
lösen to solve
der **Mai** May
manchmal sometimes
mangelhaft inadequate
der **März** March
die **Mathematik** (or: **Mathe**) mathematics
die **Musik** music
nächst next
natürlich of course, natural(ly)
neu new
die **Note,-n** (school) grade, mark
der **November** November

der **Oktober** October
die **Physik** physics
die **Physikaufgabe,-n** physics problem
praktisch practical
das **Regal,-e** shelf
die **Reise,-n** trip
ruhig quiet, peaceful
sauer angry, annoyed
der **Schlaukopf,-̈e** genius, smartie
schön beautiful
der **Schüler,-** pupil, student (at elementary and secondary school)
die **Seite,-n** page
der **September** September
sitzen to sit
der **Sommer,-** summer
der **Sport** sport
das **Sprachlabor,-s** language lab
der **Status** status
stehen to stand, be located
die **Straße,-n** street
der **Student,-en** student (at university)
studieren to study (at university)
das **Studium,-dien** studies
suchen to look for, search
die **Tür,-en** door
üben to practice
die **Übung,-en** exercise, practice
    Übung macht den Meister! Practice makes perfect.
ungeduldig impatient
ungenügend unsatisfactory
die **Uni** the 'U' (abbreviation for **Universität**), university
die **Universität,-en** university
der **Verkehr** traffic
verlieren to lose
    Verlier keine Worte! Don't waste any words!
verstehen to understand
viele many
vielleicht perhaps
die **Vokabel,-n** (vocabulary) word
der **Vorschlag,-̈e** suggestion
was für what kind of
weiter further
    Sie gehen weiter. They keep going.
wenig little
der **Winter,-** winter
wirklich really
woher where from
wohin where to
die **Wohnung,-en** apartment
das **Wort,-e** word (saying, quotation)
    Verlier keine Worte! Don't waste any words!
das **Wort,-̈er** word
das **Wörterbuch,-̈er** dictionary

Dialog

Gehen wir ins Kino!

ANGELIKA: Grüß Gott!

DIANA: Grüß Gott, Angelika!

ANGELIKA: Möchtest du ins Kino gehen?

DIANA: Ja, das ist eine prima Idee.

ANGELIKA: Dieser Film soll ganz toll sein.

DIANA: Die Vorstellung beginnt schon um drei.

ANGELIKA: Ich rufe noch schnell Rainer und Gerd an. Vielleicht kommen sie mit.

DIANA: Wo bleiben die beiden denn?

ANGELIKA: Sie sind wie immer unpünktlich.

DIANA: Na, endlich seid ihr da. Wir warten schon lange.

RAINER: Das ist nicht unsere Schuld.

GERD: Warum ruft ihr uns so spät an?

RAINER: Jetzt bin ich aber gespannt. Welcher Film läuft denn hier?

...rican movies are quite ...lar in Germany.

ANGELIKA: *Conan der Barbar,* ein Film aus Amerika.

DIANA: Und er beginnt gleich. Los, kommt!

...t prices are different, ...nding on the location of ... Admission to movies is ...ed only between ...rmances.

ANGELIKA: Vier Karten zu acht Mark, bitte.

VERKÄUFERIN: Das macht 32 Mark.

ANGELIKA: Danke schön.

DIANA: Das Kino ist ja ganz leer.

PLATZANWEISER: Ihr könnt hier sitzen.

GERD: Der Film ist wirklich klasse.

DIANA: Du hast recht.

RAINER: Angelika will ihn sogar noch einmal sehen.

ANGELIKA: Ja! Vielleicht nächste Woche.

Fragen über den Dialog

1. Was ist eine prima Idee?
2. Wann beginnt der Film?
3. Wen ruft Angelika an?
4. Kommen Rainer und Gerd pünktlich?
5. Warum ist es nicht Rainers und Gerds Schuld?
6. Welcher Film läuft heute?
7. Wieviel kostet eine Karte?
8. Ist das Kino schon voll?
9. Was möchte Angelika nächste Woche tun?

Let's Go to the Movie Theater!

ANGELIKA: Hello!

DIANA: Hello, Angelika!

ANGELIKA: Would you like to go to a movie?

DIANA: That's a great idea.

ANGELIKA: This movie is supposed to be fantastic.

DIANA: The show will be starting already at three.

ANGELIKA: I'll call up Rainer and Gerd right now. Perhaps they'll come along.

DIANA: Where are those two?

ANGELIKA: As usual, they're not on time.

DIANA: Well, finally you're here. We've already been waiting a long time.

RAINER: That's not our fault.

GERD: Why do you call us so late?

RAINER: I'm really wondering now. Which movie is playing here?

ANGELIKA: *Conan, the Barbarian,* a movie from America.

DIANA: And it starts right away. Come on, let's go!

ANGELIKA: Four tickets at eight marks, please.

SALES CLERK: That's 32 marks.

ANGELIKA: Thank you.

DIANA: The movie theater is quite empty.

USHER: You can sit here.

GERD: The movie is really great.

DIANA: You're right.

RAINER: Angelika even wants to see it again.

ANGELIKA: Yes, perhaps next week already.

Nützliche Ausdrücke

Review these expressions after students have thoroughly covered the *Dialog* and *Lesestück 1.*

Möchtest du…?	Would you like…?
Das ist eine prima Idee.	That's a great idea.
Der Film soll toll sein.	The movie is supposed to be fantastic.
Endlich seid ihr da.	Finally you're here.
Das ist unsere Schuld.	That's our fault.
Ich bin gespannt.	I'm wondering. I'm anxious.
Welcher Film läuft heute?	Which movie is playing today?
Los, kommt!	Come on, let's go!
Der Film ist klasse.	The movie is great.
Ich wohne erst einen Monat hier.	I've been living here only a month.
Er arbeitet in der Stadt.	He works downtown.
Sein Auto steht vor dem Haus.	His car is in front of the house.
Er sitzt am Tisch.	He is sitting at the table.
Sie geht einkaufen.	She goes shopping.
Er macht seine Hausaufgaben.	He does his homework.
Er spielt mit seinen Freunden.	He plays with his friends.
Der Pullover soll bald fertig sein.	The pullover is supposed to be finished soon.
Er geht spät zu Bett.	He goes to bed late.
Sie sehen fern.	They watch TV.

Sie gehen einkaufen. (Wiesbaden)

Sie sitzen am Tisch.

Ergänzung

Have students describe one of their rooms at home. You may want to introduce some additional words to expand the students' vocabulary.

1. Welche Zimmer gibt es in einer Wohnung?

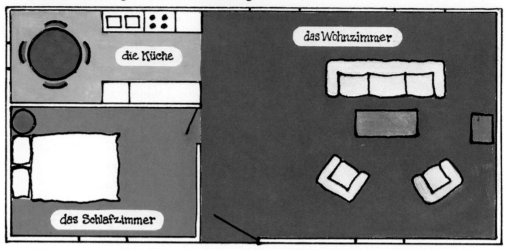

2. Welcher Tag ist heute? Heute ist Montag, der 2. (zweite) Februar.

Wann hast du Geburtstag? Ich habe am 19. (neunzehnten) Juli Geburtstag.

Welches Datum haben wir heute? Heute haben wir den 25. (fünfundzwanzigsten) September.

Use a calendar (or write the dates on the board or on flashcards) to ask the students: Welcher Tag ist heute? Wann hast Geburtstag?, Welches Datum haben wir heute?, etc. Have students ask each other, too.

3. Herr Uwe Schmidt ist Ralfs und Julias Vater.
   Frau Renate Schmidt ist Ralfs und Julias Mutter.
   Herr und Frau Schmidt sind Ralfs und Julias Eltern.
   Ralf ist Julias Bruder.
   Julia ist Ralfs Schwester.
   Ralf und Julia sind Geschwister.

   Ralf ist der Sohn von Herrn und Frau Schmidt.
   Julia ist die Tochter von Herrn und Frau Schmidt.
   Ralf ist der Enkel von Herrn und Frau Neumann.
   Julia ist die Enkelin von Herrn und Frau Neumann.

   Herr Walter Neumann ist Ralfs und Julias Großvater.
   Frau Gerda Neumann ist Ralfs und Julias Großmutter.
   Herr und Frau Neumann sind Ralfs und Julias Großeltern.

   Der Bruder von Herrn Uwe Schmidt ist Ralfs und Julias Onkel.
   Die Schwester von Frau Renate Schmidt ist Ralfs und Julias Tante.

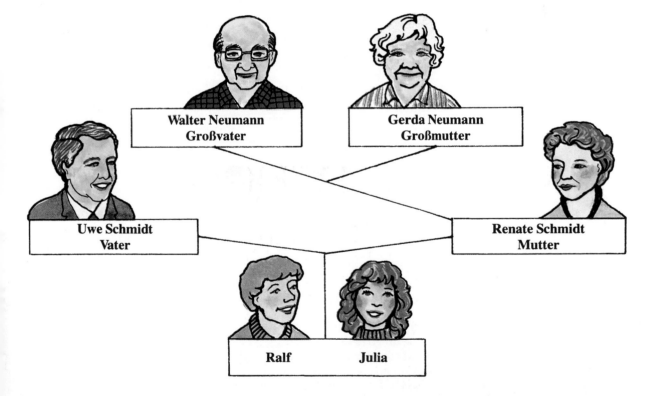

Walter Neumann
Großvater

Gerda Neumann
Großmutter

Uwe Schmidt
Vater

Renate Schmidt
Mutter

Ralf   Julia

4. 1 DM (Deutsche Mark) hat 100 Pfennige.
   1 km (Kilometer) ist ungefähr 0,6 Meilen.
   1 Kilometer (km) hat 1 000 Meter (m).

Köln 20 km

Lektion 5

Aussspracheübung

Have students repeat words at a rapid pace. You may want to explain the formation of the sounds by using the description provided.

short / u /	long / u /
und	du
um	gut
muß	ruft
Lust	sucht
Mutter	Zug
uns	nur
zum	Juni
durch	Uhr
Musik	klug

short / e /	long / e /
essen	lest
denn	der
Westen	sehr
Ecke	seht
gern	leer
sechs	Idee
Bett	mehr
Berg	Weg
fertig	gebt

[u] short *u* — sound (*Lust*): The lips are slightly protruded. The tongue arches upward in the predorsal region and remains approximately at the same height all the way back.

[ɛ] short *e* — sound (*denn*): The mouth is opened slightly. The lips and tongue have their approximate rest position.

[u:] long *u* — sound (*gut*): The lips are rounded and protruded. The tongue arches toward the back of the mouth. The tip of the tongue lies against the inner surface of the lower incisors or is slightly drawn back.

[e:] long *e* — sound (*geht*): The mouth is slightly open and lips are spread. The tip of the tongue lies against the lower teeth, but arches steeply upward from the predorsal region toward the hard palate.

Übungen

The Modal Auxiliaries: *dürfen, können, mögen*, müssen, sollen, wollen*

Modal auxiliaries (sometimes called helping verbs) help to set the mood of the particular sentence in which they occur. Let's take one sentence in English and change the modal auxiliary.

He **is allowed to** go to the movie.	*Er darf ins Kino gehen.*
He **can (is able to)** go to the movie.	*Er kann ins Kino gehen.*
He **likes to** go to the movie.	*Er mag ins Kino gehen.*
He **must (has to)** go to the movie.	*Er muß ins Kino gehen.*
He **is supposed to** go to the movie.	*Er soll ins Kino gehen.*
He **wants to** go to the movie.	*Er will ins Kino gehen.*

As you can see, the meaning or "mood" in each of these sentences is different. The same is true in German. You will notice, however, that the word order remains constant in these sentences.

---

*Mögen is used most commonly to express liking or preference in the sense of *gern haben* (like to have), *gern essen* or *trinken* (like to eat or drink). Today it is quite frequently used in the negative, often without the main verb. *Er mag das Buch nicht.* (He doesn't like the book). A more common form derived from *mögen* is *möchten* (would like to). *Er möchte nach Deutschland fahren.* (He would like to go to Germany).

It is very important to remember that the infinitive is placed at the end of the sentence. The modal auxiliary appears in the position normally held by the verb when it is a single word.

Example:

		modal auxiliary		infinitive
statement	*Paul*	*will*	*in die Stadt*	*gehen.*
question		*Will*	*Paul in die Stadt*	*gehen?*

If a modal auxiliary is used with a verb containing a separable prefix, the prefix is not separated from the verb.

Examples: *Wir wollen Christine heute abend anrufen.*

Except for *sollen*, all other modal auxiliaries show a vowel change from the singular to the plural.

	dürfen may, be permitted to	**können** can, to be able to	**mögen** to like	**müssen** must, to have to	**sollen** to be supposed to	**wollen** to want to
ich	darf	kann	mag	muß	soll	will
du	darfst	kannst	magst	mußt	sollst	willst
er **sie** **es**	darf	kann	mag	muß	soll	will
wir	dürfen	können	mögen	müssen	sollen	wollen
ihr	dürft	könnt	mögt	müßt	sollt	wollt
sie	dürfen	können	mögen	müssen	sollen	wollen
Sie	dürfen	können	mögen	müssen	sollen	wollen

Point out that modal auxiliaries have no ending when using them with *ich, er, sie* and *es*. Mention that *mögen* is mostly used in the negative. *(Ich mag das nicht.)*

NOTE: A frequently used form of „*mögen*" is „*möchten*" (would like to). The verb forms are as follows: *ich, er, sie, es möchte; du möchtest; wir, sie* (pl.), *Sie möchten; ihr möchtet.*

Folgt den Beispielen!

1. Rainer will das nicht wissen.

Variation: *Will Rainer das wissen? Ja,…/Nein,…*

    wir
    ich
    die Studenten
    der Herr
    du

Rainer will das nicht wissen.
Wir wollen das nicht wissen.
Ich will das nicht wissen.
Die Studenten wollen das nicht wissen.
Der Herr will das nicht wissen.
Du willst das nicht wissen.

2. Kannst du das Buch lesen?

    wir / die Zeitung

    die Schüler / die Wörter

    ihr / die Ausdrücke

    Angelika / die Karte

    der Beamte / den Fahrplan

Kannst du das Buch lesen?

Können wir die Zeitung lesen?

Können die Schüler die Wörter lesen?

Könnt ihr die Ausdrücke lesen?

Kann Angelika die Karte lesen?

Kann der Beamte den Fahrplan lesen?

Variation: Change sentences to questions similar to *Übung 1.*

3. Ich muß die Verkäuferin fragen.

    die Mädchen

    Gerd

    ihr

    du

    der Student

Ich muß die Verkäuferin fragen.

Die Mädchen müssen die Verkäuferin fragen.

Gerd muß die Verkäuferin fragen.

Ihr müßt die Verkäuferin fragen.

Du mußt die Verkäuferin fragen.

Der Student muß die Verkäuferin fragen.

4. Was soll ich denn tun?

    die Schüler / fragen

    der Junge / schreiben

    du / sagen

    wir / verstehen

    ihr / kaufen

    die Frau / wissen

Was soll ich denn tun?

Was sollen die Schüler denn fragen?

Was soll der Junge denn schreiben?

Was sollst du denn sagen?

Was sollen wir denn verstehen?

Was sollt ihr denn kaufen?

Was soll die Frau denn wissen?

Personalize this exercise with a question such as: *Was darfst du tun?*

5. Sie dürfen in die Stadt gehen.

    Diana und Angelika

    Peter

    ich

    Frau Müller

    du

Sie dürfen in die Stadt gehen.

Diana und Angelika dürfen in die Stadt gehen.

Peter darf in die Stadt gehen.

Ich darf in die Stadt gehen.

Frau Müller darf in die Stadt gehen.

Du darfst in die Stadt gehen.

Personalize this exercise with a question such as: *Was mögt ihr nicht?*

6. Mögt ihr das nicht?

    du

    Kerstin

    der Student

    die Jungen

    die Verkäuferin

Mögt ihr das nicht?

Magst du das nicht?

Mag Kerstin das nicht?

Mag der Student das nicht?

Mögen die Jungen das nicht?

Mag die Verkäuferin das nicht?

7. Wir möchten ins Kino gehen.

    Frau Schulz / das Buch lesen

    ich / die Musik hören

    Angelika / die Karten kaufen

    die Schüler / den Film sehen

    du / nach Hause gehen

    der Student / die Aufgaben lösen

Wir möchten ins Kino gehen.

Frau Schulz möchte das Buch lesen.

Ich möchte die Musik hören.

Angelika möchte die Karten kaufen.

Die Schüler möchten den Film sehen.

Du möchtest nach Hause gehen.

Der Student möchte die Aufgaben lösen.

8. Willst du Rainer anrufen? (können)

    Er muß bald im Büro sein. (sollen)

Kannst du Rainer anrufen?

Er soll bald im Büro sein.

Möchten Sie ins Kino gehen? (wollen)

Könnt ihr das Buch kaufen? (dürfen)

Sollen wir hier sitzen? (müssen)

Ich will das nicht. (mögen)

Wollen Sie ins Kino gehen?

Dürft ihr das Buch kaufen?

Müssen wir hier sitzen?

Ich mag das nicht.

9. **Supply the proper form of the modal auxiliaries as indicated in parentheses. Use these modal auxiliaries:** *wollen, sollen, können, dürfen, mögen, müssen.*

1. Wann (want to) _____ du Ursula anrufen?
2. Die Studenten (supposed to) _____ ein paar Bücher lesen.
3. (would like to) _____ Sie den Film aus Deutschland sehen?
4. Wir (can) _____ schon um vier ins Kino gehen.
5. Ich (permitted to) _____ heute abend in die Stadt fahren.
6. Stefan (like) _____ das gar nicht.
7. (have to) _____ du eine Arbeit schreiben?

10. **Beantwortet die Fragen!**

Encourage varied student responses.

1. Was willst du heute nachmittag machen?
2. Möchtest du ins Kino fahren?
3. Kannst du den Koffer tragen?
4. Darfst du zum Sprachlabor gehen?
5. Sollst du schon um neun nach Hause kommen?
6. Mußt du die Ausdrücke lernen?

11. **In the following sentences, provide the proper form of the modal auxiliaries as well as the main verb of the sentence.**

1. _____ ihr die Musik _____ ? (want to hear)
2. Herr Meier _____ bald in der Stadt _____ . (have to be)
3. Wann _____ die Vorstellung _____ ? (supposed to begin)
4. Ich _____ das Auto _____ . (would like to buy)
5. Wir _____ die Fremdsprache _____ . (have to learn)
6. _____ Diana die Tasche _____ ? (supposed to look for)
7. Was _____ du auf der Uni _____ ? (want to study)
8. Er _____ schon um neun Uhr _____ . (can come)
9. Du _____ das nicht _____ . (permitted to do)
10. _____ Sie den Studenten _____ ? (can ask)

12. **Construct meaningful sentences using the information given.**

1. Was / sollen / wir / heute nachmittag / tun
2. Student / können / Bedeutung / nicht / verstehen
3. Zug / sollen / halb zwei / kommen
4. Mutter / müssen / in die Stadt fahren

5. Warum / wollen / du / nicht / Beamter / fragen
6. Ich / möchten / Wörterbuch / kaufen
7. Werden / ihr / zu Hause bleiben
8. Dürfen / du / Formel / gebrauchen

Future Tense

In trying to express events that will take place any time from the present, we may use the future tense.

Examples: I will read a book.
Ich werde ein Buch lesen.

Similar to the modal auxiliaries, *werden* takes on the same word order.

werden		
ich	werde	I will
du	wirst	you will
er **sie** **es**	wird	he will she will it will
wir	werden	we will
ihr	werdet	you will
sie	werden	they will
Sie	werden	you will

Point out that the word order for *werden* + infinitive is the same as with the modal auxiliaries. Explain that (in German) the future can be expressed using either the present tense or *werden* + infinitive. *(Wir fahren am Montag nach Köln.* or *Wir werden am Montag nach Köln fahren.)*

NOTE: If the sentence contains a reference to the future, e.g. „*morgen*" or „*nächstes Jahr*," the present tense is used most of the time.

Folgt den Beispielen!

Variation: Change the statement into a question.

13. Sie werden nach Deutschland fahren.
    ich
    wir
    der Junge
    die Mädchen
    du

Sie werden nach Deutschland fahren.
Ich werde nach Deutschland fahren.

Wir werden nach Deutschland fahren.

Der Junge wird nach Deutschland fahren.

Die Mädchen werden nach Deutschland fahren.

Du wirst nach Deutschland fahren.

14. Wirst du die Verkäuferin fragen?
    er / die Wörter schreiben
    ich / den Ausdruck lernen
    wir / eine Karte kaufen
    Diana / Angelika anrufen
    die Schüler / die Bücher lesen

Wirst du die Verkäuferin fragen?
Wird er die Wörter schreiben?

Werde ich den Ausdruck lernen?

Werden wir eine Karte kaufen?

Wird Diana Angelika anrufen?

Werden die Schüler die Bücher lesen?

15. Der Film beginnt um acht.	Der Film wird um acht beginnen.
Jürgen klingelt an der Tür	Jürgen wird an der Tür klingeln.
Dort ist immer viel Verkehr.	Dort wird immer viel Verkehr sein.
Die Busse kommen bald.	Die Busse werden bald kommen.
Ich verstehe die Beschreibung.	Ich werde die Beschreibung verstehen.
Gehen Sie zu Fuß?	Werden Sie zu Fuß gehen?
Lernt ihr Deutsch?	Werdet ihr Deutsch lernen?
Wir üben die Wörter.	Wir werden die Wörter üben.

Variation: Ask questions. *(Um wieviel Uhr beginnt der Film? Was macht Jürgen?,* etc.)

16. **Change the following sentences from the present to the future tense.**

1. Wann arbeitest du heute?
2. Die Jungen hören Musik.
3. Jürgen sucht eine Kassette.
4. Was zeigt der Computer?
5. Ich verliere keine Worte.
6. Dein Vorschlag ist ganz praktisch.
7. Wir brauchen deine Hilfe.
8. Oliver weiß sehr viel.

17. **Answer each question by using the future tense.**

> **Beispiel:** *Brauchst du eine Tasche? Ja, ich…*
> *Ja, ich werde eine Tasche brauchen.*

1. Hast du Angst? Nein, ich…
2. Lernt Stefan die Vokabeln auswendig? Ja, Stefan…
3. Kommt die Straßenbahn pünktlich? Ja, sie…
4. Kauft ihr diese Karten? Nein, wir…
5. Bist du gespannt? Ja, ich…
6. Steht sein Auto vor dem Haus? Nein, es…
7. Beginnt die Vorstellung um acht? Ja, sie…
8. Verstehst du die Verkäuferin? Nein, ich…
9. Gehen die Mädchen zu Fuß? Ja, sie…
10. Wohnt Herr Braun in einem Mietshaus? Ja, er…

Personal Pronouns

Nominative (Third Person Singular)

In German, as you have learned in previous units, there are three personal pronouns *er, sie,* and *es,* which can be replaced with *der, die* and *das* respectively.

Der Junge ist hier.	*Er ist hier.* (he)
Der Zug ist hier.	*Er ist hier.* (it)
Die Frau ist dort.	*Sie ist dort.* (she)
Die Karte ist dort.	*Sie ist dort.* (it)

Das Mädchen ist da drüben.   *Es ist da drüben. (it/she)*
Das Kino ist da drüben.   *Es ist da drüben. (it)*

Accusative (Third Person Singular)

The accusative case for the pronouns *er, sie, es* is *ihn, sie, es*. Notice that only the masculine pronoun, i.e., *er,* changes to *ihn.* The other two pronouns *sie* and *es* have the same forms in the nominative as well as in the accusative case.

*Er sucht **den Jungen.***
*Er sucht **den Ball.***   *Er sucht **ihn.***
*Er sucht **einen Ball.***

*Ich sehe **die Frau.***
*Ich sehe **die Karte.***   *Ich sehe **sie.***
*Ich sehe **eine Karte.***

*Wir finden **das Mädchen.***
*Wir finden **das Buch.***   *Wir finden **es.***
*Wir finden **ein Buch.***

	masculine	feminine	neuter
nominative	er	sie	es
accusative	ihn	sie	es

Additional Personal Pronouns

In addition to the third person singular, of course, there are other personal pronouns. These, as well as the previously mentioned pronouns, are all included in the table below.

Singular		Plural	
nominative	*accusative*	*nominative*	*accusative*
ich	mich (me)	wir	uns (us)
du	dich (you)	ihr	euch (you)
er sie es	ihn (him, it) sie (her, it) es (it)	sie	sie (them)
		Sie (sg. & pl.)	Sie (you)

Folgt den Beispielen!

<table>
<tr><td>18.</td><td>Sie suchen die Zeitung.</td><td>Sie suchen sie.</td></tr>
<tr><td></td><td>Sie lesen das Buch.</td><td>Sie lesen es.</td></tr>
<tr><td></td><td>Sie schreiben den Ausdruck.</td><td>Sie schreiben ihn.</td></tr>
<tr><td></td><td>Sie kaufen die Kassette.</td><td>Sie kaufen sie.</td></tr>
<tr><td></td><td>Sie brauchen das Telefon.</td><td>Sie brauchen es.</td></tr>
<tr><td></td><td>Sie lernen die Aufgabe.</td><td>Sie lernen sie.</td></tr>
<tr><td></td><td>Sie sehen den Bahnhof.</td><td>Sie sehen ihn.</td></tr>
</table>

Personalize the exercise as follows: *Suchst du die Zeitung? — Ja, ich suche sie./Nein, ich suche sie nicht.*

Variation: Repeat exercise in the negative.

19. Brauchst du den Fahrplan?   Ja, ich brauche ihn.
    Verstehst du die Formel?   Ja, ich verstehe sie.
    Kaufst du den Koffer?   Ja, ich kaufe ihn.
    Suchst du die Straße?   Ja, ich suche sie.
    Kennst du das Haus?   Ja, ich kenne es.
    Fragst du den Studenten?   Ja, ich frage ihn.
    Lernst du die Seite auswendig?   Ja, ich lerne sie auswendig.

20. Ich kaufe eine Karte.   Ich kaufe sie.
        Auto   Ich kaufe es.
        Pullover   Ich kaufe ihn.
        Buch   Ich kaufe es.
        Zeitung   Ich kaufe sie.
        Fahrplan   Ich kaufe ihn.
        Cola   Ich kaufe sie.

21. Er fragt _____ . (ich)   Er fragt mich.
    Suchst du _____ ? (er)   Suchst du ihn?
    Ihr schreibt _____ . (es)   Ihr schreibt es.
    Wir verstehen _____ . (sie-pl.)   Wir verstehen sie.
    Ich suche _____ . (du)   Ich suche dich.
    Susanne kennt _____ . (sie-sg.)   Susanne kennt sie.
    Er findet _____ . (ihr)   Er findet euch.

22. **Provide the pronouns for the nouns indicated in parentheses.**

    Beispiel: *(Karte) Er kauft _____.*
    Er kauft sie.

    1. (Bahnhof) Suchen Sie _____?
    2. (Arbeit) Wir verstehen _____.
    3. (Platzanweiser) Frag _____ doch!
    4. (Aufgabe) Schreibt ihr _____?
    5. (Mark) Brauchst du _____?
    6. (Junge) Ich mag _____ nicht.
    7. (Schlaukopf) Wir kennen _____.
    8. (Buch) Kauft ihr _____?
    9. (Film) Werden Sie _____ sehen?
    10. (Café) Die Touristen wollen _____ finden.

23. **Supply the proper personal pronouns in German for those in parentheses.**

    1. Kann ich (you) _____ etwas fragen, Herr Peters?
    2. Wir werden (her) _____ morgen anrufen.
    3. Braucht ihr (him) _____ nicht.
    4. Sie werden (me) _____ nicht verstehen?

5. Sag (us) _____ das bitte!

6. Ich werde (you) _____ schon finden, Jörg.

7. Wir brauchen (you) _____, Petra und Andrea.

Verbs with Separable Prefixes

You can combine verbs with prefixes and thus change their meaning. In most cases such prefixes are prepositions, just as in English (to take — to undertake).

Examples: *(einsteigen) Sie steigt ein.* She gets in.
(aussteigen) Sie steigt aus. She gets out.

These prefixes, which you can add or eliminate, are called *separable*. The prefixes are separated from their verbs and placed at the end of the sentence.

Examples: *(anrufen) Angelika **ruft** um vier Uhr **an**.*
*(fernsehen) Wir **sehen** heute abend **fern**.*
*(mitkommen) Warum **kommt** ihr nicht ins Kino **mit**?*
*(einkaufen) Frau Müller **kauft** gern am Freitag **ein**.*

Folgt dem Beispiel!

24. Die Jungen kommen mit.

This material is treated more thoroughly in *Lektion 10*.

    fernsehen

    einkaufen

    anrufen

    einsteigen

Die Jungen kommen mit.

Die Jungen sehen fern.

Die Jungen kaufen ein.

Die Jungen rufen an.

Die Jungen steigen ein.

25. **Complete each sentence by filling in the appropriate verb with its separable prefix.**

    1. (to call up) Warum _____ er nicht _____?

    2. (to watch TV) Ich _____ gern _____.

    3. (to get in) _____ Sie schnell in die S-Bahn _____!

    4. (to come along) Wir möchten nicht _____.

    5. (to shop) Was _____ du heute _____?

Er steigt in die Straßenbahn ein.

Lesestück 1

Bei Familie Höhne

Familie Höhne wohnt in Marzahn, einem Vorort von Ost-Berlin. Die Mietshäuser° in dieser Gegend° sind ganz neu. Herr und Frau Höhne und ihr Sohn Klaus wohnen erst ein Jahr hier in einem Mietshaus.

apartment buildings/area

Jeden Tag muß Herr Höhne schon um sieben Uhr zur Arbeit gehen. Er arbeitet in einem Büro in der Stadt. Sein Auto steht vor dem Haus. Es dauert ungefähr fünfzehn Minuten bis Herr Höhne im Büro ist.

Klaus sitzt um halb acht am Tisch und frühstückt°. Ein paar Minuten später sagt er „Tschüs!" zu seiner Mutter und geht aus dem Haus. Die Schule ist nicht weit und er kann zu Fuß dorthin gehen.

has breakfast

Frau Höhne arbeitet jeden Tag ein paar Stunden. Sie arbeitet in einem Café gleich um die Ecke. Nach der Arbeit geht sie oft einkaufen. Eine HO-Kaufhalle° ist in der Nähe. Dort kann sie kaufen, was sie für die Familie braucht.

supermarket

Um ein Uhr kommt Klaus aus der Schule. Zuerst° muß er seine Hausaufgaben machen. Das dauert meistens° eine Stunde. Dann spielt er oft mit seinen Freunden oder auch gern mit seinen Autos.

first
mostly

Was macht Klaus?

Klaus und sein Vater spielen ein Spiel.

Frau Höhne häkelt.

Herr Höhne kommt um fünf Uhr nach Hause. Dann möchte er immer zuerst die Zeitung° lesen. Eine Stunde später sitzen alle drei am Tisch und essen Abendbrot°. Meistens gibt es Kalte Platte°. Nach dem Abendbrot arbeitet Frau Höhne eine Weile in der Küche. Dort ist immer viel zu tun. Nach der Arbeit sitzt Frau Höhne gern im Wohnzimmer und häkelt°. Sie häkelt einen Pullover. Er soll in zwei Wochen fertig sein.

newspaper

eat supper/ cold cuts

crochets

Klaus und sein Vater spielen unterdessen° ein Spiel. Wer wird gewinnen°? Herr Höhne gewinnt meistens, aber manchmal hat auch Klaus Glück. Um neun Uhr muß Klaus ins Bett. Herr und Frau Höhne sitzen dann oft in Wohnzimmer und sehen fern.

meanwhile

win

Fragen über das Lesestück

1. Wie lange wohnt Familie Höhne schon in dem Mietshaus?
2. Um wieviel Uhr geht Herr Höhne zur Arbeit?
3. Wo arbeitet er?
4. Muß Klaus weit zur Schule gehen?
5. Wo arbeitet Frau Höhne?
6. Wo geht sie einkaufen?
7. Was macht Klaus nach der Schule?
8. Wann kommt Herr Höhne nach Hause?
9. Was macht er zuerst?
10. Was essen Höhnes heute?
11. Was machen Klaus und sein Vater später? Und Frau Höhne?
12. Was tun Herr und Frau Höhne nach neun Uhr?

Erweiterung

26. Wie heißt das auf deutsch?

1. Would you like to go to Germany?
2. The performance is very popular.
3. Can we sit here?
4. The newspaper is supposed to be well-known.
5. Is Mrs. Schmidt going shopping tomorrow?
6. I'm watching TV.
7. My birthday is…(Give your birthday.)
8. Today is…(Give today's date.)
9. I'm working downtown.
10. We eat supper at 7:30.

27. Welcher Tag ist heute? Heute ist der...

You may want to expand this exercise adding more dates.

1. ninth of November
2. thirtieth of August
3. fifteenth of January
4. first of March
5. eleventh of June

28. Give the male or female counterpart including the appropriate article.

1. die Mutter - _____
2. der Sohn - _____
3. der Junge - _____
4. die Freundin - _____
5. der Großvater - _____
6. die Tante - _____
7. der Bruder - _____
8. die Enkelin - _____

29. Beantwortet die Fragen!

Encourage different answers.

Welcher Film läuft heute?

Wie soll der Film sein?

Was machst du heute abend?

Welches Datum haben wir heute?

Hast du Brüder? Wie viele?

Hast du Schwestern? Wie viele?

Wohnst du in der Stadt oder in einem Vorort?

Wohnst du in einem Mietshaus oder in einem Haus?

Wo gehst du manchmal einkaufen?

Rückblick

If students have problems completing any of these exercises, you may want to go back to the particular lesson in which the grammar point or other topic was covered.

I. Provide the article for each noun and then give the plural form.

> **Beispiel:** _____ Junge: _____
>
> *der Junge: die Jungen*

1. _____ Freundin: _____
2. _____ Kino: _____
3. _____ Tisch: _____
4. _____ Zimmer: _____
5. _____ Vater: _____
6. _____ Mutter: _____
7. _____ Büro: _____
8. _____ Kassette: _____
9. _____ Haus: _____
10. _____ Stadt: _____
11. _____ Sohn: _____
12. _____ Ecke: _____
13. _____ Bett: _____
14. _____ Land: _____
15. _____ Verkäuferin: _____
16. _____ Vorstellung: _____
17. _____ Film: _____
18. _____ Auto: _____
19. _____ Bruder: _____
20. _____ Buch: _____

II. Convert these sentences into commands.

Beispiel: *Sie sehen den Film.*
Sehen Sie den Film!

1. Ihr schreibt die Arbeit.
2. Du sitzt am Tisch.
3. Sie sind pünktlich.
4. Du hast keine Angst.
5. Ihr fragt den Platzanweiser.
6. Sie suchen den Platz.
7. Du verlierst keine Worte.
8. Du bist bald da.
9. Ihr kauft die Karten.
10. Sie kommen heute abend.

III. Restate these sentences in the negative.

1. Die Reise dauert sehr lange.
2. Die Vorstellung beginnt um sechs Uhr.
3. Ich brauche eine Kassette.
4. Sven ist Student.
5. Herr Höhne arbeitet in München.
6. Die Jungen spielen zu Hause.
7. Hast du Angst?
8. Sie geht heute nachmittag einkaufen.
9. Haben Sie ein Auto?
10. Verstehst du die Aufgabe?

IV. Match the last part (right side) with the first part (left side) to form a new meaningful noun. Also provide the article and the meaning of this noun.

1. _____ Nachbar _____   -brot
2. _____ Miets _____   -stelle
3. _____ Fremd _____   -sprache
4. _____ Schlau _____   -fest
5. _____ Geburts _____   -land
6. _____ Musik _____   -diele
7. _____ Sprach _____   -aufgabe
8. _____ Eis _____   -sportler
9. _____ Wohn _____   -tag
10. _____ Haus _____   -weg
11. _____ Groß _____   -vater
12. _____ Fahr _____   -kopf
13. _____ Abend _____   -stadt
14. _____ Halte _____   -haus
15. _____ Winter _____   -labor
16. _____ Feld _____   -zimmer
17. _____ Haupt _____   -plan

V. Supply the missing months. Keep the proper sequence.

Januar, _____, März, April, _____, _____, Juli, August, _____, _____, November, _____

VI. Wie heißen die vier Jahreszeiten?

Lesestück 2

Österreich

Österreich ist eine Republik. Das Land liegt in der Mitte von Europa. Österreich ist ungefähr so groß wie der Staat Maine. Es hat mehr als sieben Millionen Einwohner. Fast° 99% sprechen Deutsch als Muttersprache°. Sieben Länder grenzen an Österreich — die Schweiz, Liechtenstein, Italien, Jugoslawien, Ungarn, die Tschechoslowakei und die Bundesrepublik Deutschland. Österreich hat neun Bundesländer. Die Nationalfahne ist rot-weiß-rot.

almost

mother tongue

Österreich ist im Winter sehr beliebt.

In Österreich gibt es viele Berge.

Graz liegt im Süden Österreichs.

Lektion 5

Das Land liegt zum größten Teil° in den Alpen. Die Berge° *mostly/mountains*
verlaufen° von Westen nach Osten. Der höchste° Berg in Österreich *runs/highest*
ist der Großglockner. Er ist 3 798 m (Meter) hoch. Die Donau ist
der längste Fluß°. Sie fließt° von Westen nach Osten und hat in *longest river/flows*
Österreich eine Länge° von 347 Kilometern. *length*

Die Hauptstadt von Österreich ist Wien. Mehr als 20% der
Österreicher wohnen in der Hauptstadt. Wien liegt im Osten Öster-
reichs. Dort ist das Land flach°. Die Donau fließt durch° Wien. Im *flat/through*
Süden liegt Graz, eine andere große Stadt. Linz liegt im Nordosten.
Die Donau fließt auch durch Linz. Nach Wien, Graz und Linz
kommt Salzburg im Nordwesten. Salzburg ist eine beliebte° Stadt. *popular*
Viele Touristen kommen jedes Jahr im Sommer zum Musikfest° *music festival*
nach Salzburg. Innsbruck ist die fünftgrößte Stadt in Österreich.
Diese Stadt liegt im Westen und ist während° jeder Jahreszeit be- *during*
liebt. Besonders schön ist es dort im Winter. Viele Wintersportler
besuchen° dann Innsbruck und Umgebung°. *visit/area*

Der größte See° ist der Neusiedlersee. Er liegt im Osten. Es *lake*
gibt viele Seen in Österreich. Ein anderer bekannter° See ist der *well-known*
Mondsee. Er liegt im Nordwesten von Österreich. Im Winter wie
auch im Sommer ist Österreich ein beliebtes Ferienland°. *vacation country*

Fragen über das Lesestück

1. Wie groß ist Österreich?
2. Wie heißen die Nachbarländer von Österreich?
3. Wie viele Bundesländer hat Österreich?
4. Wie heißt der höchste Berg? Wie hoch ist er?
5. Fließt die Donau von Norden nach Süden?
6. Wo liegt Wien?
7. Wie heißen die drei größten Städte in Österreich?
8. Warum ist Salzburg so beliebt?
9. Wo liegt Innsbruck?
10. Ist Österreich nur im Sommer beliebt?

Sprachspiegel

I. Develop your own dialog using the information given strictly as a guideline. Be as creative as possible!

You suggest to your two friends that you go to a movie. Friend A wants to see a movie from France, but Friend B prefers one from Germany. Friend B wins this argument, especially since the tickets are cheaper. You inquire about the movie schedule. Friend B suggests that you go in the afternoon. The tickets will not be very expensive at that time. Friend A mentions that you should ask Friend C to come along. You talk to him/her over the phone, but s/he tells you that s/he has too much homework and won't be able to join you. Friend A indicates that you should take the streetcar, because otherwise you'll miss the early show. All of you agree and go to the next streetcar stop.

II. **Describe what you do during a typical day. The description doesn't need to be long. Use the vocabulary and structure that you have learned so far. Your description should include the following information:**

After students have written their description, ask for volunteers to read it to the class. Have other students ask questions to review the material read.

1. where you live (city/suburb, house/apartment)
2. time you go to school and how far you have to go
3. how you get there (car, walk, etc.)
4. how long you are at school and time you come home
5. what you do after school
6. time you eat supper and with whom
7. what you do after supper
8. when you go to bed

Wie sagt man's?

Students should be encouraged to read the short dialogs aloud with the proper expression. Ask questions or have students ask each other about the content.

Wie alt bist du, bitte?
Fünfzehn.
Dann kannst du diesen Film sehen.

Ihre Karte, bitte.
Bitte sehr.
Sie können hier sitzen.
Vielen Dank.

Der nächste Film beginnt um sieben.
Warten wir doch hier!
Wir haben noch so viel Zeit.
Dann gehen wir jetzt ins Café.

Tschüs!
Wohin gehst du denn?
In die Kaufhalle.
Warte, ich komme mit.

Du hast immer Glück.
Beim Spiel schon.
Da hast du recht, aber nicht in der Schule.

Der Film soll klasse sein.
Das weiß ich. Da werde ich wenig verstehen.
Etwas Englisch verstehst du vielleicht.

Das ist meine Familie.
Sie ist sehr groß.
Das können Sie wohl sagen.

Der Film soll klasse sein.

Und wer ist das?
Mein Freund Herbert. Er kommt aus Wiesbaden.
Meine Eltern wohnen auch in Wiesbaden.
Wie interessant.

Was für ein Film ist es?
Aus Frankreich. Er spielt schon fünf Wochen hier.
Dann muß er ja ganz toll sein.
Das glaube ich auch.

Gehst du gern ins Kino?
Ja, besonders am Sonntag nachmittag.
Warum gerade sonntags?
Dann kosten die Karten nur fünf Mark.

Zungenbrecher

This tongue twister will be challenging. See how many times your students can say it.

In Ulm und um Ulm und um Ulm herum.
(In Ulm and around Ulm and all around Ulm.)

Kulturecke

Entertainment and Leisure-Time Activities

Germans love to be entertained. This is obvious to the visitor who sees numerous posters announcing the various events taking place, particularly in the bigger cities. Besides these billboards, big, round columns (*Litfaßsäulen*) covered with posters can be seen in the streets.

The larger cities provide the most opportunities for different types of entertainment. Neighborhood movie theaters feature both German and foreign films. American movies are particularly popular. There are more than 185 theaters that receive subsidies from state and local governments. Many of the major theaters today, as in Düsseldorf, for example, have been built in striking contemporary styles. These major theaters offer a fantastic selection of performances that will suit almost everyone. Most Germans buy their theater tickets well in advance. Besides the indoor theaters, there are numerous outdoor theaters presenting plays during the summer months for local audiences, tourists and vacationers. Small-time entertainment is provided by young adults, particularly students, who play their musical instruments in major shopping areas.

Every large city has a zoo, and there are a number of American and European troupes touring the country every year. As in the U.S., German cities hold fairs at least once or twice a year offering carnival attractions of many types and the traditional rides for thrill-seekers.

There are numerous festivals in Germany throughout the year. These festivals always include a parade with local bands. Dressed in their folk costumes, these groups provide color and entertainment for the townspeople and visitors. The largest bands and crowds can be seen at the annual *Oktoberfest* in München, where over a million people congregate in an atmosphere that the Germans call *Gemütlichkeit*. The *Oktoberfest* takes place from late September to early October, but the famous *Karneval* in Köln is usually held during the month of February. Hundreds of thousands of people line the streets to witness the parade.

The German people enjoy many leisure-time activities. From September through May, millions of German fans watch the major and minor soccer matches throughout the country every week. During the summer, many Germans head for the water for swimming, sailing or fishing. Some rent boats of various types and explore the rivers and lakes on their own. Every city has one or more outdoor swimming pools that are modern and offer many facilities to the public. Germans also enjoy going to indoor swimming pools, especially during the colder season. The winter months offer other entertainment opportunities. Ice-skating, for example, has become very popular in recent years, particularly among the young. Furthermore, Germans head south to the mountainous area and go skiing — downhill or cross-country.

Every eighth German is a hiker. Major parks and forests have numerous hiking paths that are usually outlined on large boards right at the entrance of the path. Picnic facilities are also available along these hiking trails and are welcomed by those who spend several hours hiking. Bicycling has always been a favorite diversion among all age groups. There are many well-marked bicycle paths in the cities and towns and throughout the countryside. Some people enjoy horseback riding in the city parks and in the country.

People who don't care to exert themselves in active sports can stroll around in the beautifully landscaped parks scattered throughout Germany. After a long walk, it is no problem to find a place to sit down. Benches have been provided for people to relax and watch the world go by. Ice cream stands add further delight for people of all ages.

Outdoor cafés have long been traditional German gathering places. Here, people can order a cup of coffee or cola and sit for an hour or two without an obligation to order anything else. Outdoor chess games have become quite popular. Chess figures two or three feet high are moved on one-foot squares. Minigolf courses have sprung up throughout Germany. Unusual to Americans will be the concrete putting area. Most Germans consider yard work a leisure-time activity. Those who are not fortunate to have their own yard may have a *Kleingarten* on the edge of town. On this rented plot, they can spend hours and hours tending flowers, trees, fruits and vegetables.

Germans enjoy reading. There are newspaper stands all over. Many Germans, regardless of age, can be seen reading outdoors, particularly as they relax on public benches. As soon as the working parent comes home from work, it is quite customary to read the local paper.

The most common leisure-time activity in Germany is watching television. Although most Germans have a wide range of interests, more than one-fourth consider television viewing as their only pastime. Similar to American teenagers, many young people in Germany enjoy listening to popular music. Others learn and practice their own instruments, and a few play along with recorded music instruction. In all German communities, it is traditional for men to meet frequently at the local tavern to play cards.

Bicycling is a favorite German pastime.

Germans enjoy the rivers.

Germans head south to go skiing. (Alpen)

Some people enjoy horseback riding.

An outdoor swimming pool. (Kochel)

A map of the hiking paths. (Frankfurt)

You can camp all over Germany.

Vokabeln

das **Abendbrot** supper
die **Alpen** Alps
Amerika America
anrufen to call up
arbeiten to work
außerhalb outside
das **Auto,-s** car
bei at
das **Bett,-en** bed
    Er muß ins Bett. He has to go to bed.
der **Bruder,-** brother
das **Bundesland,-er** Federal District
das **Café,-s** café, coffee shop
das **Datum, Daten** date (calendar)
die **Donau** Danube
dorthin (to) there
dürfen to be permitted to, may
einkaufen to shop
    einkaufen gehen to go shopping
die **Eltern** (pl.) parents
der **Enkel,-** grandson
die **Enkelin,-nen** granddaughter
erst only, first
essen to eat
Europa Europe
die **Familie,-n** family
fernsehen to watch TV
fertig ready, done, finished
der **Film,-e** movie, film
frühstücken to have breakfast
der **Geburtstag,-e** birthday
die **Gegend,-en** area
die **Geschwister** (pl.) siblings
gespannt sein to wonder, be curious
gewinnen to win
der **Großvater,-** grandfather
die **Großmutter,-** grandmother
die **Großeltern** (pl.) grandparents
Grüß Gott! Hello!
häkeln to crochet
die **Hausaufgabe,-n** homework
    die Hausaufgaben machen to do homework
die **HO-Kaufhalle,-n** (government-owned) supermarket
hoch high
ihn it, him
Italien Italy
Jugoslawien Yugoslavia
die **Karte,-n** ticket
das **Kino,-s** movie theater
klasse sein to be great
können to be able to, can

die **Küche,-n** kitchen
laufen to run
leer empty
lieber rather
Liechtenstein Liechtenstein
Los! Come on!
    Los, kommt! Come on, let's go!
mehr als more than
meistens mostly, most of the time
das **Mietshaus,-er** apartment building
mitkommen to come along
möchten to would like to
mögen to like
müssen must, to have to
die **Mutter,-** mother
nochmal once more
oder or
der **Onkel,-** uncle
der **Platzanweiser,-** usher
der **Pullover,-** pullover
die **Republik,-en** republic
das **Schlafzimmer,-** bedroom
die **Schuld** fault
die **Schwester,-** sister
sein his
der **Sohn,-e** son
sollen to be supposed to, should
das **Spiel,-e** game
spielen to play
die **Tante,-n** aunt
der **Tisch,-e** table
die **Tochter,-** daughter
toll fantastic, wild, terrific
der **Tourist,-en** tourist
Ungarn Hungary
unpünktlich late, not on time
uns us
unsere (form of *unser*) our
unterdessen meanwhile, in the meantime
der **Vater,-** father
die **Verkäuferin,-nen** sales clerk (female)
vor in front of, before
die **Vorstellung,-en** performance, show
weiß white
der **Wintersportler,-** winter sportsman
das **Wohnzimmer,-** living room
wollen to want to
die **Zeitung,-en** newspaper
zuerst first
zum (or: **zu dem**) to the

Lesestück

Ein Tag bei Grubers

Familie Gruber wohnt in Mülheim, einem Vorort von Köln. Sind Grubers eine typische deutsche Familie? Vielleicht. Herr Gruber steht schon um sechs Uhr auf°. Eine halbe Stunde später sitzt er in der Küche. Da kann er die Zeitung ruhig lesen. Frau Gruber deckt den Tisch°, kocht° Kaffee und wartet auf Heike und Kerstin, ihre beiden Töchter.

    Heike, 16 Jahre alt, kommt zuerst in die Küche. Sie ist noch etwas müde°. Dann kommt Kerstin. Sie ist 13 Jahre alt. Kerstin ist auch noch nicht munter°. Um sieben Uhr frühstückt die Familie. Was gibt's heute? Brot°mit Butter, Marmelade, Milch und Kaffee.

    Um halb acht geht Herr Gruber zur Arbeit. Er muß nur zehn Minuten zu Fuß gehen. Etwas später verlassen° Heike und Kerstin das Haus. Heike besucht ein Gymnasium und Kerstin geht auf eine Realschule. Heikes Schule ist gleich um die Ecke. Kerstin muß mit der Straßenbahn fahren.

    Um halb ein Uhr macht Frau Gruber das Mittagessen°. Heike und Kerstin kommen kurz° nach eins aus der Schule. Das Mittagessen ist dann immer fertig. Heike und Kerstin sind sehr hungrig°. Sie sitzen in der Küche am Tisch und warten auf das Essen°. Frau Gruber bringt es auch bald. Heute essen sie Beefsteak mit Soße°, Kartoffeln°, Karotten, Erbsen°, und zum Nachtisch° Apfelmus°.

    Nach dem Essen macht Kerstin ihre° Hausaufgaben. Sie hat heute viel zu tun. Sie muß einen Aufsatz°schreiben. Das ist nicht so leicht. Später ruft sie Marion, ihre Freundin, an. Marion hat aber heute keine Zeit. Sie kann Kerstin nicht besuchen. Kerstin hat viele Kassetten. Sie hört gern Musik.

    Heike sitzt in ihrem Zimmer. Sie muß ein Buch lesen und dann viele Fragen beantworten°. Die Fragen sind sehr schwer. Heike ist erst um vier mit den Hausaufgaben fertig. Dann spielt sie gern Gitarre°.

    Um sechs Uhr steht das Abendbrot auf dem Tisch. Meistens essen Grubers Kalte Platte — Brot mit Butter, Schinken°, Wurst°, Käse° und Tomaten. Dazu° trinken sie Tee. Frau Gruber stellt° alles auf den Tisch.

    Am Abend sitzen alle im Wohnzimmer. Was gibt's denn heute im Fernsehen°? Herr Gruber möchte die Nachrichten° im Ersten Programm sehen. Das interessiert Frau Gruber und Kerstin nicht. Heike zeigt auch wenig Interesse. Sie strickt° einen Pullover und wartet gespannt auf das nächste Programm — einen Spielfilm° aus Amerika.

Margin glosses:
steht...auf *gets up*

sets the table/cooks

tired
awake
bread

leave

lunch
shortly
hungry
meal
gravy/potatoes peas/for dessert/ apple sauce

her
essay

answer questions

guitar

ham/sausage cheese/with it/ puts

on TV/news

knits
feature film

You may want to select only particular sections of this unit for review. The new words introduced are listed in the margin of the line in which they appear. If your students have some difficulties in completing the exercises, you may want to go back to the lesson in which the particular grammar point or topic was discussed.

Fragen über das Lesestück

1. Wo liegt Mülheim?
2. Um wieviel Uhr sitzt Herr Gruber in der Küche?
3. Was macht Herr Gruber zuerst? Und Frau Gruber?
4. Wie alt sind die beiden Töchter?
5. Was essen sie alle heute morgen?
6. Muß Herr Gruber zur Arbeit fahren?
7. Wie weit ist Heikes Schule entfernt?
8. Um wieviel Uhr kommen Kerstin und Heike aus der Schule?
9. Was gibt es heute zum Mittagessen?
10. Was muß Kerstin nach dem Essen machen?
11. Warum kann Marion Kerstin heute nicht besuchen?
12. Was hört Kerstin gern?
13. Was muß Heike heute nachmittag tun?
14. Was spielt sie später?
15. Was essen Grubers zum Abendbrot?
16. Wo sitzen alle am Abend?
17. Was möchte Herr Gruber sehen?
18. Was macht Heike?

Übungen

I. Select the proper question word *(wo, wohin, wie, was, woher).*

1. _____ ist eine Eisdiele?
2. _____ kommen Sie, Herr Hoffmann?
3. _____ heißt das Mädchen da?
4. _____ wollt ihr später gehen?
5. _____ macht die Familie später?
6. _____ wirst du denn dort kaufen?
7. _____ fahren die Studenten?
8. _____ wartet Kerstin?

II. Beantwortet diese Fragen!

1. Wohin willst du später gehen?
2. Was möchtest du heute abend essen?
3. Wo kannst du eine Kassette kaufen?
4. Was sollst du lesen?
5. Was mußt du jetzt tun?
6. Wohin darfst du denn fahren?

III. Change the following sentences from the singular to the plural.

Beispiel: *Ich brauche den Fahrplan.*
Wir brauchen die Fahrpläne.

1. Der Junge fragt den Beamten.
2. Suchst du die Kassette?
3. Der Student schreibt die Arbeit.
4. Wird er die Tante besuchen?
5. Das Mädchen spielt die Gitarre.
6. Der Tag ist sehr schön.
7. Kennt die Schwester den Onkel?
8. Die Vorstellung beginnt bald.
9. Der Film kommt aus Amerika.
10. Ich lerne die Vokabel.

IV. Provide the proper answer by selecting from the information listed below.

1. _____ ist ein Fluß in der BRD und fließt von Süden nach Norden.
2. _____ liegt in der DDR.
3. _____ ist die Hauptstadt von Österreich.
4. _____ liegt im Norden von Deutschland.
5. _____ ist eine Stadt und liegt in der Nähe von Wiesbaden.
6. _____ ist die Hauptstadt von Bayern.
7. _____ grenzt an die Schweiz.
8. _____ fließt durch Linz.
9. _____ ist die Hauptstadt der Bundesrepublik.
10. _____ ist ein Berg in Österreich.

Berlin	Bonn
Österreich	die Donau
Mainz	München
Wien	der Rhein
der Großglockner	Dänemark

St. Pölten, eine Stadt in Österreich

Was bedeutet dieses Schild?

Wo ist die Autobahn nach Kassel? (Würzburg)

V. Supply the correct form of the definite or indefinite article, where necessary.

1. Fragen Sie d_____ Platzanweiser!
2. Hast du ein_____ Idee?
3. D_____ Auto kostet viel Geld.
4. Wann kommt d_____ Straßenbahn?
5. Möchtest du ein_____ Buch kaufen?
6. Kann ich d_____ Fahrplan sehen?
7. Wo steht d_____ Computer?
8. Wir wollen ein_____ Film aus Deutschland sehen.
9. Der Schüler kann d_____ Aufgabe gut verstehen.
10. Herr Höhne wird ein_____ Zeitung lesen.
11. Kennen Sie d_____ Familie?
12. Sie häkelt ein_____ Pullover.

VI. Form questions by asking for the italicized words.
Use the question words *wer, wen, was, wo* or *wohin*.

1. Wir verstehen *die Wörter* nicht.
2. Die Schüler warten *in der Schule*.
3. Stuttgart liegt *in Baden-Württemberg*.
4. *Herr Gruber* arbeitet in Köln.
5. Ich werde *den Beamten* fragen.
6. *Viele Touristen* kommen zum Musikfest nach Salzburg.
7. Wir fahren vielleicht später *in die Stadt*.
8. Andreas braucht *das Geld* nicht.
9. Angelika und Diana gehen heute *ins Kino*.
10. Er ruft *Jürgen* zu Hause an.

VII. Complete each sentence.

1. Dieser Film _____.
2. Verstehst du _____?

3. Er geht _____.

4. Um wieviel Uhr _____?

5. Jeden Tag muß ich _____.

6. Nach der Schule will ich _____.

7. Was machst du _____?

8. Wirst du später _____?

VIII. Situation A

Beckers möchten nach Deutschland fahren. Herr Becker will gern nach München in Bayern fahren, aber Frau Becker will lieber nach Köln am Rhein fahren. Herr Becker macht den Vorschlag: „Warum fahren wir nicht zuerst nach Köln und dann nach München?" Frau Becker ist das recht. Zwei Monate später kommen sie nach Hamburg. Von dort fahren sie über Hannover weiter nach Köln. Sie bleiben drei Tage in Köln und fahren dann über Stuttgart nach München.

Fragen

1. Wohin möchte Frau Becker fahren?

2. Wo liegt Köln?

3. Wohin kommen sie zuerst?

4. Wie viele Tage bleiben sie in Köln?

5. Wohin fahren sie zuletzt?

Situation B

Herr Wenzel arbeitet schon zehn Jahre in einem Büro in der Stadt. Jeden Morgen muß er schon um sieben Uhr sein Haus verlassen. Bis in die Stadt sind es nur fünfzehn Minuten. Er geht meistens zu Fuß. Es ist zu viel Verkehr in der Stadt und für sein Auto gibt es dort keinen Parkplatz. Er ist immer der erste im Büro. Herr Wenzel geht um vier Uhr wieder nach Hause.

Fragen

1. Wo arbeitet Herr Wenzel?

2. Um wieviel Uhr geht er zur Arbeit?

3. Wie kommt er in die Stadt?

4. Hat Herr Wenzel ein Auto?

5. Was macht er um vier Uhr?

IX. Substitute an appropriate pronoun for the italicized words.

Beispiel: *Der Zug* kommt in fünf Minuten.
Er kommt in fünf Minuten.

1. Wo ist *die Haltestelle?*

2. Kennen Sie *Herrn Fellner?*

3. *Das Kino* ist gleich um die Ecke.

4. Fragen Sie *die Verkäuferin!*

5. *Die Zeitung* kostet 80 Pfennig.
6. *Frau Höhne* arbeitet heute nicht.
7. *Der Student* studiert Mathematik.
8. Wir brauchen *den Koffer-Kuli.*
9. Verstehst du *die Frau?*
10. Ich lese *das Buch* gern.

Nützliche Ausdrücke

Here is a summary of some phrases that you may find useful to know when starting a conversation in German:

Sprechen Sie Englisch?	Do you speak English?
Verstehen Sie mich?	Do you understand me?
Ich spreche nur wenig Deutsch.	I speak only a little German.
Bitte, sprechen Sie etwas langsamer.	Please, speak a little more slowly.
Wiederholen Sie bitte!	Please repeat.
Ich verstehe Sie sehr gut.	I understand you very well.
Ich bin Amerikaner.	I am an American (male).
Ich bin Amerikanerin.	I am an American (female).
Woher kommen Sie?	Where are you from?
Ich komme aus...	I come from...
Ich bin seit zwei Wochen in Deutschland	I have been in Germany for two weeks.
Mein Name ist...(Ich heiße...)	My name is...

Ich komme aus Leipzig.

Cultural Notes

Greetings

Guten Tag! (Hello!)	is the most commonly used greeting throughout the day. *Tag!* is more commonly heard in conversations.
Grüß Gott! (Hello!)	is used by people in Southern Germany when greeting each other.
Grüß dich! (Hello!)	is frequently heard among young adults in Southern Germany.
Servus! (Hello!)	is used occasionally by young people in Southern Germany and Austria. Sometimes *"Servus!"* is used to say "Hello!" and "Good-bye!"
Grüzü! (Hello!)	is heard primarily in the northern part of Switzerland. It means the same as *"Grüß dich!"*
Guten Morgen! (Good morning!)	is used during the morning hours. *Morgen!* is more casual and heard quite frequently.
Guten Abend! (Good evening!)	is used during the evening hours until midnight. Many Germans, however, will simply say *'n Abend!*
Auf Wiedersehen! (Good-bye!)	is the most commonly used good-bye phrase. In conversation, Germans will simply say *Wiedersehen!*
Auf Wiederhören! (Good-bye!)	is used when ending a telephone conversation. It means "hope to hear you again." More casually, a person will say *Wiederhören!*
Tschüs! (Good-bye!)	is the most common good-bye phrase in Northern Germany. It is very casual, however, and only used among good friends and relatives. *Tschüs* originated from the French *adieu.*
Pfüat di! (Good-bye!)	is used mostly in Austria and means *"Behüt dich Gott!"*

Telephone

When answering the phone, whether at home or in the office, it is customary in Germany to give one's family name. *(Weber!* or *Hier Weber!)* Young people usually answer the phone with their first and last name.

When calling someone you know, you would say, *Hier ist...* If you don't know the person, you should start out with, *Mein Name ist...*

Asking to be transfered to someone else, the caller may say, for instance, *Guten Tag, hier ist Weber, ich möchte Herrn Müller sprechen, bitte!* or *Könnte ich bitte Herrn Müller sprechen?* or *Bitte verbinden Sie mich mit Herrn Müller.*

Company operators often answer calls with an additional *Guten Tag* or *Grüß Gott.* When transferring a call they will say, *Moment (Augenblick), bitte* or *ich verbinde* (I'll connect you).

The official word for telephone is *Fernsprecher,* but everyone says *Telefon.* The word for phone booth is *die Telefonzelle.* These public phone booths are easily recognized by their bright yellow color. There are always public phones in local post offices and railroad stations.

Most phones have dialing instructions clearly posted. In calling you should follow these steps:

1. Lift the receiver.
2. Put your coins in the slot (two 10 pfennig coins for local calls).
3. Wait for the dial tone.
4. Dial the number.

Long distance calls to other German cities or foreign countries can be made from any phone booth marked *Ausland.* Of course, these calls can be made from any post office, hotel or private phones. If you place a long distance call, you should know the *Vorwahl* or *Vorwahlnummer* (area code). In case you don't know this number, you can either look it up in a telephone directory or call the *Auskunft* (information). The number for the *Auskunft* is: 118.

Long distance calls are measured by units *(1 Einheit = 23 Pfennig).* For instance, a person from Munich may call his/her friend in Hamburg for 1 mark but only be able to talk to him/her for a very short time. The caller must feed the coin-operated phone with additional coins, whenever there is little money left as indicated by lit-up numbers; otherwise s/he will be disconnected immediately.

ein
Fernsprecher

eine
Telefonzelle

Money

There are eight different coins in German money (BRD).

    1 Pfennig
    2 Pfennig
    5 Pfennig
  10 Pfennig (called *ein Groschen*)
  50 Pfennig
    1 Mark (100 Pfennig)
    2 Mark
    5 Mark

There are seven different banknotes (BRD).

    5 DM (Deutsche Mark)
  10 DM
  20 DM
  50 DM
 100 DM
 500 DM
1 000 DM

Deutsche Mark

Train Stations

In German train stations you will find two large schedules prominently posted. One is marked *Ankunft* (arrival), the other *Abfahrt* departure). There are several columns on the *Ankunft* schedule with the following heading: *Zeit* (time), *Zug Nr.* (train number), *aus Richtung* (from) and *Gleis* (track). The *Abfahrt* schedule indicates the same type of information for departing trains.

Tickets are bought at the window marked *Fahrkarten* (tickets). In case you have any questions you would simply inquire at the office marked *Information* or *Auskunft* (information). You could also ask the official *(Beamte)* in the blue uniform wearing a cap with a yellow band inscribed with the word *Information*.

der Hauptbahnhof in München

der Beamte

Streetcars and Subways

In most cities tickets for streetcars must be bought in advance. You can buy your ticket from an automat, which is usually right at the streetcar stop.

There are several German cities with subway systems (Berlin, Hamburg, Munich, Frankfurt). Some Germans buy their tickets from an automat if they travel by subway infrequently. Others have *Zeitkarten* (season or subscription tickets valid for a week or a month) which are used by daily commuters. In Hamburg and Munich, a practical system has been introduced; the same ticket is valid for all means of transportation — the subway *(U-Bahn)*, city train *(S-Bahn)*, streetcars *(Straßenbahnen)*, buses *(Busse)* and in Hamburg even river boats and ferries.

Purchase tickets at an automat.

eine Straßenbahn in Freiburg

Dialog

In der Bank

1. ANGESTELLTER:	Guten Tag!
DAME:	Guten Tag! Ich möchte Reiseschecks einlösen.
1. ANGESTELLTER:	Für welchen Betrag?
DAME:	100 Dollar, bitte.
1. ANGESTELLTER:	Kann ich bitte Ihren Paß sehen?
DAME:	Bitte schön.
1. ANGESTELLTER:	Vielen Dank.
DAME:	Wie steht der Kurs heute?
1. ANGESTELLTER:	Der Dollar steht bei 2 Mark 62. Gehen Sie mit dem Abschnitt an die Kasse, bitte.
DAME:	Hier ist mein Abschnitt.
2. ANGESTELLTER:	Wie möchten Sie das Geld haben?
DAME:	In Fünfzigern und Zwanzigern.
2. ANGESTELLTER:	50... 100... 150... 200... 220... 240... 260. Die Gebühr ist 2 Mark.
DAME:	So, jetzt kann ich wenigstens einkaufen gehen.
2. ANGESTELLTER:	Ja, mit dem Geld können Sie schon etwas kaufen.
DAME:	Das hoffe ich auch.
2. ANGESTELLTER:	Viel Spaß!

You may want to review different denominations of coins and bank notes (Lektion A).

Fragen über den Dialog

1. Was will die Dame in der Bank tun?
2. Wie viele Dollar möchte sie einlösen?
3. Was will der Angestellte sehen?
4. Wohin soll die Dame mit dem Abschnitt gehen?
5. Wie viele Mark bekommt sie?
6. Was will die Dame mit dem Geld machen?

...hange American traveler's checks, it is quite common to go to one counter first, have the check approved, get a numbered slip of paper, go to the ...ier and pick up the cash. A small fee is usually required, unless the check has already been converted to marks. Of course, then you may go ...ctly to the cashier and get the cash right away.

At the Bank

EMPLOYEE 1:	Hello!
LADY:	Hello! I would like to cash traveler's checks
EMPLOYEE 1:	For what amount?
LADY:	100 dollars, please.
EMPLOYEE 1:	Can I see your passport, please?
LADY:	Here you are.
EMPLOYEE 1:	Thank you very much.
LADY:	What's the exchange rate today?
EMPLOYEE 1:	The dollar is at 2 marks 62. Go to the cashier with the slip, please.
LADY:	Here is my slip.
EMPLOYEE 2:	How would you like to have the money?
LADY:	In fifties and twenties.
EMPLOYEE 2:	50… 100… 150… 200… 220… 240… 260. The fee is 2 marks.
LADY:	So, at least I can go shopping now.
EMPLOYEE 2:	Yes, with the money you can buy something all right.
LADY:	I hope so, too.
EMPLOYEE 2:	Have fun!

Nützliche Ausdrücke

Review these expressions after students have covered the material in the *Dialog* and *Lesestück 1*.

Wie steht der Kurs heute?	What's the exchange rate today?
Der Dollar steht bei…	The dollar is at…
Gehen Sie an die Kasse, bitte.	Go to the cashier, please.
Das hoffe ich auch.	I hope so, too.
Viel Spaß!	Have fun!
Er hat viel vor.	He is planning a lot.
Ich parke bei der Parkuhr.	I'm parking at the parking meter.
Wie ist die Auswahl?	How is the selection?
Sie begutachten die Waren.	They are looking the goods over.
Die Hose gefällt Heike.	Heike likes the pants.
Die Hose steht Heike gut.	The pants look good on Heike.
Ich bin an der Reihe.	It's my turn.

Sie begutachtet die Waren.

124

Personalize the questions by having students ask each other these questions: *Was hat Peter an?, Was hat Helga an?*, etc. Other questions: *Wie ist die Bluse? Sie ist schön.* If possible, use pictures students have cut out of magazines to further illustrate clothing items.

Ergänzung

1. Kleidungsstücke

Was hat er an?
Er hat einen Pullover an.
Was hat sie an?
Sie hat einen Rock an.

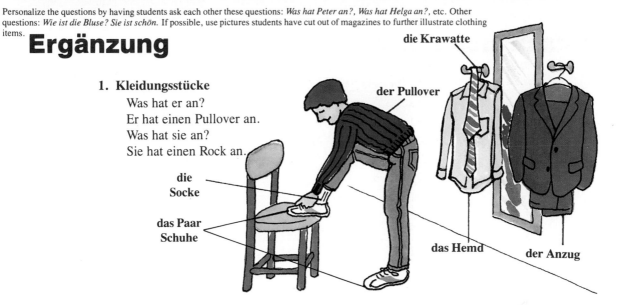

die Krawatte
der Pullover
die Socke
das Paar Schuhe
das Hemd
der Anzug

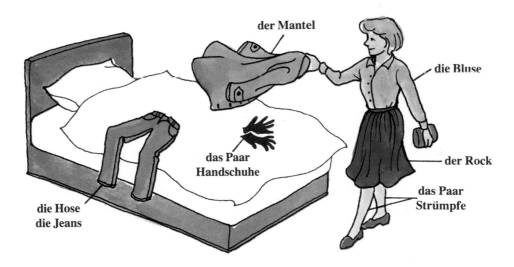

der Mantel
die Bluse
das Paar Handschuhe
der Rock
das Paar Strümpfe
die Hose
die Jeans

2. Farben

Welche Farbe hat die Hose?
Sie ist schwarz.

schwarz	grau
weiß	gelb
blau	grün
braun	rosa
rot	orange

Include colors in the questions above: *Welche Farbe hat Pauls Hose?, Ist Ursulas Pullover rot oder grün?*, etc.

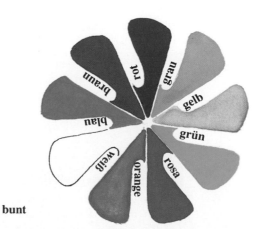

rot
grau
braun
gelb
blau
grün
weiß
orange
rosa

bunt

Aussprachҽübung

Practice the sound by having students repeat words at a fast pace. Use the description of sound formation, if needed.

/ sch /		
schon	sprechen	Stadt
schnell	Spaß	Straße
schade	Sprache	Stunde
schwarz	später	Strumpf
schreiben	Spiel	stellen
Geschichte	Sport	Studium
Geschwister	gespannt	bestimmt
Vorschlag	besprechen	bestehen

[ʃ] s — sound (*schon*): The lips are rounded and protrude distinctly. The apex is slightly retracted and the tongue arches, thus making contact with the palate.

Übungen

Dative

Indirect object

In the sentence *Ich kaufe ein Buch*, you know that *Ich* is the subject, *kaufe* is the verb, and *ein Buch* is the direct object or accusative. Now consider this sentence: *Ich kaufe dem Freund eine Karte.*

In this sentence *dem Freund* is called the indirect object or dative. Whereas *eine Karte* is directly connected with the action of the verb, *dem Freund* is indirectly connected with the verb and therefore called the indirect object. The easiest way to identify the indirect object is to determine if "to" or "for" can be put before the noun. In the above example, it would be "I am buying a ticket *for* the friend." (or: "I am buying the friend a ticket.")

	Singular			Plural
	masculine	*feminine*	*neuter*	
nominative	der	die	das	die
	ein	eine	ein	
accusative	den	die	das	die
	einen	eine	ein	
dative	dem	der	dem	den
	einem	einer	einem	

To form the dative plural noun an -*n* or -*en* is added to the plural, unless the plural noun already ends in -*n* or -*s*. The dative plural article is always *den*, regardless of the gender of the noun.

Folgt den Beispielen!

1. Ich zeige der Dame den Paß.

Variation: Ask the question:
*Was zeigt du der Dame?
(Herr — Was zeigst du dem
Herrn?)*

	Ich zeige der Dame den Paß.
Herr	Ich zeige dem Herrn den Paß.
Mädchen	Ich zeige dem Mädchen den Paß.
Beamter	Ich zeige dem Beamten den Paß.
Angestellter	Ich zeige dem Angestellten den Paß.
Verkäuferin	Ich zeige der Verkäuferin den Paß.
Onkel	Ich zeige dem Onkel den Paß.

2. Geben Sie dem Bruder die Karte!

	Geben Sie dem Bruder die Karte!
Schwester	Geben Sie der Schwester die Karte!
Junge	Geben Sie dem Jungen die Karte!
Platzanweiser	Geben Sie dem Platzanweiser die Karte!
Mädchen	Geben Sie dem Mädchen die Karte!
Dame	Geben Sie der Dame die Karte!
Verkäuferin	Geben Sie der Verkäuferin die Karte!

3. Wir zeigen dem Herrn die Stadt.

Variation: Ask the question:
Wem zeigen wir die Stadt?
*(…dem Herrn,…dem
Besucher).* You may want to
introduce *Wem?* at this point
(following *Übung 8.*)

	Wir zeigen den Herren die Stadt.
Besucher	Wir zeigen den Besuchern die Stadt.
Dame	Wir zeigen den Damen die Stadt.
Tourist	Wir zeigen den Touristen die Stadt.
Student	Wir zeigen den Studenten die Stadt.
Frau	Wir zeigen den Frauen die Stadt.
Mädchen	Wir zeigen den Mädchen die Stadt.

4. Gebt doch den Besuchern einen Fahrplan!

	Gebt doch den Besuchern einen Fahrplan!
Amerikaner	Gebt doch den Amerikanern einen Fahrplan!
Student	Gebt doch den Studenten einen Fahrplan!
Tourist	Gebt doch den Touristen einen Fahrplan!
Junge	Gebt doch den Jungen einen Fahrplan!
Dame	Gebt doch den Damen einen Fahrplan!

Verbs Followed by the Dative Case

There are a number of verbs in German that require the dative case. Some of these verbs are *antworten* (to answer), *glauben* (to believe), *gefallen* (to like, please), *passen* (to fit, suit).

Examples: *Antworten Sie dem Herrn!*
Er glaubt der Verkäuferin.

Folgt den Beispielen!

5. Glaubst du dem Jungen nicht?

Variation: Glaubst du dem Jungen nicht? Doch, ich glaube dem Jungen.

Amerikanerin	Glaubst du dem Jungen nicht?
Tourist	Glaubst du der Amerikanerin nicht?
Mädchen	Glaubst du dem Touristen nicht?
Schüler	Glaubst du dem Mädchen nicht?
Frau	Glaubst du dem Schüler nicht?
Verkäuferin	Glaubst du der Frau nicht?
	Glaubst du der Verkäuferin nicht?

6. Er antwortet dem Touristen.

Variation: Antwortet sie dem Touristen? Ja, sie...

Student	Er antwortet dem Touristen.
Freund	Er antwortet dem Studenten.
Dame	Er antwortet dem Freund.
Verkäuferin	Er antwortet der Dame.
Mädchen	Er antwortet der Verkäuferin.
	Er antwortet dem Mädchen.

7. Die Jeans gefallen dem Mädchen.

Schüler	Die Jeans gefallen den Mädchen.
Amerikanerin	Die Jeans gefallen den Schülern.
Verkäuferin	Die Jeans gefallen den Amerikanerinnen.
Dame	Die Jeans gefallen den Verkäuferinnen.
Tourist	Die Jeans gefallen den Damen.
Besucher	Die Jeans gefallen den Touristen.
	Die Jeans gefallen den Besuchern.

8. **Construct meaningful sentences using the cue words given.**

   1. Ich / glauben / Dame / kein / Wort
   2. Student / zeigen / Tourist / Stadt
   3. Kaufen / du / Mädchen / Paar Handschuhe
   4. Warum / antworten / Sie / Beamter / nicht
   5. Wir / geben / Angestellter / Geld
   6. Können / du / Herr / Zeit / sagen
   7. Hose / passen / Junge / sehr gut
   8. Stehen / Tante / Kleid

The Question Word: *Wem?*

You are already familiar with the question word *wer*? (who), which refers to the subject (person), and the question word *wen*? (whom), which refers to the direct object (person). The question word *wem*? (to whom or for whom) refers to the dative case (person).

Examples: *Sie glauben **dem** Mädchen. **Wem** glauben sie?*
*Wir kaufen **der** Tante eine Bluse. **Wem** kaufen wir eine Bluse?*

Folgt dem Beispiel!

Variation: Have students
provide the complete answer.

9. Wem wirst du es zeigen?   Der Dame.
   (Dame)

Wem wirst du es bringen?   Dem Freund.
   (Freund)

Wem wirst du es sagen?   Der Verkäuferin.
   (Verkäuferin)

Wem wirst du es glauben?   Der Freundin.
   (Freundin)

Wem wirst du es bringen?   Dem Vater.
   (Vater)

Wem wirst du es zeigen?   Der Schwester.
   (Schwester)

Dative Prepositions

The dative case always follows these prepositions:

aus	out of, from
außer	besides, except
bei	with, near, at
mit	with
nach	after, to
seit	since
von	from, of
zu	to, at

Examples: *Er kommt aus der Schule.*
         Ich habe außer einem Bruder auch eine Schwester.
         Herr Schulz wohnt beim See.
         Kommst du mit einer Freundin?
         Wohin gehen wir nach dem Film?
         Seit einem Jahr wohne ich hier.
         Ich komme vom Kino.
         Sie fahren zum Bahnhof.

Contractions

These dative prepositions and articles are contracted as long as there is no special emphasis on the article.

bei	+	dem	=	beim
von	+	dem	=	vom
zu	+	dem	=	zum
zu	+	der	=	zur

Folgt den Beispielen!

10. Sie wartet beim Eingang.   **Sie wartet beim Eingang.**

Variation: *Wo wartet er? Er wartet beim Eingang.*

    Kino   **Sie wartet beim Kino.**

    Uni   Sie wartet bei der Uni.

    Kasse   Sie wartet bei der Kasse.

    Bank   Sie wartet bei der Bank.

    Schule   Sie wartet bei der Schule.

    Haus   Sie wartet beim Haus.

11. Wohin gehst du? (Bahnhof)   **Ich gehe zum Bahnhof.**

    Wohin gehst du? (Bank)   Ich gehe zur Bank.

    Wohin gehst du? (Haus)   Ich gehe zum Haus.

    Wohin gehst du? (Schule)   Ich gehe zur Schule.

    Wohin gehst du? (Universität)   Ich gehe zur Universität.

    Wohin gehst du? (Eingang)   Ich gehe zum Eingang.

12. Was kaufst du außer einem Anzug?   **Was kaufst du außer einem Anzug?**

Variation: Answer the question instead. *(Ich brauche außer einem Anzug noch einen Mantel.)*

    Mantel   **Was kaufst du außer einem Mantel?**

    Hose   Was kaufst du außer einer Hose?

    Buch   Was kaufst du außer einem Buch?

    Krawatte   Was kaufst du außer einer Krawatte?

    Hemd   Was kaufst du außer einem Hemd?

13. Woher kommst du? (Haus)   **Aus dem Haus.**

Variation: Have students answer with different responses.

    Woher kommst du? (Kino)   Aus dem Kino.

    Woher kommst du? (Schule)   Aus der Schule.

    Woher kommst du? (Stadt)   Aus der Stadt.

    Woher kommst du? (Büro)   Aus dem Büro.

    Woher kommst du? (Bank)   Aus der Bank.

14. Was machen wir nach der Klasse?   **Was machen wir nach der Klasse?**

    Film   **Was machen wir nach dem Film?**

    Vorstellung   Was machen wir nach der Vorstellung?

    Schule   Was machen wir nach der Schule?

    Reise   Was machen wir nach der Reise?

    Kino   Was machen wir nach dem Kino?

15. Komm doch mit dem Freund!   **Komm doch mit den Freunden!**

    Komm doch mit dem Mädchen!   Komm doch mit den Mädchen!

    Komm doch mit dem Jungen!   Komm doch mit den Jungen!

    Komm doch mit der Freundin!   Komm doch mit den Freundinnen!

    Komm doch mit dem Besucher!   Komm doch mit den Besuchern!

    Komm doch mit dem Angestellten!   Komm doch mit den Angestellten!

16. Provide the proper preposition and the correct form of the definite article. Use these prepositions: *aus, außer, bei, mit, nach, seit, von, zu.*

1. Wir kommen _____ Geschäft.
2. Wohnst du weit _____ Bahnhof?
3. Ich bin _____ Monat Juni nicht mehr zu Hause.
4. Sie stehen direkt _____ Eingang.
5. Ursula geht _____ Freundin ins Kino.
6. Ich werde eine Karte _____ Herrn bekommen.
7. _____ Uni fahren wir _____ Eisdiele.
8. Parken Sie Ihren Wagen _____ Parkuhr!
9. _____ Geld kannst du bestimmt etwas kaufen.
10. Warum kommt ihr so spät _____ Schule?

17. Complete the following sentences.

1. Wir fahren mit _____.
2. Er kommt aus _____.
3. Antworte _____.
4. Kannst du _____ sagen?
5. Die Schüler gehen nach _____ zur _____.
6. Sie werden beim _____ warten.
7. Ich sage _____ auf deutsch.
8. Die Schuhe gefallen _____.

18. Beantwortet diese Fragen!

Students should be encouraged to come up with varied answers.

1. Mit wem kommst du?
2. Von wem wirst du etwas hören?
3. Wem paßt die Hose?
4. Wem zeigst du die Stadt?
5. Bei wem wohnst du?
6. Wem möchtest du die Karten kaufen?

19. Change the following sentences from the singular to the plural.

> **Beispiel:** *Sie kommt aus dem Kino.*
> *Sie kommen aus den Kinos.*

1. Ich wohne beim Fluß.
2. Der Tourist kommt von der Stadt.
3. Glaubst du dem Mädchen nicht?
4. Das Kleid steht der Amerikanerin gut.
5. Der Beamte antwortet dem Besucher.
6. Er parkt das Auto bei der Parkuhr.
7. Der Schüler geht zum Zug.

20. **Supply the definite article for the dative or accusative. Contract the preposition and the article wherever possible.**

1. Geben Sie _____ Verkäuferin _____ Geld!
2. Sie kommen aus _____ Geschäft.
3. Die Studenten gehen mit _____ Kassetten zu _____ Sprachlabor.
4. Können Sie _____ Buch lesen?
5. Wir sagen es _____ Platzanweiser.
6. Sprechen Sie doch mit _____ Angestellten!
7. Kannst du _____ Schüler _____ Computer zeigen?
8. Die Touristen fahren zu _____ Bergen.
9. Was kaufst du außer _____ Bluse?
10. Bei _____ Besuchern gibt es immer viel Spaß.
11. Mußt du heute nicht zu _____ Uni gehen?
12. Und was macht ihr nach _____ Vorstellung?

Expression of Quantity: *Wieviel?* (How much?) — *Wie viele?* (How many?)

Generally speaking, *wieviel?* is used when expressing a mass or a sum.

Examples: *Wieviel Uhr ist es?*
Wieviel kostet der Pullover?

On the other hand, *wie viele?* is used when referring to items that can be counted.

Examples: *Wie viele Karten brauchen wir?*
Wie viele Freunde hast du?

NOTE: The words *ein paar* (a few) and *ein Paar* (a pair) also express quantity. Note that the "*P*" in "ein *Paar*" (meaning "a matching pair") is always capitalized.

Folgt dem Beispiel!

21. Wir kaufen *vier* Karten.   Wie viele Karten kaufen wir?

Ask different questions. (Wer kauft vier Karten?, Was kaufen wir?)

Ich habe *etwas* Geld.   Wieviel Geld habe ich?
Die Dame kauft *zwei* Kleider.   Wie viele Kleider kauft die Dame?
Die Klasse beginnt um *elf* Uhr.   Um wieviel Uhr beginnt die Klasse?
Zehn Touristen fahren nach Deutschland.   Wie viele Touristen fahren nach Deutschland?
Drei plus fünf ist *acht*.   Wieviel ist drei plus fünf?
Er braucht *fünf* Reiseschecks.   Wie viele Reiseschecks braucht er?

22. *Wieviel?* oder *Wie viele?*

1. _____ Zeit hast du morgen?
2. _____ Geld brauchen wir denn?

3. _____ Tage bleiben Sie in Europa?

4. _____ Studenten studieren in Würzburg?

5. _____ Reiseschecks wollen Sie einlösen?

6. _____ Krawatten wirst du kaufen?

7. _____ ist neun und acht?

8. _____ kostet diese Reise?

Compound Nouns

The article of a compound noun is determined by the article of the last word in the compound.

Examples: der Nachbar, das Land = das Nachbarland
die Reise, der Scheck = der Reisescheck
das Haus, die Aufgabe = die Hausaufgabe

23. **Match the words on the right with those on the left to determine the proper compound noun. Also provide the article and the meaning of each compound noun.**

1. die Straße	die Sprache	If you have German newspapers or magazines, have students look for additional compound nouns. They may have to use a dictionary to determine the meaning.
2. der Winter	der Anweiser	
3. die Kleidung	der Sportler	
4. der Platz	die Abteilung	
5. die Dame	der Scheck	
6. die Geburt	der Tag	
7. die Mutter	der Schuh	
8. die Reise	die Aufgabe	
9. die Bank	das Stück	
10. das Haus	die Bahn	
11. die Hand	der Angestellte	
12. der Abend	das Brot	

Die Schweiz ist ein Nachbarland der BRD.

Lesestück 1

Heike und Birgit gehen einkaufen

Heike und Birgit gehen gern zusammen einkaufen. Zur Innenstadt° ist es zu Fuß zu weit. Deshalb° sprechen sie mit Heikes Vater. Herr Gruber hat heute sowieso° vor, in die Stadt zu fahren. Manchmal ist es nicht leicht im Zentrum einen Parkplatz zu finden. Heute hat Herr Gruber aber Glück. Er parkt den Wagen° direkt an einer Parkuhr.

Birgit möchte lieber im Kaufhof° einkaufen. Da ist die Auswahl immer groß. Herr Gruber will auch etwas kaufen. Er sagt den Mädchen, sie sollen in einer halben Stunde beim Eingang° warten.

Im Schaufenster° begutachten Birgit und Heike die vielen Waren. Birgit gefällt besonders eine Handtasche°. Vielleicht wird sie diese kaufen. In der Damenabteilung° findet Heike eine Hose. Sie ist rot und gefällt Heike gut. Birgit glaubt auch, daß die Hose Heike gut steht. Soll sie die Hose anprobieren°? Birgit zeigt auf den Preis. Die Hose ist sehr preiswert°. Heike zieht die Hose in einer Umkleidekabine° an°. Birgit muß zugeben°, daß Heike die Hose gut paßt.

Birgit möchte ein Paar Socken kaufen. Die Socken sind weiß. Sie sind auch nicht teuer°. Heike und Birgit gehen an die Kasse. Dort bezahlen° sie für die Hose und die Socken.

Herr Gruber hat vor, in drei Wochen mit der Familie in den Schwarzwald° zu fahren. Deshalb sucht er in der Bücherabteilung eine Karte von Süddeutschland. Er findet sie auch sofort° und wartet an der Kasse, bis er an der Reihe ist. Die Karte ist nicht sehr preiswert, aber auf der Reise kann er sie bestimmt° gut gebrauchen. Später kommen Herr Gruber, Heike und Birgit wieder aus dem Geschäft° und gehen zum Auto zurück°.

downtown
therefore
anyhow

car

name of department store

entrance

display window
purse
ladies' department

try on
reasonable/zieht... an *put on/fitting room/admit*

expensive
pay

Black Forest
right away

undoubtedly
store/gehen... zurück *go back*

Soll Heike die Hose anprobieren?

Fragen über das Lesestück

1. Warum wollen Heike und Birgit mit dem Auto in die Stadt fahren?
2. Wo parkt Herr Gruber das Auto?
3. Warum kauft Birgit gern im Kaufhof ein?
4. Wie lange werden Heike und Birgit einkaufen gehen?
5. Was möchte Birgit vielleicht kaufen?
6. Was probiert Heike an?
7. Was muß Birgit zugeben?
8. Sind die Socken preiswert?
9. Was kauft Birgit? Und Heike?
10. Wohin werden Grubers fahren?
11. Was kauft Herr Gruber?
12. Warum muß Herr Gruber warten?

Erweiterung

24. Which word from the list best describes each statement?

1. Dort studieren die Studenten.	Bank
2. Ich muß da bezahlen.	Geld
3. Ein Zug kommt dort pünktlich an.	Innenstadt
4. Wir probieren die Jeans dort an.	Mietshaus
5. Dort werde ich Reiseschecks einlösen.	Universität
6. Ich brauche es. Dann kann ich einen Mantel kaufen.	Umkleidekabine
7. Dort kann man Kleidungsstücke kaufen.	Gymnasium
8. Mein Wagen steht dort.	Haltestelle
9. Die Schüler lernen dort.	Bahnhof
10. Viele wohnen da.	Geschäft
11. Die Straßenbahn steht da.	Kasse
12. Dort gibt es viel Verkehr.	Parkplatz

25. Write a sentence in German defining the following words.

Beispiel: *Kino*
Dort läuft ein Film.

1. Büro
2. Fluß
3. Land
4. Kleidungsstück
5. Buch
6. Familie
7. Haus
8. Sprache
9. Koffer
10. Schule

26. Beantwortet die folgenden Fragen!

Beispiel: *Ist das Hemd weiß? Nein,…*
Nein, das Hemd ist nicht weiß. Es ist blau.

1. Ist die Krawatte bunt? Ja,…
2. Ist der Pullover grün? Nein,…
3. Sind die Handschuhe preiswert? Nein,…
4. Sind die Socken schwarz? Ja,…
5. Ist der Mantel teuer? Nein,…
6. Ist die Bluse braun? Nein…

27. Wie heißt das auf deutsch?

1. Go to the cashier's counter!
2. I would like to see your passport.
3. Do you have a slip (of paper)?
4. I'm wearing a suit.
5. Does she wear a blouse?
6. They would rather listen to music.
7. Wait at the entrance, please.
8. I have to admit that it fits well.
9. It's his turn.
10. We hope that, too.

28. Beantwortet die Fragen! Encourage varied responses.

Wie steht der Dollar heute?
Was sollst du mit dem Abschnitt machen?
Wem mußt du das sagen?
Was hast du heute an?
Was möchtest du kaufen?
Um wieviel Uhr kommst du aus der Schule?
Was machst du dann?
Was ist sehr preiswert?
Und was ist teuer?

Rückblick If any of these exercises are difficult, you may want to go back to the lesson in which the particular grammar point was explained.

I. Form questions asking for the italicized words. Use the question words *wer, wen, wem* or *was*.

1. Wir zeigen *den Besuchern* den Computer.
2. *Der Zug* steht schon da.
3. *Wir* haben Lust, heute abend ins Kino zu gehen.
4. Du sollst *der Tante* das Wörterbuch geben.
5. Ich kann *die Bedeutung* nicht verstehen.
6. Peter wird mit *den Studenten* sprechen.
7. Marion und Angelika kaufen *eine Gitarre*.

8. Du mußt *dem Beamten* glauben.

9. Die Geschwister werden *beim Onkel* wohnen.

10. *Die Verkäuferinnen* gehen um fünf nach Hause.

11. Die Mädchen besuchen *Heike*.

12. Ich kann *Jürgen* kein Wort sagen.

II. Change the following sentences from the present to the future tense.

1. Der Film aus Amerika läuft lange.

2. Ist das der Dame recht?

3. Wir gehen heute nachmittag zur Bank.

4. Gewinnen Sie das Spiel?

5. Ich löse ein paar Reiseschecks ein.

6. Birgit und Heike geben zu, daß die Hose gut paßt.

7. Hast du keine Zeit?

8. Warum fahren wir nicht nach Deutschland?

III. Complete the sentences using the modal auxiliary given plus a verb form of your choice where needed.

Beispiel: (*wollen*) _____ *du ein Hemd* _____?
Willst du ein Hemd kaufen?

1. (sollen) Susanne _____ bis morgen das Buch _____.

2. (mögen) _____ ihr die Kalte Platte nicht?

3. (werden) Uwe _____ die Kassette _____.

4. (können) _____ Sie die Reiseschecks _____?

5. (wollen) Wir _____ kein Englisch _____.

6. (dürfen) Ich _____ um drei in die Stadt _____.

7. (müssen) _____ ihr schon so bald _____?

IV. Complete each sentence with the proper form of one of these modal auxiliaries: *dürfen, können, müssen, sollen, wollen.*

1. Könnt ihr heute nachmittag ins Kino gehen? Wir haben Lust, aber wir _____ die Hausaufgaben machen.

2. Zuerst muß ich das Buch lesen, dann _____ ich zur Eisdiele mitkommen.

3. Frau Müller, ich habe keine Zeit. Ich _____ nicht mit Gabriele in die Stadt fahren.

4. _____ du nach Deutschland fahren? Ja, aber eine Reise ist sehr teuer.

5. Dein Vater sagt, du _____ um zehn Uhr zu Hause sein.

V. Select the proper verb form from the list on the next page and complete each sentence. Be sure to separate the prefix, where appropriate.

1. Was _____ ihr heute nachmittag _____? Das wissen wir noch nicht.

2. _____ Sie doch _____ in die Stadt, Herr Schmidt! Wir werden ein paar Kleidungsstücke kaufen.

3. Ich muß _____, die Physikaufgaben sind sehr leicht.

4. Um sieben Uhr _____ ich _____. Der Spielfilm soll sehr interessant sein.

5. Paßt die Hose? Ich weiß nicht. Ich _____ sie lieber erst _____.

6. Der Zug steht schon da. _____ Sie bald _____!

7. Wo ist das Telefon? Ich will Werner sofort _____.

8. Ich _____ nur einen Reisescheck _____. Ich brauche nicht viel Geld.

9. Wo ist die Universität? Ich komme direkt aus der Stadt. Schade. _____ Sie _____! Die Uni ist nur einen Kilometer von hier.

10. _____ du lieber im Zentrum _____? Ja, die Auswahl ist dort viel größer.

anprobieren	einsteigen
einkaufen	anrufen
fernsehen	vorhaben
zugeben	zurückgehen
einlösen	mitkommen

VI. Supply the proper form of *kennen* or *wissen*.

1. Ich _____ nicht, wo sie wohnt.

2. _____ Sie die Amerikanerin?

3. Wie heißt das auf deutsch? _____ du das?

4. Wir _____ Würzburg sehr gut.

5. _____ ihr, wie das Mädchen heißt?

6. Willst du mit Ursula ins Kino gehen? Aber ich _____ sie doch gar nicht.

7. Jörg _____ nicht, was er jetzt machen soll.

Lesestück 2

Die Schweiz

Die Schweiz ist ein sehr beliebtes Land. Jedes Jahr kommen viele Besucher° in die Schweiz. Dieses kleine Land paßt ungefähr 190 mal in die Vereinigten Staaten (ohne Alaska und Hawaii). Die Schweiz ist halb so groß wie der Staat South Carolina. — *visitors*

Die Schweiz hat fünf Nachbarländer: Frankreich, Italien, Österreich, Liechtenstein und die Bundesrepublik Deutschland. Mehr als sechs Millionen Menschen° wohnen in diesem Land. 65% sprechen Deutsch, 18% Französisch, 12% Italienisch und 5% andere Sprachen°. Die Nationalfahne ist rot und hat ein weißes Kreuz° in der Mitte. — *people* / *languages* / *cross*

Der größte Teil der Schweiz liegt in den Bergen. Die Alpen erreichen° eine Höhe° von über 4 600 m (Monte Rosa). Der Rhein ist der längste Fluß in der Schweiz. Er fließt 376 Kilometer durch das Land und dann weiter durch die Bundesrepublik Deutschland und die Niederlande zur Nordsee°. — *reach/height* / *North Sea*

Die größte Stadt der Schweiz ist Zürich. Diese Stadt liegt am Zürichsee. Die zweitgrößte Stadt ist Basel. Wie Zürich liegt auch Basel im Norden der Schweiz. Der Rhein fließt durch Basel. Genf ist eine weitere Großstadt. Diese Stadt liegt im Süden am Genfer See, direkt an der Grenze° zu Frankreich. Bern, die Hauptstadt der Schweiz, ist die viertgrößte Stadt und liegt im Westen. Eine andere — *border*

Bern ist Hauptstadt der Schweiz.

Viele Besucher kommen im Winter in die Schweiz.

Basel liegt im
Norden der Schweiz.

große und beliebte Stadt ist Luzern. Diese Stadt liegt in der Mitte
der Schweiz.

Während der Sommermonate besuchen viele Touristen die
Schweiz sehr gern. Hier können sie viel in den Bergen wandern°.   *hike*
Besonders im Winter zeigen Besucher viel Interesse in die Schweiz
zu kommen. Während der Wintermonate ist die Schweiz ein Paradies für Wintersportler.

Fragen über das Lesestück

1. Besuchen viele Touristen die Schweiz?
2. Wie groß ist die Schweiz?
3. Wie heißen die Nachbarländer der Schweiz?
4. Wie viele Einwohner hat die Schweiz?
5. Sprechen alle Deutsch?
6. Ist das Land in der Schweiz flach?
7. Wohin fließt der Rhein von der Schweiz aus weiter?
8. Wie heißen die drei größten Städte in der Schweiz?
   Wo liegen sie?
9. Wie heißt die Hauptstadt der Schweiz?
10. Wo liegt Luzern?
11. Kommen Besucher nur im Sommer in die Schweiz?

Sprachspiegel

I. Write one or two paragraphs describing the following sequence of events:

Have some of the students read their version. Students may want to ask some questions about it.

You're driving to the center of the city to look for a bank. There is a lot of traffic, but finally you find a parking meter close to the bank. You go into the bank where you wait at a counter. Finally, it's your turn. You inquire about today's currency exchange rate and decide how many traveler's checks you wish to change. The clerk asks for your passport. S/he tells you that you speak German very well. S/he gives you a slip of paper and asks you to go to another counter. There you tell another clerk the denominations in which you would like to receive your money. S/he complies with your request and you thank him or her. Then you leave the bank and decide to do some shopping.

II. Answer the following questions with as much detail as possible.

1. Du hast 200 Mark. Was möchtest du kaufen?
2. Was hast du heute an? Welche Farben haben die Kleidungsstücke?
3. Wo gehst du gern einkaufen? Warum?
4. Probierst du gern Kleidungsstücke an? Warum? Warum nicht?

Die Mädchen gehen gern einkaufen.

Welche Farben haben die Blusen? (Bonn)

Wie sagt man's?

Have students act out some of these mini-dialogs.

Ich möchte einen Reisescheck einlösen.
Darf ich Ihren Paß sehen?
Ja, hier bitte.

Der Kurs ist heute zwei Mark siebzig.
Gut. Dann löse ich 50 Dollar ein.
Bitte sehr. Zwei Fünfziger, ein Zwanziger und das Kleingeld.

Gibt es eine Bank in der Nähe?
Ja, direkt am Bahnhof.
Und wo ist der?
Gehen Sie Richtung Stadtmitte. Dann fragen Sie noch einmal.

Ich suche etwas als Geschenk für meinen Bruder.
Wir haben diese Krawatten. Gar nicht teuer.
Ja, sie sind sehr preiswert.
Möchten Sie die blaue hier?
Nein, geben Sie mir lieber die bunte.

Wo kann ich hier Bücher kaufen?
Suchen Sie etwas besonderes?
Ja, ein Wörterbuch.

Wie gefällt Ihnen diese Bluse?
Ganz gut. Sie ist aber nicht sehr preiswert.
Kommen Sie nächste Woche. Dann kostet sie nur 50 Mark.

Zeigen Sie mir bitte Kassetten!
Besondere Musik?
Moderne Musik aus Amerika.
Kommen Sie bitte hierher!

Wo bekomme ich einen Anzug?
In der Herrenabteilung.
Und eine Landkarte?
In der Bücherabteilung dort drüben.

Willst du die Hose anprobieren?
Sie ist viel zu teuer.
Aber sie steht dir gut.
Ich glaube auch.

Zungenbrecher

Find out how many times your students can say this tongue twister without any mistakes.

Sieben Schneeschaufler schaufeln sieben Schaufeln Schnee.
(Seven snow shovelers shovel seven shovels snow.)

Kulturecke

Shopping

Americans planning to shop in Germany should become familiar with the German monetary system. There are six different bills: 500 marks, 100 marks, 50 marks, 20 marks, 10 marks and 5 marks, which is not much in circulation any longer. The denominations are easily recognized — the larger the size of the bill, the greater the value. There are eight different coins: 5 marks, 2 marks, 1 mark, 50 pfennigs, 10 pfennigs, 5 pfennigs, 2 pfennigs and 1 pfennig.

German shops are not open as many hours as American stores. Although stores are open Monday through Friday from about 8:00 or 9:00 A.M. until about 6:00 P.M., they close on Saturday at 2:00 P.M., except on the the first Saturday of each month and the four Saturdays before Christmas. Banks and small stores usually close for a two-hour break at noon.

Most Germans go shopping several times a week to take care of their daily needs. Signs posted outside the shops indicate what kind of commodity is being sold. Germans usually buy their breads and rolls fresh at the local bakery (*Bäckerei*). There are some 200 different kinds of bread (*Brot*), 30 kinds of rolls (*Brötchen oder Semmeln*) and no less than 1,200 different kinds of pastries. Wherever there is a bakery, the butcher shop (*Metzgerei*) is not far away. There are many different types of butcher shops, most of which highlight their own homemade sausages. There are more than 1,500 different kinds of German sausages — raw, boiled, smoked, seasoned in various ways and shaped in all kinds of forms.

Two thirds of all Germans like to do some of their shopping at the local market (*Markt*), which is usually in the vicinity of the main shopping area of the town or city. Market day (*Markttag*) is held once or twice a week. Germans prefer to buy their fresh vegetables and fruits at the market. And they love flowers. Therefore, it is not surprising to see colorful flower stands at every market.

Most of the shopping, however, is done in the supermarkets (*Supermarkt*) found throughout the country. At these chain-operated stores, the shopper can purchase all items necessary for daily living. The big, American-style department store (*Kaufhaus*) also plays an important role, particularly in the larger towns and cities. As a matter of fact, American influence is readily noticed in stores throughout much of Germany.

There are still differences, however. A *Drogerie* is not the same as an American drugstore. A *Drogerie* will sell toilet articles, household cleaners, baby food, camera supplies, wallpapers, paints and even seeds. It does not fill prescriptions, though, and you will not find a lunch counter or soda fountain either. An *Apotheke* (pharmacy) sells both prescription and non-prescription medicines.

To buy clothes and shoes, an American should study the German measurement system carefully. The measurements are considerably different and can easily create problems, unless there is some reference to the American system. In cities, you will find a great variety of shoe stores (*Schuhgeschäfte*) and clothing stores (*Kleidergeschäfte*). American-made jeans have been popular among Germans for many years. Every average-sized town and city has specialty jeans shops. The American influence on dry-cleaning stores becomes quite apparent. More and more Germans take their clothes to a dry-cleaner (*Reinigung*).

Germans enjoy more leisure time than ever before. Therefore, it is not surprising to find numerous stores catering to leisure-time activities. A store marked *Spiel und Freizeit* attracts that group of people. German parents buy many toys for their children. Numerous toy stores (*Spielwaren*) attest to that fact. Reading is an important pastime. There are many newspaper stands where local, national and sometimes international newspapers and magazines, as well as postcards and stamps are sold. Many bookstores (*Buchhandlungen*) display their books outside of the shop so that people can browse and decide which book they want to buy.

ein Kaufhaus (Heidelberg)

Die meisten Deutschen gehen ein paar
Mal die Woche einkaufen. (Freiburg)

eine Bäckerei (Essen)

Heute ist Markttag. (Freiburg)

Was kauft
diese Dame?

For the camera buff, German cameras have long been known for their superior quality. Camera equipment and film can be bought at camera shops (*Fotogeschäfte*) found all over. American music has always been popular with Germans. Record shops (*Schallplattenge-schäfte*) sell many recordings of current American hits. These stores, of course, also sell audio cassettes and have added video cassettes in recent years. As a matter of fact, there are now specialty stores in Germany that rent video cassettes to the home market.

Every week millions of Germans participate in the various national lotteries ranging from the number lottery (*Lotto*) to the soccer lottery (*Toto*). They buy their lottery tickets in a *Lotteriegeschäft*. During the summer months, the highways are overcrowded because many Germans go on vacation trips. The travel business is brisk, and numerous travel bureaus (*Reisebüros*) offer specialty rates.

As a traveler, you will be impressed with the abundance of specialty shops. For example, candy stores offer a huge selection of sweets, both typical and exotic, to whet your appetite. You might come by a shop that sells only different kinds of teas (*Teeladen*) or a store that offers a variety of different kinds of fruits (*Früchtehaus*). And, finally, you may be in the heart of the Black Forest and stand in front of a clock shop (*Uhrengeschäft*) where the whole store front has been turned into one gigantic cuckoo clock.

ein Schallplattengeschäft (Neuß)

ein Lotteriegeschäft (Darmstadt)

Was kann man in diesem Geschäft kaufen? (Wiesbaden)

Vokabeln

der **Abschnitt,-e** slip (of paper)
der **Angestellte,-n** employee (male)
    anhaben to have on
    anprobieren to try on
    anziehen to put on (clothes)
der **Anzug,-̈e** suit
    außer besides, except
die **Auswahl** selection, choice
die **Bank,-en** bank
    begutachten to look over, evaluate
    bestimmt undoubtedly, certainly
der **Betrag,-̈e** amount
    bezahlen to pay
    bitte please
    blau blue
die **Bluse,-n** blouse
    braun brown
die **Bücherabteilung,-en** book department
    bunt colorful
die **Dame,-n** lady
die **Damenabteilung,-en**
    ladies' department
    daß that
    deshalb therefore
    direkt direct, immediate, straight
der **Dollar,-s** dollar
der **Eingang,-̈e** entrance
    einlösen to cash (in)
die **Farbe,-n** color
    Französisch French (language)
die **Gebühr,-en** fee
    gefallen to like
        Es gefällt mir. I like it.
    gelb yellow
das **Geschäft,-e** store
    grau gray
    grün green
der **Handschuh,-e** glove
die **Handtasche,-n** purse
das **Hemd,-en** shirt
    hoffen to hope
die **Hose,-n** pants, slacks
    Ihr your (formal)
die **Innenstadt,-̈e** downtown, center of city
    Italienisch Italian (language)
die **Jeans** (pl.) jeans
die **Kalte Platte** cold-cut platter
die **Karte,-n** map
die **Kasse,-n** cashier's counter
der **Kaufhof** name of department store
das **Kleid,-er** dress
das **Kleidungsstück,-e** article of clothing
die **Krawatte,-n** tie
der **Kurs,-e** exchange

der **Mantel,-̈** coat
    orange orange
das **Paar,-e** pair
das **Paradies,-e** paradise
    parken to park
der **Parkplatz,-̈e** parking space, parking lot
die **Parkuhr,-en** parking meter
der **Paß,-̈sse** passport
der **Preis,-e** price
    preiswert reasonable
die **Reihe,-n** row
        Er ist an der Reihe. It's his turn.
der **Reisescheck,-s** traveler's check
der **Rock,-̈e** skirt
    rosa pink
das **Schaufenster,-** display window
der **Schuh,-e** shoe
der **Schwarzwald** Black Forest
die **Socke,-n** sock
    sofort right away, immediately
der **Sommermonat,-e** summer month
    sowieso anyhow, anyway
der **Spaß** fun
        Viel Spaß! Have fun!
der **Strumpf,-̈e** stocking
    teuer expensive
die **Umkleidekabine,-n** fitting room
    vorhaben to plan, intend
der **Wagen,-** car
die **Ware,-n** product, goods
    wenigstens at least
der **Wintermonat,-e** winter month
    zeigen auf to point to
das **Zentrum,-tren** center
    zugeben to admit
    zurückgehen to go back

Dialog

This is a first-class German hotel in Deggendorf, a southern German city.

Im Hotel

FRAU BINDER:	Endlich sind wir da!
HERR BINDER:	Ich kann gleich hier beim Eingang parken.
FRAU BINDER:	Hast du das Gepäck?
HERR BINDER:	Was heißt Gepäck? Wir haben nur einen Koffer. Ich bringe ihn gleich mit.
FRAU BINDER:	Das stimmt. Wir bleiben ja nur zwei Tage hier.
JAN BINDER:	Das Hotel ist aber toll! Ganz elegant!
HERR BINDER:	Kommt! Gehen wir hinein!

_han law requires that all guests must fill out a _ration form._

HERR BINDER:	Haben Sie noch Zimmer frei? Wir sind drei Personen.
ANGESTELLTE:	Für drei Personen? Ja, das geht. Bitte füllen Sie das Anmeldeformular aus.
FRAU BINDER:	Du meine Güte! Was Sie alles wissen wollen!
ANGESTELLTE:	So, hier ist Ihr Zimmerschlüssel. Sie haben Zimmer 28. Fahren Sie am besten mit dem Fahrstuhl. Oder warten Sie! Ich komme mit und zeige Ihnen das Zimmer.

_ets are not very common _rman hotels._

ANGESTELLTE:	Zimmer 28, bitte schön.
FRAU BINDER:	Es sieht ja ganz gemütlich aus.
JAN BINDER:	Aber das Beste ist doch der Fernsehapparat.

Fragen über den Dialog

1. Wo parkt Herr Binder?
2. Wie viele Koffer haben Binders?
3. Wie viele Tage wollen sie im Hotel bleiben?
4. Was muß Herr Binder ausfüllen?
5. Wie kommen Binders zum Zimmer 28?
6. Wer zeigt Binders das Zimmer?
7. Wie sieht das Zimmer aus?
8. Was gefällt Jan?

In the Hotel

MRS. BINDER: We are finally here.

MR. BINDER: I can park right here at the entrance.

MRS. BINDER: Do you have the luggage?

MR. BINDER: What do you mean by luggage? We only have one suitcase. I'll bring it along right away.

MRS. BINDER: That's true. We'll stay here for only two days.

JAN BINDER: Wow, the hotel is great. Very elegant.

MR. BINDER: Come on. Let's go inside.

MR. BINDER: Do you still have rooms? There are three of us.

CLERK: For three persons? Yes, that's possible. Please fill out the registration form.

MRS. BINDER: My goodness! All the details you want to know.

CLERK: So, here is your room key. You have Room 28. It's best that you take the elevator. Or wait! I'll come along and show you the room.

CLERK: Here you are, Room 28.

MRS. BINDER: It looks quite pleasant.

JAN BINDER: But the best is still the TV set.

Nützliche Ausdrücke

Review these expressions with your students after they have learned them in the *Dialog* and *Lesestück 1*.

Das stimmt.	That's true. That's right.
Gehen wir hinein!	Let's go inside.
Das geht.	That's possible.
Füllen Sie das Formular aus!	Fill out the form!
Du meine Güte!	My goodness!
Gehen Sie am besten…	It's best that you go…
Es sieht ganz gemütlich aus.	It looks quite pleasant.
Er stempelt den Ausweis.	He stamps the identification card.
Sie bereiten das Essen zu.	They prepare the meal.
Sie essen dasselbe.	They eat the same.
Wir machen einen Klassenausflug.	We are going on a class trip.
Ich habe Hunger.	I'm hungry.
Räumt das Geschirr ab!	Clear the dishes!
Macht die Tische sauber!	Clean the tables!

Sie macht den Tisch sauber.

Ergänzung

Ask other questions: *Wie soll das Wetter morgen sein?, Scheint die Sonne heute?, Wie ist das Wetter im Winter? (Sommer, Herbst, Frühling)*

1. Wie ist das Wetter heute?

Es ist kalt. (kühl, warm, heiß)
Es ist schön. (schlecht)
Die Sonne scheint. (Es regnet. Es schneit.)

Es ist kalt.

Es ist heiß.

2. Verkehrsmittel   Have students ask each other this question: *Wie kommst du zur Schule? (mit dem Bus, Auto, Fahrrad).*

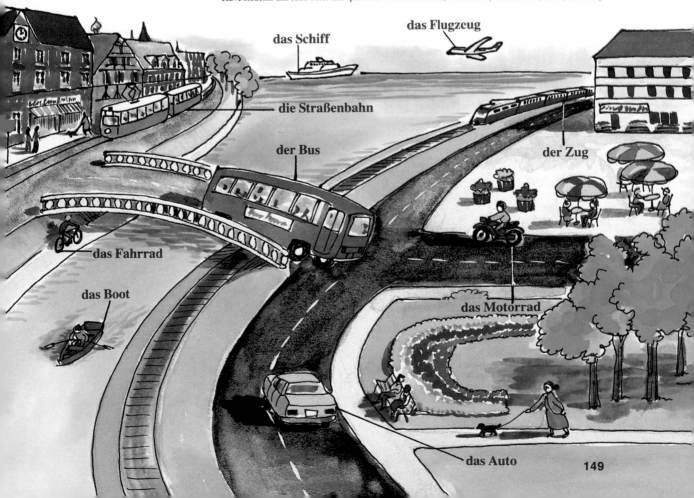

das Schiff

das Flugzeug

die Straßenbahn

der Bus

der Zug

das Fahrrad

das Boot

das Motorrad

das Auto

149

Ausspracheübung

Have students pronounce these words at a rapid pace. As this sound usually causes problems, you may want to describe the sound formation as provided.

short / ü /	long / ü /
Glück	drüben
müssen	Übung
fünf	kühl
Flüsse	Brüder
pünktlich	Schüler
dürft	Süden
gründlich	Züge
Jürgen	für
Küche	Bücher
Würste	Frühling
zurück	Güte
Günter	Tür

[Y] **short** *ü* — **sound** (*fünf*): The tongue has the same position to that of the short *i*-sound. However, the lips are positioned for a short *u*-sound.

[y:] **long** *ü* — **sound** (*Süden*): The tongue has the same position as with the long *i*-sound. However, the lips are not spread but have the same formation as for the long *u*-sound.

Übungen

Dative (Indirect Object) — Personal Pronouns

As you have already seen in the previous unit, the direct object (accusative) is the result of the action (verb) of the sentence, whereas the indirect object receives the action indirectly through the direct object.

Examples:

	dir. obj.	
Ich kaufe	eine Karte	

	indir. obj.	dir. obj.
Ich kaufe	dem Freund	eine Karte

Now substitute a personal pronoun for the indirect object in the last sentence.

	indir. obj	dir. obj.
Ich kaufe	ihm	eine Karte

Notice that there is no change in word order but simply a substitution of an indirect (dative) object pronoun. For review, the pronouns you have already learned are *also* included in the table following.

Singular			Plural		
nominative	*accusative*	*dative*	*nominative*	*accusative*	*dative*
ich	mich	mir	wir	uns	uns
du	dich	dir	ihr	euch	euch
er sie es	ihn sie es	ihm ihr ihm	sie Sie(sg. & pl.)	sie Sie	ihnen Ihnen

Folgt den Beispielen!

1. Bringst du dem Touristen das Gepäck?   Ja, ich bringe ihm das Gepäck.

Bringst du der Verkäuferin das Geld?   Ja, ich bringe ihr das Geld.

Bringst du der Mutter die Zeitung?   Ja, ich bringe ihr die Zeitung.

Bringst du der Freundin die Reiseschecks?   Ja, ich bringe ihr die Reiseschecks.

Bringst du dem Bruder den Anzug?   Ja, ich bringe ihm den Anzug.

Variation: Bringst du dem Touristen das Gepäck? (Koffer) Nein, ich bringe ihm den Koffer.

2. Zeig dem Schüler doch das Wörterbuch!   **Zeig ihm doch das Wörterbuch!**

Zeig dem Besucher doch den Fahrplan!   Zeig ihm doch den Fahrplan!

Zeig der Angestellten doch die Hose!   Zeig ihr doch die Hose!

Zeig dem Lehrer doch die Aufgabe!   Zeig ihm doch die Aufgabe!

Zeig dem Studenten doch die Kassette!   Zeig ihm doch die Kassette!

Zeig der Dame doch die Straße!   Zeig ihr doch die Straße!

Variation: Change to questions. (Zeigst du dem Schüler das Wörterbuch? Ja, ich...)

3. Kauft er mir ein Hemd?   **Kauft er mir ein Hemd?**

ihr   **Kauft er euch ein Hemd?**

Sie (form.)   Kauft er Ihnen ein Hemd?

sie (sg.)   Kauft er ihr ein Hemd?

du   Kauft er dir ein Hemd?

wir   Kauft er uns ein Hemd?

Variation: You may want to substitute objects such as Buch or Hose.

4. Geben sie uns etwas Zeit?   **Geben sie uns etwas Zeit?**

ich   **Geben sie mir etwas Zeit?**

ihr   Geben sie euch etwas Zeit?

Sie (form.)   Geben sie Ihnen etwas Zeit?

er   Geben sie ihm etwas Zeit?

sie (sg.)   Geben sie ihr etwas Zeit?

5. Es geht ihm gut.   **Es geht ihm gut.**

wir   **Es geht uns gut.**

du   Es geht dir gut.

Variation: Personalize questions. (Geht es dir/ihm/ ihr/Ihnen gut?)

ihr	Es geht euch gut.
Sie (form.)	Es geht Ihnen gut.
sie (sg.)	Es geht ihr gut.

6. Die Hose steht dir gut.

Variation: Was steht dir/ihm/ ihr gut?

Die Hose steht dir gut.	Die Hose steht dir gut.
das Kleid / sie (sg.)	Das Kleid steht ihr gut.
der Mantel / ich	Der Mantel steht mir gut.
das Hemd / er	Das Hemd steht ihm gut.
die Bluse / Sie (form.)	Die Bluse steht Ihnen gut.
der Rock / du	Der Rock steht dir gut.

7. Sprechen Sie mit der Dame!

Variation: Form questions and answers.

Sprechen Sie mit der Dame!	Sprechen Sie mit ihr!
Sprechen Sie mit dem Herrn!	Sprechen Sie mit ihm!
Sprechen Sie mit dem Angestellten!	Sprechen Sie mit ihm!
Sprechen Sie mit dem Studenten!	Sprechen Sie mit ihm!
Sprechen Sie mit der Verkäuferin!	Sprechen Sie mit ihr!
Sprechen Sie mit der Schwester!	Sprechen Sie mit ihr!

8. Wohnt der Amerikaner bei Ihnen?

Variation: Answer the question with either Ja,... or Nein,...

Wohnt der Amerikaner bei Ihnen?	Wohnt der Amerikaner bei Ihnen?
er	Wohnt der Amerikaner bei ihm?
wir	Wohnt der Amerikaner bei uns?
ihr	Wohnt der Amerikaner bei euch?
sie (sg.)	Wohnt der Amerikaner bei ihr?

9. Er kauft die Gitarre von mir.

Er kauft die Gitarre von mir.	Er kauft die Gitarre von mir.
die Karte / wir	Er kauft die Karte von uns.
das Fahrrad / du	Er kauft das Fahrrad von dir.
das Buch / ihr	Er kauft das Buch von euch.
der Pullover / Sie (form.)	Er kauft den Pullover von Ihnen.
die Bluse / sie (sg.)	Er kauft die Bluse von ihr.

10. Sollen wir mit dem Jungen spielen?

Variation: Ask additional questions using modal auxiliaries.

Sollen wir mit dem Jungen spielen?	Sollen wir mit ihm spielen?
Darf ich bei der Tante wohnen?	Darf ich bei ihr wohnen?
Wollt ihr zu der Dame kommen?	Wollt ihr zu ihr kommen?
Werden Sie bei den Freunden bleiben?	Werden Sie bei ihnen bleiben?
Möchtest du zu der Großmutter fahren?	Möchtest du zu ihr fahren?
Wird er mit dem Lehrer sprechen?	Wird er mit ihm sprechen?

11. Change the italicized nouns with their corresponding articles into pronouns.

Beispiel: *Ich zeige **dem Touristen** die Stadt.*
*Ich zeige **ihm** die Stadt.*

You may want to ask several questions about each sentence. Example for number 1: *Wer kauft der Freundin eine Bluse?, Wem kauft sie eine Bluse?, Was kauft Petra der Freundin?*

1. Petra kauft *der Freundin* eine Bluse.
2. Ich glaube *dem Herrn* nicht.
3. Kannst du *der Dame* die Zeitung bringen?
4. Wie oft kommt ihr zu *der Tante?*

5. Herr Hoffmann wohnt schon zwei Wochen bei *dem Amerikaner*.
6. Antworte *dem Lehrer* doch!
7. Er wird *der Dame* die Tasche bringen.
8. Die Kleidungsstücke gefallen *den Besuchern*.
9. Wir gehen mit *dem Onkel* ins Kino.
10. Außer *den Jungen* kommen noch viele Mädchen.

12. Supply the appropriate missing pronoun.

1. Geben Sie (me) _____ fünf Mark bitte!
2. Ich zeige (you) _____ den Weg, Herr Schulz.
3. Glaubst du (her) _____ nicht, Angelika?
4. Der Lehrer wird mit (you) _____ sprechen, Jan und Heiko.
5. Sie wohnen bei (us) _____.
6. Wir möchten es (them) _____ sagen.
7. Er kann (you) _____ das nicht kaufen, Ursula.
8. Die Schüler antworten (him) _____ nicht.

13. Answer the following questions. Use a personal pronoun in your answer.

Expand each sentence.
Example for number 1:
Warum gehst du mit ihm in die Stadt? Was macht ihr dort?

1. Gehst du mit dem Freund in die Stadt?
2. Kaufst du der Schwester eine Tasche?
3. Zeigst du dem Studenten das Gebäude?
4. Antwortest du dem Beamten?
5. Glaubst du der Verkäuferin?
6. Gefallen den Amerikanern die Berge?
7. Fahrt ihr zu der Tante?
8. Wer kommt außer dir noch mit?

Verbs with Stem Vowel Change

A number of verbs in German do not follow the regular pattern of conjugation but undergo a change in the second and third person singular. You will become familiar with two such groups of verbs, one changing from *a* to *ä*, the other one from *e* to *i* (or *ie*).

Stem vowel change *a* to *ä*
Here are the verbs with vowel changes that you already know.

	du	**er, sie, es**
fahren	fährst	fährt
tragen	trägst	trägt
verlassen	verläßt	verläßt

NOTE: When forming command forms, the familiar singular command form does not have a vowel change. For example, *Fahr nach Hause! Trag den Koffer!*

Stem vowel change *e* to *i* and *e* to *ie*

Here are the verbs with vowel changes that you already know.

	du	er, sie, es
essen	ißt	ißt
geben	gibst	gibt
sprechen	sprichst	spricht
lesen	liest	liest
sehen	siehst	sieht

Only the basic verbs (without prefixes) are listed. Verbs with separable or inseparable prefixes such as *fernsehen* or *zugeben* have the same forms as *sehen* or *geben* plus their respective prefix.

Folgt den Beispielen!

14. Wohin fährst du?

Variation: Personalize questions. *(Fährst du in die Schule/nach Hause?)*

Peter	**Wohin fährst du?**
	Wohin fährt Peter?
ihr	Wohin fahrt ihr?
der Zug	Wohin fährt der Zug?
wir	Wohin fahren wir?
die S-Bahn	Wohin fährt die S-Bahn?

15. Ich trage den Koffer.

	Ich trage den Koffer.
er	**Er trägt den Koffer.**
wir	Wir tragen den Koffer.
der Tourist	Der Tourist trägt den Koffer.
ihr	Ihr tragt den Koffer.
du	Du trägst den Koffer.

16. Er verläßt bald das Haus.

Variation: *Um wieviel Uhr verläßt du das Haus? Und du?*

	Er verläßt bald das Haus.
die Mutter	**Die Mutter verläßt bald das Haus.**
ich	Ich verlasse bald das Haus.
der Lehrer	Der Lehrer verläßt bald das Haus.
wir	Wir verlassen bald das Haus.
der Student	Der Student verläßt bald das Haus.

17. Wir sprechen Deutsch.

Variation: *Sprichst du gern Deutsch? Warum nicht?*

	Wir sprechen Deutsch.
der Herr	**Der Herr spricht Deutsch.**
ihr	Ihr sprecht Deutsch.
die Amerikanerin	Die Amerikanerin spricht Deutsch.
du	Du sprichst Deutsch.
ich	Ich spreche Deutsch.

18. Ich sehe gern fern.

Variation: *Siehst du gern fern? Welches Programm siehst du gern?*

	Ich sehe gern fern.
Jürgen	**Jürgen sieht gern fern.**
wir	Wir sehen gern fern.
die Familie	Die Familie sieht gern fern.

| ihr | Ihr seht gern fern. |
| das Mädchen | Das Mädchen sieht gern fern. |

19. Um wieviel Uhr essen wir?

Variation: Um wieviel Uhr ißt du Abendbrot? Was ißt du dann?

	Um wieviel Uhr essen wir?
die Jugendlichen	Um wieviel Uhr essen die Jugendlichen?
ihr	Um wieviel Uhr eßt ihr?
du	Um wieviel Uhr ißt du?
Herr und Frau Binder	Um wieviel Uhr essen Herr und Frau Binder?
er	Um wieviel Uhr ißt er?

20. Was lesen Sie denn?

Variation: Was liest du oft? Und du?

	Was lesen Sie denn?
die Schüler	Was lesen die Schüler denn?
du	Was liest du denn?
der Student	Was liest der Student denn?
ihr	Was lest ihr denn?
die Dame	Was liest die Dame denn?

21. Complete each sentence by providing the appropriate verb form as indicated in parentheses.

1. Die Angestellte (to speak) _____ Englisch.
2. Herr Binder (to eat) _____ schon um fünf Abendbrot.
3. (to give) _____ mir bitte etwas Geld, Susanne.
4. Die Studenten (to read) _____ das Buch sehr gern.
5. Der Junge (to admit) _____ es nicht _____.
6. Um wieviel Uhr willst du (to watch TV) _____?
7. Was (to carry) _____ du denn?
8. Die Kleidungsstücke (to like) _____ mir sehr.
9. (to see) _____ Sie die Straßenbahn?
10. Frau Reuter (to leave) _____ am Dienstag das Hotel.

Was ißt die Familie zum Abendbrot?

Lesestück 1

In der Jugendherberge

Es gibt mehr als 600 Jugendherbergen in der Bundesrepublik. Alle diese Jugendherbergen stehen in dem Buch „Deutsches Jugendherbergsverzeichnis"°. In den meisten Städten sieht man Schilder° mit dem Wort „Jugendherberge". Man braucht nur diesen Schildern zu folgen°, um eine Jugendherberge zu finden.

Register of German youth hostels/signs

follow

Viele Jugendliche° kommen mit dem Bus, mit dem Zug oder mit dem Auto. Nur wenige° kommen heute noch mit Motorrädern oder mit Fahrrädern. Für die Übernachtung° muß man einen Jugendherbergsausweis° haben. Der Herbergsvater° stempelt den Ausweis gleich nach der Ankunft° und zeigt den Jugendlichen die Zimmer, wo sie übernachten°. Viele Zimmer haben vier bis acht Betten.

young people

a few

accomodation youth hostel ID/ hostel director/ arrival

stay overnight

Man kann in einer Jugendherberge auch essen. Man bereitet das Essen in der Küche zu. Die Übernachtung und das Essen sind in einer Jugendherberge sehr preiswert. Die Jugendlichen essen in einem Speisesaal°. Natürlich gibt es keine Auswahl. Alle essen dasselbe. Viele Schüler machen Klassenausflüge zu den Jugendherbergen. Da kommen immer Lehrer° mit. Manchmal haben die Jugendlichen noch Hunger. Dann gehen sie zur Essenausgabe°. Dort bekommen sie noch etwas.

dining hall

teachers

serving counter

Eine Jugendherberge in Bonn

Die Jugendlichen essen in einem Speisesaal.

Viele Zimmer haben vier bis acht Betten.

Nach dem Essen räumen ein paar Jugendliche das Geschirr ab und bringen es in die Küche. Andere machen die Tische sauber. In einer Jugendherberge gibt es vieles°, was die Jugendlichen tun können. Einige° spielen immer wieder an den Automaten. Sie sind besonders beliebt. Andere spielen Schach°. Bei diesem Spiel muß man sehr viel denken°. Manche Jugendliche gehen lieber ins Freie°. Dort spielen sie Tischtennis° oder Fußball°.

many things
several

chess

think
outside/
table tennis/soccer

In einer Jugendherberge gibt es auch einen Briefkasten°, einen Briefmarkenautomaten°, Automaten für Getränke° und Süßigkeiten° und eine Telefonzelle°.

mailbox
stamp automat/
beverages
sweets/phone booth

Fragen über das Lesestück

1. Wie kann man eine Jugendherberge in einer Stadt finden?
2. Wie kommen die Jugendlichen zu den Jugendherbergen?
3. Was braucht man für eine Übernachtung?
4. Wie wissen die Jugendlichen, wo sie in der Jugendherberge übernachten?
5. Ist das Essen in der Jugendherberge teuer?
6. Wer kommt bei den Klassenausflügen mit?
7. Wo bekommen die Jugendlichen das Essen?
8. Wohin bringen die Jugendlichen das Geschirr?
9. Was können die Jugendlichen alles in einer Jugendherberge tun?
10. Was gibt es in einer Jugendherberge für die Briefe?

Erweiterung

22. *Wie ist das Wetter heute?* **Provide the answers in German as indicated.**

1. It's raining.
2. It's hot.
3. It's beautiful.
4. The sun is shining.
5. It's cold.
6. It's snowing.

You may wish to expand the expressions. *(Es ist nebelig, windig, wolkig; der Schauer, der Regen, die Sonne, die Luft; der bedeckte Himmel, ein klarer Tag)*

23. **Wie heißt das auf deutsch?**

1. Fill out the form please.
2. Show me your passport.
3. The room looks quite pleasant.
4. I'm preparing supper.
5. Are you hungry?
6. Clean the room!

7. It's best that you go to the bank.
8. Why are you stamping the passport?

24. Form complete sentences by using the cues given.

1. Fahren / Sie / mit / Fahrstuhl
2. Ich / können / bei / Eingang / parken
3. Lehrer / zeigen / ich / Computer
4. Jungen / kaufen / Mädchen / Kassette
5. Kleid / gut stehen / Dame
6. Angestellten / sprechen / mit / wir

25. Complete the following sentences.

Encourage students to come up with creative sentences.

1. _____ mit dem Auto?
2. _____ Bücher.
3. Um wieviel Uhr _____ Mittagessen?
4. _____ das Gepäck?
5. _____ oft Deutsch, Martin?
6. Die Touristen _____ die Berge.

26. Wie heißt das auf deutsch?

Beispiel: It's best that you go home.
Geh am besten nach Hause!

1. It's best that you go downtown.
2. It's best that you drive to Munich.
3. It's best that you see the movie.
4. It's best that you clear the dishes.
5. It's best that you ask him.
6. It's best that you prepare the meal.

27. Beantwortet die Fragen!

Students should come up with as many answers as possible.

Wo mußt du das Auto parken?
Was sollst du ausfüllen?
Wie ist das Wetter heute?
Machst du manchmal einen Klassenausflug?
Um wieviel Uhr ißt du Abendbrot?
Was spielst du gern?
Gehst du gern ins Freie? Was machst du dort?

Was machen die Jugendlichen? (Ulm)

Rückblick

If your students have any difficulties with some of the review material, you may want to go back to the lesson in which the particular grammar point was discussed. Select some of the related exercises.

I. Complete the sentences using the information given plus the infinitive form of a verb of your choice where needed.

Beispiel: *(müssen)* _____ du die Reiseschecks _____?
Mußt du die Reiseschecks einlösen?

1. (sollen) Wir _____ das Anmeldeformular _____.
2. (dürfen) _____ ihr dort _____?
3. (werden) _____ du nach Hause _____?
4. (können) Er _____ gut Gitarre _____.
5. (mögen) _____ du das nicht?
6. (müssen) Die Schüler _____ die Aufgaben _____.
7. (wollen) Ich _____ ein Motorrad _____.

II. Complete each sentence by supplying the appropriate form of the article as well as one of these prepositions: *aus, außer, bei, mit, von* or *zu*. Contract preposition and article whenever possible.

1. Die Studenten kommen _____ Sprachlabor.
2. Wohnen Sie _____ Hotel?
3. Wer kommt _____ Lehrer noch mit?
4. Fahren Sie _____ Zug nach München!
5. Wir warten _____ Eingang.
6. Die Touristen machen eine Reise _____ Bergen.
7. Um wieviel Uhr kommen die Besucher _____ Theater.
8. Ich muß noch schnell _____ Bank gehen.
9. Herr Schmidt fährt _____ Jungen und Mädchen _____ Jugendherberge.
10. Wirst du das Buch _____ Dame bekommen?

III. Complete the following sentences.

1. Das Auto steht nicht weit von _____.
2. Außer _____ spielt auch Birgit Musik.
3. Sie fahren zu _____.
4. Um wieviel Uhr kommt ihr aus _____?
5. Wir möchten ein Zimmer mit _____.
6. Nach _____ können wir zur Eisdiele gehen.
7. Die Touristen fahren von _____ zu _____.
8. Wohnt er nicht bei _____?

IV. Put each verb into the present and then into the future tense.

1. du / fahren
2. ich / fernsehen
3. ihr / lesen
4. der Lehrer / sprechen
5. die Dame / lesen

V. Provide the proper personal pronouns (dative or accusative) for the italicized words.

1. Fragen Sie *den Beamten* bitte!
2. Ich gehe mit *Hans* zur Schule.
3. Wie viele Monate wohnst du schon bei *der Dame*?
4. Der Amerikaner kann *die Verkäuferin* nicht verstehen.
5. Wir werden *den Jungen* suchen.
6. Was bekommst du von *der Mutter*?
7. Sprechen Sie doch mit *dem Herrn*!
8. Um wieviel Uhr soll ich *Frau Binder* anrufen?

VI. Unscramble each sentence and rewrite it so that each one makes sense.

1. Schule / sein / müssen / Mädchen / um / in / die / der / acht / Uhr
2. Nicht / wir / wissen / kommt / Straßenbahn / wann / die
3. Kino / Lust / ins / wir / gehen / keine / haben / zu
4. Reise / Dieter / ich / möchten / eine / Deutschland / machen / und / nach
5. Zug / Studenten / Hamburg / mit / fahren / die / dem / nach

Lesestück 2A

Bonn — die Hauptstadt der BRD

Bonn, die Hauptstadt der Bundesrepublik Deutschland, liegt links° vom Rhein. Auf der anderen Seite liegt das Siebengebirge. Die Bundeshauptstadt hat ungefähr 300 000 Einwohner. Seit 1949 ist Bonn das Zentrum der politischen Ereignisse° in der BRD. Von besonderem Interesse für Besucher sind die verschiedenen° Regierungsgebäude°. Das Bundeshaus° zum Beispiel ist sehr bekannt. Hier versammeln sich° oft der Bundestag° und der Bundesrat°. Alle Abgeordneten° haben ihre Büros im Bundeshochhaus. Der Bundespräsident wohnt in der Villa Hammerschmidt.

Bonn ist eine interessante Stadt. In der Innenstadt liegt der Marktplatz°. Dort ist ein paar Mal in der Woche Markttag. Die Leute° kommen dann in die Stadt und gehen auf dem Markt einkaufen. Am Marktplatz ist auch das Rathaus°. Es ist schon 250 Jahre alt und sieht wie ein Schloß° aus.

Bonn ist auch eine kulturelle Stadt. Sie ist zum Beispiel die Geburtsstadt von Beethoven. Viele Touristen besuchen das Beethovenhaus. Es sieht heute noch so aus wie zu Beethovens Zeit. Das Städtische Kunstmuseum° hat eine große Sammlung° von Gemälden° (1945 bis heute). Die Bonner Universität ist schon 200 Jahre alt. Sie bietet° den Studenten eine gute Möglichkeit zum Studium. Gleich in der Nähe von der Universität steht das Münster°. Es ist schon 900 Jahre alt. Der Turm° in der Mitte ist 92 Meter hoch.

left

events
various/government buildings
Federal Building
meet/House of Representatives/ Senate/representatives

market square
people
city hall
castle

City Art Museum/ collection
paintings
offers
cathedral
tower

die Universität

Das Rathaus ist direkt am Markt.

das
Bundeshochhaus

Viele Leute kommen mit dem Schiff nach Bonn. Auf dem
Rhein können sie noch viele andere Sehenswürdigkeiten° sehen.   *sights*

Fragen über das Lesestück

1. Wo liegt das Siebengebirge?
2. Wie viele Einwohner hat Bonn?
3. Warum ist das Bundeshaus so bekannt?
4. Welches Gebäude hat viele Büros für Abgeordnete?
5. Warum ist der Marktplatz so interessant?
6. Warum ist Bonn eine kulturelle Stadt? Gib ein paar Beispiele!
7. Wie alt ist das Bonner Münster?
8. Wie kommen viele Leute nach Bonn?

Lesestück 2B

Berlin (Ost) — die Hauptstadt der DDR

Berlin, die größte deutsche Stadt, liegt im Osten der DDR. Berlin hat zwei Teile, Ost und West. Ost-Berlin ist die Hauptstadt der DDR. Das Symbol von Ost-Berlin ist der Fernsehturm°; er ist der zweitgrößte in Europa. Vom Fernsehturm hat man einen guten Blick auf die ganze Stadt. In der Hauptstadt der DDR gibt es viele Regierungsgebäude, wie zum Beispiel das Staatsratsgebäude°. Der ,,Palast der Republik" ist nicht nur ein politisches, sondern auch° ein kulturelles Zentrum. Hier gibt es ein Theater, Restaurants und sogar ,,Bowling".

TV Tower

Council of State Building
nicht nur...sondern auch
not only...but also

der Alexanderplatz

Im Palast der Republik gibt es ,,Bowling".

Man hat viele Gebäude renoviert.

Der Alexanderplatz ist eine andere bekannte Sehenswürdigkeit. Der Mittelpunkt° vom Alexanderplatz ist die Weltzeituhr°. Sie zeigt die genaue° Zeit in den großen Städten der ganzen Welt°. Am Alexanderplatz sieht man viele Restaurants, Cafés und Hotels. Es gibt dort auch historische Gebäude°, wie zum Beispiel das „Rote Rathaus". Auf der anderen Seite steht die Marienkirche, die älteste° Kirche° Berlins; sie ist 700 Jahre alt.

focal point/ World Time Clock exact/world

buildings

oldest/church

Eine große und bekannte Straße heißt „Unter den Linden". In dieser Straße findet man die Deutsche Staatsoper°. Gleich gegenüber° ist die Humboldt-Universität. Dort studieren viele Studenten aus der DDR und aus anderen Ländern. Ein paar hundert Meter weiter steht das Mahnmal für die Opfer des Faschismus°. Jede Stunde kann man hier die Wachablösung° sehen. Das ist sehr interessant.

State Opera

across

Memorial for the Victims of Fascism changing of the guard

Berlin hat viele Seen und Wälder°. Touristen kommen oft zum Müggelsee und fahren mit der „Weißen Flotte"°. Es gibt eine Auswahl von verschiedenen Schiffen. Manche Besucher fahren nur eine oder zwei Stunden, andere fahren sogar den ganzen Tag auf dem See herum.

forests name of group of boats

In Ost-Berlin kann man heute noch einige alte Gebäude sehen. Die meisten Gebäude hat man aber ganz renoviert. Viele Berliner wohnen außerhalb° in neuen Wohnvierteln°.

outside (of city)/ residential areas

Fragen über das Lesestück

1. Was ist das Symbol für Ost-Berlin?
2. Was gibt es alles im „Palast der Republik"?
3. Was ist die Weltzeituhr? Und wo kann man sie finden?
4. Wo steht die Deutsche Staatsoper?
5. Was kann man beim Mahnmal für die Opfer des Faschismus sehen?
6. Wohin fahren die Touristen gern?
7. Wo wohnen viele Berliner heute?

Sprachspiegel

u may want to have dents work in groups and ate a dialog together. Have ch group act out their own rsion of their creative fort.

I. Create a dialog. You have been driving for a long time, and you are anxious to find a hotel room. Your conversation is with the hotel clerk. Be as creative as possible.

II. Answer the questions with as much detail as possible.

1. Was hast du in dem Koffer?
2. Was mußt du alles ausfüllen?
3. Gibt es in der Schule eine Essenausgabe?
4. Was spielst du gern?
5. Machst du manchmal einen Ausflug? Wohin?

III. Write or talk about the German *Jugendherberge*.

Students should be prepared to write a short paragraph or develop a dialog. If your students have too many difficulties, you may ask some questions about the *"Jugendherberge."*

Wie sagt man's?

Was kostet bei Ihnen ein Einzelzimmer?
80 Mark pro Nacht, mit Bad.
Mit Frühstück?
Ja, natürlich.

Ich brauche ein Doppelzimmer.
Für wie lange?
Für drei Tage.
Einen Moment…Ja, das geht noch.

Füllen Sie bitte dieses Formular aus?
Bitte schön, hier ist es.
Gibt es im Zimmer auch ein Telefon?
Ja, das haben Sie.

Haben Sie noch ein Zimmer frei?
Leider nicht.
Gibt es hier in der Nähe noch ein anderes Hotel?
Ja, fragen Sie mal im Hotel *Schreiber*.

Ich möchte um halb sieben aufstehen.
Gut. Ich rufe Sie um 6 Uhr 30 an.
Vielen Dank.
Gute Nacht, mein Herr.

Spiel nicht immer an den Automaten!
Es macht doch so viel Spaß.
Das schon, aber es kostet auch viel Geld.
Ich bezahle es ja.

Ich muß Sabine sofort anrufen.
Das sollst du gleich tun.
Wo gibt es denn ein Telefon hier?
Da drüben ist eine Telefonzelle.

Wann macht ihr denn einen Klassenausflug?
Am Freitag.
Und wohin werdet ihr fahren?
In die Berge.

Zungenbrecher Find out who can say this tongue twister the fastest and without making mistakes.

Ein krummer Krebs kroch über eine krumme Klammer.
(A crooked crab crawled over a crooked clip.)

Kulturecke 1

Foreign Influence in Germany

An American arriving in Germany might be surprised to see many non-German words on store fronts, billboards and in the media. Foreigners have had a tremendous impact on the German economy since the end of World War II. Americans have had the greatest influence of any foreign group. Fast food operations, for example, have sprung up all over Germany. Hamburgers, which were unknown ten years ago, can be bought in almost all German cities. American-style jeans are sold in numerous jeans shops in every German city. New technology, such as computers, is now in demand by German companies as well as by people for their homes. Other small businesses, such as those that do photocopying, are as popular in Germany as they are in this country.

The French influence has long been evident in the German clothing industry. When it comes to fashion, the Germans look to their neighbor for new styles and trends. Clothing stores with a French touch are usually more fashionable and, of course, more expensive. Germans also have an appetite for foreign foods. Italian cafés and pizzerias have become very popular. Oriental food is making an inroad into the German food business. There is no problem in finding Chinese-style restaurants.

About 5 million of the 62 million people who live in the Federal Republic of Germany are foreigners. The largest groups are the Turks, Yugoslavs, Italians and Greeks. Therefore, many restaurants cater to the demands of these ethnic groups. Most of these foreigners are so-called *Gastarbeiter*, who came to Germany during a time when unemployment was low and the demand for additional work force high.

American influence is seen throughout Germany.

Fast food operations have become quite popular.

As an example, there are more than 1.5 million Turks living in the Federal Republic. It is estimated that Kreuzberg, a district of West-Berlin, is now the third largest Turkish city in the world. The local stores cater to the Turkish population here. The Turks are able to buy the national foods that they are accustomed to. Local banks provide special service for these as well as other foreigners. Since many companies in West-Berlin employ the Turkish *Gastarbeiter*, they have given their Turkish workers an opportunity to voice their opinions on factory committees.

Most of the foreigners who have come to Germany have maintained their national identity. Although family members speak their native language at home, their children are usually assimilated into the social and cultural life of Germany. At various national festivals, these foreign groups present their national dances to the local audience. These festivals further illustrate the tremendous impact of foreigners living in Germany, and the numerous changes that have taken place in the German cultural life.

Italian foods are particularly in demand.

Foreigners in Germany have maintained their identity.

There are numerous ethnic restaurants.

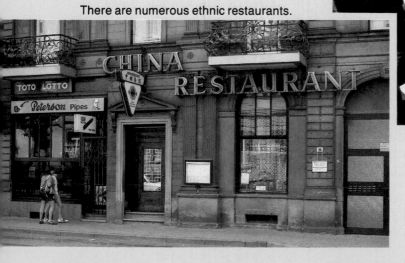

Kulturecke 2

German Influence in the United States

The first German settlers came to America over 300 years ago. Ever since their early arrival, Germans have played a significant role in our national life. One of the most famous Germans to play a historic role in America was General von Steuben, who organized the Revolutionary Army under George Washington. A monument in his honor is a Milwaukee landmark. Another well-known German is Carl Schurz, who fled to the United States where he later became a senator from Missouri and then Secretary of the Interior under President Hayes. During the summer various celebrations take place in the Carl Schurz Memorial Park in Nashota, Wisconsin.

German influence is more obvious in the many U.S. cities where streets have been named after German cities and personalities. As they enter the town of Frankenmuth, Michigan, as visitors are welcomed immediately with a German *Willkommen* sign. In the center of the city a descriptive marker summarizes the history of German settlers in the early 19th century. As you look around, it may seem as if you're in a small town in Bavaria, Germany. It's no wonder that Frankenmuth has been labeled "Michigan's Little Bavaria."

German immigrants brought along know-how in farming, fine carpentry and cheese-making as well as excellence in the art of sausage-making. Wherever there are Germans, it is safe to say that a local butcher shop — offering home-made German sausage — is not too far away. Breweries, many of which are quite well-known, also show the definite influence of Germans who introduced fine beers from Germany. Similar to other nationalities, urban German settlers generally congregated in one part of a city or town. Today cities like St. Louis and Milwaukee still show evidence of this early pattern.

Frankenmuth, Michigan

German settlers came to Frankenmuth in the 19th century.

A large population of Germans came to this country in the middle of the 19th century. Many of the newcomers looked for areas resembling the terrain of their homeland. The city of Columbus, Ohio, prides itself on a picturesque section called "German Village."

It is generally assumed that Texas reflects only Spanish and Mexican influences. However, visitors to the Texas town of Fredericksburg are surprised when they are greeted in German upon entering the town. Various stores signal the German influence — clothing stores for children called *Das Kinderhaus,* a restaurant specializing in potato pancakes called *Der Kartoffelpuffer* or again the local German butcher store called *Opa's.* Not far away from Fredericksburg is another town of German origin, New Braunfels. This town was founded in 1845 by Prinz Carl von Solms-Braunfels who came from his native town of Braunfels in Hessen, Germany. The visitors are greeted with a huge billboard that reads *In New Braunfels ist das Leben schön.* Right outside the city is *Oma's Sausage Haus & Bier Garten,* which caters strictly to the tourists passing through this German settlement.

St. Louis shows the German influence.

New Braunsfels, Texas

A sign in Fredericksburg, Texas.

Many Germans settled in Texas.

Vokabeln

abräumen to clear
die **Ankunft,-̈e** arrival
das **Anmeldeformular,-e** registraton form
    ausfüllen to fill out
    aussehen to look, appear
der **Ausweis,-e** identification (card)
das **Beispiel,-e** example
    zum Beispiel for example
    best- best
    am besten the best is
das **Bett,-en** bed
das **Boot,-e** boat
der **Briefkasten,-̈** mailbox
der **Briefmarkenautomat,-en** stamp
    automat
    dasselbe the same
    denken to think
    einige a few, several
    elegant elegant
die **Essenausgabe,-n** serving counter
das **Fahrrad,-̈er** bicycle
der **Fahrstuhl,-̈e** elevator
der **Fernsehapparat,-e** television set
das **Flugzeug,-e** airplane
    folgen to follow
    frei free, available
    Freie: ins Freie outside
der **Fußball,-̈e** football
    ganz quite
die **Geburtsstadt,-̈e** native town,
    city of birth
    gemütlich pleasant
das **Geschirr** dishes
das **Getränk,-e** beverage
die **Güte** goodness
    Du meine Güte! My goodness!
    heiß hot
der **Herbergsvater,-̈** youth hostel director
    herumfahren do drive (ride) around
    hineingehen to go inside
    historisch historical, historic
das **Hotel,-s** hotel
der **Hunger** hunger
    Hunger haben to be hungry
    immer wieder again and again
    interessant interesting
    jeder each, every
die **Jugendherberge,-n** youth hostel
der **Jugendherbergsausweis,-e** youth
    hostel identification (card)
der **Jugendliche,-n** youngster, teenager,
    youth
    kalt cold
der **Klassenausflug,-̈e** class trip

    kühl cool
    kulturell cultural
der **Lehrer,-** teacher
der **Markt,-̈e** market
der **Markttag,-e** market day
die **meisten** most
    mitbringen to bring along
die **Möglichkeit,-en** possibility
das **Motorrad,-̈er** motorcycle
die **Person,-en** person
    politisch political
    regnen to rain
    renovieren to renovate
das **Restaurant,-s** restaurant
    saubermachen to clean
das **Schach** chess
    scheinen to shine
das **Schiff,-e** ship, boat
das **Schild,-er** sign
    schneien to snow
die **Seite,-n** page, side
    sogar even
die **Sonne** sun
der **Speisesaal,-säle** dining hall
    stempeln to stamp
    stimmen to be correct
    Das stimmt. That's right.
    That's true.
die **Süßigkeiten** (pl.) sweets
das **Symbol,-e** symbol
die **Telefonzelle,-n** telephone booth
das **Theater,-** theater
das **Tischtennis** table tennis
    übernachten to stay overnight
die **Übernachtung,-en** (overnight)
    accommodation
    um in order to, to
das **Verkehrsmittel,-** means of
    transportation
    warm warm
    wenige few
das **Wetter** weather
der **Zimmerschlüssel,-** room key
    zubereiten to prepare (a meal)

Birthday parties among young adults are quite common in Germany. For this party, Michael's parents prepared the buffet meal.

Dialog

Michaels Party

MICHAEL: Tag, Leute! Ich glaube, alle sind schon da.

ALLE: Herzlichen Glückwunsch zum Geburtstag!

MICHAEL: Mann, die vielen Geschenke! . . .Besonders die Bücher . . . Da kann ich viel lesen.

KERSTIN: Aber nicht jetzt. Wir sind nämlich sehr hungrig.

MICHAEL: Ralf, ist das Essen schon fertig?

RALF: Ja, es steht schon alles auf dem Tisch. Siehst du?

MICHAEL: Mmh, der Kartoffelsalat sieht lecker aus.

RALF: Ich mag die Kalte Platte.

MICHAEL: Bring mir bitte noch etwas Schinken und Käse mit.

RALF: Jetzt aber 'ran an die Arbeit!

though Germans can begin
ir driver's instruction
fore age eighteen, they
nnot receive their driver's
enses until after they have
d their 18th birthday.

KERSTIN: Mit achtzehn kannst du jetzt Auto fahren.

MICHAEL: Ja, die Fahrprüfung liegt schon hinter mir. Ich bekomme den Führerschein nächste Woche.

KERSTIN: Da warne ich euch alle. Bleibt lieber zu Hause! Unsere Straßen sind jetzt nicht mehr sicher.

Fragen über den Dialog

1. Warum sind die Jugendlichen bei Michael?
2. Warum soll Michael die Bücher jetzt nicht lesen?
3. Was steht alles auf dem Tisch?
4. Wie alt ist Michael heute?
5. Was bekommt Michael nächste Woche? Und was kann er dann tun?

Michael's Party

MICHAEL:	Hello, guys! I think everyone is here.
EVERYONE:	Happy Birthday!
MICHAEL:	Wow, that many presents . . . Especially the books . . . I can read a lot.
KERSTIN:	But not now. We're really hungry.
MICHAEL:	Ralf, is the food ready yet?
RALF:	Yes, everything is already on the table. Look!
MICHAEL:	Mmh, the potato salad looks delicious.
RALF:	I like the cold cuts.
MICHAEL:	Please bring me some ham and cheese.
RALF:	Let's go to work now.
KERSTIN:	You're eighteen. You can drive now.
MICHAEL:	Yes, the driver's test is already behind me. I'll get the driver's license next week.
KERSTIN:	I'll warn all of you. You'd better stay home. Our streets aren't safe any more.

Nützliche Ausdrücke

Review these expressions with your students. They have been covered in the *Dialog* and *Lesestück 1.*

Herzlichen Glückwunsch zum Geburtstag!	Happy Birthday!
Es steht schon auf dem Tisch.	It's already on the table.
Es sieht lecker aus.	It looks delicious.
Jetzt aber 'ran an die Arbeit!	Let's go to work now.
Es liegt schon hinter mir.	It's already behind me.
Sie kauft Fahrkarten an einem Automaten.	She buys tickets at an automat.
Ich entwerte die Fahrkarte.	I cancel the ticket.
Bekommst du einen Sitzplatz?	Are you getting a seat?
Mußt du Eintritt bezahlen?	Do you have to pay admission?
Es gibt etwas für jeden Geschmack.	They have something for everyone's taste.
Bei der Hitze . . .	In this heat . . .
Er gibt gerade bekannt, daß . . .	He is just announcing that . . .
Welche Schallplatte legst du auf?	Which record are you putting on?
Ich mache erst einmal eine Pause.	First of all I'm taking a break.
Strengt es an?	Is it strenuous?

Ergänzung

Personalize the question. Have students ask each other questions such as: *Schreibst du mit einem Kuli oder mit einem Bleistift? (Was für ein Buch hast du?, Hast du eine Schultasche? Welche Farbe?)*

1. Was brauchst du für die Schule?
   Eine Schultasche.

ein Buch
ein Heft
ein Kuli
ein Bleistift
ein Radiergummi
Papier
ein Lineal

Ask other questions: *Spielst du Gitarre?, Frag Peter, ob er ein Musikinstrument spielt? Was für ein Musikinstrument spielt er?*

2. Was für ein Musikinstrument spielst du?
   Ich spiele Gitarre.

die Trompete
das Klavier
die Blockflöte
die Klarinette
die Geige
die Flöte
das Akkordeon
die Gitarre

[œ] **short** *ö* — **umlaut***(könnt)*: The lips are slightly protruded and have the same formation as the short *o*-sound. The tongue assumes the same position as for the short *e*-sound.

[ø] **long** *ö* — **umlaut** *(Söhne)*: The lips have the same position as the long *o*-sound. The tongue assumes the position as in the long *e*-sound.

Ausspracheübung

[ɛ] **short** *ä* — **umlaut** *(Länder)*: Formation of this sound is the same as that for the short *e*-sound. The mouth is opened slightly. The lips and tongue have their approximate rest position.

Practice these words until students can say them without difficulties. Explain sound formation, if necessary.

short / ö /	long / ö /	short / ä /	long / ä /
zwölf	Söhne	Länder	Väter
können	hören	März	Nähe
Töchter	mögen	Plätze	Universität
Röcke	Österreich	Mäntel	spät
Schlösser	schön	Fläche	Fahrpläne
möchte	größte	Geschäft	Fahrräder
Köln	Flöte	gefällt	Käse

[ɛ:] **long** *ä* — **sound** *(spät)*: The articulatory features of [ɛ:] are quite similar to [ɛ]. However, for [ɛ], the degree of opening is often somewhat less than for [ɛ:].

Übungen

Possessive Adjectives (Nominative and Accusative)

A possessive adjective is a pronoun that is used as an adjective to indicate who owns the noun that follows it. It replaces the article in front of the noun and takes on the same endings as those of the indefinite article (*ein*-words).

	Nominative Singular			Plural
	masculine	*feminine*	*neuter*	
ich	mein	meine	mein	meine
du	dein	deine	dein	deine
er	sein	seine	sein	seine
sie	ihr	ihre	ihr	ihre
es	sein	seine	sein	seine
wir	unser	unsere*	unser	unsere*
ihr	euer	euere*	euer	euere*
sie	ihr	ihre	ihr	ihre
Sie	Ihr	Ihre	Ihr	Ihre

	Accusative Singular			Plural
	masculine	*feminine*	*neuter*	
ich	meinen	meine	mein	meine
du	deinen	deine	dein	deine
er	seinen	seine	sein	seine
sie	ihren	ihre	ihr	ihre
es	seinen	seine	sein	seine
wir	unseren	unsere*	unser	unsere*
ihr	eueren	euere*	euer	euere*
sie	ihren	ihre	ihr	ihre
Sie	Ihren	Ihre	Ihr	Ihre

*The e in front of the r in **unser** and **euer** is often omitted if the ending begins with a vowel.*

Folgt den Beispielen!

1. Mein Freund ist schon da.

Variation: Wer ist noch da? Meine Freundin… Dein Bruder…

    Freundin
    Tante
    Lehrer
    Schwester
    Onkel

Mein Freund ist schon da.
Meine Freundin ist schon da.

Meine Tante ist schon da.
Mein Lehrer ist schon da.
Meine Schwester ist schon da.
Mein Onkel ist schon da.

2. Wo ist euer Geschenk?

Variation: Answer the questions using the various items.

    Mutter
    Kassette
    Mantel
    Schule
    Zimmer

Wo ist euer Geschenk?
Wo ist eu(e)re Mutter?

Wo ist eu(e)re Kassette?
Wo ist euer Mantel?
Wo ist eu(e)re Schule?
Wo ist euer Zimmer?

3. Gepäck (er)
    Buch (ich)
    Fahrkarte (Sie - form.)
    Party (wir)
    Freund (sie - sg.)
    Führerschein (du)

sein Gepäck

mein Buch
Ihre Fahrkarte
uns(e)re Party
ihr Freund
dein Führerschein

4. Hast du dein Fahrrad?

Variation: Answer the question using the cues provided.

    mein Reisescheck
    seine Aufgabe
    unser Geld
    ihr Koffer
    deine Uhr

Hast du dein Fahrrad?
Hast du meinen Reisescheck?

Hast du seine Aufgabe?
Hast du unser Geld?
Hast du ihren Koffer?
Hast du deine Uhr?

5. Wir besuchen seinen Onkel.
    Schwester / mein
    Freund / unser
    Großmutter / ihr
    Bruder / euer
    Lehrer / dein

Wir besuchen seinen Onkel.
Wir besuchen meine Schwester.

Wir besuchen uns(e)ren Freund.
Wir besuchen ihre Großmutter.
Wir besuchen eu(e)ren Bruder.
Wir besuchen deinen Lehrer.

6. Brauchst du deinen Führerschein?

Variation: Answer the question with either Ja,… or Nein,…

    Geld
    Telefon
    Tasche
    Platz
    Tisch
    Fahrkarte

Brauchst du deinen Führerschein?
Brauchst du dein Geld?

Brauchst du dein Telefon?
Brauchst du deine Tasche?
Brauchst du deinen Platz?
Brauchst du deinen Tisch?
Brauchst du deine Fahrkarte?

7. Wo sind deine Socken?
    Handschuhe / euere

Wo sind deine Socken?
Wo sind eu(e)re Handschuhe?

Geschenke / seine	Wo sind seine Geschenke?
Freundinnen / unsere	Wo sind uns(e)re Freundinnen?
Zimmer / ihre	Wo sind ihre Zimmer?
Aufgaben / meine	Wo sind meine Aufgaben?

8. Sein Auto fährt schnell.　　　　　　Seine Autos fahren schnell.

Euere Gitarre ist teuer.　　　　　　Eu(e)re Gitarren sind teuer.

Dein Zimmer sieht schön aus.　　　　Deine Zimmer sehen schön aus.

Ihr Buch ist sehr interessant.　　　　Ihre Bücher sind sehr interessant.

Unsere Reise kostet nicht viel.　　　　Uns(e)re Reisen kosten nicht viel.

Mein Bruder kommt nicht mit.　　　　Meine Brüder kommen nicht mit.

9. Siehst du mein Hemd?　　　　　　Siehst du meine Hemden?

Ich suche ihren Pullover.　　　　　　Ich suche ihre Pullover.

Wir lösen unseren Reisescheck ein.　　Wir lösen uns(e)re Reiseschecks ein.

Kennst du seinen Freund?　　　　　　Kennst du seine Freunde?

Braucht er unsere Zeitung?　　　　　Braucht er uns(e)re Zeitungen?

Frag doch deinen Lehrer!　　　　　　Frag doch deine Lehrer!

10. Wen möchtest du fragen?　　　　　Meine Freunde.
　　　(Freund)

Wen möchtest du besuchen?　　　　　Meine Großväter.
　　　(Großvater)

Was wirst du brauchen?　　　　　　　Meine Kassetten.
　　　(Kassette)

Was willst du lesen?　　　　　　　　Meine Bücher.
　　　(Buch)

Wen brauchst du?　　　　　　　　　　Meine Brüder.
　　　(Bruder)

Was mußt du haben?　　　　　　　　　Meine Pässe.
　　　(Paß)

You may want to have students provide the complete answer: Ich möchte meine Freunde fragen.

11. Complete each sentence by providing the missing endings where necessary.

1. Wann ist dein _____ Geburtstag?
2. Verstehst du sein _____ Schwester?
3. Ich muß mein _____ Reiseschecks einlösen.
4. Die Jugendlichen bekommen ihr _____ Ausweis.
5. Haben Sie schon Ihr _____ Führerschein, Herr Werner?
6. Wo sind euer _____ Schilder?
7. Wir besuchen unser _____ Tante nächste Woche.
8. Brauchst du mein _____ Computer?
9. Lies doch dein _____ Buch!
10. Siehst du sein _____ Geschenke?

12. **Supply the German equivalent for the words given in parentheses.**

1. Suchen Sie (our telephone) _____?
2. Ich möchte (your bicycle) _____ kaufen, Bernd.
3. Lest ihr (your newspapers) _____?
4. Wo wohnt (your brother) _____, Herr Mendel?
5. Warum suchst du (his books) _____?
6. (My girlfriend) _____ sucht (her cassette) _____.
7. (His teacher) _____ ist sehr beliebt.
8. (Our school) _____ ist nicht weit vom Bahnhof.
9. (Their father) _____ besucht (my uncle) _____.
10. Ich werde (her guitar) _____ kaufen.

13. **Complete the following sentences, using a possessive adjective and a noun of your choice.** Find out how many variations your students can come up with.

Beispiel: *Verstehst du _____?*
Verstehst du seinen Freund?

1. Wir brauchen _____.
2. Wo sind _____?
3. Wann bekommen Sie _____?
4. _____ fährt sehr schnell.
5. Die Jugendlichen suchen _____ .
6. _____ kostet viel Geld.
7. Sie müssen _____ lesen.
8. Kannst du _____ anprobieren?
9. Möchte er _____ besuchen?
10. Bring doch _____ mit!
11. Er stempelt _____.
12. Ich fülle _____ aus.

14. **Wie heißt das auf deutsch?**

You may want to substitute other possessive adjectives to expand this exercise.

1. his shirt
2. their tables
3. my apartment
4. her money
5. our teacher
6. my bicycles
7. their mother

Comparison of Adjectives

In adjectives of comparison there are two levels of comparing that are constructed from the basic form of the adjective, i.e., the *comparative* and the *superlative*. The formation from the basic form to the superlative is similar in both languages. For instance, take the word *fast* (schnell). The comparative is *faster* (schneller) and the superlative is *fastest* (schnellst + ending).

Examples:

das schnelle Auto	the fast car
das schnellere Auto	the faster car
das schnellste Auto	the fastest car

These examples are listed here merely to illustrate the comparison of adjectives. These adjectives (because they involve endings) will be treated specifically in later units.

When the adjective is used as part of the verb, follow this example. (Notice that *am* precedes the superlative and *-en* is added.)

Paul ist pünktlich.	Paul is punctual
Maria ist pünktlicher.	Maria is more punctual.
Herbert ist am pünktlichsten.	Herbert is most punctual.

Comparison of Adverbs

The comparison of adverbs is similar to the above. Whereas the adjective (see above) modifies the noun, the adverb (see below) modifies the verb.

Examples:

Die Straßenbahn fährt schnell.	The streetcar goes fast.
Das Auto fährt schneller.	The car goes faster.
Der Zug fährt am schnellsten.	The train goes the fastest.

EXCEPTIONS: When the adjectives or adverbs end in *d, t, tz, s, ß, sch, st, x,* or *z,* the ending in the superlative has an additional *e.*

Examples: *(am) interessantesten, heißesten*

Most one-syllable adjectives or adverbs containing an *a, o,* or *u* change to *ä, ö, ü* in the comparative and the superlative.

Examples: *warm — wärmer — am wärmsten*
 groß — größer — am größten
 dumm — dümmer — am dümmsten

A few irregular forms are also listed here:

gut	besser	am besten
viel	mehr	am meisten
hoch	höher	am höchsten
nahe	näher	am nächsten
gern	lieber	am liebsten

Illustrate forms by asking some questions such as: *Bist du älter (größer) als dein Bruder/deine Schwester?, Fährst du lieber mit dem Bus oder mit dem Zug?,* etc.

When an unequal comparison is made, use the comparative form and the word *als* (meaning "than").

Example: *Er spielt besser als Hans.* He plays better than Hans.

Folgt den Beispielen!

Variation: Turn statements into questions.

15. Der Abend ist genauso heiß wie der Nachmittag.

Der Schinken ist genauso teuer wie der Käse.

Das Auto fährt genauso schnell wie der Zug.

Der Abend ist heißer als der Nachmittag.

Der Schinken ist teu(e)rer als der Käse.

Das Auto fährt schneller als der Zug.

Das Buch ist genauso toll wie der Film.　　Das Buch ist toller als der Film.

Kerstin kommt genauso spät wie　　Kerstin kommt später als Michael.
　　Michael.

Der Winter ist genauso kalt wie　　Der Winter ist kälter als der Herbst.
　　der Herbst.

Jürgen ist genauso pünktlich wie Peter.　　Jürgen ist pünktlicher als Peter.

16. Die Vorstellung beginnt spät.　　**Der Film beginnt später.**
　　(der Film)

Variation: *Was beginnt später? Der Film oder die Vorstellung?*

Am Montag ist es kühl.　　Am Dienstag ist es kühler.
　　(Dienstag)

Das Fahrrad ist schnell　　Das Motorrad ist schneller.
　　(das Motorrad)

Der Vorort ist groß.　　Die Stadt ist größer.
　　(die Stadt)

Die S-Bahn fährt langsam.　　Die Straßenbahn fährt langsamer.
　　(die Straßenbahn)

Jörg ist klug. (Monika)　　Monika ist klüger.

Die Schule sieht schön aus.　　Die Uni sieht schöner aus.
　　(die Uni)

17. Das Auto fährt schnell.　　**Das Auto fährt schnell.**

Variation: Ask personalized questions. (*Was fährt schneller?, Wer ist größer?, Wer kommt später?*, etc.)

die S-Bahn　　**Die S-Bahn fährt schneller.**
der Zug　　**Der Zug fährt am schnellsten.**

Köln ist groß.　　Köln ist groß.
München　　München ist größer.
Berlin　　Berlin ist am größten.

Sven ist klug.　　Sven ist klug.
Petra　　Petra ist klüger.
Heike　　Heike ist am klügsten.

Herr Gruber kommt spät.　　Herr Gruber kommt spät.
Fräulein Hesse　　Fräulein Hesse kommt später.
Frau Peters　　Frau Peters kommt am spätesten.

Der Watzmann ist hoch.　　Der Watzmann ist hoch.
Die Zugspitze　　Die Zugspitze ist höher.
Der Großglockner　　Der Großglockner ist am höchsten.

Ich esse Käse gern.　　Ich esse Käse gern.
Wurst　　Ich esse Wurst lieber.
Schinken　　Ich esse Schinken am liebsten.

18. Provide the comparative and superlative forms.

　　1. schön
　　2. klug

3. groß
4. heiß
5. hoch
6. viel
7. alt
8. schlecht
9. gut
10. toll

19. Wie heißt das auf deutsch?

1. The boys are coming later.
2. Austria is not as big as Germany.
3. The spring is warmer than the fall.
4. Which mountain is higher?
5. The dress costs more than the blouse.
6. Hamburg is just as beautiful as München.
7. The cheese is more delicious than the ham.
8. My brother is older than my sister.
9. The bicycle and the motorcycle are going fast.
   The car is going fastest.
10. Ursula is smarter than Jürgen.

München

Hamburg

Additional *der*-words*

The endings for the *der*-words, i.e. *dieser* (this), *jeder* (every, each), and *welcher* (which), are the same as those of the definite article.

	Singular			Plural
	masculine	*feminine*	*neuter*	
nominative	dies*er*	dies*e*	dies*es*	dies*e*
accusative	dies*en*	dies*e*	dies*es*	dies*e*
dative	dies*em*	dies*er*	dies*em*	dies*en*

Since *jeder* does not have a plural form, you may substitute the word *alle* (all).

*Der-words are *der, dieser, jeder, welcher,* and some others which you will learn later.

20. Der Film beginnt um acht.

    Dieser Film beginnt um acht.

Variation: Ask questions.
(Um wieviel Uhr beginnt
dieser Film?)

    Die Krawatte ist bunt. — Diese Krawatte ist bunt.

    Das Geschenk ist von Uwe. — Dieses Geschenk ist von Uwe.

    Die Auswahl ist sehr gut. — Diese Auswahl ist sehr gut.

    Der Tourist kommt aus Europa. — Dieser Tourist kommt aus Europa.

    Der Student fragt oft. — Dieser Student fragt oft.

21. Die Verkäuferin ist beliebt.

    Welche Verkäuferin ist beliebt?

Variation: Welche Verkäuferin
ist beliebt? Diese Verkäuferin
ist beliebt.

    Der Computer kostet viel. — Welcher Computer kostet viel?

    Die Stadt liegt in Bayern. — Welche Stadt liegt in Bayern?

    Das Auto sieht schön aus. — Welches Auto sieht schön aus?

    Der Schüler liest die Aufgabe. — Welcher Schüler liest die Aufgabe?

    Die Zeitung ist ganz politisch. — Welche Zeitung ist ganz politisch?

22. Wir besuchen das Land.

    Wir besuchen dieses Land.

    Kaufst du das Geschenk? — Kaufst du dieses Geschenk?

    Ich brauche die Kassette. — Ich brauche diese Kassette.

    Essen Sie den Käse? — Essen Sie diesen Käse?

    Er probiert die Hose an. — Er probiert diese Hose an.

    Kennst du den Angestellten? — Kennst du diesen Angestellten?

23. Er kauft die Zeitung.

    Er kauft fast jede Zeitung.

    Ich frage den Jungen. — Ich frage fast jeden Jungen.

    Brauchst du den Pfennig? — Brauchst du fast jeden Pfennig?

    Sie kennt die Verkäuferin. — Sie kennt fast jede Verkäuferin.

    Verstehen Sie die Bedeutung? — Verstehen Sie fast jede Bedeutung?

    Wir lesen das Buch. — Wir lesen fast jedes Buch.

24. Das Fahrrad steht beim Eingang.

    Bei welchem Eingang steht das Fahrrad?

Variation: Ask questions.
(Was steht beim Eingang?,
Wer fährt mit dem Auto?)

    Herr Gruber fährt mit dem Auto. — Mit welchem Auto fährt Herr Gruber?

    Wir gehen zur Party. — Zu welcher Party gehen wir?

    Sie kommen aus der Bank. — Aus welcher Bank kommen sie?

    Der Lehrer kommt von dem Vorort. — Von welchem Vorort kommt der Lehrer.

    Seit der Reise hat er kein Geld. — Seit welcher Reise hat er kein Geld?

25. Ich glaube dem Jungen.

    Ich glaube diesem Jungen.

    Antworte dem Lehrer! — Antworte diesem Lehrer!

    Komm zu der Haltestelle! — Komm zu dieser Haltestelle!

    Was machen wir nach dem Film? — Was machen wir nach diesem Film?

    Sie geben der Verkäuferin fünfzig Mark. — Sie geben dieser Verkäuferin fünfzig Mark.

    Wir bringen dem Mädchen ein Geschenk. — Wir bringen diesem Mädchen ein Geschenk.

26. Welchen Angestellten fragt ihr?

    Welche Angestellten fragt ihr?

Variation: Answer each
question.

    Welche Gitarre kaufen Sie? — Welche Gitarren kaufen Sie?

    Welches Auto gefällt dir? — Welche Autos gefallen dir?

Welchen Anzug hast du an?   Welche Anzüge hast du an?
Welches Wort weiß er nicht?   Welche Wörter weiß er nicht?
Welchen Tanz hat sie gern?   Welche Tänze hat sie gern?

27. Was zeigt er dieser Dame?   **Was zeigt er diesen Damen?**
Ich gebe es diesem Mädchen.   Ich gebe es diesen Mädchen.
Er wohnt bei diesem Studenten.   Er wohnt bei diesen Studenten.
Sie fahren zu diesem Berg.   Sie fahren zu diesen Bergen
Wir antworten diesem Lehrer.   Wir antworten diesen Lehrern.
Glaubst du diesem Jugendlichen?   Glaubst du diesen Jugendlichen?

28. Provide the proper endings.

1. Dies _____ Film gefällt mir gar nicht.
2. Welch _____ Beamten mußt du fragen? Herrn Müller.
3. Wir fahren jed _____ Jahr zu dies _____ Stadt.
4. Welch _____ Koffer brauchen wir denn? Dies _____ zwei.
5. Warum fragen Sie jed _____ Verkäuferin?
6. Wartet bitte bei dies _____ Eingang hier!
7. Welch _____ Studenten studieren dort?
8. Ich weiß jed _____ Aufgabe.
9. Möchten Sie dies _____ Anzug anprobieren?
10. Welch _____ Freunde wirst du besuchen?

29. Beanwortet die folgenden Fragen!

Beispiel: *Möchtest du eine Krawatte kaufen?*
Ja, ich möchte diese hier.

1. Möchtest du ein Hemd haben?   Answer each question in the negative.
2. Möchtest du ein Akkordeon?
3. Möchtest du einen Fernsehapparat kaufen?
4. Möchtest du eine Bluse?
5. Möchtest du einen Pullover haben?

30. Supply the proper form of *dieser* or *welcher.*

1. _____ Musikinstrument wirst du spielen?
2. Wann sehen Sie _____ Film?
3. _____ Kassetten möchtest du hören?
4. _____ Heft sucht er denn?
5. Ich verstehe _____ Amerikanerin gar nicht.
6. _____ Mannschaft wird gewinnen?
7. Kennst du _____ Sportler? Sie sind sehr bekannt.
8. Zu _____ Städten sollen wir fahren?
9. Habt ihr mit _____ Besuchern viel zu tun?
10. Aus _____ Gebäude kommen _____ Leute?

Lesestück 1

Monika geht gern tanzen

Jede Woche, Donnerstag nachmittags, geht Monika zum Tanzunterricht°. Manchmal geht sie auch am Sonntag in die Tanzschule. Dann können die Jugendlichen dort üben. Heute, am Sonntag, möchte Monika auch etwas üben. Der S-Bahnhof° ist nicht weit von ihrem Haus.

Am Bahnhof kauft sie eine Fahrkarte an einem Automaten. Dann entwertet sie ihre Fahrkarte und geht auf den Bahnsteig°. Sie muß nicht lange warten bis die S-Bahn kommt. Sie steigt ein. Sonntags° ist die S-Bahn meistens nicht sehr voll° und Monika bekommt einen Sitzplatz. Monika fährt nur zwei Haltestellen. Die Tanzschule ist gleich in der Nähe vom S-Bahnhof.

Frau Richter, die Besitzerin°, steht hinter einer Theke°. Bei ihr muß Monika Eintritt bezahlen. Monikas Freundin Tina ist auch schon da. Beide haben immer viel Spaß zusammen. Peter, Monikas Tanzpartner, kommt heute nicht. Deshalb tanzt sie mit anderen Jungen. Die Musik ist immer sehr gut. Da gibt es Tänze für jeden Geschmack.

dancing lessons

suburban line station

platform

on Sundays/full

owner/counter

Monika geht zum Tanzunterricht.

Mit wem spricht Monika?

Es gibt Tänze für jeden Geschmack.

In der Tanzschule ist es heute sehr heiß. Bei der Hitze kann Monika nicht immer tanzen. Sie muß oftmals° aussetzen°. Jetzt spielt Frau Richter einen Walzer°. Nur wenige tanzen, die meisten tanzen lieber zu schneller Musik. Frau Richter gibt gerade bekannt, daß sie eine Schallplatte mit südamerikanischer° Musik auflegen wird. Diese Musik gefällt Monika am besten. Das weiß auch Bernd. Er fragt Monika, ob° sie mit ihm tanzen möchte. Bei einem Cha-Cha-Cha tanzen die beiden wie° Experten. Nach jedem Tanz muß Monika erst einmal eine Pause machen. Tanzen macht Spaß, aber es strengt sehr an.

often/sit out
waltz

Latin American

if
like

Fragen über das Lesestück

1. Wohin geht Monika einmal die Woche?
2. Was können die Jugendlichen am Sonntag tun?
3. Was macht Monika mit der Fahrkarte?
4. Warum muß Monika in der S-Bahn nicht stehen?
5. Wo ist die Tanzschule?
6. Wer ist Frau Richter?
7. Warum tanzt Monika nicht mit ihrem Tanzpartner?
8. Warum setzt Monika oftmals aus?
9. Warum tanzen nicht viele zu einem Walzer?
10. Welche Musik gefällt Monika am besten?

Erweiterung

31. Beantwortet die folgenden Fragen!

> **Beispiel:** *Spielst du gern Tischtennis? (Fußball)*
> *Ich spiele lieber Fußball.*

1. Spielst du gern Flöte? (Blockflöte)
2. Ißt du gern Käse? (Wurst)
3. Schreibst du gern mit einem Bleistift? (Kuli)
4. Liest du gern eine Zeitung? (Buch)
5. Sprichst du gern Englisch? (Deutsch)
6. Hörst du gern Schallplatten? (Kassetten)

32. Provide an appropriate response in German. Be sure that the whole conversation ties together and becomes meaningful.

Have students read their newly formed dialog.

1. Von wem hast du dieses Geschenk?
2. Ja, aber er hat doch gar kein Geld.
3. Das glaube ich nicht.

4. Er hat seinen Führerschein?

5. Seit Montag.

33. Define each of the words listed below. Write at least one complete sentence describing each word.

1. Geburtstag
2. Führerschein
3. Klavier
4. Schultasche
5. Schallplatte

34. Beantwortet die Fragen! Encourage varied answers.

Wann hast du Geburtstag?

Was möchtest du zum Geburtstag bekommen?

Hast du einen Führerschein?

Was für ein Musikinstrument spielst du?

Was brauchst du für die Schule?

Gehst du gern tanzen?

Welche Tänze hast du am liebsten?

Spielst du lieber Kassetten oder Schallplatten?

Rückblick

If your students have some difficulties in completing any of these exercises, go back to the particular grammar point discussed in earlier lessons. Select some of the exercises for further review.

I. Supply the appropriate German equivalents for the nouns or pronouns as listed in parentheses.

1. Frau Rübel wohnt bei (the university, a railroad station, a river, the building).
2. Glaubt (him, them, her, me) nicht!
3. Kannst du (the teacher, the girl, the ladies, the saleslady) nicht antworten?
4. Ich werde (her, them, me, him) ein Geschenk kaufen.
5. Warum gehen wir nicht mit (the boyfriend, the girl, them, her) ins Kino?
6. Sie kommen aus (the school, the house, the apartment, the movie theater).
7. Wir geben (you-sg./fam., you-form., them, her, the brother, the girlfriend) das Geld.

II. Provide the proper form of the verb provided in parentheses.

1. (sprechen) Mein Freund _____ gut Deutsch.
2. (essen) Was _____ du zum Abendbrot, Michael?
3. (fahren) Der Zug _____ direkt nach Köln.
4. (zugeben) Das stimmt. _____ es doch _____, Kerstin!
5. (gefallen) Wie _____ dir dieses Kleid?
6. (sehen) Wir _____ die Berge schon aus der Entfernung.

7. (tragen) Wer _____ meinen Koffer?

8. (lesen) Die Studenten _____ viele Bücher.

III. Complete the following sentences.

1. Ich kann bei _____ parken.

2. Um wieviel Uhr kommt ihr aus _____?

3. Außer _____ kenne ich auch noch _____.

4. Nach _____ gehen wir zu _____.

5. Wir wohnen schon seit _____ in Hamburg.

6. Hörst du manchmal von _____?

7. Er fährt mit _____.

IV. Write the opposite of each word indicated.

1. wenig: _____

2. gut: _____

3. schnell: _____

4. schwarz: _____

5. langweilig: _____

6. warm: _____

7. klein: _____

8. flach: _____

V. Complete each sentence by using the verb prefixes listed below. You may be able to use the same prefix more than once.

1. Die Jugendlichen räumen das Geschirr _____.

2. Ruf mich doch um fünf Uhr _____!

3. Steigen Sie schnell _____!

4. Meine Mutter bereitet das Essen _____.

5. Angelika probiert den Rock _____.

6. Füllen Sie bitte dieses Formular _____!

7. Wie viele Reiseschecks löst ihr _____?

8. Wir kommen zum Bahnhof _____.

9. Ich kaufe noch schnell in der Stadt _____.

10. Wann kommt dein Bruder _____? Ich muß mit ihm sprechen.

     ab   an   aus   ein   mit   zu   zurück

VI. Create a meaningful dialog by giving an appropriate response in German.

1. Grüß dich! Um wieviel Uhr fahren wir zu Sabine?

2. Schon so bald?

3. Ich kaufe noch schnell ein Geschenk.

4. Aber es ist doch ihr Geburtstag!

5. Wer kommt denn noch zur Party?

6. So viele? Die meisten kenne ich gar nicht.

7. Mir ist es recht.

8. Ja, gut. Bis bald!

Lesestück 2

Die BRD — Landschaft

Use a map to illustrate further the content of *Lesestück 2*. Point to the various geographical features described.

Im Norden grenzt die Bundesrepublik Deutschland an die Nordsee. Direkt auf der anderen Seite vom Festland°, in der Nähe von Kiel, beginnt die Ostsee°.

  mainland

  Baltic Sea

  Die BRD hat fünf verschiedene Landschaften. Im Norddeutschen *Tiefland°* liegen die Länder Schleswig-Holstein, Hamburg, Bremen, der größte Teil von Niedersachsen und ein Teil von Nordrhein-Westfalen. Die beiden letzten° Länder gehen in das *Mittelgebirgsland°* über°. Die Länder Rheinland-Pfalz, Saarland und Hessen gehören zu° dieser Landschaft. Zum Teil reichen diese Länder aber auch in das West- und Süddeutsche *Stufen- und Bergland°* hinein°. Dort und im Süddeutschen *Alpenvorland°* liegen die Länder Baden-Württemberg und Bayern. Die *Alpen* findet man nur in dem Land Bayern.

  lowlands

  last

  central highlands go into belong to/reichen… hinein reach into/ terrace and highland country Alpine foothills

  Der höchste Berg ist die Zugspitze (fast 3000 m). Die Zugspitze liegt an der Grenze zu Österreich. Der zweithöchste Berg ist der Watzmann (ungefähr 2700 m). Dieser Berg liegt im Südosten.

  Der Rhein ist der längste Fluß (867 km in der BRD). Er ist eine wichtige° Wasserstraße für den europäischen Verkehr. Der Rhein entspringt° in der Schweiz, fließt durch den Bodensee°, dann durch die BRD und die Niederlande bis in die Nordsee. Der zweitgrößte Fluß in der BRD ist die Donau (647 km). Die Donau entspringt in der Bundesrepublik und fließt von Westen nach Osten bis ins Schwarze Meer°. Der drittgrößte Fluß ist die Elbe (227 km in der BRD, 566 km in der DDR). Die Elbe kommt aus der Tschechoslowakei. Sie fließt durch die DDR, eine kurze Strecke° durch die BRD und dann in die Nordsee.

  important

  originates/Lake Constance

  Black Sea

  stretch

  Außer den Flüssen ist auch das Kanalsystem° wichtig für den europäischen Wasserverkehr. Der Mittellandkanal zum Beispiel verbindet° die Ems mit der Elbe.

  canal system

  connects

  Der Bodensee ist der größte See. Nur ein Teil vom Bodensee liegt in der BRD. Andere Teile liegen in Österreich und in der Schweiz. Es gibt aber viele kleine Seen. Die meisten Seen liegen in Süddeutschland, wie zum Beispiel der Chiemsee in Bayern oder der Schluchsee im Schwarzwald.

  Die größte Insel° ist Fehmarn. Diese Insel liegt in der Ostsee. Eine Brücke° verbindet Fehmarn mit dem Festland. Fehmarn ist auch eine wichtige Verbindung° für den Verkehr zwischen° der BRD und Dänemark. Die meisten Inseln liegen in der Nordsee. Helgoland zum Beispiel liegt am weitesten vom Festland entfernt und ist ein beliebter Ausflugsort° im Sommer. Viele kleine Inseln liegen ganz in der Nähe vom Festland. Manche° von diesen Inseln kann man bei Ebbe° sogar zu Fuß oder mit Pferden° erreichen.

  island

  bridge

  connection/between

  excursion area

  a few

  low tide/horses

Der Bodensee ist der größte See.

Die Berge sind im Süden.

Hessen liegt im
Mittelgebirgsland.

Fragen über das Lesestück

1. Welche zwei große Seen liegen im Norden der BRD?
2. Wie heißen die fünf Landschaften?
3. Wo liegt die Zugspitze? Wie hoch ist dieser Berg?
4. Fließt der Rhein nur durch die BRD?
5. Fließt die Donau von Norden nach Süden?
6. Welche Flüsse verbindet der Mittellandkanal?
7. Liegt der Bodensee nur in der BRD?
8. Wo sind die meisten Seen?
9. Wie kommt man vom Festland zur Insel Fehmarn?
10. Welche Insel liegt am weitesten vom Festland entfernt?

Sprachspiegel

After completion of the dialog or narrative, have students read their version.

I. **Create a short dialog or narrative describing a party you are attending. Be as creative as possible.**

II. **Answer each question with at least two or three sentences. Be as descriptive as possible.**

1. Was für ein Musikinstrument spielst du? (Wann? Wie oft? Wie lange? etc.)
2. Was bringst du alles in die Schule mit?
3. Was machst du bei einer Party?
4. Gehst du gern tanzen? (Wo? Wie oft? Welche Tänze tanzt du? etc.)
5. Wie sieht die Landschaft aus, wo du wohnst?

Wie sagt man's? Have students read these mini-dialogs aloud with lots of expression.

Kommt Tanja nicht?
Nein, sie hat Partys nicht gern.
Das glaub' ich nicht.
Frag sie doch!

Wann ist die Party?
Am Sonnabend um acht. Kommst du?
Wer kommt denn alles?
Bernd und seine Freunde.
Na, dann komme ich auch.

Tanzt du gern?
Ja, besonders zu moderner Musik.
Dann aber 'ran! Britta möchte bestimmt tanzen.
Hoffentlich hast du recht.

Wann beginnt der Tanz?
Um fünf. Hast du Lust mitzukommen?
Heute nicht. Vielleicht das nächste Mal.

Wer ist denn Erikas Tanzpartner?
Rolf. Er tanzt wirklich toll.
Besonders zu amerikanischer Musik.

Frag doch Jutta. Vielleicht tanzt sie mit dir.
Mir gefällt Sabine aber besser.
Warum wartest du dann?
Sie tanzt lieber mit Dieter.

Fährst du schon Auto?
Ja, ich habe jetzt meinen Führerschein.
Prima. Kannst du mich nach Hause fahren?
Na klar!

Tanzt du gern?

Was essen wir denn?
Bist du schon wieder hungrig?
Oh, das Essen sieht so lecker aus.
Ich esse auch etwas.

Zungenbrecher

Zungenbrecher Have students say the tongue twister as fast as possible. Find out who can say them the fastest.

Hinter Hermann Hannes Haus hängen hundert Hemden 'raus.
(Behind Hermann Hannes' house a hundred shirts are hanging out.)

Kulturecke

Occupations

Since World War II, Germany's economy has relied primarily on heavy industry, such as coal mining and the steel industries. Most of the heavy industry is located in the Northrhine Westphalia region. The Federal Republic of Germany is the third largest automobile producer in the world, following the U.S. and Japan.

Only seven percent of those Germans who are employed are now farmers. In order to be more competitive, most farms now have been consolidated and are part of co-operatives. Many farms are specialized and grow only certain crops such as vegetables or grapes for wine, which grow along the Rhine and Mosel rivers. About a quarter of the Federal Republic's land is forest. The law demands that forest areas must be properly managed. Land laws require forest owners to replant harvested areas or replace dead trees with new ones. Areas like Lower Saxony, Schleswig-Holstein and Bavaria are extensively involved in raising cattle and producing dairy products.

Specially trained personnel are employed in the computer industry and in related areas. Computers have had a tremendous impact on the growth of the economy. Specialists in the computer field are sought after not only by larger firms but even by smaller companies. The importance of computer technology is highly noticeable in the medical profession. There the computer is used in various specialized areas. In the Federal Republic there are about 130,000 doctors; that is one doctor to every 465 inhabitants. This makes the Federal Republic one of the best equipped countries in the world medically. Another health care occupation is the dentist or the dental technician. There are 32,000 dentists, one for every 1,916 Germans. Many pharmaceutical products tested by specialists are sold in pharmacies.

Major emphasis is placed on the importance of education. For many years, an acute shortage of teachers meant that every applicant who passed the proper examinations was accepted with open arms. Now there are many teachers without a job, which poses difficult problems for the country.

Every sixth person is employed by the federal, state or local government, providing services for the communities. For example, there are occupations concerned with public security and order, such as the police. The German Federal Post Office *(Deutsche Bundespost)* constitutes Europe's largest enterprise. Early in the morning, letter carriers can be seen leaving the main post offices to distribute the mail. Postal and telecommunications, in which thousands of people are employed, are part of the German Federal Post Office.

The German monetary system, based on the mark, has become an important factor in international trade. Financial institutions such as banks employ specialists in the different

190

Service-station attendant *(Tankwart)*.

A tree nursery *(Baumschule)*

Only 7% of employed
Germans are farmers.

Handicrafts are
traditional,
particularly
in small towns.

Women now have jobs once considered to be male
occupations.

areas of the complex financial business world. Managers in small and large companies provide the guidance and administration necessary to run their companies more effectively.

Tourism has become an important economic opportunity for Germans. Therefore, it is not surprising to find an abundance of travel agents who plan tours and vacations for groups or individuals. There are about 1.5 million jobs dependent on tourism either directly or indirectly. Some of these jobs, such as a captain on a Rhine ship, require extensive and specialized training. Lufthansa, the German Airline, requires its cabin attendants to speak at least one or two foreign languages. It is no longer rare to see women in jobs which were once considered to be typically male occupations. Almost every second woman is employed outside of the home. Tourists traveling by car have no difficulty finding service stations that can take care of the traveler's needs. Should the automobile need particular attention, authorized dealerships with specially trained auto mechanics can be found everywhere.

Americans going to a German department store with the intention of buying clothes should be aware that all clothing items are sized according to the metric system. However, experienced sales personnel can help foreigners to determine the correct size. Although many Germans go shopping in the local supermarkets today, individual shops are still extremely popular. The store owner and clerks know the individual customers, therefore providing a more personalized atmosphere. Many of these smaller stores, like the local butcher shop, are family-owned. The butcher takes special pride in offering home-made sausages and preparing the meats to the customers' special requests. Two thirds of Germans go shopping once or twice a week at the local markets. Here the clerks offer fresh fruits and vegetables, much preferred over packaged products.

The success of the restaurant business depends to a large extent on the skill of the cook. In Germany there is an abundance of various types of eating establishments, ranging from the very elegant and expensive to the simple and reasonably priced. Restaurant waiters and waitresses can be seen serving in indoor and outdoor restaurants. Many waiters or waitresses are also employed in cafés. Germans love to sit in these cafés, relax and have coffee and delicious German cake.

Germans take pride in keeping everything neat and clean. Some are employed by the sanitation department. Others, such as park attendants and gardeners, have the task of keeping the landscaped park areas beautiful and keeping everyone off the lawn.

Upon entering a town in Germany, the visitor will see a tall pole that is colorfully decorated with figures designating the trades of the town. This traditional pole dates back to the Middle Ages, a time when many apprentices and journeymen would go from town to town searching for jobs. However, times have changed and so have the methods for securing jobs.

Both the folk arts and the formal arts flourish throughout Germany. Handicrafts are traditional, particularly in smaller towns and villages. For example, the visitor will find a number of potters who create unique pottery for sale. Other artists, particularly in the town of Mittenwald, create hand-made violins that are well-respected and recognized throughout the world. In Southern Germany, the art of woodcarving is practiced by artisans who demonstrate great skill.

A woodcarver (Holzschnitzer).

Vokabeln

das **Akkordeon,-s** accordion
als than
an on
anstrengen to exert
    Es strengt an. It is exhausting.
auflegen to put on
aussetzen to sit out
der **Bahnsteig,-e** platform
bei with
bekanntmachen to announce
die **Besitzerin,-nen** owner (female)
der **Cha-Cha-Cha** cha-cha
der **Eintritt** admission
entwerten to cancel (tickets)
das **Essen** meal, food
europäisch European
der **Experte,-n** expert
die **Fahrprüfung,-en** driver's test
die **Flöte,-n** flute
der **Führerschein,-e** driver's license
die **Geige,-n** violin
das **Geschenk,-e** present
der **Glückwunsch,-̈e** congratulations (pl.)
    **Herzlichen Glückwunsch zum
    Geburtstag!** Happy Birthday!
das **Heft,-e** notebook
herzlich sincere, cordial
hinter behind
die **Hitze** heat
    bei der Hitze in this heat
der **Kartoffelsalat** potato salad
die **Klarinette,-n** clarinet
das **Klavier,-e** piano
der **Kuli,-s** (ballpoint) pen
die **Landschaft,-en** landscape
lecker delicious
das **Lineal,-e** ruler
das **Musikinstrument,-e** musical
    instrument
nämlich namely
ob if, whether
oftmals often
das **Papier** paper
die **Party,-s** party
die **Pause,-n** break
    eine Pause machen to take a break
der **Radiergummi,-s** eraser
'ran: 'Ran an die Arbeit!
    Let's go to work!
der **S-Bahnhof,-̈e** suburban line station
die **Schallplatte,-n** record
die **Schultasche,-n** school bag
sicher safe, secure
der **Sitzplatz,-̈e** seat

sonntags on Sundays
südamerikanisch South American
der **Tanz,-̈e** dance
der **Tanzpartner,-** dancing partner
die **Tanzschule,-n** dancing school
die **Theke,-n** counter
die **Trompete,-n** trumpet
der **Walzer,-** waltz
warnen to warn
die **Wasserstraße,-n** waterway
der **Wasserverkehr** water traffic
wie like

Dialog

This district championship *(Bezirksmeisterschaft)* took place in Leipzig. The best athletes from the whole area compete every year in these events.

Beim Sportwettbewerb

djective endings will be esented in Level 2. Treat is sentence *(Heute ist der oße Tag.)* as an expression this point.

UWE:	Heute ist der große Tag. Ich hoffe, ich erreiche meine Bestleistung.
ACHIM:	Beim Weitsprung bist du immer klasse.
UWE:	Das letzte Mal hast du mich aber geschlagen.
ACHIM:	Da hab' ich mehr Glück als Verstand gehabt.
UWE:	Du hast recht. Ich bin etwas zu früh gesprungen. Dabei habe ich mindestens 15 Zentimeter verloren.
ACHIM:	Ich glaube, Daniel ist in bester Form. Er hat viel trainiert.
UWE:	Wie weit bist du denn vorhin gesprungen, Daniel?
DANIEL:	Ich bin auf 5,80 gekommen.

►r specific reference on etric measures see *Lektion* *(Ergänzung)*.

ACHIM:	Jetzt bin ich dran.
UWE:	Zeig, was du kannst!
ACHIM:	Ich versuche mein Bestes.
DANIEL:	Viel Glück! . . . *(Achim springt.)* . . . Phantastisch! . . . Nicht schlecht . . . 5,66.
UWE:	Das werde ich kaum übertreffen.
DANIEL:	Du kannst es sicherlich schaffen.
UWE:	Hoffentlich. Hier kommt meine letzte Chance.

UWE:	Du bist doch besser als ich gewesen.
ACHIM:	Aber nicht der Beste. Daniel hat uns beide geschlagen.
ANSAGER:	Das Endergebnis im Weitsprung . . . Erster — Daniel Kästner, Zweiter — Achim Lehmann und Dritter — Uwe Schmidt.
UWE:	Herzlichen Glückwunsch!

Fragen über den Dialog

1. Wer ist beim Weitsprung meistens sehr gut?
2. Warum hat Uwe das letzte Mal verloren?
3. Warum ist Daniel in bester Form?
4. Wie weit ist Daniel gesprungen?
5. Wie weit springt Achim?
6. Wer ist dieses Mal der Beste?

At the Sports Competition

UWE:	Today is the big day. I hope I can match my best performance.
ACHIM:	In the broad jump you're always great.
UWE:	But you beat me the last time.
ACHIM:	I had more luck than brains.
UWE:	You're right. I jumped a bit too early. That made me lose at least 15 centimeters.
ACHIM:	I think Daniel is in great form. He has practiced a lot.
UWE:	How far did you jump before, Daniel?
DANIEL:	I got to 5.80 (5 meters and 80 centimeters).
ACHIM:	It's my turn now.
UWE:	Show what you can do.
ACHIM:	I'll try my best.
DANIEL:	Lots of luck! . . . (Achim jumps.) . . . Fantastic! . . . Not bad . . . 5.66.
UWE:	I'll hardly beat that.
DANIEL:	You can certainly make it, too.
UWE:	I hope so. Here is my last chance.
UWE:	You were better than I was.
ACHIM:	But not the best. Daniel beat both of us.
ANNOUNCER:	The final result in broad jump . . . First — Daniel Kästner, second — Achim Lehmann and third — Uwe Schmidt.
UWE:	Congratulations!

Nützliche Ausdrücke

Er hat mich geschlagen.	He beat me.
Du hast mehr Glück als Verstand.	You have more luck than brains.
Sie sind in bester Form.	They are in great form.
Ich bin dran.	It's my turn.
Kannst du das übertreffen?	Can you beat that?
Herzlichen Glückwunsch!	Congratulations!
Wann findet das Spiel statt?	When does the game take place?
Machst du mit?	Are you participating?
Sie sieht auf ihre Uhr.	She looks at her watch.
Er ist an der Spitze.	He is in front.
Sieht sie müde aus?	Does she look tired?
Wer wird es wohl sein?	Who could it be?

Ergänzung

Review these expressions. Students have learned them in going through the *Dialog* and *Lesestück 1*.

1. Welche Sportart treibst du?

    Was machst du sonst noch gern?

    Was hast du gestern gemacht?

Ich spiele Fußball. (Korbball oder Basketball, Federball, Hockey, Tennis, Tischtennis, Golf).

Ich schwimme gern.

Ich laufe gern Ski.

Ich fahre gern Rad.

Ich laufe gern Schlittschuh.

Ich wandere gern.

Ich habe Tennis gespielt.

Ich bin gewandert.

Golf

Tennis

Hockey

Tischtennis

Korbball Basketball

Federball

Fußball

Personalize questions and add others. *(Spielst du Fußball?, Wie viele Jahre hast du schon gespielt?, Wie gut ist deine Mannschaft?,* etc.)

2. Was möchtest du trinken?

Ich möchte eine Cola trinken.

(eine Tasse Kaffee, eine Tasse Tee, eine Tasse Kakao, ein Glas Wasser, Bier, Wein, Milch, Limonade)

Have students ask each other questions such as: *Was trinkst du gern?* or *Was trinkst du am Morgen/am Mittag/am Abend?*

Ausspracheübung

initial / r /	middle / r /	final / r /
Rad	andere	Sportler
rüber	unsere	Sommer
recht	Jahre	Nummer
Regal	Klarinette	später
rufen	interessant	hier
Reise	während	Uhr
Röcke	Europa	mir
Ruhe	fahren	vor
rot	Österreich	Tür
Frau	Marathon	aber
Bruder	warten	für
braun	fahren	Läufer
Freund	morgen	dort
fragen	Karte	Ort
groß	dürfen	Wort
drüben	Norden	Dorf
Straße	Arbeit	darf
Krawatte	vorbei	fährt

Have students repeat the various words at a rapid pace. Use the accompanying sound description for further clarification.
[r] or [R] — *(rot):* There are two possible *r*-sounds in German, the apicoalveolar trill [r] and the uvular trill [R]. With the [r], the mouth is slightly opened and the apex moves toward the alveolar ridge and flutters against it while interrupting the breath stream. With the [R], the apex is against the lower teeth and the back of the tongue rises toward the uvular region of the velum. The passage of air causes the two structures to vibrate against each other.

Übungen

Present Perfect Tense

To simplify matters, weak verbs are labeled "regular verbs" and strong verbs appear as "irregular verbs."

The present perfect is used more frequently in German conversation than in English. It is often called the "conversational past."

Regular verbs

haben + (*ge* + 3rd person singular)
er hat gefragt. (He has asked.)

NOTE: In English two forms (*He has asked* or *He asked*) may be used. To simplify the presentation, only the present perfect form is used throughout.

The form *gefragt* (asked) is called the past participle, which in German is placed at the end of the sentence.

Example: *Ich habe meinen Vater gefragt.*
             (I have asked my father.)

Irregular verbs

The irregular verbs, as the term suggests, do not follow the pattern above in forming their past participle. Some of them use *sein* instead of *haben*. Therefore, you must learn each present perfect form individually.

Examples: *Sie hat den Kaffee getrunken.*
(She has drunk the coffee.)
Sie ist nach Hause gefahren.
(She has driven home.)

NOTE: Verbs which use a form of *sein* must both
— indicate motion or change of condition *and*
— be intransitive, i.e. a verb that cannot have a direct object.

Here are the irregular forms for most of the verbs you have learned so far:

Students must learn these irregular verbs because most of them will be used frequently.

Infinitive	Past Participle
beginnen (to begin)	begonnen
bieten (to offer)	geboten
bleiben (to stay)	ist geblieben
bringen (to bring)	gebracht
denken (to think)	gedacht
essen (to eat)	gegessen
fahren (to drive)	ist gefahren
finden (to find)	gefunden
geben (to give)	gegeben
gefallen (to like)	gefallen
gehen (to go)	ist gegangen
gewinnen (to win)	gewonnen
haben (to have)	gehabt
helfen (to help)	geholfen
kennen (to know)	gekannt
kommen (to come)	ist gekommen
laufen (to run)	ist gelaufen
lesen (to read)	gelesen
liegen (to lie, be located)	gelegen
schlagen (to beat)	geschlagen
schreiben (to write)	geschrieben
schwimmen (to swim)	ist geschwommen
sehen (to see)	gesehen
sein (to be)	ist gewesen
sitzen (to sit)	gesessen
sprechen (to speak)	gesprochen
springen (to jump)	ist gesprungen
stehen (to stand)	gestanden
tragen (to carry)	getragen
trinken (to drink)	getrunken
tun (to do)	getan
verlassen (to leave)	verlassen
verlieren (to lose)	verloren
verstehen (to understand)	verstanden
wissen (to know)	gewußt

Verbs ending in *-ieren*

Verbs ending in *-ieren* do not have the *ge-* in the past participle.

Examples: *Maria hat Englisch studiert.*
(Maria has studied English.)
Die Studenten haben oft darüber diskutiert.
(The students have often discussed it.)

Folgt den Beispielen!

1. Hast du ihn gefragt? | Ja, ich habe ihn gefragt.

Variation: Answer questions with *Nein,…*

   Hast du sie gesucht? — Ja, ich habe sie gesucht.
   Hast du die Wurst gekauft? — Ja, ich habe die Wurst gekauft.
   Hast du ihr geglaubt? — Ja, ich habe ihr geglaubt.
   Hast du Fußball gespielt? — Ja, ich habe Fußball gespielt.
   Hast du vor dem Kino gewartet? — Ja, ich habe vor dem Kino gewartet.

2. Die Reise dauert vier Studen. | Die Reise hat vier Stunden gedauert.

Variation: Change statements to questions and have students answer them.

   Die Zuschauer hören die Musik. — Die Zuschauer haben die Musik gehört.
   Wir lernen Deutsch. — Wir haben Deutsch gelernt.
   Michael parkt das Auto. — Michael hat das Auto geparkt.
   Es regnet nicht. — Es hat nicht geregnet.
   Die Fahrräder kosten viel. — Die Fahrräder haben viel gekostet.
   Die Sportler üben oft. — Die Sportler haben oft geübt.

3. Wohnen Sie in Hamburg? | Haben Sie in Hamburg gewohnt?

Variation: Answer the questions.

   Wann tanzt ihr denn? — Wann habt ihr denn getanzt?
   Kochst du das Essen? — Hast du das Essen gekocht?
   Paßt der Anzug gut? — Hat der Anzug gut gepaßt?
   Stempelt er den Ausweis? — Hat er den Ausweis gestempelt?
   Was machen die Jungen? — Was haben die Jungen gemacht?

4. Was hast du am Montag gemacht? (Fußball spielen) | Am Montag habe ich Fußball gespielt.

Variation: Answer the questions on your own, not using the cue words provided.

   Was hast du am Samstag gemacht? (zu Hause arbeiten) — Am Samstag habe ich zu Hause gearbeitet.
   Was hast du am Donnerstag gemacht? (eine Kassette kaufen) — Am Donnerstag habe ich eine Kassette gekauft.
   Was hast du am Sonntag gemacht? (spät frühstücken) — Am Sonntag habe ich spät gefrühstückt.
   Was hast du am Dienstag gemacht? (die Aufgaben machen) — Am Dienstag habe ich die Aufgaben gemacht.

5. Ich höre diese Musik. Und du? | Ich habe diese Musik schon gehört.

Variation: *Hast du diese Musik schon gehört? Ja,…/Nein,…*

   Ich lese die Zeitung. Und du? — Ich habe die Zeitung schon gelesen.

Ich esse Abendbrot. Und du?	Ich habe Abendbrot schon gegessen.
Ich trage den Koffer. Und du?	Ich habe den Koffer schon getragen.
Ich trinke Milch. Und du?	Ich habe Milch schon getrunken.
Ich verstehe ihn. Und du?	Ich habe ihn schon verstanden.

6.
Achim bringt mir ein Geschenk.	Achim hat mir ein Geschenk gebracht.
Hast du viel Zeit?	Hast du viel Zeit gehabt?
Was denkt ihr?	Was habt ihr gedacht?
Wir schreiben eine Arbeit.	Wir haben eine Arbeit geschrieben.
Ich gebe dir meine Karte.	Ich habe dir meine Karte gegeben.
Die Sportler verlieren nicht.	Die Sportler haben nicht verloren.

7.
Das Mädchen — schwimmen	**Das Mädchen ist geschwommen.**
Die Studenten — fahren	Die Studenten sind gefahren.
Der Besucher — bleiben	Der Besucher ist geblieben.
Meine Tante — gehen	Meine Tante ist gegangen.
Daniel und Uwe — laufen	Daniel und Uwe sind gelaufen.
ich — kommen	Ich bin gekommen.

Variation: Was hat das Mädchen gemacht? Das Mädchen ist geschwommen.

8.
Gehen Sie zu Fuß?	**Sind Sie zu Fuß gegangen?**
Die Touristen fahren nach Deutschland.	Die Touristen sind nach Deutschland gefahren.
Das Spiel ist sehr interessant.	Das Spiel ist sehr interessant gewesen.
Wie weit springst du?	Wie weit bist du gesprungen?
Daniel kommt später.	Daniel ist später gekommen.
Wir schwimmen gern.	Wir sind gern geschwommen.

9. Provide the correct form of *haben* or *sein*.

1. Wann _____ ihr nach Hause gekommen?
2. Die Jugendlichen _____ Tennis gespielt.
3. Es _____ gestern viel geschneit.
4. Angelika _____ mir die Schultasche gebracht.
5. Die Studenten _____ zwei Stunden im Sprachlabor gewesen.
6. Der Lehrer _____ lange vor dem Bahnhof gewartet.
7. Um wieviel Uhr _____ ihr Abendbrot gegessen?
8. _____ Sie mit dem Zug gefahren?
9. Was _____ du am Abend getrunken?
10. _____ ihr zur Uni gelaufen?

10. *Was hast du gestern gemacht?* Beantwortet diese Frage! Folgt dem Beispiel!

    Beispiel: *ein Buch lesen*
         Ich habe ein Buch gelesen.

1. eine Trompete kaufen
2. Fußball spielen
3. in der Stadt sein

4. eine Reise machen
5. mit meinem Auto fahren
6. zum Sportwettbewerb gehen
7. deiner Freundin schreiben

11. Change the following sentences from the present to the present perfect.

1. Daniel springt weiter als Achim.
2. Was ist deine Bestleistung?
3. Ich habe viel Glück.
4. Verstehen Sie Deutsch?
5. Wir gehen um acht Uhr ins Kino.
6. Die Sportler laufen zehn Kilometer.
7. Am Sonntag regnet es nicht.
8. Warum glaubst du ihm denn?
9. Die Zuschauer hören die Musik.
10. Tragen die Touristen ihr Gepäck?
11. Der Ansager gibt das Startsignal.
12. Weißt du, wann die Vorstellung beginnt?

12. Complete each sentence by using the proper form of *haben* or *sein* as well as one of the verbs from the columns below. Be sure to use the proper form of the past participle.

1. Die Reise _____ acht Stunden _____.
2. Manche Läufer _____ älter als 50 Jahre _____.
3. Wie _____ euch der Film _____?
4. _____ die Studenten Englisch _____?
5. Ich _____ eine Tasse Kaffee _____.
6. Am Sonnabend _____ wir ins Kino _____.
7. _____ du diese Zeitung _____?
8. _____ ihr mit dem Auto _____?
9. Die Zuschauer _____ beim Sportwettbewerb _____.
10. _____ Sie die Kalte Platte schon _____?
11. _____ du deine Freundin um zwei Uhr _____?
12. Er _____ kein Wort _____.

dauern	essen
sein	sehen
trinken	fahren
lesen	gehen
gefallen	sprechen
klatschen	sagen

13. Complete the following sentences using a different verb (in the present perfect tense) each time. Find out how many different responses students will give.

1. Am Dienstag haben wir _____.
2. Warum sind die Zuschauer _____?
3. Mein Freund hat _____.

4. Hast du _____?
5. Ich bin gestern _____.
6. Die Sportler sind _____.
7. Haben die Studenten _____?
8. Uwe hat _____.

Possessive Adjectives (Dative)

	Dative Singular			Plural
	masculine	*feminine*	*neuter*	
ich	meinem	meiner	meinem	meinen
du	deinem	deiner	deinem	deinen
er	seinem	seiner	seinem	seinen
sie	ihrem	ihrer	ihrem	ihren
es	seinem	seiner	seinem	seinen
wir	unserem	unserer	unserem	unseren
ihr	euerem	euerer	euerem	eueren
sie	ihrem	ihrer	ihrem	ihren
Sie	Ihrem	Ihrer	Ihrem	Ihren

The endings for the dative possessive adjectives are the same as for the indefinite article (*ein*-words).

Folgt den Beispielen!

14. Was gibst du deiner Schwester?
   (eine Schallplatte)

Ich gebe meiner Schwester eine Schallplatte.

Variation: Have students answer the questions without using the cues.

Was kaufst du deiner Freudin?
   (eine Bluse)

Ich kaufe meiner Freundin eine Bluse.

Was bringst du deinem Lehrer?
   (das Wörterbuch)

Ich bringe meinem Lehrer das Wörterbuch.

Was sagst du deinem Freund?
   (kein Wort)

Ich sage meinem Freund kein Wort.

Was kochst du deiner Mutter?
   (das Essen)

Ich koche meiner Mutter das Essen.

15. Mit wem sprichst du denn?
   (meine Tante)

Mit meiner Tante.

Variation: Ask students to provide complete sentences.

Wem antwortest du denn?
   (sein Bruder)

Seinem Bruder.

Von wem hast du denn gehört?
   (ihre Freundin)

Von ihrer Freundin.

Wem hast du denn geglaubt?
   (deine Mutter)

Deiner Mutter.

Aus welchem Gebäude werdet ihr denn kommen?
   (unser Haus)

Aus uns(e)rem Haus.

16. Ich wohne nicht weit von meiner Schule.

    euer — Straße

    ihr — Schwester

    dein — Freund

    unser — Wohnung

    sein — Onkel

Ich wohne nicht weit von meiner Schule.

Ich wohne nicht weit von eu(e)rer Straße.

Ich wohne nicht weit von ihrer Schwester.

Ich wohne nicht weit von deinem Freund.

Ich wohne nicht weit von uns(e)rer Wohnung.

Ich wohne nicht weit von seinem Onkel.

Variation: Ask students to answer the question using the cue words.

17. Wie geht es deinem Vater?

    euer — Großmutter

    Ihr — Sohn

    sein — Angestellter

    unser — Freundin

    mein — Lehrer

Wie geht es deinem Vater?

Wie geht es eu(e)rer Großmutter?

Wie geht es Ihrem Sohn?

Wie geht es seinem Angestellten?

Wie geht es uns(e)rer Freundin?

Wie geht es meinem Lehrer?

18. Sie spricht viel von ihrem Bruder.

Hast du deiner Tante geschrieben?

Ich glaube seiner Tochter.

Er sagt es unserem Lehrer.

Kommt doch mit euerem Freund!

Ich habe von Ihrem Sohn gehört.

Sie spricht viel von ihren Brüdern.

Hast du deinen Tanten geschrieben?

Ich glaube seinen Töchtern.

Er sagt es uns(e)ren Lehrern.

Kommt doch mit eu(e)ren Freunden!

Ich habe von Ihren Söhnen gehört.

19. Er spricht viel von seiner Reise.

    Buch

    Freundin

    Lehrer

    Schallplatte

    Auto

Er spricht viel von seinen Reisen.

Er spricht viel von seinen Büchern.

Er spricht viel von seinen Freundinnen.

Er spricht viel von seinen Lehrern.

Er spricht viel von seinen Schallplatten.

Er spricht viel von seinen Autos.

20. **Supply the German equivalents for the words in parentheses.**

    1. Ich bringe (my aunt, his mother, their uncle, her girlfriends) _____ ein Geschenk.

    2. Gehst du zu (my teacher, our grandmother, his house) _____?

    3. Wie weit ist es von (our university, her apartment, their school) _____?

    4. Wir haben das (his sons, their father, her aunt) _____ nicht geglaubt.

    5. Antworte (your teacher, your brothers, your mother) _____, Michael!

21. **Form complete sentences using the information provided.**

    1. Peter / kaufen / seine Freundin / Kassette

    2. Wann / werden / Angelika / mit / ihr Lehrer / sprechen

    3. Die Angestellten / kommen / vier Uhr / aus / ihre Geschäfte

    4. Geben / du / dein Freund / ein Kugelschreiber

    5. Außer / meine Tante / besuchen / wir / unser Onkel

    6. Ansager / sprechen / viel / von / seine Sportler

    7. Student / gehen / zu / sein Zimmer

Lesestück 1

Marathonlauf in Leipzig

Jedes Jahr findet der KMU°-Marathonlauf in Leipzig statt. Mehr als 600 Sportler° machen bei diesem Sportwettbewerb mit. Schon eine Stunde vor dem Start kommen die Läufer° zur Karl-Marx-Universität. Dort wird der Marathonlauf beginnen. Manche Teilnehmer° studieren noch einmal die Strecke. Sie ist mehr als 40 Kilometer lang. *Karl-Marx-Universität* *athletes* *runners* *participants*

      Ein paar Minuten vor zwei Uhr stehen alle Läufer am Start. Die Polizei sperrt den Verkehr ab°. Niemand° darf jetzt an der Universität vorbeifahren°. Das Rote Kreuz steht auch schon bereit°. Die Zuschauer° warten ungeduldig. Es ist zwei Uhr. *sperrt...ab blocks off/no one drive by/steht... bereit is ready spectators*

      Ein Ansager gibt das Zeichen° zum Start. Zuerst starten acht Rollstuhlfahrer°. Fünf Minuten später hört man den Ansager wieder. Jetzt gibt er das Startsignal für die Läufer. Alle Teilnehmer laufen sofort los°. Sie sind in bester Form. Aber wie viele werden es schaffen, mehr als 40 Kilometer zu laufen? Vom Start laufen sie erst zweimal um die Universität herum°. Der Leiter° für den Marathonlauf sieht manchmal auf seine Uhr. Er weiß genau, wann *signal* *wheel chair drivers* *laufen...los start running* *around/person in charge*

Die Teilnehmer sind in bester Form.

Wo findet der Marathonlauf statt?

Seine Kameraden gratulieren dem Sieger.

Lektion 9

die Läufer wieder vorbeikommen°. Es dauert auch nicht lange, da kommen schon die ersten Läufer. Andreas Sprenger, Nummer 203, ist an der Spitze. Er hat schon die letzten zwei Jahre hier gewonnen. Wird er es auch dieses Mal schaffen?

come by

Nach ein paar Kilometern laufen die Sportler nicht mehr so dicht° zusammen. Außer den Männern° starten auch mehr als 40 Frauen diesen Marathonlauf. Manche Läufer sind sogar älter als 60 Jahre.

close/men

Die Richter° notieren° die Namen von den Läufern, sobald° sie vorbeikommen. Es gibt auch Aufseher°. Sie stehen auf der Straße und passen auf°, daß die Strecke für die Läufer frei bleibt. Einige Radfahrer° stehen bereit und wollen ihrer Mannschaft° helfen°.

judges/jot down/ as soon as attendants watch bicycle rider/team help

Auf der Strecke gibt es einige Stellen°, wo die Sportler etwas trinken° können. Dort stehen auch Wasserbehälter°. Bei der Hitze können sich die Läufer dort etwas abkühlen°.

places drink/water containers cool off

Nummer 203 ist noch immer an erster Stelle. Er ist jetzt schon mehr als 35 Kilometer gelaufen. Andreas Sprenger läuft sehr schnell. Er sieht gar nicht müde aus. Am Ziel° sagt der Ansager den Zuschauern, daß der erste Läufer bald ankommen wird. Wer wird es wohl sein? Plötzlich° hört man die Zuschauer klatschen°. Der erste Sportler läuft dem Ziel entgegen°. Der Sieger° heißt auch dieses Jahr wieder Andreas Sprenger. Er hat zum dritten Mal gewonnen. Seine Kameraden° gratulieren° ihm. Er hat den Marathonlauf in der Zeit von 2 Stunden und 17 Minuten gewonnen.

finish line

suddenly/applaud towards/winner

buddies/congratulate

Fragen über das Lesestück

1. Wie viele Sportler kommen zum Marathonlauf in Leipzig?
2. Wo beginnt der Marathonlauf?
3. Was macht die Polizei ein paar Minuten vor dem Start?
4. Wer startet zuerst?
5. Wo laufen die Sportler zuerst?
6. Wer hat den Marathonlauf schon zweimal gewonnen?
7. Wie viele Frauen starten im KMU-Marathonlauf?
8. Wie alt sind die ältesten Sportler?
9. Was machen die Richter? Und die Aufseher?
10. Was müssen die Läufer bei der Hitze manchmal tun?
11. Warum sieht Andreas Sprenger nicht sehr müde aus?
12. Warum klatschen die Zuschauer?
13. Wer gewinnt den Marathonlauf?
14. Wie lange ist der Sieger gelaufen?

Erweiterung

22. Wie heißt das auf deutsch?

1. Will he participate?
2. Did you beat him? No, he is much better than I am.
3. I like to play tennis.
4. Did you hike yesterday?
5. She would like to drink a glass of water.
6. It's his turn.
7. He doesn't look tired.
8. The spectators are applauding.
9. They congratulate her.
10. Who won?
11. The police are blocking off the street.
12. The athletes are waiting at the finish line.

23. Beantwortet die Fragen! Encourage varied responses. These questions could lead to a short discussion.

Welche Sportart treibst du?

Warum hast du diesen Sport gern?

Welcher Sport ist in deiner Schule sehr beliebt?

Kommen viele Zuschauer zu den Sportwettbewerben in deiner Schule? Warum?

Was trinkst du gern zum Mittagessen?

Rückblick If your students have any difficulties in completing the exercises, you may wish to review the grammar point and some of the related exercises in the particular lesson in which these were covered.

I. Complete the comparison by providing the comparative and the superlative.

1. Heute morgen ist es kalt. Später ist es _____. Am Abend ist es_____.
2. Das Museum ist alt. Das Rathaus ist _____. Das Schloß ist _____.
3. Die BRD ist klein. Die DDR ist _____. Österreich ist _____.
4. Frankfurt ist weit von München. Berlin ist _____ von München. Hamburg ist _____.
5. Das Fahrrad fährt schnell. Der Bus fährt _____. Der Zug fährt _____.
6. Die Elbe ist lang. Der Rhein ist _____. Die Donau ist _____.

II. Provide the proper form of the possessive adjective in each sentence.

1. Er geht mit (his girlfriend) _____ ins Kino.
2. Sie sind zu (their parents) _____ gefahren.
3. (Her blouse) _____ ist sehr teuer.
4. Ich antworte (my teachers) _____.

5. Wir spielen (our music) _____ sehr gern.

6. Kauf (your brothers) _____ ein paar Karten, Daniel!

7. Wir essen gern bei (your mother) _____, Kerstin und Jörg.

III. Choose the most appropriate verb from the list below to complete each phrase.

1. den Sportwettbewerb _____

2. Auto _____

3. Schach _____

4. ein Glas Limonade _____

5. Glück _____

6. einen Walzer _____

7. die Lektion _____

8. meine Hausaufgaben _____

9. Abendbrot _____

10. eine Frage _____

fahren	spielen
trinken	tanzen
haben	gewinnen
beantworten	verstehen
essen	machen

IV. Supply the appropriate forms of *dieser, jeder, welcher*.

1. _____ Buch hast du gelesen?

2. Ich habe fast _____ Film gesehen.

3. _____ Mäntel sind sehr teuer.

4. _____ Hemd kostet 40 DM.

5. _____ Karten hast du gekauft?

6. Was machst du mit _____ Kassette?

7. Er ist aus _____ Museum gekommen.

8. _____ Fahrrad habt ihr gekauft?

Lesestück 2

Die DDR — Land und Städte Use a map to further illustrate the various geographical features.

Die Deutsche Demokratische Republik grenzt im Osten an Polen, im Südosten an die Tschechoslowakei und im Westen an die Bundesrepublik Deutschland. Im Norden bildet° die Ostsee eine natürliche Grenze. Zwei Drittel der DDR bestehen aus dem *Tiefland* (im Norden) und ein Drittel besteht aus dem *Mittelgebirgsland* (im Süden). Das Erzgebirge liegt im Süden und reicht° bis in die Tschechoslowakei. Der Fichtelberg (1 214 m) ist der höchste Berg. Im Südwesten liegt der Thüringer Wald. Der Harz liegt im Westen der DDR und reicht bis in die BRD. Der höchste Berg im Harz ist der Brocken (1 142 m).

forms

reaches

75% der Bevölkerung wohnt in Städten. (Stralsund)

Die Elbe ist der längste Fluß.

Im Norden ist das Tiefland.

Die Elbe ist der längste Fluß. Die Elbe erreicht in der DDR eine Länge von 566 Kilometern. Nach der Elbe kommt die Saale mit 427 Kilometern. Der drittlängste Fluß ist die Oder (162 km). Die Oder bildet die natürliche Grenze zwischen der DDR und Polen. Der Oder-Spree-Kanal (84 km) ist der längste Kanal°. *canal*

In der DDR leben° fast 17 Millionen Menschen. 75 Prozent° der Bevölkerung° wohnt in Städten. Die größte Stadt ist Berlin (Ost), die Hauptstadt der DDR. Berlin (Ost) liegt im Osten der DDR und hat ungefähr 1,2 Millionen Einwohner. Die zweitgrößte Stadt, Leipzig (560 000 Einwohner), liegt im Süden. Jedes Jahr kommen eine halbe Million Besucher zur Messe° (Frühling und Herbst). Die nächstgrößte Stadt, Dresden (515 000 Einwohner), liegt im Südosten. Dresden hat viele Museen° und historische Gebäude. Nach Dresden kommt Karl-Marx-Stadt (315 000 Einwohner). Karl-Marx-Stadt liegt im Süden und ist eine wichtige Industriestadt°. Wie Dresden liegt auch Magdeburg an der Elbe. Magdeburg (290 000 Einwohner) liegt im Westen der DDR. *live/percent population* *Trade Fair* *museums* *industrial city*

Die Insel Rügen ist die größte Insel der DDR. Jedes Jahr verbringen° über 700 000 Menschen ihre Ferien° auf dieser beliebten Insel. *spend/vacation*

Fragen über das Lesestück

1. Welche Länder grenzen an die DDR?
2. Wie heißen die zwei Landschaften?
3. Wie heißt der höchste Berg und wie hoch ist er?
4. Wie heißen die drei größten Flüsse?
5. Wie viele Menschen wohnen in Städten?
6. Wie heißen die drei größten Städte und wo liegen sie?
7. Was für Sehenswürdigkeiten gibt es in Dresden?
8. Welche zwei Städte liegen an der Elbe.
9. Wie heißt die größte Insel und was machen viele Besucher dort jedes Jahr?

Sprachspiegel

Have some of your students read their description. Others might want to ask some questions.

I. **Describe your favorite sport in one or two paragraphs. Your description might include such items as: When do you participate (time of season)? Where do you do your sport? With whom do you play? How long have you participated in this sport?**

II. **Write at least one sentence in German defining the following:**

1. Sportwettbewerb
2. Weitsprung
3. Ansager
4. Zuschauer
5. Sportler

III. **Schreib einen kurzen Aufsatz über das Thema *Ein Marathonlauf!***

If you feel that your students may encounter some problems in writing a short description, you may want to give them some questions, using those following *Lesestück 1*.

der Ansager (Leipzig)

Wie sagt man's? Encourage students to role-play these dialogs. Ask questions about them.

Wie schnell bist du denn gelaufen?
13 Sekunden.
Im Hundert-Meter Lauf bist du immer klasse.

Kannst du 10 Kilometer schaffen?
Mit dem Auto ja, aber nicht zu Fuß.
Das kann jeder.
Aber nicht jeder hat ein Auto.

Ich habe schon viel trainiert?
Für das Tennisspiel?
Nein, wir spielen morgen Fußball.
Na, dann viel Glück!

Diesmal bist du besser gewesen.
Ich habe eben Glück gehabt.
Nein, du bist in guter Form.

Wann findet das Fußballspiel statt?
Am Freitag, um vier.
Gehst du hin?
Vielleicht.

Hast du Paul geholfen?
Er braucht meine Hilfe nicht.
Warum nicht?
Er trainiert viel mehr als früher.

Gehst du zum Sportwettbewerb?
Ich glaube nicht.
Angelika soll die Beste sein.
Im Weitsprung?
Nein, im Tausend-Meter-Lauf.

Zungenbrecher See how fast your students can say this tongue twister without stopping.

Hundert hurtige Hunde hetzen hinter hundert hurtigen Hasen her.
(A hundred speedy dogs are racing after a hundred speedy rabbits.)

Kulturecke

Sports

Germans have become more and more concerned about physical fitness. Running, jogging, hiking and walking are just some of the sports supported by the German Sports Federation *(DSB-Deutscher Sportbund)* for people of all ages. Throughout Germany, usually in a forest or park area, you can find designated exercise areas marked *"TRIMM-DICH-PFAD"* (literally meaning "Slim Down Path"). To keep physically fit or to participate in organized sports, Germans join local sports clubs. Every fourth person in the Federal Republic is a member of a sports club.

Soccer *(Fußball)* is by far the most popular sport. During the soccer season, from August to May, millions of people watch the games in the various stadiums around the country or on television at home. The national team of the Federal Republic is considered one of the best in the world.

Germany has produced world-class athletes in track and field competition *(Leichtathletik)* as well. Meets between various countries are scheduled continuously to compare athletic achievements with the rest of the world. The sport with the longest tradition in Germany is gymnastics *(Turnen)*, which became popular in the early 19th century and is today the second most popular sport with almost three million Germans participating. The sport of handball *(Handball)* is not the same as we know it. The German handball is an indoor or outdoor sport played with a ball slightly smaller than a soccer ball. Similar to soccer, the object is to get the ball between the goal posts.

For many decades in Germany, tennis *(Tennis)* was reserved only for the upper class. This is no longer true today. Tennis courts, which typically have a clay surface, are now found in all cities and most smaller towns as well. It is difficult to find golf courses in Germany. The sport of golf *(Golf)* is played by few Germans who belong to private clubs. However, the recreational sport of miniature golf *(Minigolf* or *Kleingolf)* is played by Germans everywhere. There are even championships in which the best players participate.

Various types of horse races *(Pferderennen)* take place in major cities from early spring through late fall. Horseback riding *(Reiten)* has been popular for centuries. However, this sport is expensive and practiced by only a few. In horsemanship competition, German riders have done extremely well in international competition, winning many medals in the Olympics over the last two to three decades.

The water sports, such as sailing *(Segeln)*, enjoy a tremendous popularity among Germans. The famous annual *Kieler Woche,* an international sailing regatta, has the best sailors compete for the grand prize. Others enjoy sailing more as a leisure-time sport. Sailing is particularly popular on the North Sea and Baltic Sea as well as in the few sailing lakes that Germany has to offer. Recently, surfing *(Surfen)* has been enthusiastically received by Germans. There are over one million people who participate in this sport. Those who enjoy more treacherous waters are involved in white water canoeing *(Wildwasser fahren)*, which was officially introduced as a sport in the 1972 Olympic Games held in Germany.

Over a million Germans belong to rifle and pistol clubs *(Schützenvereine)*. Many of the members enjoy the marksmanship training as well as hunting *(Jagen)* in areas that are leased to trained and licensed hunters. A less expensive sport is fishing *(Angeln)*. Germans fish not only in the lakes but also in the various rivers.

Most cities have indoor or outdoor skating facilities. Here Germans can practice and improve their skill. Germany has produced several world-class figure skaters *(Eiskunstläufer)* during the past three decades. Ice hockey *(Eishockey)* was relatively unknown twenty years ago. During the last few years, however, Germany has done quite well in international com-

Marathonlauf (Leipzig)

Segeln ist sehr beliebt.

TRIMM - DICH - PFAD
STADT
FÜRSTENFELDBRUCK

ein Trimm-
Dich-
Pfad

Was machen diese Leute? (Bayern)

Leichtathletik (Jena)

Hochsprung

Handball

Lektion 9

petition. Most sports organizations also have a youth program. During the winter months, many Germans head for the mountains in Southern Germany and go skiing *(Ski laufen)*. Those who master the skill after years of hard training can compete in local, national or even international competition. Endurance is tested not only in downhill skiing but also in cross-country skiing *(Skilanglauf)*. Some of these competitive races cover distances of up to 30 miles. Another winter sport is curling, seen mostly in the southern part of Germany.

Gliding *(Segelfliegen)* is also a popular sport in Southern Germany. There the hills and mountains provide the favorable air currents needed to stay in the air for a long time. Those who are most daring participate in a new sport called hang-gliding *(Drachen fliegen)* in which these sporting people push themselves off cliffs or hills and sit on a rod strapped to a kite-like sail. Finally, the sport of mountaineering *(Bergsteigen)* is practiced in the mountainous regions of Germany. Those who become experts eventually climb the many challenging peaks found in the Alps.

Drachen fliegen

Ski laufen

Skilanglauf

Vokabeln

sich **abkühlen** to cool off
absperren to block off
der **Ansager,-** announcer
aufpassen to watch, keep an eye on
something
der **Aufseher,-** attendant
der **Basketball,⸚e** basketball
bereitstehen to be ready, stand ready
die **Bestleistung,-en** best performance
das **Bier,-e** beer
der **Bleistift,-e** pencil
die **Blockflöte,-n** recorder
die **Chance,-n** chance
dabei in the process, while doing that
dicht close
dran sein to be one's turn
Ich bin dran. It's my turn.
das **Endergebnis,-se** final result
entgegenlaufen to run towards
der **Federball,⸚e** badminton
die **Form-en** form, shape
früh early
gestern yesterday
das **Glas,⸚er** glass
das **Golf** golf
gratulieren to congratulate
helfen to help
herumlaufen to run around
das **Hockey** hockey
hoffentlich hopefully
der **Kakao** hot chocolate, cocoa
der **Kamerad,-en** buddy
kaum hardly
klatschen to applaud
der **Korbball,⸚e** basketball
lang long
der **Läufer,-** runner
der **Leiter,-** head, person in charge
loslaufen to start running
die **Limonade,-n** soft drink
das **Mal,-e** time(s)
der **Mann,⸚er** man
die **Mannschaft,-en** team
der **Marathonlauf,⸚er** marathon run
mindestens at least
mitmachen to participate
niemand nobody, noone
notieren to jot down, make a note of
die **Nummer,-n** number
phantastisch fantastic, great
plötzlich suddenly
die **Polizei** police
das **Prozent,-e** percent

der **Radfahrer,-** bicycle rider
der **Richter,-** judge
der **Rollstuhlfahrer,-** wheel chair driver
das **Rote Kreuz** Red Cross
schaffen to manage (it), make (it)
schlagen to beat
Schlittschuh laufen to skate
schwimmen to swim
der **Sieger,-** winner
Ski laufen to ski
sobald as soon as
sonst besides, otherwise
die **Spitze,-n** top
an der Spitze sein to be in front
die **Sportart,-en** kind of sport
der **Sportwettbewerb,-e** sports competition
springen to jump
der **Start,-e** start
starten to start
das **Startsignal,-e** starting signal
stattfinden to take place
die **Stelle,-n** place, spot
die **Tasse,-n** cup
der **Teilnehmer,-** participant
das **Tennis** tennis
trainieren to train, practice
treiben to drive, do
Sport treiben to participate in
sports
trinken to drink
übertreffen to surpass, beat
der **Verstand** reason, mind
mehr Glück als Verstand haben
to have more luck than brains
versuchen to try
vorbeifahren to drive by
vorbeikommen to come by
vorhin before, earlier
der **Wasserbehälter,-** water container
der **Wein,-e** wine
der **Weitsprung,⸚e** broad jump
das **Zeichen,-** signal, sign
der **Zentimeter,-** centimeter
das **Ziel,-e** finish (line)
der **Zuschauer,-** spectator

Dialog

Beim Reisebüro
Many department stores, like this one, have their own travel agencies.

ANGESTELLTE:	Bitteschön?
KUNDE:	Meine Frau und ich möchten eine Reise machen.
ANGESTELLTE:	Wissen Sie schon, wohin?
KUNDE:	In den sonnigen Süden. Es kommt aber ganz auf den Preis an. *Adjective endings will be covered in Level 2. Treat the phrase, "In den sonnigen Süden," as an expression at this point.*
ANGESTELLTE:	Wir haben gerade ein Sonderangebot…zwei Wochen in Mallorca.
KUNDE:	Das klingt ja ganz interessant.
ANGESTELLTE:	Sehen Sie! Unser Prospekt beschreibt alles…zwei Wochen, einschließlich Flug, Hotel und zwei Mahlzeiten pro Tag.
KUNDE:	Sie machen mir schon richtig den Mund wässerig. Hm, der Preis ist sehr günstig. Haben Sie im Juli noch etwas frei?
ANGESTELLTE:	Das kann ich gleich mal nachsehen…Ja, wir haben noch ein Doppelzimmer, Abfahrt am 9. Juli. Soll ich zwei Plätze für Sie buchen?
KUNDE:	Ja, bitte, auf den Namen Krüger.
ANGESTELLTE:	Schön, Herr Krüger. Es geht in Ordnung.
ANGESTELLTE:	Sie müssen die Reise einen Monat vor der Abfahrt bezahlen.
KUNDE:	Ich nehme an, Sie schicken mir die Rechnung zu.
ANGESTELLTE:	Die bekommen Sie in ein paar Tagen. Nehmen Sie doch noch diesen Prospekt mit! Ich wünsche Ihnen eine gute Reise.
KUNDE:	Vielen Dank.

During their vacation, most Germans head south. Such countries as Spain, Italy and Yugoslavia are particularly popular.

is quite common to have ps include meals as well.

Fragen über den Dialog

1. Wohin möchten Herr und Frau Krüger fahren?
2. Von welchem Sonderangebot spricht die Angestellte?
3. Wo können sie alles über Mallorca lesen?
4. Wie findet Herr Krüger den Preis für die Reise?
5. Wann möchten Krügers die Reise machen?
6. Wann muß Herr Krüger die Reise bezahlen?
7. Was wird das Reisebüro in ein paar Tagen tun?

At the Travel Agency

CLERK:	Can I help you?
CUSTOMER:	My wife and I would like to take a trip.
CLERK:	Do you know where to?
CUSTOMER:	To the sunny south. It depends entirely on the price.
CLERK:	We're just having a special offer...two weeks in Mallorca.
CUSTOMER:	That sounds quite interesting.
CLERK:	Look! Our brochure describes everything...two weeks, including flight, hotel and two meals a day.
CUSTOMER:	You're already making my mouth water. Hm, the price is very reasonable. Do you still have something available in July?
CLERK:	I can check that right away...Yes, we still have a double room, departure July 9th. Should I book two seats for you?
CUSTOMER:	Yes, please, in the name of Krüger.
CLERK:	Fine, Mr. Krüger. It will be taken care of.
CLERK:	You'll have to pay the trip a month before departure.
CUSTOMER:	I assume you'll send me the bill.
CLERK:	You'll get it in a few days. Why don't you take this brochure along? I hope you have a good trip.
CUSTOMER:	Thank you.

Nützliche Ausdrücke

Review the expressions that students have learned in the *Dialog* and *Lesestück 1.*

Bitteschön?	Can I help you?
Es kommt auf den Preis an.	It depends on the price.
Das klingt gut.	That sounds good.
Ich sehe mal nach.	I'll check it.
Es geht in Ordnung.	It will be taken care of. That's O.K.
Ich nehme an...	I assume...
Gute Reise!	Have a good trip!
Er hält an.	He is stopping.
Wir müssen umsteigen.	We have to transfer.
Sie machen eine Rast.	They take a rest.
Wir sitzen im Freien.	We are sitting outside.

Ergänzung

Students should become familiar with these metric measures. Ask some questions such as: *Wie groß bist du?*, *Wie warm ist es heute?*, etc.

Metric—U.S. Conversion

German Metric		U.S.
1	Gramm (g)	0.035 ounce
1	Pfund (Pfd)	1.1 pounds
1	Kilogramm - *or* Kilo (kg)	2.2 pounds
1	Zentimeter (cm)	0.3937 inch
2,54	Zentimeter	1 inch
1	Meter (m)	3.281 feet
1609,3	Meter	1 mile
1	Kilometer (km)	1.094 yards
1	Liter (l)	2.113 pints

Thermometer Readings

German thermometers use the centigrade scale. To convert Fahrenheit to centigrade, subtract 32, then multiply by 5 and divide by 9. To convert centigrade to Fahrenheit, multiply by 9, divide by 5 and add 32. The chart below gives some sample readings with the conversion.

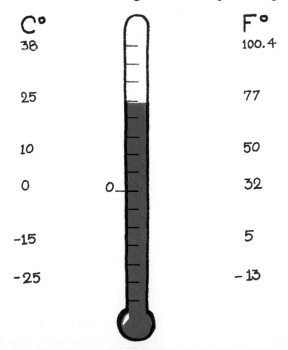

C°		F°
38		100.4
25		77
10		50
0	0	32
-15		5
-25		-13

Metric Units	
1 Pfund	500 Gramm
2 Pfund	1 Kilogramm (or: 1 000 Gramm)
1 Meter	100 Zentimeter
1 000 Meter	1 Kilometer

Ausspracheübung

/ ai /	/ oi /	/ au /
bei	neun	aus
drei	Leute	blau
Mai	teuer	kauft
weiß	euch	Auto
heißt	deutsch	laufen
Teil	heute	genau
weit	Freund	auf
ein	Läufer	brauchen
klein	Häuser	August
Zeit	Bedeutung	Haus

Have students repeat the individual words at a fast pace. You may want to use the description on sound formation, if needed.

[aI] — *(bei):* The lips, lower jaw and tongue move quickly from an approximate [a] position to an approximate [I] position.

[ɔI] — *(heute):* The lips, mandible and tongue move quickly from an approximate [ɔ] position to an approximate [I] position.

[aɔ] — *(Frau):* The lips, mandible and tongue move quickly from an approximate [a] position to an approximate [ɔ] position.

Übungen

Verbs with Separable Prefixes

With modal auxiliaries
When you use modal auxiliaries in a sentence, combine the separable prefix with the verb.

Examples: *Er muß um sechs Uhr aufstehen.*
Sie will ihre Freundin mitbringen.

Present perfect tense
In the present perfect, add the separable prefix to the past participle for regular and irregular verbs.

Examples: *Ich habe meinen Freund angerufen.*
Er hat heute nichts vorgehabt.

As you have seen in the previous lesson, you must learn the present perfect form of all irregular verbs individually. You need only learn the past participle of a particular verb, regardless of the addition of various prefixes, since the prefix changes the meaning but not the structure.

Examples: *Wir sind nicht mitgekommen.* (We didn't come along.)
Ich bin heute morgen vorbeigekommen. (I came by this morning.)
Bist du früh angekommen? (Did you arrive early?)

NOTE: The accent or emphasis is always on the separable prefix.

Here is a list of the most important irregular separable prefix verbs that you have learned so far:

Infinitive	Past Participle
anhaben (to have on)	angehabt
anhalten (to stop)	angehalten
ankommen (to arrive)	ist angekommen
annehmen (to assume)	angenommen
anrufen (to call, phone)	angerufen
aufstehen (to get up)	ist aufgestanden
aussehen (to look)	ausgesehen
aussteigen (to get off)	ist ausgestiegen
einsteigen (to get in)	ist eingestiegen
herumfahren (to drive around)	ist herumgefahren
hineingehen (to go inside)	ist hineingegangen
hierherkommen (to come here)	ist hierhergekommen
loslaufen (to start running)	ist losgelaufen
mitbringen (to bring along)	mitgebracht
mitkommen (to come along)	ist mitgekommen
mitnehmen (to take along)	mitgenommen
nachsehen (to check)	nachgesehen
stattfinden (to take place)	stattgefunden
umsteigen (to transfer)	ist umgestiegen
vorbeifahren (to drive by)	ist vorbeigefahren
vorbeikommen (to come by)	ist vorbeigekommen
vorhaben (to plan)	vorgehabt
weiterfahren (to continue driving)	ist weitergefahren
zugeben (to admit)	zugegeben
zurückgehen (to go back)	ist zurückgegangen
zurückfahren (to drive back)	ist zurückgefahren

Folgt den Beispielen!

1. Was hast du an? — Ich habe einen Anzug an.
   (einen Anzug)

   Wann kommst du vorbei? — Ich komme um sieben Uhr vorbei.
   (um sieben Uhr)

   Wer steigt ein? — Die Touristen steigen ein.
   (die Touristen)

   Wen ruft er an? (Sabine) — Er ruft Sabine an.

   Was räumen die Jungen ab? — Die Jungen räumen das Geschirr ab.
   (das Geschirr)

   Was löst der Ausländer ein? — Der Ausländer löst einen Reisescheck ein.
   (einen Reisescheck)

   Wann machst du sauber? — Ich mache später sauber.
   (später)

2. Stehst du um halb sieben auf? — Ja, ich stehe um halb sieben auf.
   Kommst du heute nachmittag rüber? — Ja, ich komme heute nachmittag rüber.

Variation: Have students answer questions on their own (without using the cue words).

Variation: Personalize questions. (*Um wieviel Uhr stehst du auf?*, *Um wieviel Uhr kommst du rüber?*, etc.)

	Legst du die Schallplatte auf?	Ja, ich lege die Schallplatte auf.
	Hast du am Samstag etwas vor?	Ja, ich habe am Samstag etwas vor.
	Hält der Zug dort an?	Ja, der Zug hält dort an.
	Steigen die Besucher beim Museum aus?	Ja, die Besucher steigen beim Museum aus.
	Bringt er seine Freundin mit?	Ja, er bringt seine Freundin mit.

3. Uwe kommt mit. — **Uwe möchte mitkommen.**

Variation: Ask questions such as: *Wer kommt mit? - Uwe kommt mit.*

Der Kunde probiert es an.	Der Kunde möchte es anprobieren.
Die Leute fahren zurück.	Die Leute möchten zurückfahren.
Wir steigen aus.	Wir möchten aussteigen.
Ich schicke dir das Geschenk zu.	Ich möchte dir das Geschenk zuschicken.
Frau Müller bereitet das Essen zu.	Frau Müller möchte das Essen zubereiten.
Sie kaufen heute ein.	Sie möchten heute einkaufen.

4. Wann kommt das Flugzeug an? — **Wann soll das Flugzeug ankommen?**

Variation: Answer questions instead.

Was zieht der Kunde an?	Was soll der Kunde anziehen?
Machst du dein Zimmer sauber?	Sollst du dein Zimmer saubermachen?
Um wieviel Uhr findet die Vorstellung statt?	Um wieviel Uhr soll die Vorstellung stattfinden?
Warum geht ihr da hinein?	Warum sollt ihr da hineingehen?
Wie sieht die Dame aus?	Wie soll die Dame aussehen?
Paßt du nicht auf?	Sollst du nicht aufpassen?

5. Ich habe den Tisch abgeräumt. Und du? — **Ich habe den Tisch nicht abgeräumt.**

Ich habe meinen Eltern zugewinkt. Und du?	Ich habe meinen Eltern nicht zugewinkt.
Ich habe beim Spiel mitgemacht. Und du?	Ich habe beim Spiel nicht mitgemacht.
Ich habe es ausgefüllt. Und du?	Ich habe es nicht ausgefüllt.
Ich habe das Abendbrot zubereitet. Und du?	Ich habe das Abendbrot nicht zubereitet.
Ich habe den Reisescheck eingelöst. Und du?	Ich habe den Reisescheck nicht eingelöst.

6. Wir haben es mitgebracht. — **Wir haben es mitgebracht.**

Variation: Ask questions such as: *Was habt ihr mitgebracht?, Wir haben...mitgebracht.*

anziehen	**Wir haben es angezogen.**
vorhaben	Wir haben es vorgehabt.
zugeben	Wir haben es zugegeben.
mitnehmen	Wir haben es mitgenommen.
annehmen	Wir haben es angenommen.

7. Sie steigen dort aus. — **Sie sind dort ausgestiegen.**

Ich fahre dort weiter.	Ich bin dort weitergefahren.
Steigt er dort ein?	Ist er dort eingestiegen?
Wann kommst du dort an?	Wann bist du dort angekommen?
Die Familie fährt dort vorbei.	Die Familie ist dort vorbeigefahren.
Wir gehen dort hinein.	Wir sind dort hineingegangen.

<table>
<tr><td>8. Paßt ihr nicht auf?</td><td>Habt ihr nicht aufgepaßt?</td></tr>
</table>

8. Paßt ihr nicht auf?   Habt ihr nicht aufgepaßt?

Variation: Answer questions
with *Ja,...* or *Nein,...*

Kaufst du heute ein?	Hast du heute eingekauft?
Was hast du denn vor?	Was hast du denn vorgehabt?
Bereitet er es gut zu?	Hat er es gut zubereitet?
Ziehst du diese Hose an?	Hast du diese Hose angezogen?
Gibt sie es zu?	Hat sie es zugegeben?
Machen sie alles sauber?	Haben sie alles saubergemacht?

9. Change the following sentences from the present to the present perfect tense.

> **Beispiel:** *Die Leute kommen mit dem Flugzeug an.*
> *Die Leute sind mit dem Flugzeug angekommen.*

1. Ich sehe gleich einmal nach.
2. Das Spiel findet um drei Uhr statt.
3. Sie steigen schnell in die S-Bahn ein.
4. Um wieviel Uhr ruft Angelika an?
5. Am Nachmittag fahre ich in die Stadt mit.
6. Warum löst du alle Reiseschecks ein?
7. Die Schüler bringen ihre Musikinstrumente mit.
8. Was haben Sie am Sonntag vor?
9. Die Polizei sperrt die Straßen ab.
10. Die Besucher winken ihnen zu.

10. Supply the proper verb form in its appropriate tense (present or present perfect) from the list below. Be sure to separate the prefix, where appropriate.

1. Wann _____ du heute morgen _____?
2. Willst du in der Stadt _____? Die Auswahl ist dort viel besser.
3. Zuerst muß ich die Mahlzeit _____.
4. Ich _____ das Kleid _____. Es paßt sehr gut.
5. Peter _____ nicht _____. Jetzt kann er die Frage nicht beantworten.
6. _____ du ihn _____? Ja, er kommt mit.
7. Die Touristen _____ am Fernsehturm _____.
8. Wir sollen dieses Anmeldeformular _____.
9. Wie _____ er denn _____? Er ist sehr groß.
10. Könnt ihr euer Zimmer _____? Wir haben keine Lust.

aufpassen	ausfüllen
aussehen	aufstehen
einkaufen	anrufen
aussteigen	zubereiten
saubermachen	anprobieren

11. Complete each of the following sentences by using an appropriate prefix.

1. Die Straßenbahn steht schon da. Er steigt gleich _____.
2. Warum ziehst du die Hose nicht _____? Vielleicht paßt sie.

3. Leg doch eine Schallplatte _____! Ich möchte etwas Musik hören.
4. Sie sind zu weit gegangen. Gehen Sie wieder _____!
5. Die Vorstellung findet um acht Uhr _____.
6. Wir werden Fußball spielen. Machst du _____?
7. Die Jugendlichen räumen das Geschirr _____.
8. Steh bitte jetzt _____! Es ist schon neun Uhr.
9. Die Schüler bringen ihre Bücher _____.
10. Meine Mutter bereitet noch schnell das Essen _____.

Verbs with Inseparable Prefixes

Present tense

There are a number of inseparable prefixes in German that remain with the verb.

Examples: *Er entwertet die Farhrkarte.*
　　　　　　　Bezahlst du das?

As you can see from these examples, the verbs containing inseparable prefixes are treated the same way as those without prefixes.

Present perfect tense

The past participle of regular verbs with inseparable prefixes has the same form as the third person singular of the present tense.

Examples: *Er hat die Fahrkarte entwertet.*
　　　　　　　Hast du das bezahlt?

Again you must learn the past participle of irregular verbs with inseparable prefixes. The list below includes the most important verbs with inseparable prefixes learned up to now. You will notice that some past participles are identical to those learned in the previous lesson, except that the prefix replaces *ge*. Here again, your students should know the basic past participle (irregular verbs) from *Lektion 9.*

Infinitive	Past Participle
beginnen (to begin)	begonnen
bekommen (to get)	bekommen
beschreiben (to describe)	beschrieben
besprechen (to discuss)	besprochen
bestehen (to consist)	bestanden
verbringen (to spend—time)	verbracht
verlassen (to leave)	verlassen
verlieren (to lose)	verloren
verstehen (to understand)	verstanden

NOTE: The accent is never on the inseparable prefix, but always on the stem of the verb.

Folgt den Beispielen!

12. Ich bekomme kein Geld.　　　　　　Ich habe kein Geld bekommen.
　　Er bespricht die Lektion.　　　　　Er hat die Lektion besprochen.
　　Wann verläßt du dein Haus?　　　Wann hast du dein Haus verlassen?
　　Erreicht sie das?　　　　　　　　Hat sie das erreicht?

Die Jungen verlieren das Spiel.   Die Jungen haben das Spiel verloren.

Wir bezahlen an der Kasse.   Wir haben an der Kasse bezahlt.

13. Hast du es beantwortet?   Hast du es beantwortet?

Variation: Ask questions such as: *Was hast du beantwortet?*, *Wen hast du begrüßt?*, etc.

begrüßen   Hast du es begrüßt?

beschreiben   Hast du es beschrieben?

verlieren   Hast du es verloren?

entwerten   Hast du es entwertet?

verstehen   Hast du es verstanden?

14. Form complete sentences using the present perfect tense.

> **Beispiel:** *Wann / zurückfahren / ihr*
> *Wann seid ihr zurückgefahren?*

1. Studenten / beantworten / Fragen
2. Leute / entwerten / Fahrkarten
3. Herr / umsteigen / bei / Bahnhof
4. Warum / du / Spiel / verlieren
5. Bus / anhalten / dort drüben
6. Was / vorhaben / Sie / gestern
7. Besichtigen / ihr / Stadt
8. Verstehen / er / Dialog
9. Ich / mitnehmen / Schultasche
10. Bekommen / du / Geld

Accusative Prepositions

The accusative case always follows these prepositions:

durch	through
für	for
gegen	against
ohne	without
um	around

Contractions

These accusative prepositions and articles are contracted as long as there is no special emphasis on the article.

durch	+	das	=	durchs
für	+	das	=	fürs
um	+	das	=	ums

Folgt den Beispielen!

15. Wir sind durch die Stadt gegangen.

    Museum

    Universität

    Tanzschule

    Rathaus

    Bahnhof

Wir sind durch die Stadt gegangen.
Wir sind durchs Museum gegangen.
Wir sind durch die Universität gegangen.
Wir sind durch die Tanzschule gegangen.
Wir sind durchs Rathaus gegangen.
Wir sind durch den Bahnhof gegangen.

16. Fährst du um das Haus? (Schule)

    Gehst du um das Gebäude? (Ecke)

    Läufst du um den Parkplatz? (Rathaus)

    Gehst du um die Jugendherberge?
    (Museum)

    Fährst du um die Bank? (Reisebüro)

Nein, ich fahre um die Schule.
Nein, ich gehe um die Ecke.
Nein, ich laufe ums Rathaus.
Nein, ich gehe ums Museum.

Nein, ich fahre ums Reisebüro.

Variation: Answer in complete sentences. You may also have students vary responses.

17. Für wen ist das Geld? (Freund)

    Für wen ist diese Kassette? (Bruder)

    Für wen ist dieser Platz?
    (Großmutter)

    Für wen ist die Karte? (Freundin)

    Für wen ist das Geschenk? (Onkel)

    Für wen ist dieses Zimmer?
    (Schwester)

Für meinen Freund.
Für meinen Bruder.
Für meine Großmutter.

Für meine Freundin.
Für meinen Onkel.
Für meine Schwester.

18. Warum kommst du ohne dein Buch?

    Fahrrad

    Geld

    Gitarre

    Freund

    Karte

Warum kommst du ohne dein Buch?
Warum kommst du ohne dein Fahrrad?
Warum kommst du ohne dein Geld?
Warum kommst du ohne deine Gitarre?
Warum kommst du ohne deinen Freund?
Warum kommst du ohne deine Karte?

19. Sie spielt gegen ihre Schwester.

    Freundin

    Lehrer

    Mannschaft

    Mutter

    Bruder

Sie spielt gegen ihre Schwester.
Sie spielt gegen ihre Freundin.
Sie spielt gegen ihren Lehrer.
Sie spielt gegen ihre Mannschaft.
Sie spielt gegen ihre Mutter.
Sie spielt gegen ihren Bruder.

Variation: Ask the questions such as: Gegen wen spielt sie?, Sie spielt gegen ihre Schwester.

20. Replace the italicized words with those listed in parentheses.

1. Wir spielen lieber ohne *ihn*. (ihr Bruder, mein Freund, du, ihr)
2. Viele Besucher kommen durch *die Stadt*. (Rathaus, Ort, Museum, Straße, Gebäude)

3. Er fährt mit seinem Auto gegen *das Haus*. (Fahrrad, Stadtmauer, Turm, Tor)

4. Kaufst du ein Geschenk für *deinen Freund?* (er, ich, sein Onkel, ihre Tante)

5. Gehen wir lieber um *die Ecke*. (Stadttor, Kino, Universität, Bahnhof, Geschäft)

21. Complete the following sentences.

Have students vary their responses as much as possible.

1. Ich will nicht ohne _____.

2. Das Reisebüro ist gleich um _____.

3. Für meine Schwester _____.

4. Ich möchte nicht gern gegen _____.

5. Auf unserer Reise sind wir durch _____.

6. Sie kaufen die Geschenke für _____.

7. Kannst du ohne _____?

8. Haben Sie etwas gegen _____?

Lesestück 1

Auf zur Zugspitze!

Die Alpen sind zu jeder Jahreszeit beliebt. Besonders gern besuchen viele Deutsche und Ausländer° jedes Jahr die Gegend um die Zugspitze. Die Zugspitze ist fast 3 000 m hoch und der höchste Berg in Deutschland. Sollen wir einmal eine Reise zur Zugspitze machen? Warum nicht. Also°, auf zur Zugspitze!   *foreigners*   *O.K. then…*

Grainau liegt in der Nähe von Garmisch-Partenkirchen.

Wir fahren direkt in die Alpen zu dem Ort° Grainau, in der *town*
Nähe von Garmisch-Partenkirchen. Schon bei der Ankunft in
Grainau begrüßt uns die Zugspitze aus der Entfernung. Der
Bahnhof ist sehr klein. Von hier können wir mit der Zahnradbahn° *cog-wheel train*
fast bis auf die Spitze fahren. Die Bahn fährt jede Stunde und kommt
immer pünktlich. Viele Touristen warten schon. Wir fahren ungefähr zehn Minuten bis zur nächsten Station—Eibsee. Auch hier
steigen noch einige Leute ein. Vom Eibsee fahren wir noch eine
halbe Stunde. Wir halten jetzt nicht mehr an. Unterwegs° haben wir *on the way*
einen schönen Blick auf den Eibsee. Er sieht wirklich märchenhaft° *fairy tale-like*
aus. Endlich kommen wir am Schneefernerhaus an°. Die Zahnrad- *kommen…an arrive*
bahn fährt nicht mehr weiter. Wir müssen in eine Seilbahn° um- *cable car*
steigen.

     Endlich sind wir da. Heute haben wir Glück. Das Wetter ist
ausgezeichnet°. Der Himmel° ist blau und es gibt nur ein paar *excellent/sky*
Wolken°. Viele Touristen sind schon da. Hier oben° gibt es viel *clouds/on top*
zu sehen. Manche Leute sind sogar ganz auf die Spitze ge-
stiegen° und machen dort oben eine Rast. Andere gehen ein paar *climbed*
Meter weiter und kommen so nach Österreich. Die Grenze ist
direkt auf der Zugspitze. Natürlich sind wir nach einer Weile
etwas hungrig. Auf der Zugspitze gibt es ein Restaurant. Kein

Was kann man alles auf der Zugspitze sehen?

anderes deutsches Restaurant liegt so hoch wie dieses. Wir können hier an einem Tisch im Freien sitzen und eine Mahlzeit essen.

Am Nachmittag fahren wir wieder mit einer Seilbahn Richtung° Eibsee. Der Eibsee ist bei den Touristen sehr beliebt. Manche kommen nur einen Tag hierher°, wandern in der Gegend oder fahren mit Booten auf dem See. Andere bleiben eine Woche oder länger am Eibsee und übernachten in den Hotels am See.

to
kommen...hierher *come here*

Die Abfahrtszeiten° vom Eibsee nach Grainau stehen deutlich° auf dem Fahrplan am Bahnhof. Eine Zahnradbahn fährt uns nach Grainau zurück°. Viele Touristen steigen in Grainau aus°, aber manche fahren direkt bis nach Garmisch-Partenkirchen weiter.

departure times
clearly
fährt...zurück *drives back*/steigen... aus *get off*

Fragen über das Lesestück

1. Wo liegt die Zugspitze? Wie hoch ist dieser Berg?
2. Wie kommt man von Grainau zur Zugspitze?
3. Wie oft fährt die Bahn?
4. Was kann man unterwegs sehen?
5. Wo müssen wir umsteigen? Warum?
6. Wie ist das Wetter heute?
7. Was machen die Touristen dort oben?
8. Welche Grenze ist direkt auf der Zugspitze?
9. Was machen die Touristen am Eibsee?
10. Warum steigen nicht alle Touristen in Grainau aus?

Erweiterung

22. Beantwortet diese Fragen! Encourage students to write about their experience (even if it's imaginary!).

1. Hast du in den letzten zwei oder drei Jahren eine Reise gemacht? Wohin?
2. Was hast du auf der Reise gemacht?
3. Wann hast du eine Reise gemacht?
4. Wo habt ihr übernachtet?
5. Wie weit bist du gefahren?

23. Use a complete sentence to define each word in German.

1. Sonderangebot
2. Prospekt
3. Rechnung

4. Reisebüro
5. Restaurant
6. Tourist

24. Provide a logical response to each statement or question.

Encourage students to be creative in writing out the various responses.

1. Bitteschön?
2. Wohin wollen Sie denn fahren?
3. Ja, dort ist es immer schön warm.
4. So teuer ist diese Reise nicht.
5. Ja, das kann ich tun. Einen Moment, bitte.

25. Wie heißt das auf deutsch?

1. It depends on the time.
2. This book describes everything.
3. Do you have a room available?
4. Send me a brochure.
5. Why is he stopping?
6. We'll have to transfer.
7. We are very hungry.
8. I would like to eat a meal.
9. Should we sit outside?
10. The tourists are getting off in Munich.

26. Complete the following information.

If you have some German newspapers or magazines, have students find references to metric units. See if they can convert them.

1. 7 kg = _____ g
2. 18 Pfund = _____ kg
3. 2,5 m = _____ cm
4. 12 000 cm = _____ km
5. 15° C = _____ ° F
6. 4 lbs. = _____ g
7. 1 ft. = _____ cm

27. Beantwortet die Fragen!

Have students respond with many different answers.

Wohin möchtest du eine Reise machen?

Warum brauchst du einen Prospekt?

Warum sitzt du im Freien?

Wie sieht das Land in deiner Gegend aus?

Wie kommst du jeden Tag zur Schule?

Rückblick

Review exercises. If your students have some difficulties, go back to the lesson in which the particular grammar point was discussed.

I. Change these sentences from the present to the present perfect tense.

Beispiel: *Am Abend essen wir meistens Wurst.*
Am Abend haben wir meistens Wurst gegessen.

1. Der Tourist fragt den Beamten.
2. Wann bist du beim Stadttor?
3. Trinkst du den Tee?
4. Mein Vater kommt um fünf Uhr nach Hause.
5. Wie gefällt dir dieses Spiel?
6. Bekommt ihr noch Karten?
7. Haben wir heute Hausaufgaben?
8. Sprechen die Ausländer deutsch?
9. Bringen Sie mir ein Geschenk?
10. Ich sage es nicht.
11. Sie fahren nach Deutschland.
12. Bezahlst du für diese Reise?

II. Supply the proper forms for the present, future or present perfect tense. Use the verbs provided in parentheses. Make sure that the whole sentence is meaningful.

1. (gehen) Die Mädchen _____ letzten Samstag zum Sportwettbewerb _____.
2. (schen) Wir _____ diesen Film nächste Woche _____.
3. (kommen) Wann _____ du zu uns?
4. (kaufen) Was _____ wir ihm morgen zum Geburtstag _____?
5. (fahren) Heute ist der 15. Mai. Schmidts _____ am 19. Mai nach Europa _____.
6. (gefallen) Dieser Mantel _____ mir nicht.
7. (warten) Erika kommt immer spät. Ich _____ das letzte Mal eine halbe Stunde auf sie _____.
8. (sein) Es ist sechs Uhr. In zwei Stunden _____ das Flugzeug hier _____.
9. (helfen) Warum _____ du ihm nicht?
10. (wissen) Köln liegt am Rhein. Das _____ ich nicht _____.

III. Supply the proper plural forms and their corresponding definite articles.

1. Die Verkäuferin zeigt ihr (Hemd, Bluse, Prospekt, Buch, Mantel).
2. Wir fahren zu (Stadt, Berg, Haus, Gebäude, Turm).
3. Die Leute kommen schon aus (Kino, Bahnhof, Theater, Museum, Reisebüro).
4. Kaufst du (Heft, Kugelschreiber, Bleistift, Buch)?
5. (Straßenbahn, Zug, Auto, Fahrrad) stehen da drüben.
6. Ich brauche die Karten für (Lehrer, Kunde, Mädchen, Dame).

IV. Supply the proper forms after the dative and accusative prepositions. The singular or plural forms in parentheses are given in the nominative case.

Beispiel: *Sprichst du mit (er) _____?*
Sprichst du mit ihm?

1. Er kommt von (die Bank) _____.
2. Wir spielen gegen (euere Klasse) _____.
3. Warum geht ihr nicht ohne (ich) _____?
4. Um fünf Uhr kommen sie aus (die Tanzschule) _____.
5. Nach (das Spiel) _____ können wir in die Stadt gehen.
6. Wir müssen um (der Marktplatz) _____ fahren.

7. Sie wohnt bei (ihre Eltern) _____.
8. Hat er etwas Geld für (wir) _____?
9. Die Touristen gehen durch (das Stadttor) _____.
10. Spielst du gern mit (dein Bruder) _____?
11. Sie fahren zu (ihre Freunde) _____.
12. Außer (ich) _____ spielt auch Ursula Klavier.

Lesestück 2

If you have a detailed map, point out the various cities along the "Romantische Straße" (from Würzburg to Füssen).

Die Romantische Straße

Zwischen Würzburg und Füssen liegt die „Romantische Straße". Diese Straße ist ungefähr 360 Kilometer lang. Millionen von Deutschen und Ausländern besuchen jedes Jahr die historischen Städte wie Würzburg, Rothenburg, Dinkelsbühl und Nördlingen. Stellen wir uns einmal eine Reise auf der Romantischen Straße vor°. Unsere Reise beginnt in Würzburg.

Würzburg ist eine Bischofs- und Universitätsstadt. Schon aus der Entfernung sehen wir die Festung° Marienburg. Diese Festung ist fast 800 Jahre alt. Sie steht hoch auf einem Hügel° und überblickt° den Main. Eine Brücke (Die Alte Mainbrücke) — man hat sie von 1453 bis 1543 erbaut° — führt° direkt in die Stadt. Verkehrsschilder° zeigen deutlich die Richtung zur Romantischen Straße.

Nach ungefähr einer Stunde Fahrt° kommen wir nach Weikersheim. Wie die anderen Städte in dieser Gegend erinnert uns auch Weikersheim an° das Mittelalter°. Diese Stadt ist früher bei den Fürsten° sehr beliebt gewesen. Sie haben Weikersheim oft besucht und manchmal auch dort gewohnt. Nur ungefähr 15 Kilometer weit von Weikersheim entfernt liegt das Städtchen Creglingen. Viele Touristen besuchen dort jedes Jahr den Marienaltar° in der Herrgottskirche. Er ist sehr berühmt°.

Rothenburg ob der Tauber ist für viele Deutsche und Ausländer der Lieblingsort° an der Romantischen Straße. Eine Stadtmauer° umgibt° diese Stadt aus dem Mittelalter. Man kann nur durch vier oder fünf Tore° in die Stadt fahren. Alle Busse müssen vor der Stadtmauer parken. In der Stadt gibt es fast keine Parkplätze.

Der Mittelpunkt von Rothenburg ist der Marktplatz. Das Rathaus ist schon mehr als 500 Jahre alt. Der Turm hinter dem Rathaus ist sogar noch älter. Rechts° vom Rathaus steht die Ratstrinkstube. Dreimal am Tag führen zwei Figuren neben° einer Uhr den „Meistertrunk" vor°. Dieser hat eine besondere geschichtliche Bedeutung für Rothenburg. Links vom Rathaus steht der St. Georgs-Brunnen. Der Brunnen° hat die Einwohner schon 1446 mit Wasser versorgt°.

stellen...vor imagine

fortress
hill
overlooks
built/leads
traffic signs

trip
erinnert...an reminds of/Middle Ages
princes

Altar of the Virgin Mary
famous

favorite place
city wall/surrounds
gates

to the right
next to
führen...vor stage

fountain
supplied

Dinkelsbühl

Die Häuser in Rothenburg
sehen märchenhaft aus.

Nördlingen

Man kann durch vier oder fünf Tore in
die Stadt Rothenburg fahren.

Schloß
Weikersheim

Lektion 10

Die Straßen und Häuser in Rothenburg sehen märchenhaft aus. Viele Blumen° verzieren° die Fenster° von den Häusern. Auf dem Weg zum Stadttor° kommen wir zum Plönlein. Dieser Stadtteil mit dem Fachwerkhaus° am Brunnen und dem Stadttor ist weltberühmt°.

flowers/decorate/windows
city gate
half-timbered house
world-famous

Von Rothenburg führt eine Landstraße an Feldern°, Bauernhöfen° und Dörfern vorbei°. Kurz vor Dinkelsbühl stehen einige Hotelschilder°. Diese geben uns Informationen über die verschiedenen Möglichkeiten, dort zu übernachten. Wie Rothenburg winkt uns auch Dinkelsbühl märchenhaft aus der Entfernung zu°. Dinkelsbühl ist mehr als eintausend Jahre alt. Heute ist diese Stadt für Besucher ein besonderer Anziehungspunkt°. Viele Häuser aus dem Mittelalter stehen noch immer dort.

fields
*farms/*führt…vorbei *goes by*
hotel signs

winkt…zu *waves at*

attraction

Weiter geht es auf der Romantischen Straße in Richtung Nördlingen, ungefähr 30 Kilometer von Dinkelsbühl entfernt. Die Stadtmauer hat drei Tore, zwei für Autos und eins für Fußgänger°. Ein Stadtplan° am Rathaus bezeichnet° diese Stadt mit den Worten „NÖRDLINGEN—DIE LEBENDE° STADT DES MITTELALTERS". Der Stadtplan zeigt deutlich, wo die Sehenswürdigkeiten sind. Wie die meisten Städte an der Romantischen Straße hat auch Nördlingen seinen mittelalterlichen° Charakter bewahrt°. Die Verkehrsschilder in der Innenstadt zeigen uns, auf welcher Straße wir weiterfahren müssen.

pedestrians/city map/labels
living

medieval

preserved

Wir verlassen Nördlingen und kommen ein paar Minuten später am Schloß Harburg vorbei. Das Schloß ist heute ein Museum. Dort kann man Kunstschätze° aus früheren Zeiten besichtigen°. Donauwörth ist eine Kleinstadt an der Donau. Viele Touristen beenden° ihre Reise hier in Donauwörth. Andere setzen ihre Reise auf der Romantischen Straße fort° und fahren über Augsburg, Landsberg, Schongau nach Füssen. Auch auf dieser Strecke können wir noch viele andere Sehenswürdigkeiten finden.

art treasures
view
end
setzen…fort *continue*

Fragen über das Lesestück

1. Wo liegt die Romantische Straße und wie lang ist sie?
2. Was kann man alles in Würzburg sehen?
3. Wer hat früher Weikersheim oft besucht?
4. Was gibt es in Creglingen zu sehen?
5. Warum können die Busse nicht in der Stadt Rothenburg parken?
6. Was ist der Mittelpunkt von Rothenburg? Was gibt es da alles zu sehen?
7. Wie sehen die Straßen und Häuser in Rothenburg aus?
8. Was findet man kurz vor Dinkelsbühl? Warum?
9. Wie weit ist Nördlingen von Dinkelsbühl entfernt?
10. Was steht auf dem Stadtplan von Nördlingen?

11. Wohnt heute noch ein Fürst im Schloß Harburg?
12. Wo liegt Donauwörth?
13. Welche anderen Städte gibt es noch an der Romantischen Straße?

Sprachspiegel

Have students use their imagination. They may want to work as teams. After the dialog or narrative has been created, have students present the material to the class.

I. Develop a dialog situation or a narrative based on the topic *"Ich möchte eine Reise machen."*

In order for you to decide on a specific trip, you may have to inquire at a travel agency, talk to your friends and/or parents and other sources. Be as creative as possible.

II. Express the answers to the following questions using only the metric system. You may have to do some figuring to come up with the right answer.

1. Wie warm ist es heute?
2. Wie groß bist du?
3. Wie weit wohnt deine Freundin

Wie sagt man's?

Ask students to read these dialogs with meaning and expression. Students could ask each other about the individual dialogs.

Wir möchten einen Ausflug auf dem Rhein machen.
Wie viele Personen?
Zwei. Was kostet die Reise?
Achtzehn Mark pro Person.

Wohin geht denn die Reise?
In den Schwarzwald.
Wie schön. Wir sind letztes Jahr dort gewesen.
Ja, es soll märchenhaft sein.

Hast du heute abend etwas vor?
Nein, ich glaube nicht.
Wollen wir ins Kino gehen?
Was läuft im Filmpalast?
Ein Spielfilm aus England.

Ich möchte nach Garmisch-Partenkirchen fahren.
Da müssen Sie in München umsteigen.
Haben Sie einen Fahrplan?
Ja, bitte schön, für Sie!

Ich nehme diesen Prospekt mit.
Darin finden Sie alles, was Sie wissen wollen.
Haben Sie Sonderangebote?
Nur während der Wintermonate.

Wir fahren nächste Woche nach Deutschland.
Ich nehme an, ihr habt alles schon geplant.
Na klar.
Wohin fahrt ihr denn?
Nach München und dann weiter in die Alpen.

Wie lange dauert die Reise?
Drei Stunden mit dem Flugzeug und zwei Stunden mit dem Bus.
Wer kommt denn alles mit?
Meine Eltern und meine Schwester.

Zungenbrecher

Go through this tongue twister first to assure good pronunciation. Then find out how fast your students can say it (and how many times) without stumbling.

Der Potsdamer Postkutscher putzt den Potsdamer Postkutschkasten.
(The Potsdam stagecoach driver is cleaning the Potsdam stagecoach.)

Kulturecke

Vacationing

Almost half the Germans go on vacation in their own country and approximately 22 million foreign tourists visit Germany every year as well. It is not surprising, therefore, to see innumerable travel agencies *(Reisebüros)* throughout the country. What are the favorite spots that tourists like to visit?

A number of islands dot the coast line of the German North Sea shore *(Nordseeküste)*. During the summer months, many Germans head north to such islands as *Sylt* or *Norderney* or take short weekend trips to the island of *Helgoland.* Along the shore of the North and the Baltic Seas *(Nord- und Ostsee)* are beautiful sandy beaches where Germans go to vacation for one or two weeks at a time. The area of *Glücksburg* near the Danish border is a particularly popular spot because of its famous castle *(Schloß Glücksburg),* which attracts visitors from all over the world.

Located south of Hamburg is a restful area, the *Lüneburger Heide.* This heather-covered region has only a few small towns. It is one of the very few secluded sections of Germany where you can hike for a long time without meeting another person. Much of it is a wildlife refuge.

Most Germans do not stay in hotels during their vacation. Instead they look for quiet, peaceful places. Vacationing on farms has become particularly popular. There the adults as well as the youngsters often have the opportunity to explore the countryside on horseback. Many of the young adults, vacationing with their classmates or friends, travel throughout Germany or stay at summer camps for two or three weeks. Wherever there are resort areas, there are modern facilities awaiting visitors. Outdoor swimming pools can be found everywhere. Of course, these resort areas also offer indoor swimming pools, including many that can make artificial waves for the enjoyment of their guests.

Along the *Rhein,* legends and fairy tales come alive for visitors passing the many castles between the cities of *Mainz* and *Koblenz.* Excursion boats provide music and other entertainment and add to the colorful surroundings. The *Mosel,* sometimes referred to as the sister of the Rhein, is another peaceful place to spend your vacation. The Mosel is located in the western part of Germany. Most tourists visit here during the months of September and October — the peak of the wine season and the festivals associated with it. One of the most popular places is the area of *Bernkastel,* where the surroundings take you back centuries.

During the summer, Germans go to lakes and rivers to explore with their own motor boats or in their kayaks. Some enjoy sitting along the river's edge and trying their fishing skill. The *Neckar River* is particularly popular on warm summer days. And, of course, the 14th century castle in *Heidelberg,* overlooking the Neckar River, is the landmark of the city.

Those who don't stay in hotels or guest-houses *(Pensionen)* travel in their own campers. Camping is the least expensive way of vacationing in Germany. There are about 1,700 camping sites to choose from. Hiking always ranks high among Germans vacationing anywhere in the country. Detailed maps of the hiking paths are usually found right at the entrance of the park or forest area. Most hikers familiarize themselves with the maps before tackling the sometimes long and strenuous hiking paths.

One of the most frequently visited towns is *Rothenburg,* located along the *Romantische Straße.* Rothenburg is a well-preserved medieval town with an encircling wall and over 30 gates and towers. Not far away from Rothenburg is *Dinkelsbühl,* a town that is more than one thousand years old.

Camping in den Alpen

an der Ostsee

Youngsters explore
the countryside
on horseback.
(Schwarzwald)

ein Picknick
im Schwarzwald

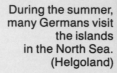

During the summer,
many Germans visit
the islands
in the North Sea.
(Helgoland)

Was machen diese
Leute? (Friedrichsau)

The Black Forest *(Schwarzwald)*, located in southwestern Germany, is just what its name implies. It really is a forest, and the trees are exceptionally dark because of their density. This vast mountain forest has a number of popular resort areas, like the town and lake of *Titisee*. The lake offers numerous opportunities for excursion rides and boating. Within 20 miles of Titisee you'll find another lake, the *Schluchsee*, which is a paradise for surfing and sailing. The sport of surfing has enjoyed a tremendous popularity during the past few years. Many vacationers visit not only the smaller peaceful lakes but also such large lakes as the *Bodensee*, located in the southwestern corner of Germany. The Bodensee is a favorite vacation spot due to its convenient location, close to Switzerland and Austria. The island of *Mainau* has one of the most beautifully landscaped parks found anywhere in Germany. The park facilities, an important prerequisite for most vacationers, are plentiful. People can be seen sitting on the benches reading a paper or book, or just watching the world go by.

For many vacationers, Bavaria *(Bayern)* is still the favorite place to spend their vacation. In recent years, a trip on the *Isar* River has been the thing to do. More than 50 people can float down this river on a raft, while being entertained by a small band. Besides the numerous attractions offered in the Bavarian capital of *München*, many people visit the various castles further south, such as *Neuschwanstein*. This castle has been immortalized in several books and movies. The Alps have numerous vacation spots. An example is the quaint little town of *Berchtesgaden*, located in the vicinity of the *Watzmann*, Germany's second largest mountain. More and more people come to the South during the winter for the skiing opportunities for all skill levels in this Alpine region. The area of the *Zugspitze*, near *Garmisch-Partenkirchen*, attracts many vacationers during the winter season. And, of course, the traditional sleigh rides in these mountain resorts, like *Mittenwald*, are still considered among the most popular activities for the visitors.

Vokabeln

die **Abfahrt,-en** departure
die **Abfahrtszeit,-en** departure time
also O.K. then…
anhalten to stop
ankommen to arrive
annehmen to assume
ausgezeichnet excellent
der **Ausländer,-** foreigner
aussteigen to get off
die **Bahn,-en** train
beschreiben to describe
dienen to serve
das **Doppelzimmer,-** double room
die **Fahrt,-en** trip
die **Figur,-en** figure
der **Flug,-̈e** flight
die **Frau,-en** wife
der **Fürst,-en** prince
gerade just
geschichtlich historical
das **Gramm,-e** gram
günstig favorable, reasonable
hierherkommen to come here
der **Himmel** sky
die **Information,-en** information
klein small
die **Kleinstadt,-̈e** small town
klingen to sound
der **Kunde,-n** customer
die **Landstraße,-n** two-lane highway
die **Mahlzeit,-en** meal
märchenhaft legendary, fairy tale-like
der **Meter,-** meter
mitnehmen to take along
der **Mund,-̈er** mouth
nachsehen to check
oben on top
die **Ordnung,-en** order
    Es geht in Ordnung. It will be taken care of.
der **Ort,-e** town, place
das **Pfund,-e** pound
pro per
der **Prospekt,-e** brochure
die **Rast,-en** rest, break
    eine Rast machen to take a rest
die **Rechnung,-en** bill, invoice
das **Reisebüro,-s** travel agency
richtig really, correct
die **Richtung,-en** direction
die **Seilbahn,-en** cable car
das **Sonderangebot,-e** special offer
sonnig sunny
der **Sportler,-** athlete

die **Station,-en** station
steigen to climb
tausend thousand
umsteigen to transfer
unterwegs on the way
vorher before, in advance
wässerig watery
weiterfahren to continue (driving)
die **Wolke,-n** cloud
womit with what
wünschen to wish
die **Zahnradbahn,-en** cog-wheel train
zurückfahren to drive back
zuschicken to send, mail (to)

Lesestück 1

In der Stadt

Jeden Samstag, außer dem ersten Samstag im Monat, sind die Geschäfte nur bis 14 Uhr geöffnet. Deshalb ist am Samstag in der Stadt immer besonders viel Verkehr. Die Leute wollen noch schnell vor 14 Uhr einkaufen.

Stephanie, Tina und Ursel gehen samstags auch gern in die Stadt. Oft treffen sie sich° vor dem Kino. Das Kino ist direkt in der Stadtmitte. Viele Geschäfte sind in der Nähe vom Kino. Die Mädchen haben noch etwas Zeit, sich die Schaufenster anzusehen°. Manchmal kaufen sie auch ein paar Kleinigkeiten°. Heute haben die drei Mädchen vor, in der Stadt zu essen. Sie kommen bei Hillers vorbei. Hillers ist eine Imbißstube°. Dort ist es immer preiswert, und das Essen schmeckt° auch gut. Auf einer Tafel° können sie auswählen°, was sie essen möchten. Alle drei essen dieses Mal Bratwurst mit Brot. Außer der Bratwurst bestellen° sie noch Cola.

Während der Mittagszeit° ist es in der Imbißstube sehr voll. Die Mädchen haben aber Glück, einen Tisch in der Ecke zu finden. Sie sprechen oft über ihre Freunde und Freundinnen. Stephanie möchte wissen, was sie ihrem Freund Georg kaufen soll. In zwei Wochen gibt Georg eine Party. Er wird dann mit seinem Abitur° fertig sein. Tina glaubt, daß Georg einen Kugelschreiber gebrauchen kann. Ursel hat einen anderen Vorschlag. „Georg kann ein Fotoalbum besser gebrauchen," sagt sie. Dieser Vorschlag gefällt auch Stephanie und Tina. Georg fotografiert° gern. Sie hoffen, daß ein Fotoalbum nicht zu teuer sein wird.

Nach dem Essen wollen sie noch schnell zu einem Kaufhaus° gehen. Das Kaufhaus ist gleich in der Nähe von der Imbißstube. Sie müssen sich beeilen. Es ist schon Viertel vor zwei und die Geschäfte machen bald zu°.

treffen…sich meet

sich…anzusehen to look at
small items

snack bar
tastes/board
select
order
noon time

final examination

takes pictures

department store

machen…zu close

Fragen über das Lesestück

1. Warum ist am Samstag meistens viel Verkehr in der Stadt?
2. Wo sind viele Geschäfte?
3. Wo wollen sie heute essen?
4. Was bestellen sie dort?
5. Warum wird Georg eine Party haben?
6. Was will Stephanie Georg kaufen?

You may want to select only particular sections of this unit for review. The only new words introduced are listed in the margin of the line in which they appear. If your students have some difficulties in completing the exercises, you may want to go back to the lesson in which the particular grammar point or topic was discussed.

Lesestück 2

Wolfgang und Günter fahren zur Jugendherberge

Wolfgang und Günter haben schon seit Wochen geplant°, eine Reise durch Süddeutschland zu machen. Sie wollen mit Wolfgangs Motorrad fahren. Sie haben genug Geld gespart° und haben vor, zwei Wochen lang durch die Gegend zu fahren. Sobald sie in einem Ort ankommen, suchen sie zuerst die Jugendherberge. Dort kann man immer preiswert übernachten. Meistens sehen sie ein Schild. Es zeigt ihnen, wo die Jugendherberge ist. Manchmal müssen sie aber fragen. *planned* *saved*

Heute kommen sie in Nürnberg an. Wie in den meisten Städten ist auch in dieser Stadt die Jugendherberge groß. Hier können mehr als 200 Jugendliche übernachten. Ein paar Motorräder, ein paar Autos und drei Busse stehen schon da. Wolfgang stellt sein Motorrad neben den Eingang. Dann gehen sie beide in die Jugendherberge hinein.

Sie müssen dem Herbergsvater ihren Jugendherbergsausweis zeigen. Der Herbergsvater zeigt den beiden Jungen die Jugendherberge. Die Jugendherberge ist sehr modern. Sie hat viele Schlafzimmer und auch zwei große Speisesäle. Sie können hier für zwölf Mark pro Person übernachten. Gleich in der Nähe von der Jugendherberge ist ein Sportplatz°. Dort spielen immer viele Fußball. Andere bleiben in der Jugendherberge und spielen Tischtennis, Karten, Schach oder andere Spiele. Ein Mädchen spielt sogar Gitarre und einige Jugendliche singen. *athletic field*

Viele Jugendliche kommen in kleinen oder großen Gruppen°. Für Wolfgang und Günter ist es nicht schwer, andere Jungen und Mädchen kennenzulernen°. Es ist besonders interessant, denn die Jugendlichen kommen aus allen Teilen Deutschlands und sogar aus anderen Ländern. Außer Deutsch hören sie noch Englisch und Französisch. Wolfgang und Günter bleiben hier nur einen Tag und fahren dann in Richtung München weiter. *groups* *to get to know*

Fragen über das Lesestück

1. Wohin fahren Wolfgang und Günter?
2. Was suchen sie zuerst in einem Ort?
3. Wie finden sie eine Jugendherberge?
4. Was steht alles vor der Jugendherberge?
5. Was müssen sie dem Herbergsvater zeigen?
6. Was machen die Jugendlichen in der Jugendherberge?
7. Woher kommen die Jugendlichen?

Wo ist die
Jugendherberge?

ein Jugendherbergsausweis

eine Jugendherberge

Wann ist diese
Jugendherberge
geschlossen?

In diesem
Buch stehen
alle deutschen
Jugendherbergen.

Dialog

Auf dem Weg in die Stadt

FRAU SENDER:	Guten Tag, Frau Böll. Wohin gehen Sie denn so früh am Morgen?
FRAU BÖLL:	Guten Tag, Frau Sender. Ich will in die Stadt gehen und ein Geschenk für meinen Mann kaufen. Er hat morgen Geburtstag.
FRAU SENDER:	Fahren Sie mit der Straßenbahn?
FRAU BÖLL:	Nein, ich gehe zu Fuß. Es dauert nur eine halbe Stunde, bis ich in der Stadt bin.
FRAU SENDER:	Was kaufen Sie Ihrem Mann denn?
FRAU BÖLL:	Das weiß ich noch nicht genau. Vielleicht ein Hemd und eine Krawatte oder ein Buch.
FRAU SENDER:	Das ist eine gute Idee. Mein Bruder hat nächste Woche Geburtstag. Er liest auch sehr gern Bücher.
FRAU BÖLL:	Wollen Sie mitkommen?
FRAU SENDER:	Nein, heute habe ich leider keine Zeit.

Fragen über den Dialog

1. Was will Frau Böll für ihren Mann kaufen?
2. Warum will sie etwas kaufen?
3. Wie kommt Frau Böll in die Stadt?
4. Was möchte Frau Sender kaufen?
5. Warum kann Frau Sender heute nicht mit Frau Böll in die Stadt gehen?

Übungen

I. **Provide an appropriate response in German. Be sure that the whole conversation ties together and becomes meaningful.**

A. Heute habe ich wirklich Lust, an den See zu gehen.

B: Ich habe heute leider keine Zeit mitzukommen.

A: _____

B: Ich muß mit meinen Eltern zum Bahnhof fahren.

A: _____

B: Mein Onkel und meine Tante.

A: _____

B: Aus Stuttgart.

A: _____

B: Sie bleiben ungefähr drei Wochen bei uns.

A: _____

II. **Form complete sentences using first the future and then the present perfect tense.**

1. Jungen / spielen / Montag / Tennis
2. Familie Lesemann / fahren / Sommer / Österreich
3. Ich / kaufen / Hose / und / Hemd
4. Sprechen / du / Deutsch / oder / Englisch
5. Wir / Spiel / gewinnen
6. Welcher / Film / ihr / sehen
7. Zug / acht Uhr / München / ankommen

III. **Define each of the following words in German. Form at least one complete sentence describing each word.**

1. die Stadt
2. der Tag
3. die Imbißstube
4. das Reisebüro
5. der Zug
6. das Geld
7. die Universität
8. die Mutter
9. das Wort
10. das Kino

IV. **Complete each sentence by supplying the correct form of the possessive adjective indicated.**

1. Hast du (my) _____ Bruder gesehen?
2. Wo habt ihr (our) _____ Karten gekauft?
3. Ich kann (his) _____ Schwester nicht verstehen.
4. Der Lehrer wird den Schülern (their) _____ Bücher geben.
5. Wohin haben Sie (your) _____ Frau gefahren, Herr Wiemann?

das Reisebüro

6. Sie kommt mit (her) _____ Eltern nach Europa.

7. Maria bekommt das Buch von (her) _____ Freunden.

8. Seit zwei Jahren habe ich (your) _____ Onkel nicht gesehen, Walter.

9. Ich habe von (your) _____ Brüdern lange nicht gehört, Elisabeth und Barbara.

10. Was machen Sie denn nach (your) _____ Reise?

11. Haben Sie mit (my) _____ Mutter gesprochen?

12. Peter hat (his) _____ Freundin nichts von dem Geschenk gesagt.

V. Find the matching word pairs using the words listed below.

1. Tischtennis: _____

2. Walzer: _____

3. Mittwoch: _____

4. Mahlzeit: _____

5. Reisescheck: _____

6. Wasser: _____

7. Herbst: _____

8. Blockflöte: _____

9. Straßenbahn: _____

10. Zimmer: _____

11. Rock: _____

12. Film: _____

Tag	Musikinstrument	Jahreszeit
Bank	Verkehrsmittel	Kleidungsstück
Kino	Fluß	Restaurant
Sport	Tanz	Hotel

VI. Change the following sentences to the present perfect tense.

1. Herr Schmidt spricht gut Deutsch.

2. Ich werde ein paar Prospekte mitbringen.

3. Seine Eltern sind nicht zu Hause.

4. Werden sie heute in Köln ankommen?

5. Wir besuchen die Stadtmauer.

6. Habt ihr die Karten?

7. Um wieviel Uhr wirst du aufstehen?

8. Wo bleibt er denn nur?

9. Ich finde das Buch sehr schwer.

10. Warum fragst du ihn nicht?

VII. Supply the proper present tense forms of the verbs provided in parentheses.

Beispiel: *(sprechen) _____ du Deutsch?*
Sprichst du Deutsch?

1. (geben): _____ er dir sein Fahrrad?

2. (lesen): Paul _____ das Buch. Es ist toll.

3. (anhalten): Der Bus _____ hier _____.

4. (fahren): Familie Meier _____ in die Schweiz.

5. (sehen): _____ du das Flugzeug?

6. (mitnehmen): Petra _____ ihre Schwester in die Stadt _____.

7. (essen): Was _____ ihr denn?

8. (gefallen) Diese Stadt _____ mir besonders gut.

VIII. **Substitute the proper form of one of the three words which best completes the sentence.**

1. Sie _____ zu Fuß in die Stadt. (fahren, gehen, sehen)

2. Ich möchte gern diesen Film _____. (laufen, sehen, spielen)

3. Die Dame will einen Platz _____. (lesen, machen, buchen)

4. Wir können die Vokabeln nicht _____. (verstehen, kaufen, kommen)

5. _____ wir am besten unsere Reise! (warten, gehen, besprechen)

6. Die Prospekte _____ die mittelalterliche Stadt sehr gut. (sagen, einkaufen, beschreiben)

7. In Mainz müssen wir in einen anderen Zug _____. (umsteigen, gehen, anrufen)

8. Meine Mutter wird das Essen _____. (anprobieren, einsteigen, zubereiten)

9. Wir wollen meinen Onkel _____. (glauben, besuchen, interessieren)

10. Mußt du das Gepäck _____? (liegen, versuchen, tragen)

Welche Filme zeigt man in diesen Kinos?

Sie haben
viel Spaß.

Nützliche Ausdrücke

Here are some phrases that are particularly helpful when buying clothing items:

Bitte sehr?	May I help you?
Ich möchte ein paar Schuhe, Größe 41, bitte.	I would like a pair of shoes, size 9, please.
Welche Größe haben Sie?	What size do you wear?
Welche Farbe?	Which color?
Wollen Sie das Kleid anprobieren?	Do you wish to try the dress on?
Gehen Sie bitte in die Kabine.	Please go to the fitting room.
Es ist zu eng.	It is too tight.
Was kostet das?	What does that cost?

Cultural Notes

Popular English Words in the German Language

German borrowed many words from English. Here are some of the English words with their corresponding German articles. The pronunciation of these words in German is usually as close to English as possible, depending on the speaker's familiarity with English.

die Band	das Happening	der Manager	das Sit-in
die City	das Hobby	die Party	die Snackbar
der Computer	die Jeans	die Pipeline	der Teenager
das Feature	der Job	das Popcorn	der Trend
der Gag (joke)	das Makeup	die Publicity	das Understatement

Hier kann man Jeans kaufen.

Was kauft man in diesem Geschäft?

Welcher Film läuft hier?

Origin of Town Names

Many town and city names in Germany have suffixes that can easily identify their origin. Once you know a little about their origin, you may look at these places with different eyes. Many town names go back to the Roman and Germanic times.

The ending syllable *-furt* (as in Frankfurt) means that the town originated at a ford, where a river could be crossed by wading or with a wagon.

Some German town names end or begin with *-reuth, -reut, -reute, -rode, -rod,* or *-rath* (as *Bayreuth, Wernigerode* or *Benrath*). These towns originated in a wooded area that had to be cleared of trees and stumps (*"roden"* in German) before houses could be built and fields could be made arable.

Many towns in southern and western Germany originated as Roman settlements in the earliest centuries A.D. The end syllable *-kastel* (as in *Bernkastel)* goes back to the Latin "castellum" (castle, fortified camp).

If a name ends with *-burg* (as *Hamburg*), this shows that the town grew near or around a *Burg,* a castle.

Towns originating around abbeys, convents, etc. often still carry the word *Kloster* (cloister) or *Mönch* (monk) in their names (*Klosterreichenbach, München*).

Town names ending with *-ingen (Sigmaringen)* usually lie in Swabia, those with *-ing* (Dingolfing) in Bavaria. The name *Sigmaringen* tells that the settlement was founded by a Teuton called Sigmar and his kin.

Wie heißen die Städte auf dem Schild?

Kloster Ettal (Bayern)

Ravensburg grew near a *Burg.*

At a German Hotel

Finding a Room

The safest way to get a room is to reserve one in advance. However, if you arrive without a room reservation, in most German cities you can make use of the services of a room referral agency, called *"Zimmernachweis"* which often is in or near the railroad station. It charges a small fee for locating a room for you.

Bath Must be Ordered

Moderately priced German hotels do not furnish soap and wash cloths. All hotels supply towels, but only the more expensive ones supply soap. Rooms with a private bath and toilet must be specifically ordered; they cost usually about 50% more than a room without these facilities. Usually, there is at least one bathroom with shower at the disposal of all hotel guests. However, hotel guests have to let the hotel know when they want to use it, as a fee will be charged. A toilet is generally found on each floor and can be used by those who do not have one included in their room.

Registration

Every hotel guest must fill out a hotel registration form, which is not as detailed and complex as it used to be. Some hotels have even abolished lengthy registration forms.

Paying the Bill

In all German hotels you pay when you check out. A service charge will be included in the bill.

Continental Breakfast

The "continental breakfast" is the traditional German breakfast served in German hotels. It consists of *Kaffee* or *Tee* (your choice), *Brötchen, Schwarzbrot* (brown bread), *Marmelade* (jam) and, on requests, a soft boiled egg *(weich gekochtes Ei),* served in a little egg cup. In some hotels you may also find a small assortment of *Aufschnitt* (assorted cold cuts and cheese) for breakfast. Most hotels expect you to have breakfast at their hotel. Consequently, breakfast is usually included in the hotel bill.

Zimmernachweis oder Tourist Information

Hotels usually furnish towels but not always soap.

Personal Pronouns

SINGULAR	Nominative	Accusative	Dative
1st person	ich	mich	mir
2nd person	du	dich	dir
3rd person	er sie es	ihn sie es	ihm ihr ihm
PLURAL			
1st person	wir	uns	uns
2nd person	ihr	euch	euch
3rd person	sie	sie	ihnen
formal form (plural or singular)	Sie	Sie	Ihnen

Definite Article

	Singular			Plural
	Masculine	*Feminine*	*Neuter*	
Nominative	der	die	das	die
Accusative	den	die	das	die
Dative	dem	der	dem	den

Der-Words

	Singular			Plural
	Masculine	*Feminine*	*Neuter*	
Nominative	dieser	diese	dieses	diese
Accusative	diesen	diese	dieses	diese
Dative	diesem	dieser	diesem	diesen

Other *der*-words introduced here are *welcher* and *jeder*.

Question Words: *Wer? Was?*

Nominative	wer	was
Accusative	wen	was
Dative	wem	

Indefinite Article

	Singular			Plural
	Masculine	*Feminine*	*Neuter*	
Nominative	ein	eine	ein	keine
Accusative	einen	eine	ein	keine
Dative	einem	einer	einem	keinen

Regular Verb Forms — Present Tense

	gehen	**finden**	**heißen**
ich	gehe	finde	heiße
du	gehst	findest	heißt
er, sie, es	geht	findet	heißt
wir	gehen	finden	heißen
ihr	geht	findet	heißt
sie, Sie	gehen	finden	heißen

Irregular Verb Forms — Present Tense

	haben	**sein**	**wissen**
ich	habe	bin	weiß
du	hast	bist	weißt
er, sie, es	hat	ist	weiß
wir	haben	sind	wissen
ihr	habt	seid	wißt
sie, Sie	haben	sind	wissen

Command Forms

Familiar (singular)	Geh!	Warte!	Sei!	Hab!
Familiar (plural)	Geht!	Wartet!	Seid!	Habt!
Formal (singular/plural)	Gehen Sie!	Warten Sie!	Seien Sie!	Haben Sie!
Wir-form (Let's…)	Gehen wir!	Warten wir!	Seien wir!	Haben wir!

Plural of Nouns

	Singular	Plural
no change or add umlaut	das Zimmer die Mutter	die Zimmer die Mütter
add -*n*, -*en*, or -*nen*	die Ecke der Automat die Freundin	die Ecken die Automaten die Freundinnen
add -*e* or ¨*e*	der Tag die Stadt	die Tage die Städte
add ¨*er*	das Buch	die Bücher
add -*s* (adopted foreign words)	das Café das Büro	die Cafés die Büros

Inverted Word Order

1. Formation of questions beginning with the verb
    Spielst du heute Fußball?
2. Formation of questions beginning with a question word
    Wohin gehen Sie heute nachmittag?
3. Command forms
    Hab keine Angst!
    Lauft schnell!
    Passen Sie auf!
    Gehen wir!
4. Sentence beginning with a word other than the subject
    Am Sonntag fahren wir zu meiner Tante.

Negation

Verbs *(nicht)* Kommen Sie nicht zu uns?
Nouns *(kein)* Ich habe keine Karte.

Modal Auxiliaries

	dürfen	können	mögen	müssen	sollen	wollen
ich	darf	kann	mag	muß	soll	will
du	darfst	kannst	magst	mußt	sollst	willst
er, sie, es	darf	kann	mag	muß	soll	will
wir	dürfen	können	mögen	müssen	sollen	wollen
ihr	dürft	könnt	mögt	müßt	sollt	wollt
sie, Sie	dürfen	können	mögen	müssen	sollen	wollen

Future tense *(werden* + infinitive)

ich	werde
du	wirst
er, sie, es	wird
wir	werden
ihr	werdet
sie, Sie	werden

Sie werden nächstes Jahr nach Deutschland fahren.
Wirst du morgen ins Kino gehen?

Verbs with Stem Vowel Change (2nd & 3rd person singular only)

	a to *ä*	*e* to *i*	*e* to *ie*
ich	fahre	spreche	sehe
du	fährst	sprichst	siehst
er, sie, es	fährt	spricht	sieht
wir	fahren	sprechen	sehen
ihr	fahrt	sprecht	seht
sie, Sie	fahren	sprechen	sehen

Prepositions

Dative	Accusative	Contraction
aus	durch	durch das = durchs
außer	für	für das = fürs
bei	gegen	bei dem = beim
mit	ohne	—
nach	um	um das = ums
seit		—
von		von dem = vom
zu		zu dem = zum / zu der = zur

Verbs Followed by Dative Case

helfen antworten gefallen passen glauben
Gabi hilft ihrer Mutter.
Der Anzug gefällt mir.
The verb *glauben* may take either the dative or accusative. If used with a person, the dative follows *(Ich glaube ihm)*. If used with an object, the accusative is used *(Ich glaube das nicht)*.

Possessive Adjectives

	Singular			Plural
	Masculine	*Feminine*	*Neuter*	
Nominative	mein	meine	mein	meine
Accusative	meinen	meine	mein	meine
Dative	meinem	meiner	meinem	meinen

The endings of possessive adjectives are the same as those of the indefinite article *(ein*-words). Possessive adjectives are *mein, dein, sein, ihr, sein, unser, euer, ihr, Ihr.*

Comparison of Adjectives and Adverbs

Adjective/Adverb	schnell	warm	gut	hoch
Comparative	schneller	wärmer	besser	höher
Superlative	schnellst-	wärmst-	best-	höchst-

Numbers

0 = null	11 = elf	22 = zweiundzwanzig
1 = eins	12 = zwölf	30 = dreißig
2 = zwei	13 = dreizehn	40 = vierzig
3 = drei	14 = vierzehn	50 = fünfzig
4 = vier	15 = fünfzehn	60 = sechzig
5 = fünf	16 = sechzehn	70 = siebzig
6 = sechs	17 = siebzehn	80 = achtzig
7 = sieben	18 = achtzehn	90 = neunzig
8 = acht	19 = neunzehn	100 = einhundert
9 = neun	20 = zwanzig	101 = hunderteins
10 = zehn	21 = einundzwanzig	

Time

1:00 Es ist ein Uhr.
2:00 Es ist zwei Uhr.
3:30 Es ist halb vier Uhr.
10:15 Es ist Viertel nach zehn.
11:45 Es ist Viertel vor zwölf.
5:10 Es ist zehn Minuten nach fünf.
7:58 Es ist zwei Minuten vor acht.

Irregular Verbs — Present Perfect Tense (Past Participle)

The following list contains all the irregular verbs used in *DEUTSCH: AKTUELL 1*. Verbs with separable or inseparable prefixes are not included when the basic verb form has been introduced (Example: *kommen, ankommen*). If the basic verb has not been introduced, then the verb is included with its prefix. Verbs with stem vowel changes have also been indicated.

Infinitive	Stem Vowel Change	Past Participle	Meaning
anhalten	hält an	angehalten	to stop
anrufen		angerufen	to call (phone)
anziehen		angezogen	to put on (clothes)
beginnen		begonnen	to begin
bekommen		bekommen	to get
beschreiben		beschrieben	to describe
bieten		geboten	to offer
bleiben		ist geblieben	to stay, remain
bringen		gebracht	to bring
denken		gedacht	to think
essen	ißt	gegessen	to eat
fahren	fährt	ist gefahren	to drive, go
finden		gefunden	to find
fließen		ist geflossen	to flow, run
geben	gibt	gegeben	to give
gefallen	gefällt	gefallen	to like
gehen		ist gegangen	to go, walk
gewinnen		gewonnen	to win
haben	hat	gehabt	to have
heißen		geheißen	to be called
helfen	hilft	geholfen	to help
kennen		gekannt	to know (a person)
klingen		geklungen	to sound
kommen		ist gekommen	to come
laufen	läuft	ist gelaufen	to run, walk
lesen	liest	gelesen	to read
liegen		gelegen	to lie
nehmen	nimmt	genommen	to take
scheinen		geschienen	to shine
schlagen	schlägt	geschlagen	to beat, hit
schreiben		geschrieben	to write
schwimmen		ist geschwommen	to swim
sehen	sieht	gesehen	to see
sein	ist	ist gewesen	to be
singen		gesungen	to sing
sitzen		gesessen	to sit
sprechen	spricht	gesprochen	to speak, talk
springen		ist gesprungen	to jump
stehen		gestanden	to stand
steigen		ist gestiegen	to climb
tragen	trägt	getragen	to carry

Infinitive	Stem Vowel Change	Past Participle	Meaning
treffen	trifft	getroffen	to meet
treiben		getrieben	to do (sports)
trinken		getrunken	to drink
tun		getan	to do
verlassen	verläßt	verlassen	to leave
verlieren		verloren	to lose
verbinden		verbunden	to connect
wissen	weiß	gewußt	to know

All the words introduced in DEUTSCH: AKTUELL 1 have been summarized in this section. The numbers following the meaning of individual words or phrases indicate the particular lesson in which they appear for the first time. In cases in which there is more than one meaning for a word or phrase and it has appeared in different lessons, both lesson numbers are listed. (Example: die *Frau,-en* Mrs., woman 1; wife 5)
Nouns have been listed with their respective articles and plural forms.

A

der **Abend,-e** evening 2
das **Abendbrot** supper 5
aber but 2
die **Abfahrt,-en** departure 10
die **Abfahrtszeit,-en** departure time 10
der **Abgeordnete,-n** representative 7
das **Abitur,-e** final examination (secondary school) B
sich **abkühlen** to cool off 9
abräumen to clear 7
der **Abschnitt,-e** slip (of paper) 6
absperren to block off 9
acht eight 1
achtzehn eighteen 2
das **Akkordeon,-s** accordion 8
alle all 2; everyone 8
alles everything 3
die **Alpen** Alps 5
das **Alpenvorland** Alpine foothills 8
als than 8
also O.K. then... 10
alt old 4
ältest- oldest 7
am (or: **an dem**) at the, on the 2
Amerika America 5
der **Amerikaner,-** American (male) A
die **Amerikanerin,-nen** American (female) A
an at 3; on 8
ander- other, different 4
der **Angestellte,-n** employee (male) 6
die **Angst,-̈e** fear 2; *Hab keine Angst!* Don't worry! Don't be afraid! 2
anhaben to have on 6
anhalten to stop 10
ankommen to arrive 10
die **Ankunft,-̈e** arrival 7
das **Anmeldeformular,-e** registration form 7
anprobieren to try on 6
anrufen to call up 5

der **Ansager,-** announcer 9
sich **ansehen** to look at B
anstrengen to exert 8; *Es strengt an.* It is exhausting. 8
antworten to answer 3
anziehen to put on (clothes); dress 6
der **Anziehungspunkt,-e** attraction 10
der **Anzug,-̈e** suit 6
das **Apfelmus** apple sauce A
der **April** April 4
die **Arbeit,-en** work 2; *eine Arbeit schreiben* to take a test 2
arbeiten to work 5
auch also, too 1
auf to, on 2
die **Aufgabe,-n** problem, exercise 4
auflegen to put on 8
aufpassen to watch, keep an eye on something 9
der **Aufsatz,-̈e** essay, composition A
der **Aufseher,-** attendant 9
aufstehen to get up A
der **August** August 4
aus from, out of 2
der **Ausdruck,-̈e** expression 4
der **Ausflugsort,-e** excursion area 8
ausfüllen to fill out 7
ausgezeichnet excellent 10
der **Ausländer,-** foreigner 10
ausreichend sufficient 4
aussehen to look, appear 7
außer besides, except 6
außerhalb outside 5
aussetzen to sit out 8
aussteigen to get off 10
die **Auswahl** selection, choice 6
auswählen to choose, select B
der **Ausweis,-e** identification (card) 7
auswendig lernen to memorize, learn by heart 4
das **Auto,-s** car 5

der **Automat,-en** automat 3

B

die **Bahn,-en** train 10
der **Bahnhof,-̈e** (train) station 3
der **Bahnsteig,-e** platform 8
bald soon 2
die **Bank,-̈e** bench 4
die **Bank,-en** bank 6
der **Basketball,-̈e** basketball 9
der **Bauernhof,-̈e** farm 10
beantworten to answer A; *eine Frage beantworten* to answer a question A
die **Bedeutung,-en** meaning, significance 4
sich **beeilen** to hurry 3; *Beeilen wir uns!* Let's hurry. 3
beenden to end, finish 10
befriedigend satisfactory 4
beginnen to begin 3
begrüßen to greet 3
begutachten to look over, evaluate 6
bei at 5; with 8
beide both 2
das **Beispiel,-e** example 7; *zum Beispiel* for example 7
bekannt well-known 5
bekanntgeben to announce 8
Belgien Belgium 3
beliebt popular 5
bekommen to get, receive 2
bequem comfortable 3
bereitstehen to be ready, stand ready 9
der **Berg,-e** mountain 5
berühmt famous 10
beschreiben to describe 10
die **Beschreibung,-en** description 4
besichtigen to view, look over 10

die **Besitzerin,-nen** owner (female) 8
besonder- special, unusual 4
besonders especially 4
besprechen to discuss 4
best- best 7; *am besten* the best is 7
bestehen aus to consist of 4
bestellen order B
bestimmt undoubtedly, certainly 6
die **Bestleistung,-en** best performance 9
besuchen to visit 5
der **Besucher,-** visitor 6
der **Betrag,-̈e** amount 6
das **Bett,-en** bed 5; *Er muß ins Bett.* He has to go to bed. 5
die **Bevölkerung,-en** population 9
bewahren to preserve 10
bezahlen to pay 6
bezeichnen to label, designate 10
das **Bier,-e** beer 9
bieten to offer 7
bilden to form 9
die **Biologie** biology 4
bis until 2
bitte please 6
blau blue 6
bleiben to stay, remain 2
der **Bleistift,-e** pencil 8
der **Blick** view 4
die **Blockflöte,-n** recorder 9
die **Blume,-n** flower 10
die **Bluse,-n** blouse 6
der **Bodensee** Lake Constance 8
das **Boot,-e** boat 7
die **Bratwurst,-̈e** bratwurst, fried sausage B
brauchen to need 2
braun brown 6
der **Briefkasten,-̈** mailbox 7
der **Briefmarkenautomat,-en** stamp automat 7
bringen to bring A
das **Brot,-e** bread A
die **Brücke,-n** bridge 8
der **Bruder,-̈** brother 5
der **Brunnen,-** fountain, well 10
das **Buch,-̈er** book 4
buchen to book 10
die **Bücherabteilung,-en** book department 6
die **Bundeshauptstadt** federal capital 7
das **Bundeshaus** Federal Building (in Bonn) 7
das **Bundeshochhaus** Federal Office Building for Representatives 7

das **Bundesland,-̈er** Federal State 5
der **Bundespräsident** Federal President 7
der **Bundesrat** similar to Senate 7
die **Bundesrepublik Deutschland** Federal Republic of Germany 3
der **Bundestag** similar to the House of Representatives 7
bunt colorful 6
das **Büro,-s** office 4
der **Bus,-se** bus 4
die **Butter** butter A

C

das **Café,-s** café, coffee shop 5
der **Cha-Cha-Cha** cha-cha 8
die **Chance,-n** chance 9
der **Charakter,-e** character 10
die **Chemie** chemistry 4
die **Cola,-s** cola 2
der **Computer,-** computer 3

D

da there 1; *da drüben* over there 1
dabei in the process, while doing that 9
dafür for that, for it 4
die **Dame,-n** lady 6
die **Damenabteilung,-en** ladies' department 6
Dänemark Denmark 3
der **Dank** thanks 10; *Vielen Dank.* Many thanks. 10
danke thanks 1; *Danke schön.* Thank you 5
dann then 2
das the, that 1
daß that 6
dasselbe the same 7
das **Datum, Daten** date (calendar) 5
dauern to last, take (time) 3
dazu with it A
decken to cover A; *den Tisch decken* to set the table A
dein your 4
denken to think 7
denn used for emphasis 2; *Wieviel Geld brauchst du denn?* Well, how much money do you need? 2
deshalb therefore 6
deutlich clearly 10

deutsch German 1
das **Deutsch** German (the language, subject in school) 4
die **Deutsche Demokratische Republik** German Democratic Republic 3
Deutschland Germany 3
der **Dezember** December 4
dicht close 9
der **Dienstag** Tuesday 2
diese (form of *dieser*) this 3
dieser this 3
direkt direct, immediate, straight 6
doch used for emphasis 3
der **Dollar,-s** dollar 6
die **Donau** Danube 5
der **Donnerstag** Thursday 2
das **Doppelzimmer,-** double room 10
dort there 3
dorthin (to) there 5
dran sein to be one's turn 9; *Ich bin dran.* It's my turn. 9
drei three 1
dreizehn thirteen 2
du you (familiar singular) 1
durch through 5
dürfen to be permitted to, may 5

E

die **Ebbe,-n** low tide 8
eben just 4
die **Ecke,-n** corner 1
eigentlich actual(ly), real(ly) 3
ein(e) a, an 2
einfach simple, one-way (ticket) 3
der **Eingang,-̈e** entrance 6
einige a few, several 7
einkaufen to shop 5; *einkaufen gehen* to go shopping 5
einlösen to cash (in) 6
einmal once 3; *wieder einmal* once again 3; *noch einmal* one more time 5
eins one 1
einschließlich including 10
einsteigen to get in(to), board 2
der **Eintritt** admission 8
der **Einwohner,-** inhabitant 3
die **Eisdiele,-n** ice cream parlor 2
elegant elegant 7
elf eleven 2
die **Eltern** (pl.) parents 5
das **Ende** end 3
das **Endergebnis,-se** final result 9

endlich finally *2*
England England *4*
das **Englisch** English (language, subject in school) *4*
englisch English *4*
der **Enkel,-** grandson *5*
die **Enkelin,-nen** granddaughter *5*
entfernt away, distant *4*
die **Entfernung,-en** distance *3*
entgegenlaufen to run towards *9*
entspringen to originate (river) *8*
entwerten to cancel (tickets) *8*
er he *1*
erbauen to build, construct *10*
die **Erbse,-n** pea *A*
die **Erdkunde** geography *4*
das **Ereignis,-se** event *7*
erinnern an to remind of *10*
erreichen to reach *6*
erst only, first *5*
es it *1*
das **Essen** meal *A;* food *8*
essen to eat *5*
die **Essenausgabe,-n** serving counter *7*
etwas some, a little *2*
Europa Europe *5*
europäisch European *8*
der **Experte,-n** expert *8*

F

das **Fach,-̈er** (school) subject *4*
das **Fachwerkhaus,-̈er** half-timbered house *10*
fahren to drive, go *3*
die **Fahrkarte,-n** ticket *3*
der **Fahrplan,-̈e** schedule *3*
die **Fahrprüfung,-en** driver's test *8*
das **Fahrrad,-̈er** bicycle *7*
der **Fahrstuhl,-̈e** elevator *7*
die **Fahrt,-en** trip *10*
die **Familie,-n** family *5*
die **Farbe,-n** color *6*
der **Faschismus** fascism *7*
fast almost *5*
der **Februar** February *4*
der **Federball,-̈e** badminton *9*
das **Feld,-er** field *10*
der **Feldweg,-e** field path *4*
das **Fenster,-** window *10*
die **Ferien** (pl.) vacation *9*
das **Ferienland,-̈er** vacation country *5*
der **Fernsehapparat,-e** television set *7*

Fernsehen: im Fernsehen on TV *A*
fernsehen to watch TV *5*
der **Fernsehturm,-̈e** television tower *7*
fertig ready, done, finished *5*
das **Festland,-̈er** mainland *8*
die **Festung,-en** fortress *10*
die **Figur,-en** figure *10*
der **Film,-e** movie, film *5*
finden to find *4*
flach flat *5*
die **Fläche,-n** area, surface *3*
fleißig hard-working, industrious *4*
fließen to flow, run *5*
die **Flöte,-n** flute *8*
der **Flug,-̈e** flight *10*
das **Flugzeug,-e** airplane *7*
der **Fluß,-̈sse** river *5*
folgen to follow *7*
die **Form,-en** form, shape *9*
die **Formel,-n** formula *4*
fortsetzen to continue *10; eine Reise fortsetzen* to continue a trip *10*
das **Fotoalbum,-ben** photo album *B*
fotografieren to photograph *B*
die **Frage,-n** question *A*
fragen to ask *2*
Frankreich France *3*
Französisch French (language) *6*
die **Frau,-en** Mrs., woman *1;* wife *10*
das **Fräulein,-** Miss *1*
frei free, available *7*
Freie: ins Freie outside *7; im Freien* outdoors *10*
der **Freitag** Friday *2*
die **Fremdsprache,-n** foreign language *4*
der **Freund,-e** boyfriend, friend *1*
die **Freundin,-nen** girlfriend *3*
froh happy, glad *2*
früh early *9*
der **Frühling,-e** spring *4*
frühstücken to have breakfast *5*
führen to lead *10*
der **Führerschein,-e** driver's license *8*
fünf five *1*
fünfzehn fifteen *2*
für for *3*
der **Fürst,-en** prince *10*
der **Fuß,-̈e** foot *3; zu Fuß* on foot, walk *3; zu Fuß gehen* to walk *3*
der **Fußball,-̈e** soccer *7*
der **Fußgänger,-** pedestrian *10*

G

ganz quite *3;* whole *7*
gar nicht not at all *4*
das **Gebäude,-** building *7*
geben to give *4; es gibt* there is (are) *4*
gebrauchen to use, apply *4*
die **Gebühr,-en** fee *6*
die **Geburtsstadt,-̈e** native town, city of birth *7*
der **Geburtstag,-e** birthday *5*
gefallen to like *6; Es gefällt ihr.* She likes it. *6*
die **Gegend,-en** area *5*
gegenüber across *7*
gehen to go *1; Wie geht's?* How are you? (familiar) *1; zu Fuß gehen* to walk *3; Das geht.* That's possible. *7*
gehen über to go into, merge with *8*
gehören zu to belong to *8*
die **Geige,-n** violin *8*
gelb yellow *6*
das **Geld** money *2*
das **Gemälde,-** painting *7*
gemütlich pleasant *7*
genau exact *7*
genauso wie just like/as *4*
geöffnet open *B; Das Geschäft ist geöffnet.* The store is open. *B*
das **Gepäck** luggage, baggage *3*
gerade just *10*
gern gladly, with pleasure *4; gern gehen* like (enjoy) to walk *4*
das **Geschäft,-e** store *6*
das **Geschenk,-e** present *8*
die **Geschichte** history *4*
geschichtlich historical *10*
das **Geschirr** dishes *7*
der **Geschmack,-̈e** taste *8*
die **Geschwister** (pl.) siblings *5*
gespannt sein to wonder, be curious *5*
gestern yesterday *9*
das **Getränk,-̈e** beverage *7*
gewinnen to win *5*
die **Gitarre,-n** guitar *A*
das **Glas,-̈er** glass *9*
glauben to believe, think *3*
gleich immediately, right away *1; gleich um die Ecke* right around the corner *1*
das **Gleis,-e** track *3*
das **Glück** luck *2; Glück haben* to be lucky *2*

der **Glückwunsch,⸚e** congratulations (pl.) 8; *Herzlichen Glückwunsch zum Geburtstag!* Happy Birthday! 8; *Herzlichen Glückwunsch!* Congratulations! 9

gold gold 4

das **Golf** golf 9

das **Gramm,-e** gram 10

gratulieren to congratulate 9

grau gray 6

die **Grenze,-n** border 6

grenzen an to border on 4

groß big, large 3

größt- biggest, largest 4

die **Großeltern** (pl.) grandparents 5

die **Großmutter,⸚** grandmother 5

der **Großvater,⸚** grandfather 5

grün green 6

gründlich thorough, careful 4

die **Gruppe,-n** group B

Grüß dich! Hi! 1; *Grüß Gott!* Hello! 5

günstig favorable, reasonable 10

gut good, well, O.K. 1

die **Güte** goodness 7; *Du meine Güte!* My goodness! 7

das **Gymnasium,-sien** secondary school 2; *Sie geht auf ein Gymnasium.* She goes to a secondary school. 2

H

haben to have 2

häkeln to crochet 5

halb half 3

die **Haltestelle,-n** stop (for bus or streetcar) 2

der **Handschuh,-e** glove 6

die **Handtasche,-n** purse 6

die **Hauptstadt,⸚e** capital (city) 3

das **Haus,⸚er** house 2; *nach Hause gehen* to go home 2; *zu Hause* at home 2

die **Hausaufgabe,-n** homework 5; *die Hausaufgaben machen* to do homework 5

das **Heft,-e** notebook 8

heiß hot 7

heißen to be called, named 1; *Wie heißt du?* What's your name? 1

helfen to help 9

das **Hemd,-en** shirt 6

der **Herbergsvater,⸚** youth hostel director 7

der **Herbst,-e** fall, autumn 4

der **Herr,-en** Mr., gentleman 1

herumfahren to drive (ride) around 7

herumlaufen to run around 9

herzlich sincere, cordial 8

heute today 2; *heute abend* this evening, tonight 2

hier here 1

hierherkommen to come here 10

die **Hilfe** help, assistance 4

der **Himmel** sky 10

hin und zurück round trip 3

hineingehen to go inside 7

hineinreichen to reach into 8

hinter behind 8

historisch historical, historic 7

die **Hitze** heat 8; *bei der Hitze* in this heat 8

hoch high 5

höchst- highest 5

das **Hockey** hockey 9

hoffen to hope 6

hoffentlich hopefully 9

die **Höhe,-n** height 6

die **HO-Kaufhalle,-n** (government-owned) supermarket 5

hören to listen, hear 4

die **Hose,-n** pants, slacks 6

das **Hotel,-s** hotel 7

das **Hotelschild,-er** hotel sign 10

der **Hügel,-** hill 10

der **Hunger** hunger 7; *Hunger haben* to be hungry 7

hungrig hungry 4

I

ich I 1

die **Idee,-n** idea 2

ihn it, him 5

ihr you (familiar plural) 1, their 4, her 4

Ihr your (formal) 6

im (or: **in dem**) in the 4

die **Imbißstube,-n** snack bar B

immer always 2; *immer wieder* again and again 7

in in 1

die **Industriestadt,⸚e** industrial city 9

die **Information,-en** information 10

die **Innenstadt,⸚e** downtown, center of city 6

ins (or: **in das**) in(to) the 4

die **Insel,-n** island 8

interessant interesting 7

das **Interesse,-n** interest A

interessieren to interest A

ist is 1

Italien Italy 5

Italienisch Italian (language) 6

J

ja yes 1

das **Jahr,-e** year 2

die **Jahreszeit,-en** season 4

der **Januar** January 4

die **Jeans** (pl.) jeans 6

jeden form of **jeder** each, every 2

jeder each, every 7

jetzt now 1

die **Jugendherberge,-n** youth hostel 7

der **Jugendherbergsausweis,-e** youth hostel identification (card) 7

der **Jugendliche,-n** youngster, teenager, youth 7

Jugoslawien Yugoslavia 5

der **Juli** July 4

der **Junge,-n** boy 1

der **Juni** June 4

K

der **Kaffee** coffee A

der **Kakao** hot chocolate, cocoa 9

kalt cold 7

die **Kalte Platte** cold-cut platter 5

der **Kamerad,-en** buddy 9

der **Kanal,⸚e** canal 9

das **Kanalsystem,-e** canal system 8

die **Karte,-n** ticket 5, map 6; card B

die **Kartoffel,-n** potato A

der **Kartoffelsalat** potato salad 8

der **Käse** cheese A

die **Kasse,-n** cashier's counter 6

die **Kassette,-n** cassette 4

kaufen to buy 3

das **Kaufhaus,⸚er** department store B

der **Kaufhof** name of department store 6

kaum hardly 9

kein no 2; *keine Zeit* no time 2

kennen to know (someone) 1

kennenlernen to get to know B

der **Kilometer,-** kilometer 3

das **Kino,-s** movie theater 5

der **Kiosk,-e** kiosk 2

die **Kirche,-n** church 7

klar clear, O.K. 3

die **Klarinette,-n** clarinet 8

die **Klasse,-n** class 3; *zweiter Klasse* second class 3

klasse sein to be great 5

der **Klassenausflug,⸚e** class trip 7

klatschen to applaud 9

das **Klavier,-e** piano 8

das **Kleid,-er** dress 6

das **Kleidungsstück,-e** article of clothing 6

klein small, little 10

die **Kleinigkeit,-en** small item, thing B

kleinst- smallest 4

die **Kleinstadt,⸚e** small town 10

klingeln to ring 4; *an der Tür klingeln* to ring the doorbell 4

klingen to sound 10

klug smart 3

kochen to cook A

der **Koffer,-** suitcase 3

der **Koffer-Kuli,-s** luggage cart 3

kommen to come 1; *Komm doch mit.* Why don't you come along? 1; *Es kommt auf... an.* It depends on... 10

können to be able to, can 5

der **Korbball,⸚e** basketball 9

kosten to cost 4

die **Krawatte,-n** tie 6

das **Kreuz,-e** cross 6

die **Küche,-n** kitchen 5

kühl cool 7

der **Kuli,-s** (ballpoint) pen 8

kulturell cultural 7

der **Kunde,-n** customer 10

die **Kunst** art 4

der **Kunstschatz,⸚e** art treasure 10

der **Kurs,-e** exchange 6

kurz short(ly) A

L

das **Land,⸚er** country, land 3; "state" in the *BRD* 4

die **Landschaft,-en** landscape 8

die **Landstraße,-n** two-lane highway 10

lang long 9

lange long 3

die **Länge,-n** length 5

langsam slow(ly) A

längst- longest 5

langweilig boring 2

laufen to run 5

die **Läufer,-** runner 9

leben to live 9

lebend living 10

lecker delicious 8

leer empty 5

der **Lehrer,-** teacher 7

leicht easy 3

leider unfortunately B

der **Leiter,-** head, person in charge 9

lernen to learn 4; *auswendig lernen* to memorize, learn by heart 4

lesen to read 4

letzt- last 8

die **Leute** (pl.) people 7

lieber rather 5

der **Lieblingsort,-e** favorite place 10

Liechtenstein Liechtenstein 5

liegen to lie, be located 3

die **Limonade,-n** soft drink 9

das **Lineal,-e** ruler 8

links left, on(to) the left 7

los: was ist los? What's the matter? 2; *Los!* Come on! 5; *Los, kommt!* Come on, let's go! 5

lösen to solve 4

loslaufen to start running 9

die **Lust** pleasure, joy 2; *Sie hat Lust...* She would like to... 2

Luxemburg Luxembourg 3

M

machen to do, make 1; *Das macht fünf Mark.* That's five marks. 3

das **Mädchen,-** girl 1

die **Mahlzeit,-en** meal 10

das **Mahnmal** memorial 7

der **Mai** May 4

mal times 3

das **Mal,-e** time(s) 9

man one, they, you, people 3

manche a few 8

manchmal sometimes 4

mangelhaft inadequate 4

der **Mann,⸚er** man 9

die **Mannschaft,-en** team 9

der **Mantel,⸚** coat 6

der **Marathonlauf,⸚e** marathon run 9

märchenhaft legendary, fairy tale-like 10

die **Mark** mark (German monetary unit) 2

der **Markt,⸚e** market 7

der **Marktplatz⸚e** market square 7

der **Markttag,-e** market day 7

die **Marmelade** jam A

der **März** March 4

die **Matheaufgabe** math problem 3

die **Mathematik** (or: **Mathe**) mathematics 4

mehr als more than 5

mein my 1

die **meisten** most 7

meistens mostly, most of the time 5

der **Mensch,-en** person, human being 6

die **Messe,-n** trade fair 9

der **Meter,-** meter 10

das **Mietshaus,⸚er** apartment building 5

die **Milch** milk A

die **Million,-en** million 3

mindestens at least 9

minus minus, less 2

die **Minute,-n** minute 2

mit with 3

mitbringen to bring along 7

mitkommen to come along 5

mitmachen to participate 9

mitnehmen to take along 10

der **Mittag,-e** noon 2

das **Mittagessen** lunch A

die **Mittagszeit,-en** noon time, lunch time B

die **Mitte,-n** middle, center 4

das **Mittelalter** Middle Ages 10

mittelalterlich medieval 10

das **Mittelgebirgsland** central highlands 8

der **Mittelpunkt,-e** focal point 7

der **Mittwoch** Wednesday 2

möchten would like to 5

modern modern B

mögen to like 5

möglich possible 2

die **Möglichkeit,-en** possibility 7

der **Moment,-e** moment 3

der **Monat,-e** month 2

der **Montag** Monday 2

morgen tomorrow 2

der **Morgen** morning 2; *heute morgen* this morning 2

das **Motorrad,⸚er** motorcycle 7

müde tired A

der **Mund,⸚er** mouth 10

das **Münster,-** cathedral 7

munter awake A

das **Museum,-seen** museum 9

die **Musik** music 4

das **Musikfest,-e** music festival 5

das **Musikinstrument,-e** musical instrument 8

müssen must, to have to 5

die **Mutter,⸚** mother 5

die **Muttersprache,-n** mother tongue 5

N

na well 2

nach to, after 3

das **Nachbarland,-̈er** neighboring country *3*

der **Nachmittag,-e** afternoon *2*

die **Nachrichten** (pl.) news *A*

nachsehen to check *10*

nächst next *4*

der **Nachtisch,-e** dessert *A*

die **Nähe** nearness, proximity *2; in der Nähe* nearby *2*

der **Name,-n** name *1*

nämlich namely *8*

die **Nationalfahne,-n** national flag *4*

natürlich of course, natural(ly) *4*

neben next to, besides *10*

nein no *1*

neu new *4*

neun nine *1*

neunzehn nineteen *2*

nicht not *1*

die **Niederlande** Netherlands *3*

niemand nobody, noone *9*

noch still, yet *2*

nochmal once more *5*

der **Norden** north *3*

die **Nordsee** North Sea *6*

die **Note,-n** (school) grade, mark *4*

notieren to jot down, make a note of *9*

der **November** November *4*

null zero *1*

die **Nummer,-n** number *9*

nur only, just *3*

O

ob if, whether *8*

oben on top *10*

oder or *5*

oft often *2*

oftmals often *8*

ohne without *3*

der **Oktober** October *4*

der **Onkel,-** uncle *5*

das **Opfer,-** victim *7*

orange orange *6*

die **Ordnung,-en** order *10; Es geht in Ordnung.* It will be taken care of. *10*

der **Ort,-e** town, place *10*

der **Osten** east *3*

Österreich Austria *3*

die **Ostsee** Baltic Sea *8*

P

paar: ein paar a few, some *3*

das **Paar,-e** pair *6*

das **Papier** paper *8*

das **Paradies,-e** paradise *6*

parken to park *6*

der **Parkplatz,-̈e** parking space, parking lot *6*

die **Parkuhr,-en** parking meter *6*

die **Party,-s** party *8*

der **Paß,-̈sse** passport *6*

passen to fit *3*

die **Pause,-n** break *8; eine Pause machen* to take a break *8*

die **Person,-en** person *7*

das **Pferd,-e** horse *8*

das **Pfund,-e** pound *10*

phantastisch fantastic, great *9*

die **Physik** physics *4*

die **Physikaufgabe,-n** physics problem *4*

planen to plan *B*

der **Platz,-̈e** seat, place *3*

der **Platzanweiser,-** usher *5*

plötzlich suddenly *9*

plus plus *1*

politisch political *7*

die **Polizei** police *9*

praktisch practical *4*

der **Preis,-e** price *6*

preiswert reasonable *6*

prima great, splendid *3*

pro per *10*

das **Programm,-e** program *A*

der **Prospekt,-e** brochure *10*

das **Prozent,-e** per cent *9*

der **Pullover,-** pullover *5*

pünktlich punctual, on time *2*

R

der **Radfahrer,-** bicycle rider *9*

der **Radiergummi,-s** eraser *8*

'ran: 'Ran an die Arbeit! Let's go to work! *9*

die **Rast,-en** rest, break *10; eine Rast machen* to take a rest *10*

das **Rathaus,-̈er** city hall *7*

die **Realschule,-n** secondary school (grades 4-10) *A*

die **Rechnung,-en** bill, invoice *10*

recht right *1; Das ist mir recht.* That's all right (O.K.) with me. *1; Du hast recht.* You're right. *3*

rechts right, on(to) the right *10*

das **Regal,-e** shelf *4*

das **Regierungsgebäude,-** government building *7*

regnen to rain *7*

reichen to reach, extend *9*

die **Reihe,-n** row *6; Er ist an der Reihe.* It's his turn. *6*

die **Reise,-n** trip *4*

das **Reisebüro,-s** travel agency *10*

der **Reisescheck,-s** traveler's check *6*

renovieren to renovate *7*

die **Republik,-en** republic *5*

das **Restaurant,-s** restaurant *7*

der **Richter,-** judge *9*

richtig really, correct *10*

die **Richtung,-en** direction *10*

der **Rock,-̈e** skirt *6*

der **Rollstuhlfahrer,-** wheel chair driver *9*

rosa pink *6*

rot red *4*

das **Rote Kreuz** Red Cross *9*

rüberkommen (colloquial) to come over *2*

die **Ruhe** peace, silence *3; Immer mit der Ruhe!* Take it easy. *3*

ruhig quiet, peaceful *4*

S

die **S-Bahn,-en** city train, suburban express train *2*

der **S-Bahnhof,-̈e** suburban line station *8*

sagen to say, *2*

die **Sammlung,-en** collection *7*

der **Samstag** Saturday *2*

saubermachen to clean *7*

sauer angry, annoyed *4*

das **Schach** chess *7*

schade too bad *2*

schaffen to manage (it), make (it) *9*

die **Schallplatte,-n** record *8*

der **Schalter,-** (ticket) counter *3*

das **Schaufenster,-** display window *6*

scheinen to shine *7*

das **Schiff,-e** ship, boat *7*

das **Schild,-er** sign *7*

der **Schinken** ham *A*

das **Schlafzimmer,-** bedroom *5*

schlagen to beat *9*

der **Schlaukopf,-̈e** genius, smartie *4*

schlecht bad *1*

Schlittschuh laufen to skate *9*

das **Schloß,-̈sser** castle *7*

schmecken to taste *B*

schneien to snow *7*

schnell fast, quick(ly) *2*

schon already *2; schon wieder* again *2*

schön beautiful *4*

schreiben to write *2*
der **Schuh,-e** shoe *6*
die **Schuld** fault *5*
die **Schule,-n** school *2*
der **Schüler,-** pupil, student (at elementary and secondary school) *4*
die **Schultasche,-n** school bag *8*
der **Schulweg,-e** way to school *3*
schwarz black *4*
das **Schwarze Meer** Black Sea *8*
der **Schwarzwald** Black Forest *6*
die **Schweiz** Switzerland *3*
schwer difficult, hard *3*
die **Schwester,-n** sister *5*
schwimmen to swim *9*
sechs six *1*
sechzehn sixteen *2*
der **See,-n** lake *5*
sehen to see, look *3; Mal sehen...* Let's see... *3; Seht mal!* Look! *4; sehen auf* to look at *4*
die **Sehenswürdigkeit,-en** sight(s) *7*
sehr very *3*
die **Seilbahn,-en** cable car *10*
sein to be *3*
sein his *5*
seit since, for *A*
die **Seite,-n** page *4;* side *7*
die **Sekunde,-n** second *2*
der **September** September *4*
sicher safe, secure *8*
sie she, they *1*
Sie you (formal) *1*
sieben seven *1*
siebzehn seventeen *2*
der **Sieger,-** winner *9*
singen to sing *B*
sitzen to sit *4*
der **Sitzplatz,-̈e** seat *8*
Ski laufen to ski *9*
so so *3*
so... wie as... as *3*
sobald as soon as *9*
die **Socke,-n** sock *6*
sofort right away, immediately *6*
sogar even *7*
der **Sohn,-̈e** son *5*
sollen to be supposed to, should *5*
der **Sommer,-** summer *4*
der **Sommermonat,-e** summer month *6*
das **Sonderangebot,-e** special offer *10*
sondern but *7; nicht nur... sondern auch* not only... but also *7*
der **Sonnabend** Saturday *2*

die **Sonne** sun *7*
sonnig sunny *10*
der **Sonntag** Sunday *2*
sonntags on Sundays *8*
sonst besides, otherwise *9*
die **Soße,-n** gravy *A*
sowie as well as *10*
sowieso anyhow, anyway *6*
sparen to save *B*
der **Spaß** fun *6; Viel Spaß!* Have fun! *6; Es macht Spaß.* It is fun. *8*
spät late *2; Wie spät ist es?* What time is it? How late is it? *2*
später later *2*
der **Speisesaal,-säle** dining hall *7*
das **Spiel,-e** game *5*
spielen to play *5*
der **Spielfilm,-e** feature film *A*
die **Spitze,-n** top *9; an der Spitze sein* to be in front *9*
der **Sport** sport *4*
die **Sportart,-en** kind of sport *9*
der **Sportler,-** athlete *9*
der **Sportplatz,-̈e** athletic field *B*
der **Sportwettbewerb,-e** sports competition *9*
die **Sprache,-n** language *6*
das **Sprachlabor,-s** language lab *4*
sprechen to speak, talk *2; sprechen über* to talk about *2*
springen to jump *9*
der **Staat,-en** state *3*
die **Staatsoper** State Opera *7*
das **Staatsratsgebäude** Council of State Building (DDR) *7*
die **Stadt,-̈e** city *1; in die Stadt gehen* to go downtown *1*
das **Städtische Kunstmuseum** City Art Museum *7*
die **Stadtmauer,-n** city wall *10*
der **Stadtplan,-̈e** city map *10*
das **Stadttor,-e** city gate *10*
der **Start,-s** start *9*
starten to start *9*
das **Startsignal,-e** starting signal *9*
die **Station,-en** station *10*
stattfinden to take place *9*
der **Status** status *4*
stehen to stand, be located *4; Es steht ihr gut.* She looks good in it. *6*
steigen to climb *10*
steigen: Sie steigt ein. She gets in(to). *2*
die **Stelle,-n** place, spot *9*
stellen to put, place *A*
stempeln to stamp *7*

stimmen to be correct *7; Das stimmt.* That's right. That's true. *7*
die **Straße,-n** street *4*
die **Straßenbahn,-en** streetcar *3*
die **Strecke,-n** stretch, distance *8; auf der Strecke* on the track (road) *9*
stricken to knit *A*
der **Strumpf,-̈e** stocking *6*
der **Student,-en** student (at university) *4*
studieren to study (at university) *4*
das **Studium, -dien** studies *4*
das **Stufen- und Bergland** terrace and highland country *8*
die **Stunde,-n** hour *2*
suchen to look for, search *4*
südamerikanisch South American, Latin American *8*
der **Süden** south *3*
die **Süßigkeiten** (pl.) sweets *7*
das **Symbol,-e** symbol *7*

T

die **Tafel,-n** board *B*
der **Tag,-e** day *1; Tag!* Hello! (conversational), Hi! *1; Guten Tag!* Hello! *1*
die **Tante,-n** aunt *5*
der **Tanz,-̈e** dance *8*
tanzen to dance *8*
der **Tanzpartner,-** dancing partner *8*
die **Tanzschule,-n** dancing school *8*
der **Tanzunterricht** dancing lessons (pl.) *8*
die **Tasche,-n** bag *3*
die **Tasse,-n** cup *9*
tausend thousand *10*
der **Tee** tea *A*
der **Teil,-e** part, section *5; zum größten Teil* for the most part, mostly *5; zum Teil* partly, in part *8*
der **Teilnehmer,-** participant *9*
das **Telefon,-e** telephone *2*
die **Telefonzelle,-n** telephone booth *7*
das **Tennis** tennis *9*
teuer expensive *6*
das **Theater,-** theater *7*
die **Theke,-n** counter *8*
das **Tiefland** lowlands *8*
der **Tisch,-e** table *5*
das **Tischtennis** table tennis *7*
die **Tochter,-̈** daughter *5*
toll fantastic, wild, terrific *5*

die **Tomate,-n** tomato *A*
das **Tor,-e** gate *10*
der **Tourist,-en** tourist *5*
tragen to carry *3*
trainieren to train, practice *9*
sich **treffen** to meet *B*
treiben to drive, do *9; Sport treiben* to participate in sports *9*
trinken to drink *9*
die **Trompete,-n** trumpet *8*
die **Tschechoslowakei** Czechoslovakia *3*
Tschüs! See you! (sometimes spelled Tschüss! or Tschüß!) *2*
tun to do *2*
die **Tür,-en** door *4*
der **Turm,-̈e** tower *7*
typisch typical *A*

U

üben to practice *4*
über over, above *3;* about *10*
überblicken to overlook *10*
übernachten to stay overnight *7*
die **Übernachtung,-en** (overnight) accommodation *7*
übertreffen to surpass, beat *9*
die **Übung,-en** exercise, practice *4; Übung macht den Meister!* Practice makes perfect. *4*
die **Uhr,-en** clock, watch *2; Wieviel Uhr ist es?* What time is it? *2; Es ist vier Uhr.* It's four o'clock. *2*
um at *2;* around *1;* in order to, to *7; Um wieviel Uhr?* At what time? *2*
umgeben to surround *10*
die **Umgebung,-en** surrounding, vicinity *5*
die **Umkleidekabine,-n** fitting room *6*
umsteigen to transfer *10*
und and *1*
Ungarn Hungary *5*
ungeduldig impatient *4*
ungefähr approximate(ly) *3*
ungenügend unsatisfactory *4*
die **Uni** "U" (abbreviation for **Universität**) university *4*
die **Universität,-en** university *4*
unpünktlich late, not on time *5*
uns us *5*
unsere (form of **unser**) our *5*

unterdessen meanwhile, in the meantime *5*
unterwegs on the way *10*

V

der **Vater,-̈** father *5*
verärgert angry *2*
verbinden to connect *8*
die **Verbindung,-en** connection *8*
verbringen to spend (a vacation) *9*
die **Vereinigten Staaten** United States *3*
die **Verkäuferin,-nen** sales clerk (female) *5*
der **Verkehr** traffic *4*
das **Verkehrsmittel,-** means of transportation *7*
das **Verkehrsschild,-er** traffic sign *10*
verlassen to leave *A*
verlaufen to run, extend *6*
verlieren to lose *4; Verlier keine Worte!* Don't waste any words!*4*
sich **versammeln** to gather, meet *7*
verschieden different, various *7*
versorgen to supply, provide *10*
der **Verstand** reason, mind *9; mehr Glück als Verstand haben* to have more luck than brains *9*
verstehen to understand *4*
versuchen to try *9*
verzieren to decorate *10*
viel much *2*
viele many *4*
vielleicht perhaps *4*
vier four *1*
das **Viertel,-** quarter *3; Es ist Viertel nach acht.* It's a quarter after eight. *3*
vierzehn fourteen *2*
die **Vokabel,-n** (vocabulary) word *4*
voll full *3*
von from, of *2*
vor in front of, before *5*
vorbeifahren to drive by *9*
vorbeiführen to go past *10*
vorbeikommen to come by *9*
vorführen to perform, stage *10*
vorhaben to plan, intend *6*
vorher before, in advance *10*
vorhin before, earlier *9*
der **Vormittag,-e** forenoon *2*
der **Vorort,-e** suburb *3*
der **Vorschlag,-̈e** suggestion *4*
sich **vorstellen** to imagine *10*

die **Vorstellung,-en** performance, show *5*

W

die **Wachablösung** changing of the guard *7*
der **Wagen,-** car *6*
während during *5*
der **Wald,-̈er** forest *7*
der **Walzer,-** waltz *8*
wandern to hike *6*
wann when *2*
die **Ware,-n** product, goods *6*
warm warm *7*
warnen to warn *8*
warten to wait *2; warten auf* to wait for *A*
warum why *2*
was what *1*
was für what kind of *4*
der **Wasserbehälter,-** water container *9*
wässerig watery *10*
die **Wasserstraße,-n** waterway *8*
der **Wasserverkehr** water traffic *8*
der **Weg,-e** way *2; auf dem Weg* on the way *2*
die **Weile** while *2; eine Weile* a while *2*
der **Wein,-e** wine *9*
weiß white *5*
weiter further *4; Sie gehen weiter.* They keep going. *4*
weiterfahren to continue (driving) *10*
weitest- farthest *3*
der **Weitsprung,-̈e** broad jump *9*
welcher which *2*
die **Welt,-en** world *7*
weltberühmt world-famous *10*
die **Weltzeituhr** World Time Clock *7*
wenig little *4*
wenige few *4*
wenigstens at least *6*
wer who *2*
der **Westen** west *3*
das **Wetter** weather *7*
wichtig important *8*
wie how *1;* like *8; Wie geht's?* How are you? (familiar) *1; wie viele?* how many *3*
wieder again *2*
wiederholen to repeat *A*
wieviel how much? *2; Um wieviel Uhr?* At what time? *2*
der **Winter,-** winter *4*

der **Wintermonat,-e** winter month 6
der **Wintersportler,-** winter sportsman 5
wir we 1
wirklich really 4
wissen to know, be familiar with 3
wo where 1
woher where from 4
wohin where to 4
wohnen to live 1
die **Wohnung,-en** apartment 4
das **Wohnviertel,-** residential area 7
das **Wohnzimmer,-** living room 5
die **Wolke,-n** cloud 10
wollen to want to 5
womit with what 10
das **Wort,-e** word (saying, quotation) 4; *Verlier keine Worte!* Don't waste any words. 4

das **Wort,-̈er** word 4
das **Wörterbuch,-̈er** dictionary 4
wünschen to wish 10
die **Wurst,-̈e** sausage A

Z

die **Zahnradbahn,-en** cog-wheel train 10
zehn ten 1
das **Zeichen,-** signal, sign 9
zeigen to show 3; *zeigen auf* to point to 6
die **Zeit,-en** time 2
die **Zeitung,-en** newspaper 5
der **Zentimeter,-** centimeter 9
das **Zentrum, -tren** center 6
das **Ziel,-e** finish (line) 9
das **Zimmer,-** room 2
der **Zimmerschlüssel,-** room key 7

zu at, too, to 2; *zu Hause* at home 2
zubereiten to prepare (a meal) 7
zuerst first 5
der **Zug,-̈e** train 3
zugeben to admit 6
zum (or: **zu dem**) to the 5
zumachen to close B
zur (or: **zu der**) to the 2
zurückbekommen to get back 2
zurückfahren to drive back 10
zurückgehen to go back 6
zusammen together 2
der **Zuschauer,-** spectator 9
zuschicken to send, mail (to) 10
zuwinken to wave at 10
zwanzig twenty 2
zwei two 1
zwischen between 8
zwölf twelve 2

All the words introduced in DEUTSCH: AKTUELL 1 have been summarized in this section. The numbers following the meaning of individual words or phrases indicate the particular lesson in which they appear for the first time. In cases in which there is more than one meaning for a word or phrase and it has appeared in different lessons, the corresponding lesson numbers are listed.

A

a eine(e) *2*
able: to be able to können *5*
about über *10*
above über *3*
accommodations (overnight) die Übernachtung,-en *7*
accordion das Akkordeon,-s *8*
across gegenüber *7*
actual(ly) eigentlich *3*
admission der Eintritt *8*
to **admit** zugeben *7*
afraid: to be afraid Angst haben *2*
after nach *3*
afternoon der Nachmittag,-e *2*
again wieder *2; again and again* immer wieder *7*
airplane das Flugzeug,-e *7*
all alle *2*
almost fast *5*
Alps die Alpen *5*
already schon *2*
also auch *1*
always immer *2*
America Amerika *5*
American der Amerikaner,- (male), die Amerikanerin,-nen (female) *A*
amount der Betrag,¨e *6*
an ein(e) *2*
and und *1*
angry verärgert *2; sauer 4*
to **announce** bekanntgeben *8*
announcer der Ansager,- *9*
annoyed sauer *4*
to **answer** antworten *3; beantworten A; to answer a question* eine Frage beantworten *A*
anyhow sowieso *6*
anyway sowieso *6*
apartment die Wohnung,-en *4*
apartment building das Miets-haus,¨er *5*

to **applaud** klatschen *9*
apple sauce das Apfelmus *A*
approximate(ly) ungefähr *3*
April der April *4*
area die Fläche,-n *3;* dic Ge-gend,-en *5*
around um *1*
arrival die Ankunft,¨e *7*
to **arrive** ankommen *10*
art die Kunst *4*
article of clothing das Kleidungs-stück,-e *6*
art treasure der Kunstschatz,¨e *10*
as... as so... wie *3*
to **ask** fragen *2*
to **assume** annehmen *10*
at um, an *2; bei 5; At what time?* Um wieviel Uhr? *2; at home* zu Hause *2*
athlete der Sportler,- *9*
athletic field der Sportplatz,¨e *B*
attendant der Aufseher,- *9*
attraction der Anziehungs-punkt,-e *10*
August der August *4*
aunt die Tante,-n *5*
Austria Österreich *3*
automat der Automat,-en *3*
available frei *7*
awake munter *A*
away entfernt *4*

B

bad schlecht *1; too bad* schade *2*
badminton der Federball,¨e *9*
bag die Tasche,-n *3*
baggage das Gepäck *3*
ballpoint pen der Kuli,-s *8*
Baltic Sea die Ostsee *8*

bank die Bank,-en *6*
basketball der Basketball,¨e; der Korbball,¨e *9*
to **be** sein *3*
to **beat** übertreffen *9; schlagen 9*
beautiful schön *4*
bed das Bett,-en *5*
bedroom das Schlafzimmer,- *5*
beer das Bier,-e *9*
before vor *5; vorher 10*
to **begin** beginnen *3*
behind hinter *8*
Belgium Belgien *3*
to **believe** glauben *3*
to **belong to** gehören zu *8*
bench die Bank,¨e *4*
beside neben *10*
besides außer *6; sonst 9*
best best- *7; the best is* am besten *7*
between zwischen *8*
beverage das Getränk,-e *7*
bicycle das Fahrrad,¨er *7*
bicycle rider der Radfahrer,- *9*
big groß *3*
bill die Rechnung,-en *10*
biology die Biologie *4*
birthday der Geburtstag,-e *5 Happy Birthday!* Herzlichen Glückwunsch zum Geburts-tag! *8*
black schwarz *4*
Black Forest der Schwarzwald *6*
Black Sea das Schwarze Meer *6*
to **block off** absperren *9*
blouse die Bluse,-n *6*
blue blau *6*
board die Tafel,-n *B*
boat das Boot,-e *7; das Schiff,-e 7*
book das Buch,¨er *4; book de-partment* die Bücherab-teilung,-en *6*
to **book** buchen *10*

border die Grenze,-n 6
to **border on** grenzen an 4
boring langweilig 2
both beide 2
boy der Junge,-n 1
boyfriend der Freund,-e 1
bratwurst die Bratwurst,-̈e B
bread das Brot,-e A
break die Pause,-n 8; to take a break eine Pause machen 8
breakfast: to have breakfast frühstücken 5
bridge die Brücke,-n 8
to **bring** bringen A
to **bring along** mitbringen 7
broad jump der Weitsprung,-̈e 9
brochure der Prospekt,-e 10
brother der Bruder,-̈ 5
brown braun 6
buddy der Kamerad,-en 9
to **build** erbauen 10
building das Gebäude,- 7
bus der Bus,-se 4
but aber 2; sondern 7; not only... but also nicht nur... sondern auch 7
butter die Butter A
to **buy** kaufen 3

C

cable car die Seilbahn,-en 10
café das Café,-s 5
to **call (up)** anrufen 5
called: to be called heißen 1
can können 5
canal der Kanal,-̈e 9
canal system das Kanalsystem,-e 8
to **cancel (tickets)** entwerten 8
capital (city) die Hauptstadt,-̈e 3
car das Auto,-s 5; der Wagen,- 6
card die Karte,-n B
to **carry** tragen 3
to **cash (in)** einlösen 6
cashier's counter die Kasse,-n 6
cassette die Kassette,-n 1
castle das Schloß,-̈sser 7
cathedral das Münster,- 7
center die Mitte,-n 4; das Zentrum,-tren 6
centimeter der Zentimeter,- 9
certainly bestimmt 6
chance die Chance,-n 9
character der Charakter,-e 10
to **check** nachsehen 10

cheese der Käse A
chemistry die Chemie 4
chess das Schach 7
chocolate: hot chocolate der Kakao 9
choice die Auswahl 6
to **choose** auswählen B
church die Kirche,-n 7
city die Stadt,-̈e 1
city gate das Stadttor,-e 10
city hall das Rathaus,-̈er 7
city map der Stadtplan,-̈e 10
city wall die Stadtmauer,-n 10
clarinet die Klarinette,-n 8
class die Klasse,-n 3; second class zweiter Klasse 3
class trip der Klassenausflug,-̈e 7
to **clean** saubermachen 7
clear klar 3
to **clear** abräumen 7
clearly deutlich 10
to **climb** steigen 10
clock die Uhr,-en 2
close dicht 9
to **close** zumachen B
cloud die Wolke,-n 10
coat der Mantel,-̈ 6
cocoa der Kakao 9
coffee der Kaffee A
cog-wheel train die Zahnradbahn,-en 10
cola die Cola,-s 2
cold kalt 7
cold-cut platter die Kalte Platte 5
collection die Sammlung,-en 7
color die Farbe,-n 6
colorful bunt 6
to **come** kommen 1; Come on! Los! 5
to **come along** mitkommen 5
to **come by** vorbeikommen 9
to **come here** hierherkommen 10
to **come over** rüberkommen 2
comfortable bequem 3
competition der Wettbewerb,-e 9; sports competition der Sportwettbewerb 9
composition der Aufsatz,-̈e A
computer der Computer,- 3
to **congratulate** gratulieren 9
congratulations (pl.) der Glückwunsch,-̈e 8; Congratulations! Herzlichen Glückwunsch! 9
to **connect** verbinden 8
connection die Verbindung,-en 8
to **consist of** bestehen aus 4
to **construct** erbauen 10

to **continue** fortsetzen 10; to continue a trip eine Reise fortsetzen 10; to continue (driving) weiterfahren 10
to **cook** kochen A
cool kühl 7
to **cool off** sich abkühlen 9
corner die Ecke,-n 1
correct richtig 10; to be correct stimmen 7
to **cost** kosten 4
counter die Theke,-n 8; counter (ticket) der Schalter,- 3
country das Land,-̈er 3
course: of course natürlich 4
to **cover** decken A
to **crochet** häkeln 5
cross das Kreuz,-e 6
cultural kulturell 7
cup die Tasse,-n 9
customer der Kunde,-n 10
Czechoslovakia die Tschechoslowakei 3

D

dance der Tanz,-̈e 8
to **dance** tanzen 8
dancing lessons (pl.) der Tanzunterricht 8
dancing partner der Tanzpartner,- 8
dancing school die Tanzschule,-n 8
Danube die Donau 5
date (calendar) das Datum, Daten 5
daughter die Tochter,-̈ 5
day der Tag,-e 1
December der Dezember 4
to **decorate** verzieren 10
delicious lecker 8
Denmark Dänemark 3
department store das Kaufhaus,-̈er B
departure die Abfahrt,-en 10
departure time die Abfahrtszeit,-en 10
to **describe** beschreiben 10
description die Beschreibung,-en 4
to **designate** bezeichnen 10
dessert der Nachtisch,-e A
dictionary das Wörterbuch,-̈er 4
different verschieden 7
difficult schwer 3
dining hall der Speisesaal,-säle 7

direct direkt *6*

direction die Richtung,-en *10*

to **discuss** besprechen *4*

dishes das Geschirr *7*

display window das Schaufenster,- *6*

distance die Entfernung,-en *3;* die Strecke,-n *8*

distant entfernt *4*

to **do** machen *1;* tun *2*

dollar der Dollar,-s *6*

door die Tür,-en *4*

downtown die Innenstadt,⁺e *6*

dress das Kleid,-er *6*

to **drink** trinken *9*

to **drive** fahren *3*

to **drive around** herumfahren *7*

to **drive back** zurückfahren *10*

to **drive by** vorbeifahren *9*

driver's license der Führerschein,-e *8*

driver's test die Fahrprüfung,-en *8*

during während *5*

E

each jeder *7*

earlier vorhin *9*

early früh *9*

east der Osten *3*

easy leicht *3*

to **eat** essen *5*

eight acht *1*

eighteen achtzehn *2*

elegant elegant *7*

elevator der Fahrstuhl,⁺e *7*

eleven elf *2*

employee der Angestellte,-n *6*

empty leer *5*

end das Ende *3*

to **end** beenden *10*

England England *4*

English englisch *4;* das Englisch *4*

entrance der Eingang,⁺e *6*

eraser der Radiergummi,-s *8*

especially besonders *4*

essay der Aufsatz,⁺e *A*

Europe Europa *5*

European europäisch *8*

even sogar *7*

evening der Abend,-e *2; this evening …* heute abend *2*

event das Ereignis,-se *7*

every jeder *7*

everyone alle *8*

everything alles *3*

exact genau *7*

example das Beispiel,-e *7; for example* zum Beispiel *7*

excellent ausgezeichnet *10*

except außer *6*

exchange (money) der Kurs,-e *6*

excursion der Ausflug,⁺e *8*

exercise die Übung,-en *4*

expensive teuer *6*

expert der Experte,-n *8*

expression der Ausdruck,⁺e *4*

F

fairy tale-like märchenhaft *10*

fall der Herbst,-e *4*

family die Familie,-n *5*

famous berühmt *10*

fantastic toll *5;* phantastisch *9*

farm der Bauernhof,⁺e *10*

fascism der Faschismus *7*

fast schnell *2*

father der Vater,⁺ *5*

fault die Schuld *5*

favorable günstig *10*

fear die Angst,⁺e *2*

feature film der Spielfilm,-e *A*

February der Februar *4*

Federal Republic of Germany die Bundesrepublik Deutschland *3*

fee die Gebühr,-en *6*

few wenige *7;* einige *7; a few* ein paar *3;* manche *8*

field das Feld,-er *10*

field path der Feldweg,-e *4*

fifteen fünfzehn *2*

figure die Figur,-en *10*

to **fill out** ausfüllen *7*

film der Film,-e *5*

finally endlich *2*

to **find** finden *4*

finish (line) das Ziel,-e *9*

to **finish** beenden *10*

first erst *5;* zuerst *5*

to **fit** passen *3*

fitting room die Umkleidekabine,-n *6*

five fünf *1*

flat flach *5*

flight der Flug,⁺e *10*

to **flow** fließen *5*

flower die Blume,-n *10*

flute die Flöte,-n *8*

to **follow** folgen *7*

food das Essen *8*

foot der Fuß,⁺e *3; on foot* zu Fuß *3*

for für *3;* seit *A*

foreign language die Fremdsprache,-n *4*

foreigner der Ausländer,- *10*

forenoon der Vormittag,-e *2*

forest der Wald,⁺er *7*

form die Form,-en *9*

to **form** bilden *9*

formula die Formel,-n *4*

fortress die Festung,-en *10*

fountain der Brunnen,- *10*

four vier *1*

fourteen vierzehn *2*

France Frankreich *3*

free frei *7*

French (language) Französisch *6*

Friday der Freitag,-e *2*

friend der Freund,-e *1*

from von *2;* aus *2*

front: in front of vor *5*

full voll *3*

fun der Spaß *6; Have fun!* Viel Spaß! *6; It is fun.* Es macht Spaß. *8*

further weiter *4*

G

game das Spiel,-e *5*

gate das Tor,-e *10*

to **gather** sich versammeln *7*

genius der Schlaukopf *4*

gentleman der Herr,-en *1*

geography die Erdkunde *4*

German deutsch *1;* Deutsch (language) *4*

German Democratic Republic die Deutsche Demokratische Republik *3*

Germany Deutschland *3*

to **get** bekommen *2*

to **get in(to)** einsteigen *2*

to **get off** aussteigen *10*

to **get up** aufstehen *A*

girl das Mädchen,- *1*

girlfriend die Freundin,-nen *3*

to **give** geben *4*

glad froh *2*

gladly gern *4*

glass das Glas,⁺er *9*

glove der Handschuh,-e *6*

to **go** gehen *1;* fahren *3; to go into* gehen über *8*

to **go back** zurückgehen *6*

to **go inside** hineingehen *7*

to **go past** vorbeiführen *10*

gold gold *4*

golf das Golf *9*

good gut *1*

goodness die Güte *7; My goodness!* Du meine Güte! *7*

grade (school) die Note,-n *4*

gram das Gramm,-e *10*

granddaughter die Enkelin,-nen *5*

grandfather der Großvater,- *5*

grandmother die Großmutter,- *5*

grandparents die Großeltern (pl.) *5*

grandson der Enkel,- *5*

gravy die Soße,-n *A*

gray grau *6*

great prima *3;* phantastisch *9; to be great* klasse sein *5*

green grün *6*

to **greet** begrüßen *3*

group die Gruppe,-n *B*

guitar die Gitarre,-n *A*

H

half halb *3*

ham der Schinken *A*

happy froh *2*

hard schwer *3*

hardly kaum *9*

to **have** haben *2*

to **have on** anhaben *6*

to **have to** müssen *5*

he er *1*

head der Leiter,- *9*

to **hear** hören *4*

hearty herzlich *8*

heat die Hitze *8; in this heat* bei der Hitze *8*

height die Höhe,-n *6*

Hello! Grüß dich!, Guten Tag! *1*

help die Hilfe *4*

to **help** helfen *9*

her ihr *A*

here hier *1*

Hi! Grüß dich!, Tag! *1*

high hoch *5*

highway die Landstraße,-n *10*

to **hike** wandern *6*

hill der Hügel,- *10*

his sein *5*

historic(al) historisch *7;* geschichtlich *10*

history die Geschichte *4*

hockey das Hockey *9*

home: at home zu Hause *2; to go home* nach Hause gehen *2*

homework die Hausaufgabe,-n *5; to do homework* die Hausaufgaben machen *5*

to **hope** hoffen *6*

hopefully hoffentlich *9*

horse das Pferd,-e *8*

hot heiß *7*

hotel das Hotel *7*

hotel sign das Hotelschild,-er *10*

hour die Stunde,-n *2*

house das Haus,-er *2; half-timbered house* das Fachwerkhaus,-er *10*

how wie *1; How are you?* Wie geht's? *1; how many?* wie viele? *3; how much?* wieviel? *2*

Hungary Ungarn *5*

hunger der Hunger *7*

hungry hungrig *A*

to **hurry** sich beeilen *3; Let's hurry.* Beeilen wir uns! *3*

I

I ich *1*

ice cream parlor die Eisdiele,-n *2*

idea die Idee,-n *2*

identification (card) der Ausweis,-e *7*

if ob *8*

to **imagine** vorstellen *10*

immediately gleich *1;* sofort *6*

impatient ungeduldig *4*

important wichtig *8*

in in *1*

inadequate mangelhaft *4*

including einschließlich *10*

industrial city die Industriestadt,-e *9*

industrious fleißig *4*

information die Information,-en *10*

inhabitant der Einwohner,- *3*

interest das Interesse,-n *A*

to **interest** interessieren *A*

interesting interessant *7*

island die Insel,-n *8*

it es *1*

Italian Italienisch (language) *6*

Italy Italien *5*

J

jam die Marmelade *A*

January der Januar *4*

jeans die Jeans (pl.) *6*

to **jot down** notieren *9*

judge der Richter,- *9*

July der Juli *4*

to **jump** springen *9*

June der Juni *4*

just nur *3;* eben *4;* gerade *10; just like/as* genauso wie *4*

K

kilometer der Kilometer,- *3*

kiosk der Kiosk,-e *2*

kitchen die Küche,-n *5*

to **knit** stricken *A*

to **know (someone)** kennen *1;* wissen *3; to get to know* kennenlernen *B*

L

to **label** bezeichnen *10*

ladies' department die Damenabteilung,-en *6*

lady die Dame,-n *6*

lake der See,-n *5*

landscape die Landschaft,-en *8*

language die Sprache,-n *6*

language lab das Sprachlabor,-s *4*

large groß *3*

last letzt- *8*

to **last** dauern *3*

late spät *2; How late is it?* Wie spät ist es? *2*

late, not on time unpünktlich *5*

to **lead** führen *10*

to **learn** lernen *4; to learn by heart* auswendig lernen *4*

least: at least wenigstens *6;* mindestens *9*

to **leave** verlassen *A*

left links *7*

legendary märchenhaft *10*

length die Länge,-n *5*

to **lie** liegen *3*

Liechtenstein Liechtenstein *5*

like wie *8*

to **like** gefallen *6;* mögen *5; She likes it.* Es gefällt ihr. *6; to like to walk* gern gehen *4; Would you like to…?* Hast du Lust…? *2*

to **listen** hören *4*

little wenig *4;* klein *10; a little* etwas *2*

to **live** wohnen *1;* leben *9; living* lebend *10*

living room das Wohnzimmer,- *5*

located: to be located liegen *3;* stehen *4*

long lange *3,* lang *9*

to **look** sehen *3; Look!* Seht mal! *4; to look at* sehen auf *4*

to **look at** sich ansehen *B*
to **look for** suchen *4*
to **look over** begutachten *6;* besichtigen *10*
to **lose** verlieren *4*
  luck das Glück *2; to be lucky* Glück haben *2*
  luggage das Gepäck *3*
  luggage cart der Koffer-Kuli,-s *3*
  lunch das Mittagessen *A*
  lunch time die Mittagszeit,-en *B*
  Luxembourg Luxemburg *3*

M

to **mail (to)** zuschicken *10*
  mailbox der Briefkasten,⸚ *7*
  mainland das Festland,⸚er *8*
to **make** machen *1; to make it* schaffen *9*
  man der Mann,⸚er *9*
  many viele *4*
  map die Karte,-n *6*
  marathon run der Marathonlauf,⸚e *9*
  March der März *4*
  mark die Mark *2*
  market der Markt,⸚e *7*
  market day der Markttag,-e *7*
  market square der Marktplatz,⸚e *7*
  mathematics die Mathematik (Mathe) *4*
  math problem die Matheaufgabe,-n *3*
  matter: What's the matter? Was ist los? *2*
  may dürfen *5*
  May der Mai *4*
  meal das Essen *A;* die Mahlzeit,-en *10*
  meaning die Bedeutung,-en *4*
  meanwhile unterdessen *5*
  medieval mittelalterlich *10*
to **meet** sich treffen *B;* sich versammeln *7*
  memorial das Mahnmal *7*
to **memorize** auswendig lernen *4*
  meter der Meter,- *10*
  middle die Mitte,-n *4*
  Middle Ages das Mittelalter *10*
  milk die Milch *A*
  million die Million,-en *3*
  minus minus *2*
  minute die Minute,-n *2*
  Miss das Fräulein,- *1*
  modern modern *B*

moment der Moment,-e *3*
Monday der Montag *2*
money das Geld *2*
month der Monat,-e *2*
more than mehr als *5*
morning der Morgen *2; this morning* heute morgen *2*
most die meisten *7*
mostly meistens *5*
mother die Mutter,⸚ *5*
mother tongue die Muttersprache,-n *5*
motorcycle das Motorrad,⸚er *7*
mountain der Berg,-e *5*
mouth der Mund,⸚er *10*
movie der Film,-e *5*
movie theater das Kino,-s *5*
Mr. der Herr,-en *1*
Mrs. die Frau,-en *1*
much viel *2*
museum das Museum,-seen *9*
music die Musik *4*
music festival das Musikfest,-e *5*
musical instrument das Musikinstrument,-e *8*
must müssen *5*
my mein *1*

N

name: to be named heißen *1; What's your name?* Wie heißt du? *1*
name der Name,-n *1*
namely nämlich *8*
national flag die Nationalfahne, -n *4*
natural(ly) natürlich *4*
nearby in der Nähe *2*
to **need** brauchen *2*
neighboring country Nachbarland,⸚er *3*
Netherlands die Niederlande *3*
new neu *4*
news die Nachrichten (pl.) *A*
newspaper die Zeitung,-en *5*
next nächst *4*
next to neben *10*
nine neun *1*
nineteen neunzehn *2*
no nein *1; kein 2; no time* keine Zeit *2*
nobody niemand *9*
noon der Mittag,-e *2*
noon time die Mittagszeit,-en *B*
north der Norden *3*
North Sea die Nordsee *6*
not nicht *1; not at all* gar nicht *4*

notebook das Heft,-e *8*
November der November *4*
now jetzt *1*
number die Nummer,- *9*

O

October der Oktober *4*
of von *2*
to **offer** bieten *7*
office das Büro,-s *4*
often oft *2; oftmals 8*
O.K. Gut! *1; klar 3*
old alt *4*
on auf *2; an 8*
once einmal *3; once again* wieder einmal *3; one more time* noch einmal *5; once more* nochmal *5*
one eins *1; man 3*
one-way (ticket) einfach *3*
only nur *3; erst 5*
open geöffnet *B; The store is open.* Das Geschäft ist geöffnet. *B*
or oder *5*
orange orange *6*
to **order** bestellen *B*
order die Ordnung,-en *10*
to **originate (river)** entspringen *8*
other andere *4*
otherwise sonst *9*
our unser *5*
out of aus *2*
outside außerhalb *5; ins Freie 7; im Freien 10*
over über *3*
to **overlook** überblicken *10*
overnight: to stay overnight übernachten *7*
owner der Besitzer,- (male), die Besitzerin,-nen (female) *8*

P

page die Seite,-n *4*
painting das Gemälde,-n *7*
pair das Paar,-e *6*
pants die Hose,-n *6*
paper das Papier *8*
paradise das Paradies,-e *6*
parents die Eltern (pl.) *5*
to **park** parken *6*
parking lot der Parkplatz,⸚e *6*
parking meter die Parkuhr,-en *6*
part der Teil,-e *5; for the most part* zum größten Teil *5*
participant der Teilnehmer,- *9*
to **participate** mitmachen *9*

partly zum Teil *8*
party die Party,-s *8*
passport der Paß,-̈sse *6*
to pay bezahlen *6*
pea die Erbse,-n *A*
peace die Ruhe *3*
pedestrian der Fußgänger,- *10*
pencil der Bleistift,-e *8*
people die Leute (pl.) *7*
per pro *10*
per cent das Prozent,-e *9*
to perform vorführen *10*
performance die Vorstellung,-en
5; die Leistung,-en *9*
perhaps vielleicht *4*
permitted: to be permitted to
dürfen *5*
person der Mensch,-en *6;* die
Person,-en *7*
photo album das Fotoalbum,-ben
B
to photograph fotografieren *B*
physics die Physik *4*
piano das Klavier,-e *8*
pink rosa *6*
to place stellen *A*
place der Platz,-̈e *3;* der Ort,-e
10; die Stelle,-n *9*
to plan vorhaben *6;* planen *B*
platform der Bahnsteig,-e *8*
to play spielen *5*
pleasant gemütlich *7*
please bitte *6*
pleasure die Lust *2*
plus plus *1*
police die Polizei *9*
political politisch *7*
popular beliebt *5*
population die Bevölkerung-en *9*

possibility die Möglichkeit,-en *7*
possible möglich *2; That's possible. Das geht. 7*
potato die Kartoffel,-n *A*
potato salad der Kartoffelsalat *8*
pound das Pfund *10*
practical praktisch *4*
to practice üben *4*
practice die Übung,-en *4; Practice makes perfect.* Übung
macht den Meister! *4*
to prepare (a meal) zubereiten *7*
present das Geschenk,-e *8*
to preserve bewahren *10*
price der Preis,-e *6*
prince der Fürst,-en *10*
problem die Aufgabe,-n *4*
product die Ware,-n *6*
program das Programm,-e *A*

to provide versorgen *10*
pullover der Pullover,- *5*
punctual pünktlich *2*
pupil der Schüler,- *4*
purse die Handtasche,-n *6*
to put stellen *A*
to put on (clothes) anziehen *6; to
put on (records)* auflegen *8*

Q

quarter das Viertel,- *3; It's a
quarter after eight.* Es ist
Viertel nach acht. *3*
question die Frage,-n *A*
quick(ly) schnell *2*
quiet ruhig *4*
quite ganz *3*

R

to rain regnen *7*
rather lieber *5*
to reach erreichen *6*
to reach into hineinreichen *8*
to read lesen *4*
ready fertig *5*
really wirklich *4;* richtig *10*
reasonable preiswert *6;* günstig
10
to receive bekommen *2*
record die Schallplatte,-n *8*
recorder die Blockflöte,-n *9*
red rot *4*
Red Cross das Rote Kreuz *9*
registration form das Anmeldeformular,-e *7*
to remain bleiben *2*
to remind of erinnern an *10*
to renovate renovieren *7*
to repeat wiederholen *A*
representative der Abgeordnete,-n *7*
republic die Republik,-en *5*
rest die Rast,-en *10; to take a rest*
eine Rast machen *10*
restaurant das Restaurant,-s *7*
result das Ergebnis,-se *9; final
result* das Endergebnis,-se *9*
right rechts *10; That's all right
with me.* Das ist mir recht. *1;
You're right.* Du hast recht. *3;
That's right.* Das stimmt. *7*
right away gleich *1;* sofort *6*
to ring (bell) klingeln *4*
river der Fluß,-̈sse *5*
room das Zimmer,- *2*

room key der Zimmerschlüssel,-
7
row die Reihe,-n *6; It's his turn.*
Er ist an der Reihe. *6*
ruler das Lineal,-e *8*
to run laufen *5; to run (river) 5*
to run around herumlaufen *9*
to run towards entgegenlaufen *9*
runner der Läufer,- *9*

S

safe sicher *8*
sales clerk (female) die Verkäuferin,-nen *5*
the same dasselbe *7*
satisfactory befriedigend *4*
Saturday der Sonnabend *2;* der
Samstag *2*
sausage die Wurst,-̈e *A*
to save sparen *B*
to say sagen *2*
schedule der Fahrplan,-̈e *3*
school die Schule,-n *2*
school bag die Schultasche,-n *8*
season die Jahreszeit,-en *4*
seat der Platz,-̈e *3;* der Sitzplatz,-̈e *8*
second die Sekunde,-n *2*
to see sehen *3; Let's see...* Mal sehen... *3; See you!* Tschüs! *2*
to select auswählen *B*
selection die Auswahl *6*
to send (zu)schicken *10*
September der September *4*
seven sieben *1*
seventeen siebzehn *2*
several einige *7*
shape die Form,-en *9*
she sie *1*
shelf das Regal,-e *4*
to shine scheinen *7*
ship das Schiff,-e *7*
shirt das Hemd,-en *6*
shoe der Schuh,-e *6*
to shop einkaufen *5; to go shopping*
einkaufen gehen *5*
short(ly) kurz *A*
should sollen *5*
to show zeigen *3*
show die Vorstellung,-en *5*
siblings die Geschwister (pl.) *5*
side die Seite,-n *7*
sight(s) die Sehenswürdigkeit,-en
7
sign das Schild,-er *7;*das Zeichen,- *9*

signal das Zeichen,- 9

significance die Bedeutung,-en 4

silence die Ruhe 3

simple einfach 3

since seit A

sincere herzlich 8

to **sing** singen B

sister die Schwester,-n 5

to **sit** sitzen 4

to **sit out** aussetzen 8

six sechs 1

sixteen sechzehn 2

to **skate** Schlittschuh laufen 9

to **ski** Ski laufen 9

skirt der Rock,¨e 6

sky der Himmel 10

slip (of paper) der Abschnitt,-e 6

slow(ly) langsam A

small klein 10

smart klug 3

snack bar die Imbißstube,-n B

to **snow** schneien 7

so so 3

soccer der Fußball,¨e 7

sock die Socke,-n 6

soft drink die Limonade,-n 9

to **solve** lösen 4

some etwas 2; ein paar 3

sometimes manchmal 4

son der Sohn,¨e 5

soon bald 2; as soon as sobald 9

to **sound** klingen 10

south der Süden 3

South American südamerika-nisch 8

to **speak** sprechen 2

special besonders 4

special offer das Sonderangebot, -e 10

spectator der Zuschauer,- 9

spring der Frühling,-e 4

sport der Sport 4; kind of sport die Sportart,-en 9

spot die Stelle,-n 9

to **stamp** stempeln 7

stamp automat der Briefmarken-automat,-en 7

to **stand** stehen 4

start der Start,-s 9

to **start** starten 9

starting signal das Startsignal,-e 9

to **start running** loslaufen 9

state der Staat,-en 3

station die Station,-en 10; der Bahnhof,¨e 3

to **stay** bleiben 2

still noch 2

stocking der Strumpf,¨e 6

stop (bus or streetcar) die Halte-stelle,-n 3

to **stop** anhalten 10

store das Geschäft,-e 6

street die Straße,-n 4

streetcar die Straßenbahn,-en 3

stretch die Strecke,-n 8

student der Schüler,- (through high school) 4; der Student,-en (at university) 4

studies das Studium,-dien 4

to **study (at university)** studieren 4

subject (school) das Fach,¨er 4

suburb der Vorort,-e 3

suddenly plötzlich 9

sufficient ausreichend 4

suggestion der Vorschlag,¨e 4

suit der Anzug,¨e 6

suitcase der Koffer,- 3

summer der Sommer,- 4

sun die Sonne 7

Sunday der Sonntag 2; on Sun-days sonntags 8

sunny sonnig 10

supermarket (DDR) die HO-Kaufhalle,-n 5

supper das Abendbrot 5

to **supply** versorgen 10

supposed: to be supposed to sol-len 5

to **surpass** übertreffen 9

to **surround** umgeben 10

surrounding die Umgebung,-en 5

sweets die Süßigkeiten (pl.) 7

to **swim** schwimmen 9

Switzerland die Schweiz 3

symbol das Symbol,-e 7

T

table der Tisch,-e 5

table: to set the table den Tisch decken A

table tennis das Tischtennis 7

to **take (time)** dauern 3

to **take along** mitnehmen 10

to **take place** stattfinden 9

to **talk** sprechen 2; to talk about sprechen über 2

taste der Geschmack,¨e 8

to **taste** schmecken B

tea der Tee A

teacher der Lehrer,- 7

team die Mannschaft,-en 9

telephone das Telefon,-e 2

telephone booth die Telefon-zelle,-n 7

television: on television im Fern-sehen A

television set der Fernsehappa-rat,-e 7

television tower der Fernseh-turm,¨e 7

ten zehn 1

tennis das Tennis 9

terrific toll 5

test die Arbeit,-en 2; to take a test eine Arbeit schreiben 2

than als 8

thanks der Dank 10; danke 1; Danke schön. 5; Many thanks. Vielen Dank. 10

that das 1; daß 6

the der, die, das 1

theater das Theater,- 7

their ihr 4

then dann 2

there da 1; dort 3; dorthin 5; over there da drüben 1; there is (are) es gibt 4

therefore deshalb 6

they sie 1; man 3

to **think** denken 7

thirteen dreizehn 2

this dieser 3

thorough gründlich 4

thousand tausend 10

three drei 1

through durch 5

Thursday Donnerstag 2

ticket die Fahrkarte,-n 3; die Karte,-n 5

tide: low tide die Ebbe,-n 8

tie die Krawatte,-n 6

time die Zeit,-en 2; time(s) das Mal,-e 9 What time is it? Wieviel Uhr ist es?, 9; Wie spät ist es? 2; on time pünktlich 2

times mal 3

tired müde A

to auf 2; zu 2; nach 3; um 7

today heute 2

together zusammen 2

tomato die Tomate,-n A

tomorrow morgen 2

tonight heute abend 2

too auch 1; zu 2

top die Spitze,-n 9; to be on top an der Spitze sein 9; on top oben 10

tourist der Tourist,-en *5*
tower der Turm,¨e *7*
town der Ort,-e *10*
track das Gleis,-e *3*
trade fair die Messe,-n *9*
traffic der Verkehr *4*
traffic sign das Verkehrsschild, -er *10*
train der Zug,¨e *3; city train* die S-Bahn,-en *2;* die Bahn,-en *10*
to **train** trainieren *9*
to **transfer** umsteigen *10*
travel agency das Reisebüro,-s *10*
traveler's check der Reisescheck,-s *6*
trip die Reise,-n *4;* die Fahrt,-en *10; round trip* hin und zurück *3*
trumpet die Trompete,-n *8*
to **try** versuchen *9*
to **try on** anprobieren *6*
Tuesday der Dienstag *2*
twelve zwölf *2*
twenty zwanzig *2*
two zwei *1*
typical typisch *A*

U

uncle der Onkel,- *5*
to **understand** verstehen *4*
unfortunately leider *B*
United States die Vereinigten Staaten *3*
university die Universität,-en *4*
unsatisfactory ungenügend *4*
until bis *2*
us uns *5*
to **use** gebrauchen *4*
usher der Platzanweiser,- *5*

V

vacation die Ferien (pl.) *9*
vacation country das Ferienland,¨er *5*
very sehr *5*
victim das Opfer,- *7*

view der Blick *4*
to **view** besichtigen *10*
violin die Geige,-n *8*
to **visit** besuchen *5*
visitor der Besucher,- *6*
vocabulary word die Vokabel,-n *4*
vorhin before *9*

W

to **wait** warten *2; to wait for* warten auf *A*
to **walk** zu Fuß gehen *3*
waltz der Walzer,- *8*
to **want to** wollen *5*
warm warm *7*
to **warn** warnen *8*
watch die Uhr,-en *2*
to **watch** aufpassen *9; to watch TV* fernsehen *5*
water container der Wasserbehälter,- *9*
water traffic der Wasserverkehr *8*
waterway die Wasserstraße,-n *8*
watery wässerig *10*
to **wave at** zuwinken *10*
way der Weg,-e *2; on the way* auf dem Weg *2;* unterwegs *10; way to school* der Schulweg, -e *3*
we wir *1*
weather das Wetter *7*
Wednesday der Mittwoch *2*
well na *2*
well-known bekannt *5*
west der Westen *3*
what was *1; what kind of* was für *4*
wheel chair der Rollstuhl,¨e *9; wheel chair driver* der Rollstuhlfahrer,- *9*
when wann *2*
where wo *1; where to* wohin *4; where from* woher *4*
whether ob *8*
which welcher *2*
while die Weile *2; a while* eine Weile *2*
white weiß *5*
who wer *2*

whole ganz *7*
why warum *2*
wife die Frau,-en *10*
to **win** gewinnen *5*
window das Fenster,- *10*
wine der Wein,-e *9*
winner der Sieger,- *9*
winter der Winter *4*
to **wish** wünschen *10*
with mit *3;* bei *8*
without ohne *3*
woman die Frau,-en *1*
to **wonder** gespannt sein *5*
word das Wort,¨er *4*
work die Arbeit,-en *2*
to **work** arbeiten *2; Let's go to work!* 'Ran an die Arbeit! *8*
world die Welt,-en *7*
world-famous weltberühmt *10*
would: would like to möchten *5*
to **write** schreiben *2*

Y

year das Jahr,-e *2*
yellow gelb *6*
yes ja *1*
yesterday gestern *9*
yet noch *2*
you du *1;* ihr *1;* Sie *1;* man *3*
youngster der Jugendliche,-n *7*
your dein *4;* Ihr *6*
youth hostel die Jugendherberge,-n *7*
youth hostel director der Herbergsvater,¨ *7*
youth hostel identification (card) der Jugendherbergsausweis,-e *7*
Yugoslavia Jugoslawien *5*

Z

zero null *1*

Abbreviations

A . . . . Review Unit A
B . . . . . . Review Unit B
E . . . . . . Ergänzung
K . . . . . . Kulturecke
L1 . . . . . Lesestück 1
L2 . . . . . Lesestück 2

Acknowledgments

The author wishes to express his gratitude to the many people in Germany *(BRD* and *DDR)*, Austria and Switzerland who assisted in the photography scenes for the textbook and the filmstrips. Particularly helpful was Panorama DDR, an organization that set up all the requested photography sessions in the German Democratic Republic. Special thanks should also go to those people who cooperated in setting up photography sessions in the other German-speaking countries: Familie Heinz Devrient (Köln), Professor Ulrich Froehlich (Würzburg), Herr Rudolf Hocker (Neustadt/Weinstraße), Herr Dieter Messner (Lienz), Herr Donatus Moosauer (Deggendorf), Herr und Frau Robert O'Reilly (EMC), Herr Horst Penner (Bergisch-Gladbach), Familie Ingomar Stainer (München), Herr und Frau Helmut Strunk (Essen).

Furthermore, the author would like to pay tribute to those professionals who contributed in the creative effort beyond the original manuscript: Rosemary J. Barry (Editor), Cyril John Schlosser (Designer) and Chris Wold Dyrud (Illustrator).

Last but not least, the author would like to thank his wife, Rosie, and his two daughters, Heidi and Marci, for showing such tremendous patience during the development of this series and for their valuable contributions before, during and after the extensive trip throughout German-speaking countries.

The following German instructors provided valuable comments for the revision of *Deutsch:Aktuell 1:*
Norma Ackley, South High School, Milwaukee, Wisconsin; *Sandra K. Benzer,* Urban Junior High School, Sheboygan, Wisconsin; *F. P. Boost,* McNary Senior High School, Salem, Oregon; *Edward H. Bray, Jr.,* Wissachickon Middle School, Ambler, Pennsylvania; *Anita Brückler,* Muskingum College, New Concord, Ohio; *Marge Burk,* Covington Latin School, Covington, Kentucky; *James Caputo,* Wooster High School, Wooster, Ohio; *Lydia Colson,* Cuyahoga Community College, Parma, Ohio; *Fred Covey,* Drake University, Des Moines, Iowa; *Leslie F. Durmek,* University of Arizona, Tucson, Arizona; *William R. Davis,* University of New Hampshire, Durham, New Hampshire; *Craig Deville,* University of Arizona, Tucson, Arizona; *Lucie M. Dilger,* Yorktown High School, Arlington, Virginia; *Lee Duty,* Sauk Prairie High School, Sauk City, Wisconsin; *Wendell Frye,* Hartwick College, Oneonta, New York; *Christa M. Fumea,* Northeast High School, St. Petersburg, Florida; *Karl-Heinz Gabbey,* Buffalo Grove High School, Buffalo Grove, Illinois; *Jacqueline S. Gnagi,* Perry A. Tipler Middle School, Oshkosh, Wisconsin; *Inez Good,* Roanoke College, Salem, Virginia; *Larry Hall,* Sewickley Academy, Sewickley, Pennsylvania; *Jerome P. Harper,* Carson-Newman College, Jefferson City, Tennessee; *Barbara A. Heck,* Arlington High School, Arlington Heights, Illinois; *Richard C. Helt,* University of Arizona, Tucson, Arizona; *Ursula F. Hildebrandt,* Libertyville High School, Libertyville, Illinois; *Frank D. Hirschbach,* University of Minnesota, Minneapolis, Minnesota; *Bradley A. Holtman,* Monroe High School, Monroe, Wisconsin; *Jörg Homberger,* Warwick High School, Lititz, Pennsylvania; *Kim P. Icsman,* Ursuline Academy, Cincinnati, Ohio; *Marie E. Ingram-Helt,* University of Arizona, Tucson, Arizona; *G. F. Jeffries,* North Hills High School, Pittsburgh, Pennsylvania; *Al Johnson,* Austin High School, Austin, Minnesota; *Thomas Kamla,* University of Scranton, Scranton, Pennsylvania; *Guido Kauls,* Minnehaha Academy, Minneapolis, Minnesota; *John Kelly,* Trinity High School, Manchester, New Hampshire; *Nancy M. King,* Parkview High School, Lilburn, Georgia; *Peter E. Klose,* Grand Blanc High School, Grand Blanc, Michigan; *George Kopecky,* West Torrance High School, Torrance, California; *Helga Lange,* Cuyahoga Valley Christian Academy, Cuyahoga Falls, Ohio; *Lowell E. Lee,* St. Louis Park Junior High School, St. Louis Park, Minnesota; *Jane Lienau,* Lutheran High School West, Detroit, Michigan; *A. H. Loewenstein,* Scottsdale High School, Scottsdale, Arizona; *Maimu Looke,* Harrison High School, Farmington, Michigan; *Mary Mateer,* DeWitt Middle School, Ithaca, New York; *Reverend J. Anthony Meis,* Bishop McNamara High School, Kankakee, Illinois; *Paul J. Nagy,* North Iowa Area Community College, Mason City, Iowa; *Lisa Oas,* Lakeview Christian Academy, Duluth, Minnesota; *Heinz J. Otto,* The Blake Schools, Minneapolis, Minnesota; *Reverend Ronald V. Perry,* Fairfield Prep School, Fairfield, Connecticut; *Martha Pleggenkuhle,* St. Ansgar Senior High School, St. Ansgar, Iowa; *Patricia Priolo,* Central High School, Scranton, Pennsylvania; *Donald E. Ruhde,* Iowa Falls High School, Iowa Falls, Iowa; *Mary Sexton,* Hamilton High School, Hamilton, Montana; *Gerlinde Sly,* Rockland Community College, Suffern, New York; *Wlliam Small,* University of Maine, Orono, Maine; *Debra Starkey,* Mitchell High School, Mitchell, Nebraska; *Michael Still,* De La Salle High School, Concord, California; *Reverend Keven Storek,* Lutheran High School, Rockford, Illinois; *Terry Mitchell Strohm,* West Chicago High School, West Chicago, Illinois; *Elvira Stromberg,* Shorecrest High School, Seattle, Washington; *Ronald Swanson,* Oshkosh North High School, Oshkosh, Wisconsin; *Ingrid von Reitzenstein,* Mundelein High School, Mundelein, Illinois; *Brigitte Wichmann,* Hanover College, Hanover, Indiana; *Hannelore Wilfert,* Russell Sage College, Troy, New York; *Tony Young,* Tokay High School, Lodi, California; *Hans R. Zumpft,* North High School, Sheboygan, Wisconsin.

Photo Credits

All the photos in the *Deutsch: Aktuell 1* (2nd edition) textbook not taken by the author have been provided by the following:

Austrian National Tourist Office: page 105 (left and bottom right)

Benkert, Christine: cover (flags)

Deutsche Bundespost: page 120 (top right)

Devrient, Heinz: page 100

Fremdenverkehrsverband Allgäu-Bayerisch e.V.: page 48

Fremdenverkehrsverband Bodensee-Oberschwaben e.V.: page 188 (top left)

Fremdenverkehrsverband Franken e.V.: page 121 (bottom right)

Fremdenverkehrsverband Lüneburger Heide e.V.: pages 109, 110 (top left), 192

Fremdenverkehrsverband München-Oberbayern e.V.: cover (top), pages 110 (center right), 249 (left)

Fremdenverkehrsverband Rheinland-Pfalz e.V.: pages 11 (left), 12, 76 (right)

German Information Center: pages 77 (both), 161 (top right and left), 180 (left), 191 (top right), 213 (center left and bottom right), 233 (top left), 237 (top right), 238 (top right)

German Rail: pages 53 (top and center left), 54 (bottom left and right)

Informations- und Presseamt Dortmund: page 166 (right)

Inter Nationes: page 249 (bottom right)

Landesfremdenverkehrsverband Baden-Württemberg e.V.: cover (center), pages 13, 30 (left), 58, 89 (right), 110 (center left), 191 (center and bottom right), 233 (bottom right), 237 (bottom right), 238 (top left)

Lufthansa German Airlines: pages 54 (top left), 180 (right), 188 (right), 247 (bottom right)

Moosauer, Donatus: pages 86 (both), 146 (both), 191 (top left)

Panorama DDR: pages ix (center right), 49 (right), 83 (top left), 162 (top left and bottom), 209 (top right and left), 213 (center right)

Presse- und Informationsamt der Bundesregierung (Bildstelle): pages ix (top left), 49 (left), 76 (left), 161 (bottom right), 191 (bottom left), 213 (bottom left), 214 (right top and bottom)

Stokes, Jim: page 243 (top right)

Swiss National Tourist Office: pages ix (bottom left), 110 (top right), 133, 139 (all), 213 (top right), 237 (top left)

Verkehrsbüro der Stadt Ulm: pages 29 (left), 158, 214 (top left), 238 (bottom center)